RESEARCH IN ELEMENTARY SCHOOL CURRICULUM

EDITED BY

A. Montgomery Johnston

Paul C. Burns

THE UNIVERSITY OF TENNESSEE

ALLYN AND BACON, INC.   BOSTON

CONTENTS

TOPICAL OUTLINE

CONTRIBUTING
AUTHORS

Enstrom, E. A., Director of Research, Peterson System of Directed
    Handwriting Inc., Greensburg, Pennsylvania   182

Goodwin, William L., Assistant Professor, Bucknell University,
    Lewisburg, Pennsylvania   502

Gray, Roland F., Associate Professor of Education, University of
    British Columbia, B. C., Canada   292

Hahn, Harry T., Professor of Education, Oakland University,
    Rochester, Michigan   58

Halliwell, Joseph W., Professor of Education, St. John's University,
    Jamaica, N.Y.   422

Hampleman, Richard S., Professor of Education, North Texas
    State University, Denton   453

Hillerich, Robert, Assistant Superintendent, Glenview, Illinois   47

Hodges, Richard E., Associate Professor of Education, University
    of Chicago, Illinois   167

Homze, Alma, Assistant Professor of Education, Teachers College,
    University of Nebraska, Lincoln   139

Inbody, Donald, Director of Instruction, Corinth District Schools,
    Prairie Village, Kansas   373

Jones, J. Charles, Professor of Education, Bucknell University,
    Lewisburg, Pennsylvania   484

Joyce, Bruce, Teachers College, Columbia University,
    New York   231

Kramer, Klass, Professor of Education, State University of
    Brockport, New York   322

Lambert, Philip, Professor of Education, University of Wisconsin,
    Madison   502

Long, Elizabeth   223

Lundsteen, Sara W., Associate Professor of Education, University
    of Texas, Austin   131

Mackintosh, Helen K., Retired from U. S. Office of Education,
    Washington, D.C.   115

Malmstrom, Jean, Professor of English, Western Michigan
    University, Kalamazoo   156

Mason, John M., Professor of Education, Michigan State
    University, East Lansing   430

May, Frank B., Associate Professor of Education, Washington
    State University, Pullman   145

McAulay, J. D., Professor of Elementary Education, Pennsylvania
    State University, University Park, Pennsylvania   261

McCracken, Robert A., Professor of Education, Western
    Washington State College, Bellingham   103

PREFACE

Change is taking place throughout the entire fabric of our educational system. Innovations are being introduced at an increasingly rapid rate, so rapid that educators are hard pressed to keep up with what is going on, much less make value judgments about the innovations. The number of research studies produced as a result of federal and foundation grants as well as by dissertation and other more traditional means is also increasing rapidly.

The purpose of this book is to provide seniors, graduate students, and practitioners in the field of elementary education a perspective of new developments and proven practices through critically selected reports of research.

The development of this book stems from a belief that the mature student of elementary education needs to have a thorough acquaintanceship with the research literature, to be aware of research models in basic aspects of the elementary school program, and to have sound notions as to what research will and will not tell him about the more crucial issues of the day. The research reported in this book should provide a beginning for serious thinking and growth in point of view about newer trends and issues in elementary education. And while this book does not treat all subject areas, programs, or newer trends of elementary education, it should provide the reader with important intellectual tools and motivations to attack those not specifically covered.

One of the purposes of this book is to reduce the lag between research and practice through bringing important researches to the attention of practitioners; by developing an acquaintanceship with the sources and tools of locating research; by developing an appreciation for research and its possible contributions; and by developing skills in evaluating, interpreting, and applying research.

Research is becoming an increasingly important tool to the educator because there is much more research, the quality of research is improving, and it is ever more crucial that practitioners have better answers to their problems.

The increasingly sophisticated research resulting from improved statistics, computer assistance, more highly trained researchers, and better funding is providing some useful answers about newer trends and older practices for the practicing educator. Consequently, this book should serve the educator by providing guides to the research, useful models, and clues to using the research.

A sound point of view or coordinated set of beliefs about society and education in general, and about elementary education in particular, is a vital piece of intellectual equipment for any person hoping to give leadership in elementary schools. Research can better aid the educator if he has a clearly defined set of values and hierarchy of educational goals. The introductory chapter and discussions accompanying the researches should aid the reader in clarifying his point of view about better elementary school programs.

It is anticipated that this book would serve as a useful text in senior or graduate level curriculum courses, student teaching, and courses concerned with research or newer trends in elementary education. Evaluation of research studies is often an indispensable part of such courses. By evaluating research studies, the student learns to differentiate between good practices, which he may wish to emulate, and poor practices, which should be avoided if and when he conducts research. Furthermore, class discussions of research studies (a case study technique) are of maximum value if all students have had an opportunity to study the research being discussed. Unfortunately most textbooks written for curriculum courses, student teaching, or educational research do not supply original research studies for class evaluation.

In general, it is hoped that the book will prove helpful to the practitioner who wants to remain abreast of or to make increasing use of the research in elementary education.

1

INTRODUCTION

A highly effective educational system is essential to our democratic and technical society. The first and most important phase of this system is the elementary school (kindergarten–grade 8). Too often, curriculum practices fall far short of the mark. The importance of good elementary schools is generally taken for granted, but such schools must be brought closer to reality for all children.

The curriculum, the heart of effective elementary education, is the sum total of the experiences the children have under the supervision of the school. The most important step toward improving elementary schools is insuring that these experiences are significant. They must be consistent with the best directions or goals that can be developed; must be balanced in relation to the areas of man's knowledge and problems; and must allow emphasis on individual interests, talents, and abilities.

In the final analysis, research is an attempt to find information that will lead to better answers. In this volume, some tentative answers are proposed to two questions: What experiences are best to provide children? How may these experiences best be provided?

While newness is no certain criterion of importance or quality, it is an educator's responsibility continually to develop new ideas, to examine and evaluate new trends, and, where they are deemed promising, to try new practices. This volume presents, through research reports, selected newer trends and provides the reader with attitudes, skills, and understandings with which to deal with these and future developments.

SCOPE OF THE VOLUME

A quick glance at the table of contents will indicate the major topics treated in this volume. There have been many significant studies relating to education. To choose the most important or the best-designed of them would be a controversial, if not impossible, task. Those included here have been chosen to illustrate important topics in selected areas of the elementary school program and the ways in which research procedures have been employed to cast new light on the learner and the learning processes at various stages of the child's development. The studies are not presented as perfect in structure or in execution. The researchers themselves would be the first to recognize their limitations. However, each report adds to the understanding of the possibilities of research in education.

The content and quality of the research article itself were the primary features determining selection, but the following criteria were also utilized: (1) Studies reported in other books of readings or similar sources were generally excluded; (2) Studies reflected in government reports, dissertations, long monographs, and similar sources were excluded in favor of shorter journal-published research reports; and (3) No more than one report was included for any single researcher.

The writers have tried, for the volume as a whole, to select studies which dealt with problems at various age and grade levels. These efforts resulted in a grade level distribution as follows: K–12, five studies; K–2, two studies; K, three studies; grade 1, one study; grades 1–6, five studies; grades 1–2–3, four studies; grades 3–6, eight studies; grade 3, two studies; grade 4, two studies; grade 5, one study; grade 6, six studies; grades 4–8, five studies; and grade 7, one study.

In addition to the research reports, there are short chapter introductions, topic introductions, and bibliographies. The introduction to each chapter presents its scope, cross-referencing to relevant chapters, a brief analysis of the studies (classified by the type of research and the age or grade level of the sample), a list of research sources (journals, annual lists, key bibliographies, or broad research summaries), and often ideas for further needed research. The article introductions comment on the topic, classify the study (by the type of research and the topic it treats), note some of its strengths and weaknesses, and indicate its relationship to other researches, both within and outside this volume. The bibliography following each selection, entitled "For Further Reading," includes general sources on the topic, research analyses and evaluation summaries, other recent research studies, and definitive articles related to the topic under consideration. The cross-referencing can be most useful to the reader, since a research study often cuts across more than one topic. For example, many research reports related in some way to social studies fall outside the chapter on that topic, such as: the studies of interpersonal relations in children's literature, information sources children use, the seventh and eighth grade core program.

More specific considerations were also kept in mind in compiling this anthology: (1) In each chapter, various grade levels are represented (kindergarten, primary, intermediate, and junior high school); (2) One study of historical overview is included in most of the chapters to give a time perspective on the topic; (3) The broadest possible range of topics has been selected for each chapter; (4) A wide variety of research techniques is represented, though not necessarily in any single chapter; (5) Only one research study has been presented for each topic and shorter, more recent research reports have been favored. Page limitations dictated that not every possible or even important subtopic could be treated within each chapter. In many cases a given topic (children's interests, study skills, or grade placement, for examples) is treated in only one chapter, although the applicability of such topics is mentioned in the introductions to various chapters. The reader may observe that while there is no separate chapter devoted to early childhood education, a wide variety of articles deal with this topic, including Hillerich on pre-reading skills (Chapter 2); Hahn on approaches to beginning reading (Chapter 2); Bjonerud on the arithmetic concepts of pre-schoolers (Chapter 5); Inbody on primary children's understandings of natural phenomena (Chapter 6); Hampleman on the age of admission to school (Chapter 7); and Dobbs and Neville on retention of first graders (Chapter 7). Finally, while the book does not present a chapter on "Evaluation," two research articles were selected dealing with the topic of testing and evaluating (see McCracken, Chapter 2 and Nelson and Mason, Chapter 6). And while art, music, health–physical education, and foreign language are certainly a part of the elementary school curriculum, it was decided to not include them in this volume. The writers believe that a superficial treatment leads only to frustration, and an adequate presentation of these areas would require an entire separate volume.

From this overview, the reader may see the various uses of this book. For the undergraduate or the student teacher, for example, it can provide a broad summary of selected aspects of the elementary school curriculum and an overall perspective of trends and issues in the field from a research orientation. For the teacher with four to six years of experience, who has not participated in further formal study, the volume may provide one means of self-instruction. For the graduate student, it should prove valuable in bringing researches and sources of research to his attention. For educational leaders (principals and supervisors), the book should provide an opportunity to probe more deeply into pertinent questions and problems associated with elementary education, as well as recent research on these topics.

The remainder of this introductory chapter is devoted to an examination of the nature of research and the role of research in elementary education and the presentation of a point of view which attempts to relate research implications and the basic principles of elementary education, these principles being approached from the viewpoint of the curriculum, methods of teaching, organization, materials, and evaluation.

NATURE OF RESEARCH

Research may in the final analysis merely be called problem solving. It represents a careful inquiry or examination in an attempt to discover new information or relationships or to explain or verify existing knowledge.

Common Elements of Journal-Published Research Reports

A good many researches are reported in this volume. Customarily, a report on completed research, when it appears as an article in a professional journal, follows an outline such as this:

I Presentation of the Problem
   Review of the literature, if appropriate
   Review of prior studies, if appropriate
   Summary of local issues, if appropriate
   Clear statement of solution being sought

II Procedures Employed
   Description of population or samples used
   Objectives or hypotheses being tested
   Instrumentation and statistical collection methods
   Summary tables, when appropriate
   Methods of analyzing data, including statistical tests and decisions

III Results
   Presentation of findings, including levels of statistical significance
   Logical analyses of major findings

IV Discussion
   References to objectives or hypotheses being tested
   Ideas on extended meanings of the findings for additional studies
V References
   References in standard form for bibliographical search
   Annotated references, if desired (1)

Types of Research and their Characteristics

As the reader studies each research report, he will become aware of the various types of research and their characteristics. While there is some preference for three categories of classification (historical, descriptive, and experimental), the following categories have been accepted for this volume:

Descriptive: Research in which the researcher reports on records which may have been kept by someone else; includes reviews, historical studies, and textbook analyses or comparisons

Survey: Research which attempts to find characteristics of a population by asking a sample through the use of a questionnaire or interview; includes also the status study, in which a group is investigated as it is to ascertain pertinent characteristics (measures assigned variable only)

Case study: Research in which the researcher describes in depth what is happening to one designated unit, usually one child

Action research: Research which uses nominal controls; generally teacher or school originated; procedures of actual practice may be described

Correlational: Research which studies relationships between two or more variables (2); uses correlational statistics primarily

Ex post facto: Research in which the independent variable or variables were manipulated in the past; the researcher starts with the observation of a dependent variable or variables. He then studies the independent variables in retrospect for their possible effects on the dependent variables. (He may examine interrelationships of two or more assigned variables or two or more levels of one assigned variable.)

Experimental: Research in which the independent variable or variables are manipulated by the researcher to quantitatively measure their effect on some dependent variable or variables, to test a logically derived hypothesis. (3)

Each of the above-mentioned types of research serves a particular function. Historical research provides us with a perspective on the future, as well as recording truths about the past. Descriptive research (including surveys, case studies, and correlational research as categorized above) aims at answering the general question of "What exists?" Such factual information enables the profession to make more intelligent plans for future courses of action, helps interpret the educational problems more effectively to the public, focuses attention upon needs, and can be used to justify or improve immediate school situations. In contrast, experimental research aims at the "how" and "why" questions and the observations are usually controlled in some way. Most descriptive studies portray the state of things, but less often seek to account for them. Of course, descriptive studies may involve experimentation. Studies vary in classification, primarily to fit the purpose of the investigation.

Using the categories above, the writers find that they have selected 8 studies of the descriptive type, 7 surveys, 1 case study, 2 action research studies, 1 correlational study, 9 ex post facto studies, and 17 experimental—making a total of 45 studies.

Criteria for Good Research

Some general criteria are presented below. These should be kept in mind in interpreting and evaluating the reports contained in this volume. They are not addressed to sophisticated researchers and are not intended as a substitute for a deeper study of research design and statistics, but rather to introduce the reader to some basic considerations.

1. The problem should be clearly stated and limited, and have contemporary significance or relevance. The purposes, objectives, testable hypotheses, or specific questions should be clearly presented. Crucial terms should be identified.

   Often the report should include at least a brief review of previous related studies. Familiarity with the research in the field is demonstrated by such a review and it permits comparison of the findings with those of previous investigators. (It is recognized that space-conscious journal editors often shorten or delete this part of the report.) Reference may be made to the study's theoretical orientation.

2. The manipulated, controlled, and observed variables should be described. Examples of manipulated variables are methods of teaching or length of time for practice. Controlled variables are those held constant or limited. One may control spelling content while varying teaching methods. In

descriptive research, the reporter may be dealing only with observed variables—such as vocabulary of kindergarten children.

3. The report should provide a description of the procedures utilized that is specific and clear enough to enable another person to reproduce the study. Details about the duration of the study, treatments used, and the like should be given. (In survey research, of course, there would be no treatments administered.) Judgments made concerning the length of the study, the data collected, control of the treatments, and the like should be frankly disclosed and justified if necessary.

4. Characteristics of the subjects or groups (population, number, procedures for selection of sample) should be clearly presented. Usually, for example, the investigator wants to apply his findings to all third graders (the total population), not just to one third grade. To represent this population, he will select for participation in the experiment a smaller collection (the sample) that is representative of the entire group about which he wants to draw conclusions. The nature of these pupils should be described in enough detail to permit the reader to determine for what kinds of pupils the results are applicable.

In comparing one method of instruction with another—a common experimental type of study—close attention should be devoted to pupils, teachers, methods, and school setting. Pupils (in pairs or groups) could be matched on intelligence, age, readiness factors, physical condition, set toward learning, and cultural background—to name some major items. Teachers could be matched on personality, knowledge, and experience. A common way of achieving this effect is a fair but rigorous random assignment of pupils (or groups), teachers, and methods. The technical feature that defines a random sample is simply that each member of the population has an equal chance of being selected every time a member is drawn. Of course, the broader the population represented by the sample, the broader are the generalizations that can be made from the results of the research.

If matching or random sampling is not used, a statistical device (analysis of covariance) can make adjustments for the differences among groups that exist at the start of the experiment. This statistical adjustment is roughly equivalent to the equalization of the groups which might be achieved by highly selective sampling.

The report should note the school setting—the organization of the classes and the characteristics of the school. The time allotted to instruction should be controlled, as well as the supervision or attention given to those involved in the study. The "Hawthorne effect"—that is, the fact that a new program results in gains due to novelty or enthusiasm rather than the treatment—should be guarded against. Other "hidden" classroom influences should be accounted for—the time of day the classes meet, motivation by classroom rewards, size of classes, and the like.

5. The evaluation instruments should be appropriate for the hypotheses being tested. If the test is of a standardized nature it should be so described. If a test was developed for the study, representative items used in the test may be reproduced in the report and data concerning validity and reliability should be included. The term "validity" refers to the extent to which a test does the specific job for which it is used, while "reliability" means the extent to which a test is consistent in measuring whatever it does measure—that is, whether it is dependable and stable and gives similar results time and again. A test of science would be invalid, for example, if it incorporated such a high level of reading proficiency that difficulties in understanding the vocabulary interfered with a pupil's performance on the test. However, such a test could be reliable.

There is a distinction between non-standardized and standardized tests. The test that an individual constructs is likely to be less expertly designed than that of the professional. In the standardized test, each item has been subjected to careful analysis, as have total scores, and validity and reliability have been established, based upon the performance of many subjects of various ages living in many different types of communities and geographic areas. Not only the content of the test, but also its administration and scoring have been standardized so that all those taking the test will take it under the same conditions. While this is not to claim that all standardized tests are optimum, they have been made as sound as possible in the light of what is known by experts in test construction, administration, and interpretation.

6. The most effective techniques (not necessarily the most complicated) should be applied to scores and ratings. These may be descriptive measures (means, medians, percentages, quartiles, ranks, and the like). Often the major purpose of the statistical analysis is to determine whether the obtained differences in the two or more groups can be ascribed to chance. Because there are always a number of uncontrolled factors operating in an experiment, the effects that are observed cannot all be attributed to the experimental variable. There are available a number of statistical procedures to determine the probability that an observed effect is due to these "chance" factors. This probability is referred to as the level of confidence or significance. For example, if an effect is significant at the .01 level of confidence, it means that there is only 1 chance in 100 that differences as large as those observed could have occurred by chance.

7. The results should be precisely stated in the report.

8. Few, if any, studies are "perfect" in every respect. The mature investigator recognizes the limitations of his study and states only conclusions which can be adequately supported by the findings. For example, he does not generalize beyond the limitation of the type of population from which he sampled. In the interpretation of some investigations it is not uncommon to find cause and effect inferred when, truly, relationship is

the only thing that can be inferred. Unless the investigation has been *designed* to study cause and effect, the existence of a relationship *per se* does *not* warrant a cause-effect inference.

9. Perhaps needless to add, the organization of the report should be logical and the style clear. The study should be as free as possible from bias on the part of the experimenter. His attitude should represent an honest desire to discover or test some generalization about which he believes he is not fully informed.

A summary of some characteristics of research may clarify the ideas presented to this point. Research gathers new knowledge or data. It places emphasis upon the detection of general principles, going beyond the specific groups and situations investigated and, by careful sampling procedures, inferring qualities of the entire population. Research is systematic investigation. The researcher knows what is already known about his problem. He starts from this point, carefully planning his procedures. Data are gathered, recorded, and analyzed. He uses data-gathering instruments as valid as he can find or devise. Where appropriate, he uses mechanical means to improve on the accuracy of human observation. Research is objective. The researcher strives to eliminate personal feeling and preference. He avoids the temptation to seek only the data that support his hypothesis. Rather than attempt to persuade or to prove, he emphasizes testing the hypothesis. The researcher endeavors to organize his data and express them as usefully as possible. He permits his data and logic to lead to sound conclusions. Research is carefully reported. The terms are defined, procedures are described in detail, limiting factors are recognized, and results are objectively recorded. Conclusions and generalizations are cautiously arrived at, with due consideration for all of the limitations of methodology, data collection, and errors of human interpretation.

Several other ideas for interpreting and evaluating the research reports presented in this volume are suggested to the reader:

1. Read the entire study to get an overview. Identify the portions that deal with: (a) statement of the problem, (b) procedures used to collect data, (c) analysis of the data, and (d) conclusions. Determine whether the data gathered are related to the problem as stated, and whether the conclusions are related to the evidence presented.

2. Reexamine the sections dealing with the procedures used to collect and analyze the data. Ask yourself questions: Has the population studied been adequately described? Was the method of sampling, if used, specified? Are the instruments for gathering data described? Were provisions made to control variables described?

3. Reread the results. Now that the investigator has told what he did, what did he find?

4. Reexamine each conclusion. Ask yourself questions: Has the evidence justified this conclusion? Are any others, not stated by the author, justified by the evidence? What conclusions, if any, can be generalized from the particular educational setting in which the research was done?

Guidelines for Evaluating Educational Research

For the interested reader, a bibliography of guidelines for evaluating educational research is provided below:

Books

Best, John W., *Research in Education* (Englewood Cliffs, N.J.: Prentice-Hall, Inc., 1959), pp. 278–281, 307.

Borg, Walter R., *Educational Research: An Introduction* (New York: David McKay Co., Inc., 1963), pp. 326–345.

Campbell, Donald T., and Julian C. Stanley, "Experimental and Quasi-Experimental Designs for Research on Teaching" in N. L. Gage (editor), *Handbook of Research on Teaching* (Chicago: Rand McNally and Co., 1963), Chapter 5, pp. 171–246.

Mouly, George J., *The Science of Educational Research* (New York: American Book Company, 1963), pp. 503–504.

Rummel, J. Francis, *An Introduction to Research Procedures in Education,* 2nd edition (New York: Harper & Row, Publishers, 1964), pp. 268–269.

Sax, Gilbert, *Empirical Foundations of Educational Research* (Englewood Cliffs, N.J.: Prentice-Hall, Inc., 1968) *passim.*

Travers, Robert M. W., *An Introduction to Educational Research,* 2nd edition (New York: The Macmillan Company, 1964), pp. 82–88.

Van Dalen, Deobold B., *Understanding Educational Research* (New York: McGraw-Hill Book Company, 1962), pp. 366–376.

Periodicals and Other Sources

Anderson, J. and A. H. Kerr, "A Checklist for Evaluating Educational Research", *Educational Research* 11 (November 1968) 74–75.

Dvorak, Earl A., "General Guide to a Study of Research Reports," *Peabody Journal of Education* 34 (November 1956) 141–144.

Farquhar, William W., and John D. Krumboltz, "A Check List for Evaluating Experimental Research in Psychology and Education," *Journal of Educational Research* 52 (May 1959) 353–354.

Romberg, Thomas A., "Criteria for Evaluating Educational Research", Technical Memo No. S-61-1, Wisconsin Research and Development Center for Cognitive Learning, Madison: The University of Wisconsin, January 1969.

Suydam, Marilyn N., "An Instrument for Evaluating Experimental Educational Research Reports," *Journal of Educational Research* 61 (January 1968) 200–203.

Van Dalen, D. B., "A Research Check List in Education," *Educational Administration and Supervision* 44 (May 1958) 174–181.

Major Sources for Locating Research Reports

While each chapter that follows provides research sources for its specific subject, the remaining portion of this section will deal with some of the major sources for interpreting and locating research information. The first grouping presents major locational tools and resources:

Alexander, Carter, and Arvid J. Burke, *How to Locate Educational Information and Data,* 4th edition, (New York: Bureau of Publications, Teachers' College, Columbia University, 1958). This book provides the user with hundreds of sources for locating educational information and data.

American Educational Research Association, N.E.A., *Review of Educational Research* (Washington, D.C.: U.S. Government Printing Office, 1931 to present, five issues per year). This journal reports research findings and conclusions by areas of interest. It identifiies, summarizes, and critically analyzes research studies. Research literature is ordinarily summarized in three-year cycles, although some topics have been treated regularly but less frequently and others have been introduced at irregular intervals.

Cumulative Book Index (New York: H. W. Wilson Co., 1928 to present). This monthly publication indexes all books published in the English language by author, title, and subject. It is helpful in assuring the student that all pertinent published books have been covered in his researches.

Dissertation Abstracts (Ann Arbor, Michigan: University of Michigan, monthly). This is a collection of abstracts of doctoral dissertations and monographs which are available complete on microfilm or in other forms.

Education Index (New York: H. W. Wilson Co., monthly, 1929 to present). This is a useful guide to books and periodicals in education since January 1929. It lists nearly all educational literature from significant sources.

Gage, N. L., editor, *Handbook of Research on Teaching* (Chicago: Rand McNally & Co., 1963). This book contains 23 sections written by 31 authors, each of whom is a specialist. It presents a comprehensive range of basic material for those interested in research on teaching.

Harris, Chester W., editor, *Encyclopedia of Educational Research*, 3rd edition (New York: The Macmillan Company, 1960). This volume gives the outstanding researches—early as well as recent—on a large number of educational topics. The articles have been written by outstanding specialists in their particular fields. Three editions, published in 1941, 1950, and 1960, are available. An extensive bibliography is provided for each topic.

Readers' Guide to Periodical Literature (New York: H. W. Wilson Co., 1900 to present). Prior to 1929, when the *Education Index* was established, the *Readers' Guide* covered many of the educational journals.

U.S. Department of Health, Education, and Welfare, Office of Education, *Research in Education* (Washington, D.C.: U.S. Government Printing Office, monthly). An abstract journal, indexed by subjects, authors and investigators, and institutions. It deals with research projects funded by U.S. Office of Education as well as other reports collected by the 18 clearing houses that comprise the National ERIC (Educational Resources Information Center) network. Each abstract is accompanied by information as to where, in what form, and at what price the research may be obtained.

Two specialized sources of extreme value to the researcher are the following:

Buros, Oscar K., editor, *Mental Measurements Yearbook*, 6th edition (Highland Park, N.J.: Gryphon Press, 1966). This—and the past five volumes—lists commercially available educational, psychological, and vocational tests published during the period it covers, providing evaluative comments by authorities.

Good, Carter V., editor, *Dictionary of Education* (New York: McGraw-Hill Book Company, 1959). This source is very helpful in defining some 17,000 educational terms with precision.

The following general journals are rich sources of original research reports:

American Educational Research Association, N.E.A., *American Educational Research Journal* (Washington, D.C.: U.S. Government Printing Office, January 1964–present). This journal has published reports of studies in education, each article providing information on the purposes of the investigation, its design and procedures, a description of the sample studied, results, and conclusions and a discussion. It is published four times a year.

California Journal of Educational Research (Burlingame, California: California Teachers' Association). Published five times a year, this journal reports on research directed at the solution of educational problems, as well as digests of theses and dissertations.

Division of Educational Research Services, *The Alberta Journal of Educational Research* (Edmonton, Canada: The University of Alberta Press). This is a quarterly journal devoted to the dissemination, criticism, interpretation, and encouragement of all forms of systematic inquiry into education and related fields. Particularly helpful is the Tenth Anniversary edition, which contains abstracts of articles for Volumes I–X (1955–1964) classified under appropriate headings.

Educational Research (London: Newnes Educational Publishing Co., Ltd.). Published three times per year, this journal contains a readable synthesis of valid research on the practical problems posed by the English educational system. It is adequate in length and detail to acquaint the reader with the main results of the work, the sampling on which it was based and the experimental, statistical, and other techniques used.

Educational Research Bulletin (Columbus, Ohio: Bureau of Educational Research and Service, Ohio State University). Published nine times a year, this bulletin features articles on current areas of interest in educational research.

Elementary School Journal (Chicago, Illinois: University of Chicago Press). This general journal presents current articles and research topics in the field of elementary education. Emphasis is placed on the nontechnical type of reporting in most cases.

Journal of Educational Psychology (Washington, D.C.: American Psychological Association). Published bimonthly, this periodical presents original researches about problems of learning, teaching, and the psychological development of the individual. It deals with all levels of education and all age groups.

Journal of Educational Research (Madison, Wisconsin: Dembar Publications, Inc.). This journal reports significant research being carried on in a wide variety of areas. The articles state the problems, methods of procedure, conclusions, and implications. It is published nine times a year.

Journal of Experimental Education (Madison, Wisconsin: Dembar Publications, Inc.). Published quarterly (September, December, March, and June), this journal reports scientific investigations relating to various areas of the school program.

New Research in Education (London: Newnes Educational Publishing Co., Ltd.). Initially published annually (1967–1968), this journal will, starting in 1969, be published three times a year to meet the demand for rapid communication of research still in progress, even if the findings are only of a provisional nature. In addition, it includes shorter research reports and papers, substantial abstracts of research, and technical communciations on methodology.

As an example of the use of the resources mentioned above, suppose you are planning to read or write about the responses of male and female teachers to the behavior of boys and girls as rated on a particular behavior rating schedule. First, you might list all possible headings under which this topic might be listed in the major indexes (card catalogue; *Education Index; Readers' Guide to Periodical Literature; Cumulative Book Index*) such as: teacher attitudes, teacher behavior, teaching ratings, sex differences or sex roles, behavior ratings, individual differences, rating scales. Next, you could consult general sources for more specific books, bibliographies, and references (as *Encyclopedia of Educational Research, Handbook of Research on Teaching, Review of Educational Research, What Research Says to the Teacher* Series). Thirdly, specific sources for the references could be consulted, such as *Dissertation Abstracts,* periodic journal bibliographies on the topic, summaries of researches in journals, books of readings, specific books on the topic, specific chapters in general books on the topic. Here you would give particular attention to those journals which are mentioned above as resources of original research reports. (Also note the major resources which are directed at certain areas of the elementary school program.)

Based on the findings of these steps, develop a card file of specific references. Locate, read, and take notes on them. Take care that notes are accurate so that they may be used with confidence later for quotations and footnotes. Study the footnotes and bibliographies of the articles for further relevant references. Keep on the lookout for other possible headings under which relevant information might be listed. After a thorough study of the literature, as outlined above, you should be prepared to write a paper on the topic. If you intend to do a research study, more is needed: restating the problem more precisely and in detail; stating hypotheses to be tested; outlining procedures for testing hypotheses including the sample, measuring devices, experimental program (if any), and statistical analyses. In some cases, consultation of specific literature on sampling, tests, experimental procedures, and statistical procedures would be advisable.

Some references which might assist the reader as he proceeds into the writing stage of his research are listed below:

American Psychological Association, *Publication Manual*, revised, Washington, D.C.: American Psychological Association, 1967.

Campbell, William G., *Form and Style in Thesis Writing*, Boston: Houghton Mifflin Co., 1954.

Turabian, Kate, *Manual for the Writers of Term Papers, Theses, and Dissertations*, 3rd edition, Chicago: University of Chicago Press, 1967.

ROLE OF RESEARCH IN ELEMENTARY EDUCATION

Importance of Research to Elementary Education

Over the past 50 years, the elementary schools have pioneered educational change, perhaps because there are so many of these schools; perhaps because they have been free of the restrictions of Carnegie units, college entrance requirements, and accrediting associations; and perhaps because they have been less tied to subject matter than other units of the educational system. Whatever the reason for their leadership in experimentation, it is natural that elementary schools should turn to research for continued growth. That they do so is important for at least three reasons.

First, given the major changes taking place in most areas of life today, the significant alterations in the academic disciplines, important additions to our knowledge of child development and learning, and the changing role of elementary schools in our educational system and society, continued evolution of the elementary school is imperative. This evolution can avoid random vacillation with the aid of soundly conceived scientific research and philosophic thinking.

Second, evaluation of a variety of types of in-service teacher education suggests that one of the most effective means to change a teacher's behavior is to guide him to discover, through his own research, more effective ways of teaching. In other words, educational change is more likely to occur if the teacher finds out for himself the problems and more effective solutions to them.

Third, there is a tendency in our dynamic society for the "new" to be revered for its own sake. This attitude often leads to blind alleys, wasting much effort and opportunity, unless tempered by a pragmatic, scientific attitude. A continuous demand—"let's take a look at the research evidence"—should be basis for sound progress.

Lag Between Research and Practice

It is important that elementary school teachers, principals, and supervisors be fully aware of research focusing on the questions facing the elementary school. However, there is a considerable lag between publication of the researchers' findings and awareness of them among elementary school personnel. Some estimate this gap as 50 years, but documentation would be difficult.

The many sources cited earlier in this chapter exist to make the findings of researchers more available. But despite these efforts there remains a wide gap. Some of the reasons for this lag are: (1) There is an increasing amount of research, (2) research reports are often difficult to locate, (3) the reports are frequently quite technical and a large portion of elementary school personnel are not prepared to understand and evaluate research studies, (4) the methods books widely used in educating elementary school personnel often are not research oriented, and (5) elementary school personnel are not prepared to engage in research themselves. The present volume is conceived as an attempt to bring research and practice closer together by helping teachers become acquainted with a wide variety of research reports and locate and evaluate research, and by encouraging research activities they can engage in themselves.

Research is valuable, but perhaps more in its promise than in its realization. Research in elementary school education does not contain a treasure of definitive answers about what or how to teach. In fact, answers to such questions hardly exist at all. The best researchers indicate their awareness of their limitations by being very careful to circumscribe any conclusions based on their findings, making reference to the limits of their samplings or their controls. The reader is cautioned not to select from some piece of research something that fits his "pet idea" or use it as his only justification for action. A cautious and tentative use of whatever knowledge can be established as sound is more appropriate. Perhaps the experience of Braddock, Lloyd-Jones, and Schoer (4) will underscore for the reader some of the caution needed in interpreting research findings. In 1963, they undertook to review the research on the teaching of written composition, starting with 1000 bibliographic citations, and making a more careful examination of 500, in order to identify "the dozen or so most soundly based studies." They finally found 5 acceptable researches. Such a statement is not intended to discourage the reader from consulting research for the help it can provide, nor from engaging in research himself, but it can serve as a caution regarding what research has done and may do.

Role of the Practitioner as Consumer and Producer

The practitioner in elementary education has a choice of being a follower, implementing someone else's directions, or a leader, having some share in the decision-making process. The truly professional educator is desirous and capable of making decisions, and is willing to engage in critical thinking and research to reach the best possible decisions. Too many school personnel are willing to let someone else make their decisions, thus denying their professional roles. The university researcher can be a very narrow technical specialist, who may not know the most appropriate application of his findings. The day-by-day practitioner, who sees the forces that bear upon the child and his teaching, must have an important share in the application of research findings.

A significant part of good research is asking the correct question. That this can often be done best by the practitioner suggests an important need for effective liason between the practitioner and the researcher. This liason can be accomplished in several ways, including: (1) The practitioner also being the researcher, (2) the practitioner and the researcher being on a team together, or (3) the researcher visiting or working in the classroom from time to time.

The problem of the dissemination and utilization of research findings is usually largely alleviated when the practitioner is himself the researcher. Not only does he apply his own findings but he is more inclined to seek and use the findings of other researchers. The elementary school teacher who appreciates good research and understands the criteria and techniques for scientific investigation is much more likely to be able to guide children in the inquiry method, in independent study, in increasing understanding and skill in the use and appreciation of the scientific method.

Limitations of Research

It is important to keep in mind that there are significant limitations to what research can do. Research cannot answer a great many questions, although it can answer certain kinds. For example, historical research can tell us reasonably well what has happened in the past, although it sometimes gets into difficulty when it attempts to evaluate happenings. Descriptive and survey research can tell us about existing practices, conditions, or characteristics. Similarly, experimental research can tell us moderately well what specific events will happen under certain carefully specified conditions, although, given the complexity of human beings, there are important limitations even here.

What scientific research cannot tell us is what should happen. Should foreign languages be included in the elementary school program? Should the selected language be Latin, French, or Chinese? Where should the time come from for foreign language instruction? These are important questions, and it is possible that research can contribute data to their solution, but it cannot really answer them. Philosophic thinking about values or beliefs, along with research data, must be applied to obtain sound answers.

Research, the Slave of Philosophy

In sorting out the various issues associated with the elementary school program to identify a specific problem to attack at a given time, the researcher is wearing the hat of the philosopher. He is making value judgments about what is more important or more relevant; he is seeking the more crucial issues or those that will produce significant results. Thus every researcher has a point of view which leads him to his study and guides him during it. The work of the researcher, then, should be based on a sound set of values—comprehensive, internally consistent, and ordered—and sound processes of reasoning from these values.

Similarly, at the conclusion of his research, the effective researcher seeks to spell out as best he can what he sees as the implications of his findings, again a philosophical process. He places his specific conclusions in perspective within the complex of conclusions about elementary school practice. This is a value-manipulating process, requiring that the researcher reason logically and be acquainted with the world of values. In this terminal phase of his study the researcher needs a sound set of beliefs concerning children, the learning process, knowledge, society, and the functions of schools.

POINT OF VIEW ON ELEMENTARY EDUCATION

Some of the values (or biases) of the writers have already been revealed in the preceding pages. It may be useful to the reader to identify a few others, which may enable him to understand why certain researches were selected, to be aware of some of the beliefs that might influence researchers, and to reexamine his own set of values for comprehensiveness, consistency, and orderliness. It is one of the aims of this volume to help the reader develop a better set of principles about elementary education. The critical examination of researches can be quite helpful to this development. But before this close analysis can take place, there must be some criteria. Perhaps the following discussion will further stimulate the reader to a more conscious awareness of his values, which he can then use to examine the researches in the remainder of this volume. Below is a list of some of the beliefs which have guided the writers, and which the reader may consider for himself:

1. The writers have assumed as a basic point of view that "the" answer has not yet been found; in other words, that there is always room for improvement. No methodology is considered above question—no content is "sacred." A good researcher or consumer of research should consider his conclusions to some degree tentative—subject to reexamination and experimentation.

2. There is seldom any single correct way to do anything, nor any single correct answer to a problem. There is more than one correct way to teach reading, there is more than one correct set of social studies facts to be learned. Often, proponents of a particular method, subject matter, or school organization seem to want others to believe that theirs is the only correct one. This is a danger to which researchers and practitioners alike are exposed as they become ego-involved in the conclusions or applications of research.

3. Elementary school personnel have the responsibility and should have the freedom to vary their methods and their content to seek better instructional programs. This freedom places an obligation on the teacher, the administrator, and the supervisor. The teacher must read, study, think, and identify the ideas he wishes to try in the classroom. The administrator must set a climate in which the teacher feels that such actions are expected and rewarded. He must also help the teacher find the time, the materials, and the personnel needed to experiment. The supervisor also has an obligation, not only to encourage and support such experimentation but to aid in supplying technical know-how and materials. This belief is consistent with the idea of every teacher being, as much as possible, both a consumer and a producer of research.

4. The writers stress the idea that just because an idea or technique is new is no reason to assume that it is as good or better than older ideas or techniques. New ideas have glamor and excitement, adjustment to them

is continually demanded of us, and much that is new turns out to be a significant improvement over the old. But researchers have a basic obligation to withhold judgment concerning the new until there is sufficient evidence to warrant its acceptance or rejection.

5. Methods, materials, organization, and evaluation are determined by the goals or purposes of education. More specifically, a method of teaching is only justifiable if it achieves desirable goals. Using arithmetic exercises as a method of punishment can cause the learner to dislike arithmetic. To require all members of the fifth grade to use the same social studies text when not all have a fifth grade reading ability is inexcusable for that reason alone, not to mention many other good reasons. Organizational devices must also be measured or justified in terms of their contribution to learning. Similarly, an evaluation device can be justified only if it accomplishes the desired goals and does not contribute other undesirable effects.

   As the reader considers the researches included in this volume, it is important that he evaluate their findings by their contributions to what, to him, are significant educational goals. For example, one researcher of school admission age concludes that many children have a much better chance of success in reading if they start school a few months later. The reader should ask himself what sorts of goals early and late admission achieve and draw his conclusions about what age of admission to use in terms of his evaluation of these goals. Single or multiple researches on methods, materials, organization, and evaluation cannot alone dictate a decision.

6. Not all educational goals are of equal importance. Because an educational practice contributes to a goal is not sufficient reason for its use. If a practice contributes to one goal but defeats the realization of another which is more important, then it should be avoided. For example, if it is found that programmed instruction, while teaching a specific body of subject matter, is at the same time teaching dependence and not developing independent study skills, it should be seriously questioned. This conclusion assumes that independence and command of effective study skills are more important goals than mastery of the subject matter in the program. It is important that one's point of view include some ordering of educational goals. Some of the following points constitute the writers' more important goals:

   a. One of the more important goals of elementary education is to develop as much individuality as possible while developing basic conformities. A minimum amount of general education designed to instill the society's most important values is essential for all children. At the same time the elementary school should strive to meet individual needs, adjust to individual differences in ability, encourage and develop individual interests, and nurture individual talents—either physical, social, or mental. Elementary education should make children alike only in a minimum number of basic ways—but it is fully as important to make children different in a great many ways, to foster self-realization, to encourage differentiation and specialization.

b. A second important goal of elementary education is developing in each child as much creative potential as he possesses. All children have some creative potential and it is the responsibility of the elementary school to develop any creative potential that exists. Since creativity is possible in all subjects, all should be taught so as to develop it. Two basic assumptions of this approach are that there may be more than one correct method of finding answers and there may be more than one correct answer. One of the tests of teaching methodologies in the elementary schools should be whether they foster or hinder creativity in the learners. This test applies to the findings of research on teaching strategies as well.

Creativity deserves a high place in goal priorities, since it is a crucial element in a dynamic society, it is essential to the self-realization of a person, and it is important in the developing of an effective international society.

c. A third top priority goal for elementary education is development of the ideas and skills of democracy. It is of crucial importance that educators ask themselves, about each practice incorporated in the elementary school, "Does this practice, by its content or precept, teach children democracy?" Democracy here is defined as a relationship of mutual respect between people. Everything educators do with children—all sorts of children—should say and imply that each child is of importance, he is to be respected. The methods used, the types of materials placed in their hands, and the organization of the children, should always be influenced by the desire to inculcate feelings of mutual respect. The disadvantaged child as well as the child from a minority group—racial, religious, or national in origin—must be shown in every way that he is respected so that he can participate effectively in all our democratic processes. The advantaged child, whether WASP, gifted, or rich, must also be given a realistic picture of himself and his role in a truly democratic society. The findings of research in elementary education must be measured against the criterion of democracy as a basic goal for schools.

d. A fourth priority goal for elementary schools is a balance of concern for the intellectual, emotional, social, and physical development of each child. There has been a strong tendency for schools, in their concern for excellence, to stress intellectual growth over other aspects of the child's development. This tendency has been strengthened by increased use (or misuse) of standardized tests, some grouping practice, and the recent stress on the structure of knowledge. The Association for Childhood Education International, the Association for Supervision and Curriculum Development, child development groups, and many psychologists and educators have over a period of years urged a concern for all facets of children's growth and development. The yearbook *Perceiving, Behaving, Becoming,* (5) is one of the classic statements of the ideas related to this goal. Growing concern for the disadvantaged child has reemphasized the necessity of more than the intellectual needs of the child.

7. There is a hierarchy among learning products which should guide curriculum and methods selection. In their order of importance from highest to lowest, they are: attitudes, skills, generalizations, concepts, facts, and habits. This ordering is based on the criteria of importance in influencing peoples' lives, importance to society, transfer, and retention. Attitudes are considered synonymous with values or beliefs and are emotionalized predispositions to act for or against something. (I like apples.) Skills are conceived to include such intellectual skills as problem solving, critical thinking, creative thinking, reading, writing, speaking, listening, and study skills as well as physical skills. (I can peel apples efficiently.) Generalizations are statements of relationships between concepts. (Apples are green before they are ripe.) Concepts are the integrated ideas one has regarding a thing. (All I know about apples is my concept of apples.) Facts are highly specific instances (this apple is red), and a habit is the tendency to repeat, without too much reflection, certain behavior. (I eat an apple a day.) All types of learning products are important and there should be some degree of balance among them in selecting learning goals. However, because of their more profound influence on the learner's life, their greater importance in a dynamic society, and the likelihood of greater retention and transfer, attitudes and intellectual skills should be stressed to a greater extent than other learning products.

8. Our changing society requires different learning goals than a static society. As power shifts from local to state, to federal, to international governments; as the roles and functions of the family are eroded by technology and other social agencies; as knowledge of the atom gives us awesome weapons to both save and destroy; as automation invades more and more aspects of our lives—the schools must emphasize different learning goals. Each area of the sciences and arts, due to intensive research, changed conceptions, societal demands, and the rapid accumulation of knowledge, is undergoing a metamorphosis. These changes are giving our society new tools, new ways of living, new styles, and new problems. School curricula, methods, materials, organizations, and evaluations must respond to them and to their causes and the resulting changes in society. In general the dynamic nature of our society demands greater emphasis on process goals—including more adequate self-concepts, abiding values, and inquiry techniques—than on content goals.

REFERENCES

1. Barnes, Fred P., *Research for the Practitioner in Education* (Washington, D.C.: Department of Elementary School Principals, NEA, 1964), pp. 109–110. Copyright 1964, Department of Elementary School Principals, National Education Association. All rights reserved.

2. In the above categories, the term "variable" is used. A variable is something which can change. Test scores, grades, experimental conditions, and the like are examples of typical variables in educational research. In nearly every study, the investigator has some special variable he wants to manipulate in order to see what happens to another variable as a result. The variable which the experimenter manipulates is called the "independent variable." The variable that is observed to see what happens to it as a result of this manipulation is called the "dependent variable." A simple example: Assume that we want to study the effect of handwriting practice on handwriting achievement of fifth grade children. We would manipulate the handwriting practice and observe the effect on achievement. Therefore, handwriting practice is the independent variable and handwriting achievement is the dependent variable. (Practice is of course not the only variable that can affect handwriting achievement. The ability of the subjects, their previous handwriting achievement, and probably their teacher will also affect the results. The experimenter must make sure that such relevant variables do not affect one group differently from another.)

3. Suydam, Marilyn, "An Evaluation of Journal-Published Research Reports of Elementary School Mathematics 1900–1965," unpublished doctoral dissertation (University Park: Pennsylvania State University, 1967), p. 500. Reprinted with permission.

4. Braddock, Richard, R. Lloyd-Jones, and Lowell Schoer, *Research in Written Composition* (Champaign, Illinois: National Council of Teachers of English, 1963).

5. Combs, Arthur W., chairman, *Perceiving, Behaving, Becoming*, Yearbook (Washington, D.C.: Association for Supervision and Curriculum Development, 1962).

FOR FURTHER READING

Barnes, Fred P., *Research For The Practitioner in Education* (Washington, D.C.: Department of Elementary School Principals, National Education Association, 1964).

Best, John W., *Research in Education* (Englewood Cliffs, N.J.: Prentice-Hall, Inc., 1959).

Cook, David R., *A Guide to Educational Research* (Boston: Allyn and Bacon, Inc., 1965).

Educational Policies Commission, N.E.A., *Education For All American Children* (Washington, D.C.: National Education Association, 1948).

Fleming, Robert S., *Curriculum for Today's Boys and Girls* (Columbus, Ohio: Charles E. Merrill Books, Inc., 1963).

Foshay, Arthur W., and Kenneth D. Wann, *Children's Social Values* (New York: Bureau of Publications, Teachers' College, Columbia University, 1954).

Franzblau, Abraham N., *A Primer of Statistics For Non-Statisticians* (New York: Harcourt, Brace and Co., 1958).

Gagne, Robert and William J. Gephart, editors, *Learning Research and School Subjects*, Eighth Annual Phi Delta Kappa Symposium on Educational Research (Itasca, Illinois: F. E. Peacock, Publishers, Inc., 1968).

Galfo, Armand J., and Earl Miller, *Interpreting Educational Research* (Dubuque: William C. Brown Company, Publishers, 1965).

Good, Carter V., *Introduction to Educational Research*, 2nd edition (New York: Appleton-Century-Crofts, 1963).

Herrick, Virgil E., John I. Goodlad, Frank J. Estvan, and Paul W. Eberman, *The Elementary School* (Englewood Cliffs, N.J.: Prentice-Hall, Inc., 1956).

Lee, J. Murray, and Doris May Lee, *The Child and His Curriculum*, 3rd edition (New York: Appleton-Century-Crofts, 1960).

Mouly, George J., *The Science of Educational Research* (New York: American Book Company, 1963).

Ragan, William B., *Modern Elementary School*, 3rd edition (New York: Holt, Rinehart & Winston, Inc., 1966).

Rummel, J. Francis, *An Introduction to Research Procedures in Education*, 2nd edition (New York: Harper & Row, 1964).

Travers, Robert M., *An Introduction to Educational Research* (New York: The Macmillan Company, 1964).

Van Dalen, Deobold, *Understanding Educational Research* (New York: McGraw-Hill Book Company, 1966).

Wandt, Edwin, *A Cross-Section of Educational Research* (New York: David McKay Co., Inc., 1965).

2

READING

Though school responsibilities have broadened over the years and there have been wide variations in the emphasis given to different areas of learning, elementary schools have consistently continued to stress instruction in reading. Educators have diligently sought the methods, materials, and organizational procedures that would provide optimum reading instruction for each child. Certainly more research has been conducted concerning reading than any other single area of elementary education. Yet, questions remain unanswered, some of which are reflected in the research reports in this chapter. While the following articles do not give "the answer," they do provide a clue as to how researchers have undertaken to study key aspects of reading, what tentative conclusions were reached, and what ideas deserve further study.

This chapter includes research reports on the following topics: an historical overview; pre-first grade reading; general approaches to the teaching of reading (ITA, Language Experience, Basic Readers); word recognition (phonics); rate of reading; interclass grouping; and evaluation.

The reader is reminded that cross-references are quite important to the use of this volume, since a research report often deals with more than one topic. There are several relevant reports outside this chapter: Schiller's study of study skills (Chapter 4); Smith's study of current events (Chapter 4); McAulay's study of map learnings (Chapter 4); Hampleman's study of reading achievement of early and late school starters (Chapter 7).

About half of the research reports for this chapter are of an experimental nature (Hillerich, Hahn, Bear, Powell); Smith's historical (descriptive) study opens the chapter; a correlational type of study

(Shores) is presented, as well as one classified as ex post facto (Mc-Cracken). Studies treat various grade levels, kindergarten through junior high school. Space prohibits presentation of studies representing some areas of interest to the reading teacher, such as context aids, early readers *per se*, legibility, reading interests of children, readability formulas, gifted readers, critical reading, and reading disabilities.

Some major resources directed specifically at reading which the reader will find helpful include:

Hunnicutt, C. W., and William J. Iverson, editors, *Research in the Three R's*, (New York: Harper and Brothers, 1958). This volume contains studies dealing with reading, writing, and arithmetic. The works were chosen for their influence and importance in the field.

Reading Research Quarterly (Newark, Delaware: International Reading Association, Fall 1965–present). This journal is published four times a year (Fall, Winter, Spring, and Summer) to accommodate lengthy and comprehensive reports, thus permitting depth and detail not possible in most journals of reading research. Other features include summaries of research, reviews of books on research, and critiques of the status of reading research. The same organization publishes *The Reading Teacher* which devotes considerable space and attention to the publication of research articles and includes a monthly feature entitled "What Research Says to the Reading Teacher."

The reader is advised to become familiar with the other publications of the International Reading Association (6 Tyre Avenue, Newark, Delaware 19711), the professional organization for persons concerned with improving reading at all educational levels. Publications include professional journals, annotated bibliographies on a variety of topics, a series of "prospectives in reading," convention proceedings, institute reports, reading aids, and other special publications.

A listing of other resources (journals, annual lists, key bibliographies, and research summaries) is given below for the benefit of those who are particularly interested in research in the area of reading instruction:

American Educational Research Association, *Review of Educational Research*, "Language Arts and Fine Arts" 31 (April 1961) 130–144; 34 (April 1964) 127–155; 37 (April 1967) 12–133.

American Educational Research Association, "Teaching Reading," *What Research Says to the Teacher*, No. 1 (Washington, D.C.: National Education Association, 1953).

Barton, Allen H., and David E. Wilder, "Research and Practice in the Teaching of Reading: A Progress Report" in M. B. Miles, editor, *Innovation in Education* (New York: Bureau of Publications, Teachers' College, Columbia University, 1964), pp. 361–398.

Burns, Paul C., and Vernon E. Troxel, "A Year of Research in Language Arts Instruction: 1960," *Elementary English* 38 (October 1961) 384–388.

———, "Another Year of Research in Language Arts Instruction: 1961," *Elementary English* 39 (October 1962) 549–555, 557.

Cutts, Warren G., *Research in Reading for the Middle Grades: An Annotated Bibliography*, U.S. Department of Health, Education, and Welfare, Office of Education Bulletin No. 31 (Washington, D.C.: U.S. Government Printing Office, 1963).

Durrell, Donald D., and Helen A. Murphy, "Boston University Research in Elementary School Reading, 1933–1963," *Journal of Education* 146 (December 1963).

Fay, Leo C., Weldon Bradtmueller, and Edward G. Summers, *Doctoral Studies in Reading*, 1919 through 1960, Vol. 40, No. 4 (Bloomington, Ind.: Bureau of Educational Studies, School of Education, Indiana University, 1964).

Gray, William S., *Summary of Investigations Relating to Reading*, Supplementary Educational Monographs No. 28 (Chicago: The University of Chicago Press, 1925).

———, "Summary of Reading Investigations" (1925–1932), *Journal of Educational Research* 26 (February 1933) 401–424. Similar summaries are published yearly in the February issue of the same journal, 1934–1960.

———, "Reading," in *Encyclopedia of Educational Research*, 3rd edition (New York: The Macmillan Company, 1960), pp. 1086–1135.

Gray, Miriam M., "Research and Elementary School Critical Reading Instruction," *Reading Teacher* 22 (February 1969) 453–459.

Gunderson, Doris V., *Research in Reading at the Primary Level, An Annotated Bibliography*, U.S. Department of Health, Education, and Welfare, Office of Education Bulletin No. 42 (Washington, D.C.: U.S. Government Printing Office, 1963).

Harris, Theodore L., "Summary of Investigations Relating to Reading," *Journal of Educational Research* 55, 56, 57, 58, 59, 60 (February 1962, 1963, 1964, 1965, 1966, 1967, 1968).

Karlin, Robert, "Research Results and Classroom Practices," *Reading Teacher* 21 (December 1967) 211–226.

King, Martha L., Bernice D. Ellinger, and Willavene Wolf, *Critical Reading* (Philadelphia: J. B. Lippincott Co., 1967).

Levin, Harry, "Reading Research: What, Why and For Whom?," *Elementary English* 43 (February 1966) 138–147.

Malmquist, Eve, "Reading Research in Scandinavia," in J. A. Figurel, editor, *Reading and Inquiry,* Proceedings of the International Reading Association 10 (1965) 399–404.

McCullough, Constance M., "What Does Research Reveal About Practices in Teaching Reading?," *English Journal* 46 (November 1957) 475–490.

Petty, Walter T., "A Summary of Investigations Relating to the English Language Arts in Elementary Education: 1962," *Elementary English* 40 (February 1963) 150–164, 201.

———, and Paul C. Burns, "A Summary of Investigations Relating to the English Language Arts in Elementary Education: 1963," *Elementary English* 41 (February 1964) 119–137.

———, and Paul C. Burns, "A Summary of Investigations Relating to the English Language Arts in Elementary Education: 1964," *Elementary English* 42 (April 1965) 411–430.

———, and Paul C. Burns, "A Summary of Investigations Relating to the English Language Arts in Elementary Education: 1965," *Elementary English* 43 (March 1966) 252–277.

———, and Paul C. Burns, "A Summary of Investigations Relating to the English Language Arts in Elementary Education: 1966," *Elementary English* 44 (April and May 1967) 392–401, 492–517.

Plessas, Gus P., *Sources of Reading Research: An Annotated Bibliography* (Newark, Delaware: International Reading Association, 1965).

Robinson, Helen M., "Summary of Investigations Relating to Reading," *The Reading Teacher* 17 and 18 (January 1962, January 1963, February 1964, February 1965).

———, Samuel Weintraub, and Helen K. Smith, "Summary of Investigations Relating to Reading," July 1, 1964 to June 30, 1965, *Reading Research Quarterly* 1 and 2 (Winter 1965, Winter 1966–1967).

Russell, David H., "Reading Research That Makes a Difference," *Elementary English* 38 (February 1961) 74–78.

———, "Some Research on the Impact of Reading," *English Journal* 47 (October 1958) 398–413.

———, and Henry Fea, "Research on Teaching Reading," in N. L. Gage, editor, *Handbook of Research on Teaching* (Chicago: Rand McNally & Co., 1963), pp. 865–928.

Singer, Harry, "Substrata-factor Theory of Reading: Research and Evaluation of Critiques," in J. A. Figurel, editor, *Reading and Inquiry*, Proceedings of the International Reading Association 10 (1965) 325–331.

Staiger, Ralph C., "Language Arts Research: 1964," Part I and Part II, *Elementary English* 42 (April and May 1965) 433–445, 513–526.

Summers, Edward G., "Doctoral Dissertation Research in Elementary and Secondary Reading, 1958, 1959, and 1960," *Journal of Developmental Reading* 5 (Summer 1962) 232–244.

―――, "Doctoral Dissertation Research Reported for 1961—Part I," *Journal of Developmental Reading* 6 (Winter 1963) 87–105; Part II 7 (Spring 1963), 156–175.

―――, "Doctoral Dissertation Research in Reading Reported for 1962," *Journal of Developmental Reading* 7 (Summer 1964) 223–260.

―――, and Billie Hubrig, "Doctoral Dissertation Research in Reading Reported for 1963," *Journal of Reading* 9 (April 1966 and May 1966) 295–321, 386–401.

―――, and J. Laffey, "Doctoral Dissertation Research in Reading for 1964," Parts I, II, III, and IV, *Journal of Reading* 10 (December 1966, January 1967, February 1967, March 1967) 169–184, 187; 243–257; 305–327; 383–392.

Townsend, Agatha, "What Research Says to the Reading Teacher," *Reading Teacher* 18 and 19 (monthly), 1964–65.

Traxler, Arthur E., *Summary and Selected Bibliography of Research Relating to the Diagnosis and Teaching of Reading: 1930–1937*, Educational Records Supplementary Bulletin A (New York: Educational Records Bureau, October 1937).

―――, and Margaret A. Seder, *Summary and Selected Bibliography of Research Relating to the Diagnosis and Teaching of Reading: October 1938 to September 1939* (New York: Educational Records Bureau, 1940).

―――, and Margaret A. Seder, *Ten Years of Research in Reading*, Educational Records Bulletin No. 32 (New York: Educational Records Bureau, 1941).

―――, and Agatha Townsend, *Another Five Years of Research in Reading*, Educational Records Bulletin No. 46 (New York: Educational Records Bureau, October 1946).

―――, et al., *Eight Years of Research in Reading: Summary and Bibliography*, Educational Records Bulletin No. 64 (New York: Educational Records Bureau, 1955).

————, and Ann Jungeblut, *Research in Reading During Another Four Years: Summary and Bibliography,* Educational Records Bulletin No. 75 (New York: Educational Records Bureau, 1960).

Weintraub, Sam, "What Research Says to the Reading Teacher," *Reading Teacher* 20, 21, 22 (monthly), 1966–67; 1967–68; 1968–69.

For ideas of the research needed in reading and discussions of various features of reading research, the following references are suggested:

Cleland, Donald L., "Needed Improvement in Research Design in Reading," *Improvement of Reading Through Classroom Practice,* International Reading Association Yearbook 9 (1964) 244–249.

Clymer, Theodore, "The Real Frontier in Reading Research," *The Reading Teacher* 11 (December 1958) 92–97.

Cook, Desmond L., "The Hawthorne Effect and Reading Research," *Improvement of Reading Through Classroom Practice,* International Reading Association Yearbook 9 (1964) 249–253.

Gates, Arthur I., "The Future of Research in Reading," *Education* 82 (May 1962) 545–554.

Raygor, Alton L., "Some Thoughts on the Current State of Research in Reading," *Journal of Developmental Reading* 7 (Winter 1964) 75–76.

Strang, Ruth, "Reactions to Research on Reading," *Educational Forum* (January 1962) 187–192.

What Have We Accomplished in Reading?
A Review of the Past Fifty Years*

NILA B. SMITH

Reviews of historical trends provide important information concerning the effects of certain educational practices which may suggest programs for future action. They also offer explanations of the how and why of many of the theories and practices that now prevail in the schools. They help educational workers to identify and evaluate fads and bandwagon schemes. Finally, they contribute to the understanding of the significance of education and the interrelationship between the school and the society from which the school derives its functions.

Some of these purposes are served by the first selection in this chapter. Professor Smith, possibly America's foremost reading historian, presents an overview of reading developments. Three other historical overviews (Mackintosh, Chapter 3; Wade, Chapter 4; Craig, Chapter 6) are included in this volume. See "For Further Reading" concerning the 1965 edition of Smith's *American Reading Instruction*.

This last half century stands out as a truly golden period in the progress of reading instruction. More innovations have been effected in reading during the last fifty years than during the entire three hundred years antedating this period of American history. I am sure that progress has been equally notable in the other phases of the language arts constellation. It is most appropriate that accomplishments in all of the language arts areas be reviewed upon this momentous occasion—the Golden Anniversary of The National Council of Teachers of English!

Progress in reading instruction has been marked by a succession of turning points. For a period of years reading methods and materials all over the country are quite similar—so similar, in fact, that an unbiased examiner might arrive at the conclusion that all had been turned

* From *Elementary English* 38 (March 1961) 141–150. Reprinted with permission of the National Council of Teachers of English and Nila B. Smith, Distinguished Service Professor, Glassboro State College, New Jersey.

out of the same mold, with just a slightly different crimp here and there in the contour of the pan. Then, rather suddenly, a new plan becomes popular, and we teach reading in this manner until another turning point arrives. Thus, epoch after epoch of reading instruction passes (26).

Fortunately printed records are available to which we can turn in delineating these epochs and ascertaining their characteristics. In attempting to obtain information to bring to you about reading epochs during our recent half century the following source materials, published between 1910 and 1960, were explored: prominent educational magazines that usually contain reading articles, yearbooks of learned societies, summaries of published investigations in reading, lists of unpublished master's and doctoral researches completed or under way. More than 300 pieces of materials were surveyed for the purpose of picking up the sequence of events and trends which marked the pilgrimage of reading in its upward march from 1910 to the present time. This information will be presented to you by decades.

ACCOMPLISHMENTS FROM 1910 TO 1920

The dramatic decade beginning with 1910 ushered in the first truly great breakthrough in reading progress. This was the birth of the scientific movement in education. In 1909 Thorndike made the initial presentation of his handwriting scale before a meeting of the American Association for the Advancement of Science, and in 1910 it was published (29). Generally speaking, the publication of the Thorndike scale has been recognized as the beginning of the contemporary movement for measuring educational products scientifically. In the immediately ensuing years scales and tests appeared rapidly: Courtis arithmetic tests, Hilligas' Composition Scale, Buckingham Spelling Scale—and then a reading test—The Gray Standardized Oral Reading Paragraphs (13). This test was published in 1915. Other reading tests followed shortly.

As a result of the strong new surge of interest in placing education on a scientific basis together with its correlative motives for developing instruments of measurement, we would naturally expect that the scientific study of reading problems would take a vigorous spurt. And this it did.

Through all the years up to 1910 only 34 studies had been reported in reading. During the 1910–20 decade, 200 accounts appeared, about six times as many as had been reported during the entire history of reading preceding this time. These studies had to do mostly with tests and school surveys as would be expected.

As for method: the most revolutionary thing happened that had happened since clergy began to teach reading in churches, and dames began to teach reading in kitchens. "For hundreds of years oral reading had maintained a supreme and undisputed claim on teaching methods" (25). During this decade, however, the concept of teaching *silent* reading burst into our slumbering complacency like a bombshell. It came suddenly and in the midst of a period in which school people were serenely content in the use of sentence-story methods applied to the oral reading of selections in literary readers. For the most part they continued to use these practices to the end of the decade but the startling new idea was at least launched. Discussions of the advantages of silent reading appeared for the first time in the Sixteenth (16) and in the Eighteenth (17) Yearbooks of the National Society for the Study of Education. Speakers at educational conventions began to talk about it, magazine articles began to discuss it. The idea had been born.

To sum up: developing the concept of applying scientific techniques to the study of reading, devising standardized instruments to measure reading achievement, increasing the number of studies tremendously, initiating the silent reading idea. These seem to have been the major accomplishments from 1910 to 1920.

ACCOMPLISHMENTS FROM 1920 TO 1930

The period extending from 1920 to 1930 is perhaps the most golden decade in this golden era of progress in so far as fundamental changes in reading practices are concerned. These changes were largely due to the scientific movement which had shaped up during the preceding period and which now was opening up fresh wells of information with improved and extended applications.

The new studies conducted during this decade carried with them three distinct earmarks of progress: the number increased tremendously; they covered a wider scope of problems; many of them were conducted in classrooms by teachers and other school personnel, rather than being confined to the laboratory.

As to the number of investigations: Gray's summaries reveal that 763 were reported as compared with 200 during the preceding decade. This unprecedented increase reflected the zeal and enthusiasm with which school people were searching for more information about the important subject of reading.

The studies of this period probed a variety of problems, but there were three problem areas which were most highly significant. They were significant because they resulted in sweeping changes in practice. These three areas were: (1) silent reading, (2) individual differences, and (3) remedial reading.

The first half of this decade might well be called "The Age of Silent Reading." "These years were marked with an exaggerated, often exclusive emphasis on silent reading as opposed to the traditional oral reading techniques" (25). As previously mentioned, the concept of teaching silent reading was initiated during the latter part of the preceding period, but it didn't really take hold as a nation-wide classroom practice until during the years of 1920 to 1925. This sudden and widespread reversal in practice was largely due to two influences: the development of tests which revealed that silent reading was superior to oral reading in speed and comprehension; and the publication of The Yearbooks of the National Society for the Study of Education. As already indicated, one article each appeared in the Sixteenth (16) and the Eighteenth (17) Yearbooks. The climax, however, came with the publication of the Twentieth Yearbook, Part II (19) of which was devoted entirely to the report of the "Society's Committee on Silent Reading." Following the appearance of this Yearbook, "textbook writers began to produce readers based on silent reading procedures; other authors prepared professional books on silent reading; teachers busied themselves in preparing exercises that would check comprehension of silent reading by means of drawings, true-false statements or completion sentences and so forth. The whole country for a time seemed to be obsessed with the idea of teaching silent reading" (25).

This extreme emphasis, however, was soon balanced with other factors. By 1925 the novelty of the new idea had worn off, somewhat; investigations revealed some unique uses of oral reading, school people discovered that there still were some special needs for oral reading in the school program. Perhaps, the culminating influence came with the publication of the Twenty-Fourth Yearbook, Part I (20) which appeared in 1925. This Yearbook advocated a broader program of reading instruction which among other things recognized both oral and silent reading. New courses of study, professional books and readers immediately reflected the broadened objectives of this Yearbook and methods during the years 1925–1930 were shaped largely by its contents. So during the first two decades of the last fifty years we progressed from extreme oral reading to extreme silent reading to a broader program which recognized both. In my opinion, this was an indication of real accomplishment.

As for individual differences: with the administration of the newly developed tests, a very great fundamental truth became apparent with a violent impact—the realization that there were wide individual differences in the reading achievement of children, in the same grade and in the same classroom. This discovery spurred school people to experiment with a variety of adjustments in classroom organization and instruction, designed to cope with this newly revealed variation in the learning rate of children.

There were reports of adjustments made in classrooms which maintained the regular organization such as ability grouping, flexible promotions, and differentiated assignments. But the pulsating new idea was that of breaking up class organization entirely to permit of individual progression. This plan of organization received as much attention at this time as it is receiving at the present moment. Speeches, articles, and Yearbooks dealt with the subject. San Francisco; Los Angeles; Detroit; Winnetka; Madison, Wisconsin; and other school systems reported (21) results they had obtained by individual instruction. The states of Connecticut and Illinois reported (21) experiments in individualizing instruction in rural schools.

The various plans, on the whole, were pattened after the Winnetka or the Dalton ideas, in both of which individual progression in reading and other subjects was made possible by means of assignments in which the child worked through subject material that increased in small increments of difficulty. The important point to note is that attention to individual differences in reading received its first great impetus during this decade of remarkable progress.

The concept of *remedial* reading was launched from its small island of study during this period and sent out over unexplored seas in quest of answers to disability problems. The movement was spurred on by the use of standardized tests. These tests revealed that thousands of boys and girls were failing each year to make normal progress in reading. Published reports of work in the reading disability field indicate that the chief interest at this time was in diagnosing individual cases. As for method, it was during this period that Fernald evolved her kinesthetic method, and that Orton expounded his theory on mixed dominance and the treatment that accompanied it. Remedial reading did get under way during this period.

In beginning reading there also were innovations. Experience charts first came into use. The Nineteenth Yearbook (18), published in 1920, dealt with reading materials. In it examples were given of charts based on children's experiences, and the practice of introducing children to beginning reading through the use of such material was advocated. This practice was not widely accepted until much later, but progress had been made in evolving the idea.

And last but not least, mention must be made of another mark of progress which clearly stamped itself into the later annals of this decade. The reading readiness concept began to take shape at this time.

In 1926 the International Kindergarten Union in cooperation with the United States Bureau of Education conducted an investigation on "Pupils' Readiness for Reading Instruction upon Entrance to First Grade." The first articles on this subject were published in *Childhood Education* in January, 1927. Two of these articles used the term "reading readiness." In so far as I am aware, this was the first time that this phrase crept into our reading vocabulary (27). In Gray's summaries published in 1928, he reported for the first time three studies on reading readiness. A few master's theses and a trickling of articles on this subject also appeared before the close of the decade. The new concept, however, was still in the formative stage, and little was done about it in a practical way until the following period, but the movement was on its way.

Much more could be said about the accomplishments made during this unprecedented period. I should like to dwell longer on the accumulation of information gathered about reading and the auspicious innovations in classroom practice that were inaugurated at this time, but I must pass on to other conquests and other days.

ACCOMPLISHMENTS FROM 1930 TO 1940

This period may be characterized largely as one of extension and application rather than one of revelation and initiation.

Investigations continued at an accelerated pace. In round figures about 1200 studies were reported between 1930 and 1940. Not only were these studies greater in number, but they were superior in isolation of problems, in designs, and in controls.

Some of the embryo ideas that had sprouted in the preceding decade came into full bloom and fruited profusely at this time. For example: the reading readiness interest reached its zenith in this period (27). Published investigations on this topic increased steadily during each successive year of this decade (9), reaching their climax of frequency in 1940 when Gray reported 22 studies relating to this topic in one year. Since that time the number has decreased steadily.

Turning to unpublished research, this was the hey-day of aspiring masters and doctors in finding problems for research in the readiness area. The first doctoral dissertation on readiness was reported in 1927. From that time on, the number of master and doctoral studies increased, reaching its peak in the years 1937 to 1940. Fourteen such studies were completed in 1937, 15 in 1938, 14 in 1939, and 12 in 1940. Since that time only 2 or 3 academic studies on readiness have been reported each year.

A similar trend is seen in published articles on reading readiness. Periodicals abounded with discussions on readiness topics from 1930 to 1940. Articles on this subject rarely appear in present-day literature.

In the light of this evidence, it may be concluded that this was the period of most vigorous emphasis, both on investigations of readiness and applications of the readiness theory. The concept has been accepted now and we hear little about it at the present time.

Remedial reading, which had experienced a touch-and-go recognition during the preceding period, now became established and gained stature. Many significant studies were conducted in the remedial reading areas: causes of difficulties, diagnosis, and corrective procedures. Professional books devoted exclusively to remedial reading were first published. Some laboratory studies were still made but the majority of studies now were conducted in schools. Remedial reading, which had started in laboratories, now became a topic for practical experimentation in the public schools themselves.

A new trend that began to emerge was that of giving beginning attention to high school, college, and adult reading. Studies made at these levels, however, were mostly concerned with interests in, and uses of reading, rather than with reading achievement and teaching procedure.

Every decade reviewed so far has been characterized by one or two events of great distinction. In the 1910–1920 decade, it was the application of scientific measurement and investigation to reading; in the 1920–30 era, it was the startling innovations of silent reading and of individual progression. What was the spectacular event in the nineteen-thirties?

The Activity Movement swept the country during these years, and the startling new idea in reading was to teach this skill as a part of the Activity Program. In such a program children worked freely and spontaneously and actively in following their own interests; and teachers were intrigued with the new "game" of trying to get all of their subject matter across through "Units of Work."

In so far as reading was concerned, pupils had access to a considerable number of books bearing largely on the topic of their "Unit of Work." This was the first big impetus for bringing a quantity of books into the classroom for reading. There was a profusion of charts and school-made booklets growing out of children's interests. Pupils read functionally from their co-operatively prepared materials and out of many books in doing research in connection with their Units. In a word, this was how reading proceeded in the Activity Program in the thirties.

We no longer hear of the Activity Program at this time nor of the teaching of reading in connection with this program. The Activity Movement, however, made a vigorous impact on the teaching of reading and other subjects at this time—an impact so strong that its influence still continues. The Activity Movement distracted the school public from its age-old concept of schools centered almost exclusively on subject-matter goals to schools in which consideration is given to the child, himself, his stage of development, his interests, his activities, his choices and his decisions.

In summary, we may say that progress in this decade was characterized by continuing investigations, greater in number, higher in quality than in the preceding decade; intensive application of the readiness concept; transfer of remedial activities from laboratory to classroom; beginning attention to reading at higher levels; and widespread interest in teaching reading as an integral part of the Activity Program.

ACCOMPLISHMENTS FROM 1940 TO 1950

An event resulting from progress in science overshadowed all other indications of progress during this period. The "birthday of the atomic age" is officially set as December 2, 1942, when Dr. Enrico Fermi turned on the first successful nuclear energy machine in Chicago. The first atomic bomb destroyed Hiroshima on August 6, 1945. On the face of things this terrifying discovery with its possibilities for good or for evil reduced to comparative insignificance our little scientific achievements in reading. Yet, could this achievement have been possible without reading? Can we cope adequately with its future destructive or beneficent effects, as the case may be, without more efficient reading skill and a wider reading citizenry? The atomic age and reading immediately become interactive.

But we didn't realize this at the time. We were too close to this earth-shaking event to sense its import for reading instruction. The war probably only had two *immediate* effects on reading. One of these was a diminution in the number of reading investigations. This was probably due to the fact that many of the psychologists and educators who conducted research in reading, or stimulated others to do so, were in the armed services.

The other major effect of the war was the shocking discovery that at this day and age thousands of young men in the military service could not read well enough to follow the simple printed instructions for camp life. Coupled with this discovery was the revelation that reading could be taught to these young men in army camps in an amazingly short time. Concurrently, several new investigations disclosed reading deficiencies in large numbers of high school and college students. These several influences combined to produce a spurt in attention to reading at these higher levels. Immediately following the war, a great deal of professional literature on reading emerged and among these publications several bulletins and one Yearbook appeared dealing with high school and college reading. Chief among these publications was a bulletin of the National Education Association titled *Reading Instruction in Secondary Schools* (15), and the Forty-Eighth Yearbook, Part II of The National Society for the Study of Reading, titled *Reading in High School and College* (24). The actual teaching of reading at these levels had not progressed far at this time but the idea was vigorously expanding.

During this period, reading in the content subjects also became a matter of wide discussion and the subject of a few investigations. The studies at this time pointed to the general conclusion that while good readers can read well in all subject fields, special practice in reading in particular subject areas is helpful to average and poor readers.

In the forties, wide recognition was given to the interrelationships amongst the language arts. Studies, articles, speeches were concerned with the relationship of reading to spelling, handwriting, vocabulary, and composition. As a result we came to recognize that reading was not an isolated skill independent of other skills used in the interchange of ideas, but that it was just one aspect of the total language arts constellation mutually dependent upon and interactive with all other skills in the communication dimension.

A strong new concern also sprang up in regard to the effects of three of the newer media for mass communication: comics, movies, and radio. Television did not come in for much attention until the next decade but during this period wide dissemination of entertainment through the first named agencies stirred up worry on the part of school people and parents. They feared that interest in listening to radio, looking at comics, viewing movies would reduce interest in reading and thus decrease the amount of reading done. Numerous popular articles bemoaned the situation and pointed out its dangers. Several studies were conducted directed toward the exploration of students' interests in this area and finding out how much time they devoted to the offerings of these types. Thus initial steps were taken in obtaining information to combat what was thought to be the first threat to reading.

Remedial diagnosis and treatment continued to claim a large segment of the spotlight. Mechanical instruments and devices which had been introduced during the preceding period increased in numbers and use. There were fewer studies reported on psychological factors such as dominance, handedness, eyedness, and reversals. An increasing number were devoted to personal factors as related to reading: personal interests and attitudes, personal status in social, emotional, and experiental maturity. This attention to other growth and development factors as related to reading was certainly one of the most notable advances made during this period.

To sum up: the chief points of progress during this decade were: increased attention to teaching reading at the higher levels; growing attention to reading in the content subjects; concerns about mass communications; attempts to find relationships between reading and handwriting, spelling, vocabulary and composition; and perhaps, most important of all, a growing consciousness of the profound truth that reading doesn't develop in a vacuum by itself, but that it is part and parcel of general child development and is affected by all other aspects of child growth.

ACCOMPLISHMENTS FROM 1950 TO 1960

A most exciting decade! For one thing, interest in reading instruction became almost universal during this period. There was a time when primary teachers were the only people interested in the teaching of reading. Now teachers of all subjects and at all levels want to know more about reading. Parents are asking questions, pursuing books and articles on reading. Students at high-school and college levels and adults beyond college are flocking to reading centers. Slick magazines and laymen are discussing reading freely. A great conflagration of interest has been ignited amongst teachers and students, and more especially amongst the lay public. And this is good.

During this period, however, for the first time in history, reading instruction in American schools underwent harsh and severe criticism by laymen. School people maintained that the criticisms were unfair and rose to the defense of their methods through articles, speeches, discussions, and investigations. Several comparative studies of "Then and Now" were made. These studies, on the whole, showed that we were teaching reading as well as or better than in preceding years.

Insofar as progress is concerned the criticism by laymen probably had three good effects: it caused school people to examine their present methods more carefully; it stimulated the interest of parents and other laymen in reading instruction; it offered motives and opportunities to school people to explain the research, psychology, and philosophy on which present methods are based. So in this situation, as is often the case in other situations, even criticism caused reading to move forward.

Perhaps as an off-shoot of interest and criticism, coupled with a growing awareness of the complexity of the reading process, there has been a spurt of activity in the re-instatement and increase of reading courses in the curriculums of teacher-training institutions. Concurrently with this interest in adding more courses, standards are being raised in regard to the qualifications of teachers of reading and of reading specialists. This movement toward better-trained teachers in reading is a big step forward.

As for the number of investigations: studies during this period reached incredible proportions. Gray reported over 1,000 studies in his 1960 summary, but in his introduction he said for the first time in his thirty-five years of annual summarizing, "The number of studies are increasing so rapidly that it is no longer possible to report all of them in this annual summary. Those referred to this year represent either a new or distinctive approach to a problem or suggest significant issues in need of further study." Not only was this increase apparent in the published reports of reading investigations, but it also was reflected in the reports of dissertations completed or in progress which soared to new numerical heights, the number reported averaging about 90 per year as compared with about 50 in the preceding decade.

Advance is shown in the subjects of investigation. Reading in the content fields, adult reading deficiencies, and television as related to reading came in for strong additional attention. The most gratifying trend revealed, however, is that we are at present delving more deeply into the reading process and more broadly into the factors that affect it. The former popular topic of phonics now seems to have been replaced with studies of perception. Comprehension is no longer treated as a lump sum; the emphasis at present is upon the higher thinking processes of interpretation and critical reading. The old readiness studies are replaced with investigations of prediction and expectancy. Remedial reading is not so much concerned now with studies of gadgets and specific teaching remedies as it is with organismic and personality factors. Parental personality, attitudes, and interactions with the child as related to reading entered the research scene for the first time during this period, and many reading investigations concerned with parents and their children are now being reported. Studies are made in regard to the climate of the classroom and its effect on reading. This mere glimpse at some of the subjects of the most recent studies is indicative of a trend toward probing to greater depths and in wider breadths than was evident in most of the studies preceding this period.

Special mention should be made of a clearly discernible advance in regard to reading and the other language arts. In the preceding decade we became strongly concerned about the relationships of reading to the subjects of spelling, handwriting, vocabulary, and composition. During this decade we have moved on to a concern about aspects of the language arts which perhaps are less tangible than the subject matter areas but more inclusive in their application to the entire block of communication skills. Listening studies have increased by leaps and bounds. Some of the most recent dissertation topics have to do with semantic studies of reading content, multiple meanings, figures of speech in reading, and the linguistic approach to reading. Is it not an accomplishment to have moved on from subject interrelationships to relationships dealing with listening and the various aspects of linguistics?

The innovation in reading method which has loomed large on the horizon of late is the plan known as *individualized instruction*. The amount of attention given to this plan in this decade is comparable to that given to individual instruction in the nineteen-twenties. It probably is the most popular topic of discussion at present in educational magazines and often at teacher gatherings.

This individualized plan of the present is different from individual instruction which was popular in the twenties. The earlier plan was subject matter oriented. Each child was given subject matter assignments divided into small increments of difficulty and he was permitted to progress as fast as he, personally, could complete each successive increment. The present plan is child-psychology oriented utilizing particularly Dr. Willard Olsen's theory of *seeking, self-selection,* and *pacing* in that the child seeks that which stimulates him, selects the book he desires to read, and proceeds at his own rate.

This plan has been used too recently for research reports to have crept into published summaries of investigations. Most of the research on this topic at present falls into the unpublished category of theses, dissertations, or mimeographed reports of experiments carried on in certain school systems. An examination of the most recent sources listing dissertations completed or under way indicates that a quantity of research is now taking place in regard to this topic. Much of it will undoubtedly find its way into print in the near future.

Much more could be said about this period, but because of lack of time we now shall let the curtain fall over the last scene in fifty years of reading accomplishment. As we review the stirring events of the past, we have a right to feel cheered, grateful, proud. In looking back in retrospect we might wonder whether another fifty years could possibly bring about so many changes. This was the first period in which experimentation could be conducted scientifically. In consideration of the newly developed tools, our eagerness to learn, and studies conducted, we might reason that practically all facets of reading instruction have been explored and thus another era could never be so great as this.

If we do reason to this conclusion, we probably are wrong. We pioneered during this period in unexplored territory. We chopped down and cleared away the large virgin trees, but perhaps some of the humble shrubs or creeping vines or fragile mosses may hold even more significance for us than the strikingly obvious, first-sight timbers. But these more obscure growths won't yield their significance with the use of heavy saws and axes. We shall need fresh, piercing insights in choosing which of these to select for dislodgment, and then we shall need unique, delicate tools to pry them loose from their tangled environment and to test the potency of their effect.

What I am trying to say is that while our accomplishments have been very great, indeed, it may be that we have only penetrated the first layer, the troposphere, so to speak. Undoubtedly, brilliant new insights will be revealed, ingenious new techniques of experimentation will be evolved. Possibilities of such developments portend opportunities for unlimited achievement in the future.

Most assuredly, we shall not rest complacently in the glory of achievement during this past golden age. Rather shall we look forward to still greater accomplishments in reading. Let us push on and on with more and more vigor in the next decade and the next decade, and in all of the other decades ahead!

REFERENCES

This bibliography would be too voluminous if each separate piece of material examined were listed. In case of educational journals, yearbooks, and summaries of investigations, each successive issue or publication was examined during the period of years indicated by dates accompanying the general reference. In cases in which a specific reference was made, or a quotation was stated from one particular publication, that publication is listed. Professional books on reading were examined but the titles are too numerous to include in this list.

1. Betts, Emmett Albert, and Betts, Thelma Marshall. *An Index of Professional Literature on Reading and Topics.* American Book Company, New York: 1945.
2. *Childhood Education,* 1–37, 1924–1960.
3. *College English,* 1–22, 1939–1960.
4. *Doctoral Dissertations Accepted by American Universities,* H. W. Wilson Co., New York: 1934, 1955.
5. *Educational Index,* 1–31, H. W. Wilson Co., New York: 1930–1960.
6. *Elementary School Journal,* 10–60, 1910–1960.
7. *Elementary English,* 1–37, 1924–1960.
8. *English Journal,* 1–49, 1911–1960.
9. Good, Carter V. "Doctoral Studies Completed or Under Way," *Phi Delta Kappan,* 1923–1953; (Separate publications) Lyda, Mary Louise; Jenson, Glenn; Brown, Stanley; Anderson, Harold, Phi Delta Kappa, Bloomington, Ind. 1954–1959.
10. Gray, William S. *Summary of Investigations Relating to Reading.* University of Chicago Supplementary Monograph, No. 28, Chicago: 1925.
11. Gray, William S. "Summary of Investigations Relating to Reading," *Elementary School Journal,* 26–32, 1925–1932.
12. Gray, William S. "Summary of Investigations Relating to Reading," *Journal of Educational Research,* 5–54, 1932–1960.
13. Gray, William S. *Oral Reading Paragraphs Test,* Public School Publishing Co., Bloomington, Indiana: 1915.

14. National Education Association, "Newer Practices in Reading in the Elementary School," *The National Elementary Principal,* Seventeenth Yearbook, 1938.

15. National Education Association, *Reading Instruction in Secondary Schools,* Research Bulletin, Vol. 22, No. 1, 1942.

16. National Society for the Study of Education: *Sixteenth Yearbook, Part I,* 1917.

17. *Eighteenth Yearbook, Part II,* 1919.

18. *Nineteenth Yearbook, Part I,* 1920.

19. *Twentieth Yearbook, Part II,* 1921.

20. *Twenty-Fourth Yearbook, Part I,* 1925.

21. *Twenty-Fourth Yearbook, Part II,* 1925.

22. *Thirty-Sixth Yearbook, Part I,* 1937.

23. *Forty-Eighth Yearbook, Part I,* 1949.

24. *Forty-Eighth Yearbook, Part II,* 1949.

25. Smith, Nila Banton. *American Reading Instruction,* Silver Burdett, New York: 1937.

26. Smith, Nila Banton. "Historical Turning Points in Reading," *National Education Association Journal* (May, 1952), 280–282.

27. Smith, Nila Banton. *Readiness for Reading and Related Language Arts,* National Council of Teachers of English, 1950.

28. *The Reading Teacher,* International Reading Association, 1–14, 1947–1960.

29. Thorndike, E. L. *The Thorndike Scale for Handwriting of Children,* Bureau of Publications, Teachers College, Columbia University, New York: 1910.

30. Traxler, Arthur E. Educational Records Bureau, New York: *Ten Years of Research in Reading* (with Seder, Margaret), 1941. *Another Five Years of Research in Reading* (with Townsend), 1946. *Eight More Years of Research in Reading* (with Townsend), 1955, *Research in Reading During Another Four Years* (with Jungeblut).

31. U.S. Library of Congress, Catalog Division, *American Doctoral Dissertations* Lists, Government Printing Office, Washington: 1913–1940.

FOR FURTHER READING

This and later, similarly titled sections provide some additional selected references that focus upon the topic of the preceding study. It will also provide, where appropriate, general major resources such as books; research analyses and evaluative summaries; selected research reports; and definitive articles.

Dodds, William J., "Highlights from the History of Reading Instruction, *The Reading Teacher* 21 (December 1967) 274–280.

Harris, Albert J., "Five Decades of Remedial Reading," in J. Allen Figurel, editor, *Forging Ahead in Reading*, International Reading Association Conference Proceedings, Vol. 12, Part I (Newark, Delaware: International Reading Association, 1968), pp. 25–34.

Robinson, Helen M., editor, *Innovations and Change in Reading Instruction*, 67th Yearbook of the National Society for the Study of Education, Part II (Chicago: University of Chicago Press, 1968).

Smith, Dora V., *American Reading Instruction* (Newark, Delaware: International Reading Association, 1965).

Pre-Reading Skills in Kindergarten:
*A Second Report**

ROBERT L. HILLERICH

Considerable concern is expressed today as to the most appropriate time to initiate reading instruction. Should kindergarten teachers limit their reading program to the kinds of action which promote a general readiness for learning? Or should they provide pre-reading activities which will develop skills that the child can directly apply when he begins to read? Hillerich's experimental study (with an ex post facto follow-up) is presented to provide something more than conjecture as a basis for answering this question. The study is part of the growing body of information which supports early reading instruction. The evidence in this study suggests that such instruction provides initial superiority which is maintained and that undesirable side effects need not occur. For another point of view, see the study by Hampleman (Chapter 7). Other supporting and conflicting viewpoints are found in the articles cited in "For Further Reading." (Particularly note the research sources and summaries on this topic and the Durkin reports which discuss children who learn to read at preschool age.)

Some of the strengths of the Hillerich report are: The purpose of the study is clearly set out; previous research is noted; the questions to be answered are clearly stated in a form which allows them to be easily answered by the results; the treatment is of sufficient duration; and the interpretation of the data is consistent with the results. But the report has some limitations: Lack of detail as to how the sample was drawn and its characteristics; failure to mention whether the experimental and control groups were initially comparable in certain important respects.

Continued research is needed to find what to do about reading in early instruction and how to take advantage of those pupils who are reading before school age. Other reports on pre-first grade children included in this volume are by Bjonerud (Chapter 5), Inbody (Chapter 6), and Hampleman (Chapter 7).

---

* From *Elementary School Journal* 65 (March 1965) 312–317. Reprinted with permission of the University of Chicago Press © 1965 and Robert Hillerich, Assistant Superintendent, Glenview, Illinois.

Although change has become a byword in our society, most kindergarten programs are little different from programs of thirty—or even fifty—years ago.

We firmly believe that there are legitimate reasons for revising traditional programs in kindergarten as well as at other levels. While joining with others to decry the arbitrary pushing down of content in the grades, we do see an important philosophical distinction between a sputnik-inspired pushing down of content and the changing of programs out of consideration for children's needs and experiences.

Typically, pre-reading skills are taught in first grade. Justification of this placement rests primarily on tradition. Morphett and Washburne suggested a mental age of six and a half as optimum for beginning-reading instruction (1). This recommendation, made more than three decades ago, has had a strong influence on the timing of beginning reading.

For years little serious attention was given to the idea that formal reading instruction might begin before first grade. The five-year-old's experience and vocabulary are too limited, we were told. His eyes are not mature enough for close work, and, we were warned, his vision may become impaired.

Recent research raises questions about these views. Coefficients of correlation between mental age—or intelligence—and reading achievement range from .60 to .00 (2, 3). The concern for visual maturity has been obviated by Eames (4). Observation of five-year-olds today forces us to recognize the fact that television, travel, and home background have had an effect on children's vocabularies and experience. Schramm reported that preschool television-viewing results in "vocabularies about a grade higher than children have if they are without the benefit of television" (5).

Morrison reported that 58 per cent of the reading specialists he surveyed favored provisions in kindergarten for "formal reading instruction extending *beyond readiness*" (6; italics mine).

Nicholson reported that the traditional gross-discrimination activities in kindergarten are a "waste of time" (7). Most children can match letter forms and identify capital letters before they receive instruction in school (8).

Anderson (9), using *Getting Ready To Read* (10), found that a group of kindergarten pupils who had mental ages that ranged from 52 to 65 months benefited as much as a group that had mental ages that ranged from 79 to 92 months.

The Denver study, "Reading Instruction in the Kindergarten," revealed that development of pre-reading skill in kindergarten resulted in significantly greater reading skill by the end of first grade (11).

As early as 1960, kindergarten teachers in Glenview were discussing the possibility of a more specific approach to reading readiness. These teachers reviewed the experience backgrounds and capabilities of their pupils, current research related to the five-year-old, and the appropriateness of certain activities and skills for the kindergarten child (12, 13).

In January, 1963, the Glenview schools entered into a five-year study of the effectiveness of a formal program of pre-reading skills in kindergarten. The program, based on *Getting Ready To Read* by McKee and Harrison, has as its objective the building of children's skill and interest in reading (10). In a study designed to test the attainment of this two-fold objective, Glenview kindergarten teachers sought answers to the following questions:

1. Can kindergarten children develop adequate skill in using oral context and letter-sound associations?
2. Is there a significant difference in the pre-reading skill of children who use a workbook and those who do not?
3. Regardless of the degree of skill developed, do kindergarten children retain this skill through the summer?
4. At the end of first grade are the reading skills of pupils in the experimental program significantly greater than the skills of children in the traditional program?
5. Does the early introduction of skills result in more or less interest in reading?

The Pre-Reading Study in Glenview involved twenty-two sections of kindergarten children in seven elementary schools. Eleven teachers and about 650 kindergarten pupils were included in the study. Of the 650 kindergarten children, 402 returned for first grade, and 363 completed that year.

In the first year of the study, ten sections of children used workbooks in the *Getting Ready To Read* program; twelve other sections used all the materials in the program except the workbooks. The individual kindergarten teacher determined whether or not she would use workbooks. There was no special interclass grouping for the program; six schools grouped kindergarten pupils by geographic area; one school grouped by chronological age.

Pre-reading skills were measured at the end of kindergarten (June

3–7, 1963), when each kindergarten teacher administered Part 2 of A Pre-Reading Inventory of Skills Basic to Beginning Reading. During the week of September 9–13, 1963, the same test was administered by the first-grade teacher.

To establish a criterion group in terms of reading achievement, the primary consultant and the assistant superintendent administered Level 1 of Primary Reading Profiles to the total first-grade population of 449 children in May, 1963. The classroom teacher administered Level 2 of the test to all children who exceeded the system mean of 92.9. The same procedure was followed with the experimental group in May, 1964.

An instrument to measure the degree of interest in reading is now being developed. This instrument will be administered to control groups, Grades 3 and 4, in February, 1965, and to the experimental group, Grade 3, in February, 1966.

Statistical significance of results was determined by t test for all hypotheses except the first. No criterion group was available as a statistical check of the first question, since we had never attempted previously to develop "adequate skill in using oral context and letter-sound associations" among kindergarten children. As a result, *adequate skill* was arbitrarily defined as a score on the Pre-Reading Inventory that approaches 45.0, the cut-off recommended by the test authors as adequate for beginning-reading instruction.

Table 1 reports the degree of skill developed by kindergarten children. The mean score of 48.0 for all kindergarten pupils exceeded the authors' suggested cut-off score of 45.0. Kindergarten mean scores exceeded the suggested cut-off scores on all subtests except the fourth, which required the combined use of oral context and letter-sound association.

Of the total group, 70 per cent, or 280 pupils, achieved at or above the suggested cut-off score: 88 per cent of the children who used workbooks achieved at or above the cut-off score, as compared with 50 per cent of those who did not use workbooks.

Further comparison of the groups that used workbooks with groups that did not indicated a difference in mean total score of 8.7 in favor of the groups that used workbooks. This difference was significant at the .01 level. In every subtest, the mean score of the group that used workbooks exceeded the cut-off score. In fact, there was only a slight overlap between the mean scores (subtest and total test) of the lowest section that used workbooks and mean scores of the highest section that did not use workbooks.

TABLE 1
Mean Scores on the Pre-Reading Inventory at the End of Kindergarten

Subtests	Cut-Off—Maximum Possible Score	Workbook Group			Non-Workbook Group			All Kinder-garteners
		Highest Section	Lowest Section	Total Group	Highest Section	Lowest Section	Total Group	
Using context	6–8	7.7	7.6	7.6	6.8	5.5	6.4	7.0
Finding letters	14–18	17.3	15.7	16.7	16.9	14.4	15.5	16.1
Listening for letter sounds	10–14	13.8	10.2	12.6	11.6	9.4	10.4	11.5
Matching letters and sounds	15–18	17.4	14.4	15.4	13.2	10.7	11.4	13.4
Total*	45–58	56.3	47.9	52.3†	48.4	40.0	43.6†	48.0

* The discrepancies between total scores and total of subtest scores arise because total scores were treated separately to determine mean of the total test.
† The difference between total scores for the workbook group and total scores for the non-workbook group is significant at the .01 level ($t = 10.3227$).

On the basis of these findings, the first two questions were answered in the affirmative: children did develop adequate skills in kindergarten, and the children who used workbooks developed significantly more skill than those who did not. As a result, in 1963–64, workbooks were used in all kindergarten classes.

In June, 1964, at the end of the second year's experience with the program, the second group of kindergarten pupils was tested. Of this group, 83 per cent scored at or above the cut-off score for beginning reading.

At the end of first grade, the Primary Reading Profiles were administered to the experimental group. The results provided further evidence in favor of the use of workbooks in kindergarten. The children who had used workbooks in kindergarten had a mean total score of 160.94 as opposed to a mean total score of 138.45 for those who had not used workbooks. This difference was significant at the .01 level. The result indicated that differences in the pre-reading skill of workbook groups and non-workbook groups were reflected a year later as differences in reading skill.

Table 2 shows mean scores on the Pre-Reading Inventory at the end of kindergarten and mean scores on the same test at the beginning of first grade. Over the summer vacation, mean loss for the total group on the 58-item test was 2.6 points. While the greatest loss was found among the workbook group, many children in this group had received perfect scores on the initial testing. It was not surprising, therefore, to find the mean score of that group lower on the retest.

There was no pattern to explain the gains or losses of individual children. The scores of a few children dropped fourteen points over the summer; scores of others increased fourteen points. Generally the results showed the typical statistical tendency for scores to regress toward the mean: children who scored very high on the first test tended to score lower on retest; children who scored very low on the first test tended to gain on retest.

In general, retention of skill over the summer vacation was excellent. The mean loss of 2.6 points, although statistically significant (.01 level), was considerably less than one might expect. The mean score in first grade was still above the authors' suggested cutoff score of 45 points. As a result, the third question was also answered in the affirmative: kindergarten children did retain the pre-reading skills over the summer.

Table 3 shows results of the Primary Reading Profiles administered to experimental and control groups at the end of Grade 1. The mean

TABLE 2

Mean Scores on the Pre-Reading Inventory in Kindergarten and Grade 1

| Subtests | Workbook Group | | Non-Workbook Group | | Total Group | |
	Kinder-garten	Grade 1	Kinder-garten	Grade 1	Kinder-garten	Grade 1
Using context	7.6	7.0	6.4	6.2	7.0	6.7
Finding letters	16.7	16.2	15.5	15.1	16.1	15.6
Listening for letter sounds	12.6	11.9	10.4	10.4	11.5	11.1
Matching letters and sounds	15.4	13.1	11.4	10.8	13.4	12.0
Total*	52.3	48.1	43.6	42.6	48.0	45.4
t	5.7719†		1.0565		4.0284†	

* The discrepancies between total scores and total subtest scores arise because total scores were treated separately to determine mean of the total test.
† Significant at .01 level.

TABLE 3

*Mean Reading Achievement and Aptitude Scores of Experimental
and Control Groups at the End of Grade 1*

Test and Group	Number of Pupils	Mean Score	t
Aptitude Experimental	363	20.0882	
			2.7431*
Control	449	20.8486	
Total Reading Experimental	363	150.2837	
			3.7471*
Control	449	135.4788	

* Significant at .01 level.

score of the experimental group was slightly lower in aptitude than that of the control group. Nevertheless, the experimental group scored considerably higher in reading achievement. Both differences were significant at the .01 level.

The results shown in Table 3 clearly indicate that the children who had the formal-skills program in kindergarten scored better on the reading test than the children who did not have the program in kindergarten.

It is doubtful that the Hawthorne effect was operating in this study, since the children were not aware of any experimentation. Likewise, the investigator's bias was probably counterbalanced by the initial reservations of a number of kindergarten and first-grade teachers.

Apparently the earlier start in formal reading, based on a foundation of specific skills, made it possible for the children to get greater experience in reading outside the basal reader. More first-grade children read more library books, and read them sooner, than did first-grade children of previous years.

Two unforeseen aspects of the program have aroused considerable interest. The first has to do with speech problems.

All first-grade children are examined by speech therapists early in each school year. In comparing the experimental group with first-grade pupils of the previous year, speech therapists reported that the experimental group showed 36 per cent fewer minor articulation problems (substitution of *w* for *l*, *f* for *th*, *s* for *th*, *b* for *v*).

The second unexpected finding had to do with the reading achievement of boys and girls. There is a possibility that the more formal program in kindergarten may reduce differences in the reading achievement of boys and girls. A preliminary study which involved pre- and post-tests of readiness skills revealed that girls scored higher than boys on both tests, but the gain was the same for both (14). In the second year of the program, there was no significant difference between the scores of boys and those of girls on the Pre-Reading Inventory at the end of kindergarten.

Study of a formal program of teaching pre-reading skills in kindergarten, conducted by the Glenview schools, has led to the following conclusions:

1. Kindergarten pupils developed pre-reading skills to the point of using context and letter-sound associations to unlock a printed word.

2. These skills were developed more adequately with a workbook than without.

3. The skills were retained over the summer vacation.

4. Children who had formal training in kindergarten were better readers at the end of first grade than children who had not had such training.

Although the investigation still continues, observations to date suggest that the formal program in kindergarten has resulted in more proficient and more avid readers in first grade. These pupils will be studied through the grades with the expectation that what we learn from the program can benefit not only these children, but all children who follow them.

REFERENCES

1. Mabel Morphett and Carleton Washburne. "When Should Children Begin To Read?" *Elementary School Journal,* XXXI (March, 1931), 496–503.

2. Eunice Shaad Newton. Unpublished speech presented at the Science Research Associates' Conference in Chicago, 1960.

3. Dolores Durkin. "An Earlier Start in Reading?" *Elementary School Journal, LXIII* (December, 1962), 147–51.

4. Thomas Eames. "Physical Factors in Reading," *Reading Teacher,* XV (May, 1962), 432.

5. Wilbur Schramm, J. Lyle, and E. Parker. "Television in the Lives of Our Children." Palo Alto, California: Stanford University Press, 1961.

6. Coleman Morrison. "A Comparison between Reported and Recommended Practices Related to Selected Aspects of the Kindergarten and Beginning Reading Program." Paper presented at Chicago: American Educational Research Association, February 21, 1964.

7. Alice Nicholson. "Background Abilities Related to Reading Success in Beginning Reading." Unpublished doctoral dissertation, Boston University, 1957.

8. Arthur Olson, Jr. "Growth in Word Perception as It Related to Success in Beginning Reading." Unpublished doctoral dissertation, Boston University, 1957.

9. Dorothy Anderson. "A Study To Determine if Children Need a Mental Age of Six Years and Six Months To Learn To Identify Strange Printed Word Forms When They Are Taught To Use Oral Context and the Initial Sound of the Word." Unpublished doctoral dissertation. Greeley: Colorado State College, 1960.

10. Paul McKee and Lucille Harrison. *Getting Ready To Read.* Boston: Houghton Mifflin, 1962.

11. Denver Public Schools. "Reading Instruction in the Kindergarten." Denver, Colorado: Denver Public Schools, November 21, 1962 (mimeographed).

12. Robert Hillerich. "Dare We Evaluate Paradise?" *Illinois Education,* LI (April, 1963), 326, 345.

13. Robert Hillerich. "Reading Readiness in Kindergarten," *Cook County Educational Digest,* XXV (June, 1963), 5–6.

14. Robert Hillerich. "A Report on Results of the McKee Reading Readiness Program in Four Sections of Kindergarten, Glenview, 1960–61." Glenview School's Bulletin, June 15, 1961 (ditto).

FOR FURTHER READING

Barrett, Thomas C., "The Relationship Between Measures of Pre-reading Visual Discrimination and First Grade Reading Achievement: A Review of the Literature," *Reading Research Quarterly* 1 (Fall 1965) 51–76.

Brzeinski, Joseph E., "Beginning Reading in Denver," *The Reading Teacher* 18 (October 1964) 16–21.

Dykstra, Robert, "Auditory Discrimination Abilities and Beginning Reading Achievement," *Reading Research Quarterly* 1 (Spring 1966) 5–34.

Durkin, Dolores, "A Study of Children Who Learned to Read Prior to First Grade," *California Journal of Educational Research* 10 (May 1959) 109–113.

———, "Children Who Read Before Grade 1: A Second Study," *Elementary School Journal* 64 (December 1963) 143–148.

———, "Early Readers—Reflections After Six Years of Research," *The Reading Teacher* 18 (October 1964) 3–7.

———, "A Fifth-Year Report on the Achievement of Early Readers," *Elementary School Journal* 65 (November 1964) 76–80.

———, "The Achievement of Pre-School Readers: Two Longitudinal Studies," *Reading Research Quarterly* 1 (Summer 1966) 5–36.

———, *Reading and the Kindergarten,* Annotated Bibliography Series (Newark, Delaware: International Reading Association, 1966).

Georgiady, Nicolas P., Louis Romano, and Arthur Baranewski, "To Read or Not to Read—in Kindergarten," *Elementary School Journal* 65 (March 1965) 306–311.

Gunderson, Doris V., *Research in Reading Readiness,* U.S. Department of Health, Education, and Welfare, Office of Education Bulletin No. 8 (Washington, D.C.: U.S. Government Printing Office, 1964).

Harrison, M. Lucille, *Reading Readiness* (Boston: Houghton Mifflin Company, 1936).

Hillerich, Robert L., "Kindergartners are Ready! Are We?" *Elementary English* 42 (May 1965) 569–573.

———, "An Interpretation of Research in Reading Readiness," *Elementary English* 43 (April 1966) 359–364.

Monroe, Marion, *Growing into Reading* (Chicago: Scott, Foresman & Company, 1951).

Moskowitz, Sue, "Should We Teach Reading in the Kindergarten?" *Elementary English* 42 (November 1965) 798–804.

Schoephoerster, Hugh, Richard Barnhart, and Walter M. Loomer, "The Teaching of Pre-reading Skills in Kindergarten," *The Reading Teacher* 19 (February 1966) 352–357.

Sutton, Marjorie Hunt, "First Grade Children Who Learned to Read in Kindergarten," *The Reading Teacher* 19 (December 1965) 192–196.

———, "Children Who Learned to Read in Kindergarten: A Longitudinal Study," *Reading Teacher* 22 (April 1969) 595–602.

Vernon, Magdalen D., *Visual Perception and Its Relation to Reading: An Annotated Bibliography* (Newark, Delaware: International Reading Association, 1966).

———, "Ten More Important Sources of Information on Visual Perception in Relation to Reading," *The Reading Teacher* 20 (November 1966) 134–135.

Three Approaches to Beginning Reading Instruction— ITA, Language Experience, and Basic Readers— Extended into Second Grade*

HARRY T. HAHN

In 1964–1965 there were 27 first grade reading studies sponsored by the U.S. Office of Education. These studies were made in different localities and were concerned with different problems. All used some of the same pretests and posttests and all ran for approximately 140 days. In making a general conclusion about the studies, it was found that they could not be compared because a large number of variables were not uniformly controlled; the methods were not clearly different; the tests used for measurement caused much concern (some were of the homemade variety with no established validity or reliability); and the statistical procedures were not uniform. Thus each study must be examined on its own. The U.S. Office of Education extended 14 of the studies through the second and third grade. The Hahn study was one of these. (Reports of all the first- and second-year studies may be found in the three issues of *The Reading Teacher* cited in "For Further Reading.")

The results of the first year of this study can be summarized as follows: They were limited to reports of test given in May of the school year. *The Stanford Achievement Test, Primary Form,* and the *San Diego County Reading Attitude Tests* were administered. Individual tests, including the *Gilmore Oral Reading Paragraphs* and three word lists, were given to a random sample of 55 pupils in each of the three approaches. Children in the three approaches showed no significant differences in reading attitudes. All were enthusiastic in response to the *Reading Inventory* survey. The ITA and language experience pupils wrote freely and extensively throughout most of the school year. The time for writing seemed restricted in the basic reader approach and less writing was evident. Pupils of the ITA and language experience approaches had significantly higher scores than those of the basic reader approach on the word reading test. Language experience and basic reader approaches provided significantly better spellers. No differences were found among the three approaches when ITA spelling was accepted. On oral (individual) reading tests there

* From *The Reading Teacher* 20 (May 1967) 711–715. Reprinted with permission of the International Reading Association and Harry T. Hahn, Professor of Education, Oakland University, Rochester, Michigan.

were no significant differences in speed or accuracy recorded. ITA children recognized significantly more words on the Fry and Gates word lists when given ample time to sound through each word. There was evidence that ITA children employed a broader range of word attack skills. The capacity-achievement relationships were strongest for language experience in Paragraph Meaning and for ITA and language experience in Word Study. Girls and boys had comparable test scores on group data, but boys lagged behind the girls in reading achievement.

In the study, the initial intelligence quotients for the three groups were found not to be significantly different, most test instruments are respected ones, and the procedures are explained in some detail. Questions that may come to readers' minds in interpreting the data might include: Was the sampling random? What was the socio-economic level of the pupils of the various groups? Since teachers volunteered for the experimental groups and pupils knew they were doing something different, how might these factors have biased the results (the Hawthorne effect)?

Some books dealing with ITA and language experience are included in the "For Further Reading" section, as well as books on another influence, linguistics and reading.

"Provide boys and girls in the primary grades with many opportunities to read and write on their own." This dictum emerges from an examination of the progress of the young participants involved in three approaches to beginning reading and related language arts instruction —Initial Teaching Alphabet (ITA), Language Experience (LE), and Basal Reader and related language development programs (BR).

The study was initiated in September 1964 by twelve school districts in Oakland County, Michigan: Bloomfield Hills, Clarenceville, Farmington, Hazel Park, Lamphere, Madison Heights, Oak Park, Pontiac, Royal Oak, Troy, Walled Lake, and Waterford. The districts had agreed to provide three first grade classrooms, one for each approach, from three elementary schools in comparable socioeconomic areas within each district. Competent teachers, chosen from among those who volunteered for the three approaches, agreed to use new and relatively unfamiliar programs and materials and to participate in extensive in-service training sessions which were to continue throughout the school year. Teachers of the BR children, the control group, followed practices suggested in the teacher's manuals of the textbooks selected and endeavored to enrich and extend their programs within the framework provided. ITA and LE children were given intensive instruction in methods of relating sounds to symbols, and the teachers developed their programs using as a basic instructional source the dictated and written materials of the boys and girls. Individualized reading and writing practice was encouraged as pupils demonstrated control of symbolic language.

At the close of the first year children in the two experimental groups tended to make higher scores on the various evaluation devices used. However, the differences in achievement between ITA and LE children were not extensive. It was noted that many ITA children who had made the transfer to TO still continued to use the ITA in their compositions and on spelling tests.

During the second year ITA and LE children followed similar instructional programs, except for use of Sir James Pitman's alphabet when it was needed. The programs focused on methods for providing pupils with purposeful reading, writing, listening, and speaking activities, integrated to assist them in discovery of the power of self-expression. Experimental language experience units prepared by R. Van Allen, later published by Encyclopaedia Britannica Press under the title, *An Introduction to Language-Experience Program, Level II,* were used, together with similar units prepared by the teachers. Individualized reading practices, incorporating the concepts of self-selection, pacing, and individual teacher conferences, were started in September 1965. Small-group directed reading-thinking instruction supplanted the time devoted to individualized reading in October. Stories for group work were chosen to accord with the needs and interests of the participants. Instruction emphasized skill in asking questions, making predictions before and during reading, discovering story organization, content and plot, reconstructing endings, and related activities intended to reveal the role of the effective writer, as well as the active and intelligent reader, in the communication process. The plan provided that children would alternate month after month between group and individualized instruction to give them time to develop strong independent reading and work habits and to profit from group experience, as well as from the expert guidance of the teacher. The teachers involved were pleased with these arrangments.

The new Stanford Achievement Test, Primary Battery II was administered to the entire student population in May 1966. The mean scores and standard deviations are reported for each approach in Table 1. The significance of the differences in the means noted was determined by tests programmed through the 1620 IBM computer. No significant differences were found between the two experimental groups. ITA pupils were significantly higher, at the .05 level, than the BR children on tests of Spelling and Word Study. In first grade, ITA children had scored significantly lower in Spelling. Comparing LE with BR children, LE

TABLE 1
Summary of Results of Stanford Achievement Test, Primary Battery II
May 1966

Tests	ITA (N = 221)		LE (N = 212)		BR (N = 216)		t Tests		
	Mean	SD	Mean	SD	Mean	SD	ITA-LE	ITA-BR	LE-BR
Word Meaning	20.19	7.65	21.29	7.09	19.42	6.47	-1.54	1.13	2.84**
Paragraph Meaning	32.53	13.01	34.10	11.32	30.99	10.85	-1.33	1.33	2.89**
Science-S.S. Concepts	19.96	5.71	20.75	5.08	19.31	5.58	-1.51	1.20	2.78**
Spelling	15.68	8.02	15.90	7.91	14.09	7.60	-0.28	2.12*	2.40*
Word Study	40.78	12.74	40.40	11.34	38.09	12.12	0.32	2.25*	2.03*
Language	38.06	10.59	39.69	9.16	37.58	10.25	-1.70	0.48	2.23*
Arithmetic Computation	20.97	9.05	21.78	7.66	21.73	8.63	-1.00	-0.89	0.06
Arithmetic Concepts	20.74	9.44	21.34	7.83	20.33	8.83	-0.71	0.46	1.24

* Significant at .05 level.   ** Significant at .01 level.

61

children consistently made higher scores, at the .05 level, for Spelling, Word Study, and Language. The similarity in the scores among the three approaches in Arithmetic, in which the programs within districts tended to be quite similar, might be interpreted to show that the abilities of children among the approaches used were quite comparable.

The native ability of the boys and girls in the study is shown by the mean scores on the Pintner-Cunningham Intelligence Test in Table 2. The test was administered in first grade, and the results indicate that the mean differences among the three groups were not significant.

A random sample of pupils from each classroom was given the Gilmore Oral Reading Paragraphs and the Gates Word List. The mean scores for these tests are reported in Table 3. No significant differences were found among the three approaches in Rate and Accuracy of oral reading. However, the experimental groups of children recognized a significantly larger number of words on the Gates Word List.

Table 4 was prepared to show the mean differences in the number of books read in one month and the results on a test intended to reveal attitudes toward reading. LE children read significantly more books. BR boys and girls made significantly higher scores, at the .05 level, than ITA pupils on the Attitudes Survey, while differences between BR and LE means were not significant.

Near the close of second grade all the children were invited to write an ending to a story which was read to them. Word counts were made on the stories and the mean scores are reported in Table 5. LE children wrote significantly longer stories, used more different words, more polysyllabic words, and spelled more words correctly. BR children, however, demonstrated somewhat stronger mechanical skills in writing: their score was significantly higher, at the .05 level, on the Mechanics Ratio Scale.

RESULTS

The pattern of differences in performance among children in the three approaches which was noted in first grade continued to show at the close of second grade. Here is a summary of the significant differences which can be reported at this time:

ITA-LE. No differences were found on standardized tests. LE pupils read more books and wrote longer stories.

ITA-BR. ITA pupils made higher scores in Spelling and Word Study on the Stanford battery and recognized more words on the Gates Word List. BR

TABLE 2
Summary of Results for the Pintner-Cunningham Test
September 1964

	ITA		LE		BR		t Tests		
Pintner-Cunningham	Mean	SD	Mean	SD	Mean	SD	ITA-LE	ITA-BR	LE-BR
Raw Scores	40.19	8.70	41.04	6.94	39.75	7.76	−1.11	0.55	1.80

TABLE 3
Summary of Results for the Gilmore Oral Reading Paragraphs and the Gates Word List
May 1966

Test	ITA (N = 62)		LE (N = 65)		BR (N = 49)		t Tests		
	Mean	SD	Mean	SD	Mean	SD	ITA-LE	ITA-BR	LE-BR
Gilmore Oral Reading Paragraphs									
Accuracy	37.89	18.58	39.50	15.99	36.67	13.57	−0.91	0.69	1.78
Rate (wpm)	87.3	34.3	90.0	35.6	93.8	31.1	−0.75	−1.84	−1.06
Gates Word List Word Pronunciation	26.38	8.80	26.12	8.35	23.58	6.73	0.29	3.29**	3.12**

** Significant at .01 level.

TABLE 4

Summary of Results of Survey of Books Read in One Month
and San Diego Pupil Attitude Inventory

	ITA		LE		BR		t Tests		
Measure	Mean	SD	Mean	SD	Mean	SD	ITA-LE	ITA-BR	LE-BR
Number of Books Read Completely	7.67	6.65	15.56	13.27	8.16	7.46	-7.85***	-0.72	7.11***
San Diego Pupil Attitude Inventory	17.67	5.11	18.16	4.61	18.71	4.61	-1.04	-2.22*	-1.23

* Significant at .05 level.   ** Significant at .01 level.   *** Significant at .001 level.

TABLE 5

Summary of Results of Writing Samples
May 1966

	ITA		LE		BR		t Tests		
Story Samples	Mean	SD	Mean	SD	Mean	SD	ITA-LE	ITA-BR	LE-BR
Running Words	59.0	33.4	73.6	43.7	59.6	35.1	-3.66***	-0.16	3.29**
No. of Different Words	36.08	13.59	42.66	18.13	36.37	16.05	-4.00***	-0.18	3.44***
No. of Words Spelled Correctly	50.8	32.6	64.4	40.3	53.3	33.2	-3.62***	-0.70	2.80**
No. of Polysyllabic Words	14.34	7.43	16.91	11.84	14.63	8.83	-2.53*	-0.33	2.02*
Mechanics Ratio Scale	51.6	19.4	51.4	17.4	56.3	19.2	2.10	-2.26*	-2.53*

* Significant at .05 level.   ** Significant at .01 level.   *** Significant at .001 level.

pupils made higher scores on a Reading Attitude Test and a Writing Mechanics Ratio Scale.

LE-BR. LE pupils made higher scores on Word Meaning, Paragraph Meaning, Science-Social Studies Concepts, Spelling, Word Study, and Language tests. They also recognized more words on a word list, read more books, and wrote longer stories. BR children were stronger on the Writing Mechanics Ratio Scale.

CONCLUSION

1. The young learners in this study who were given ample time for purposeful writing, speaking, and listening together with many opportunities to read books of their own choice have thus far demonstrated greater control over the basic skills than those boys and girls involved in structured programs which focused on those skills daily. It must be noted that the basal reader children had many opportunities to read independently and write extensively, but the framework of the basal program did not permit the freedom and opportunity for personal commitment to learning found in the language experience approach.

2. In those classrooms where instruction was focused on children's thoughts, ideas, and varied methods for self-expression, it was observed that the teacher served as a catalyst to initiate learning and as a ready resource to keep it going. In such an environment it was apparent that the boys and girls had more opportunity to become independent and self-reliant workers. They found a great deal of satisfaction in their own achievement, as well as in the achievements of others.

3. It doesn't appear in this study that the use of the initial teaching alphabet has given children an advantage over those using a comparable instructional approach with traditional orthography. It must be noted, however, that ITA-oriented boys and girls do not appear to be handicapped by their unique learning experience. It was felt that, for research purposes, the new alphabet provided ITA teachers and children with a lively and exciting examination of a provocative method for reading and writing, which both found beneficial. In this writer's opinion, there is a constant need for spirited, research-oriented instruction which will challenge all of us to take a hard look at practices and programs which are too often taken for granted. The use of ITA offered this type of instruction.

Perhaps the greatest problem in the use of ITA as another approach to beginning reading is an administrative one. As John Downing reported in his recent tour of the United States, some children do not master the simpler alphabet in two, three, four, and possibly more years. How does one encourage and sustain an interest in ITA among third, fourth, and fifth grade teachers in order to accommodate a few who need it? What is more, where does one scrounge for materials to provide teachers with ITA texts and tradebooks needed for this long stretch of time?

FOR FURTHER READING

Bond, Guy L., "First Grade Reading Studies: An Overview," *Elementary English* 43 (May 1966) 464–470.

Campbell, Paul B., Henry C. Heusner, and June J. Slobedian, "An Analysis of Eight Different Reading Instructional Methods Used with First Grade Students," in J. Allen Figurel, editor, *Forging Ahead in Reading*, International Reading Association Conference Proceedings, No. 12, Part I (Newark, Delaware: International Reading Association, 1968), pp. 468–477.

Downing, John A., *Initial Teaching Alphabet Reading Experiment: Three Lectures on Research in Beginning Reading* (Chicago: Scott, Foresman & Company, 1965).

Duncan, Roger L., "What's the Best Way to Teach Reading?" *School Management* 8 (December 1964) 46–47.

Fries, Charles C., *Linguistics and Reading* (New York: Holt, Rhinehart & Winston, Inc., 1963).

Lee, Doris May, and R. Van Allen, *Learning to Read Through Experience* (New York: Appleton-Century-Crofts, 1963).

Lefevre, Carl A., *Linguistics and the Teaching of Reading* (New York: McGraw-Hill Book Company, 1964).

Robinson, Helen M., "Assessing the Experimental Evidence for Various Beginning Reading Plans," *Modern Educational Developments: Another Look*, Report of 30th Educational Conference Sponsored by Educational Records Bureau, pp. 167–176.

Stauffer, Russell G., "The Verdict: Speculative Controversy," *Reading Teacher* 19 (May 1966) 563–564, 575.

"U.S. Office of Education First Grade Reading Studies," *The Reading Teacher* 20 (May and October 1966); 21 (May 1967).

Walker, Frederick R., "Evaluation of Three Methods of Teaching Reading—7th Grade," *Journal of Educational Research* 54 (May 1961) 356–358.

Two Methods of Teaching Phonics: A Longitudinal Study*

DAVID E. BEAR

Bear's experimental study (and its extension into an ex post facto study) has been selected to represent an area of considerable controversy: the role of "code-breaking" as a word recognition technique in reading instruction. Here the question is not "phonics or no phonics?" or "which phonics?" but "analytic versus synthetic" instruction as defined by the researcher.

Very limited evidence is available about the various facets of phonic instruction, particularly for grades 4, 5, and 6. In her reflection after studying much research on the topic, Jeanne Chall (see "For Further Reading") stated her belief that systematic phonics is probably more effective for slow-learning children and those of average intelligence since it can be made easier than intrinsic phonics. Further, she concluded that systematic phonics tends to produce generally better reading and spelling achievement at the very beginning than intrinsic phonics—at least through grade 3. More specifically, Chall wrote that children beginning with systematic phonics: (1) achieved early superiority in word recognition and by grades 2 and 3 increased ability to read for meaning, (2) may be slower readers in grades 1 and 2, and (3) may have limited use of phonics after grade 4 since at that point other factors, such as intelligence, experience, and language maturity, may be more crucial to the reading process.

The reader can decide for himself which of these conclusions is supported by the Bear study. In this study, the initial population and sample are important considerations in interpreting the data. Since a period of years intervened between the first and the present study, the different experiences of the children—and their order and intensity—are important variables.

The Chall reference provides a very complete research bibliography for this topic. Several reviews of research are cited in "For Further Reading." Other articles cited deal with the usefulness of specific phonic generalizations (Bailey, Burmeister, Clymer); and one (Mills) seeks to determine the technique—visual, phonic, kinesthetic,

* From *Elementary School Journal,* 64 (February 1964) 273–279. Reprinted with permission of the University of Chicago Press © 1964 and David E. Bear, Professor of Education, Southern Illinois University, Edwardsville.

or a combination—most effective in teaching word recognition to different types of pupils. Finally, the reader is reminded of other word recognition techniques as described by writers of professional reading textbooks.

There is very little controversy today over the importance of phonics in a well-balanced reading program. Authorities in the field of reading method agree that children need a knowledge of phonics if they are to become independent readers. But authorities disagree on which is the best method to use, how much phonics should be taught, and when phonics instruction should begin.

Phonics programs in use before 1920 were synthetic in nature. Instruction began by teaching the sounds of letters and the blending of these sounds into larger units. These synthetic phonic methods made use of drill on letters and sound units in a special period set aside for this purpose. The actual reading process itself, which dealt with the interpretation of whole words and sentences, was usually delayed until the child had achieved a high degree of mastery of phonics. These early reading programs were highly mechanistic in that great emphasis was placed on phonics and word structure to the neglect of important skills in comprehension.

The programs neglected many important skills needed for efficient reading. Because of the neglect, a few prominent authorities in reading method became highly critical of synthetic phonic methods. Most of these critics believed that synthetic methods over-emphasized phonics instruction and that the overemphasis resulted in the following:

Word-calling

Overemphasis on the mechanics of reading to the neglect of reading for meaning

Lessened interest in reading

Unnatural articulation

Little transfer of learning to normal reading situations

Difficulty in teaching phonics to beginners because of the unphonetic character of the English language

Lack of carry-over of letter-type phonics to the pronunciation of multi-syllabic words

Poor spelling because of the unphonetic character of the English language

Retarded development of adequate speed in reading

The imbalance in the reading programs of this early period and the influence of the critics ushered in a reaction against phonics which almost eliminated it from reading instruction in the United States during the 1920's (1). Silent reading skills received increased attention during the twenties, and the sight method emerged as the major approach in introducing pupils to reading material in the first grade.

Along with this development, a new method of teaching phonics, known as intrinsic phonics, was introduced. By this method a child acquires a sight vocabulary before he is introduced to phonics. After the child learns a small stock of words by the sight method, he begins to compare these words for similarities and thus builds phonic generalizations.

For instance, after a child has learned two or three sight words that begin alike, such as *bird, ball,* and *boy,* he is taught to notice that the words begin with the same letter and also sound alike at the beginning. In this manner, the child makes generalizations that will help him identify this sound at the beginning of other words. This method is known as an analytic method because the identification of a strange word begins with the whole word, which is then analyzed into its pronounceable units.

In describing the phonic methods in use in most basal reading programs today, Emmett Betts made a clear distinction between the synthetic method and the analytic method. He wrote: "*Sounding* methods of phonics have given way to *pronouncing* methods. The *synthesizing* of sounds into words (called the synthetic method) has given way to the *analysis* of whole words (called the analytic method). In recent teacher's manuals, the emphasis has been on the nonseparation, or whole word, method" (2).

The controversy in phonics today centers on these two methods. Each method has its strong proponents, and they are usually quite vocal in their criticism of the method they oppose. Research has failed to give conclusive evidence of the superiority of one method over the other, yet educators continue to take strong positions on the issue.

In the study reported here, a synthetic method of teaching phonics was compared with an analytic method. The study was first reported by Bear in April, 1959 (3). The 1959 report presented test results after one year of instruction of two matched groups of first-grade pupils. This report, which is the second, presents the results of a testing program for the same pupils at the end of Grade 6. The follow-up study was made to determine the long-range effects of two methods of teaching phonics to first-graders. I hoped to learn whether the differences found at the end of first grade were still present at the end of sixth grade.

The original experiment began in September, 1956, in fourteen first-grade classrooms in the public school system in Alton, Illinois. The seven classes that made up the experimental group were given instruction in phonics in a special thirty-minute period each day. This group used the phonics primer and workbook mataerial, *Reading with Phonics,* 1954 edition, published by the J. B. Lippincott Company, more popularly known as the Hay-Wingo system (4). This material is typical of a synthetic method and similar to that used in some of the reading programs in the early 1900's.

Seven other classes known as the control group received instruction in phonics in accordance with the teacher's manuals that accompanied the basal reading series of the Row-Peterson Company which was published in 1954 (5).

In the fourteen classrooms, 136 pupils in the experimental group and 139 pupils in the control group finished the school year. The two groups were found to be equal in intelligence, in reading-readiness scores, and on the Warner Index of Status Characteristics. More details on the experimental design can be found in the first report (3).

Both the experimental and the control group used the Row-Peterson basal reading program with one major variation: the method of teaching phonics. The control group received instruction in phonics according to the directions in the teacher's manuals accompanying the basal readers. For the experimental group, this instruction in phonics was eliminated. Even the workbook pages dealing with visual discrimination and auditory discrimination were eliminated. Instead, a special thirty-minute period each day was used for teaching phonics using the materials published by the Lippincott Company.

After one semester of instruction in the first grade, the mean scores on the Gates Primary Reading Tests were almost identical. The *t* ratios indicated no differences that were considered statistically significant.

The testing program at the end of the first grade revealed that the pupils who used the synthetic method achieved much higher scores than those who used the analytic method. The *t* ratios were sufficiently high to reject the null hypothesis on both the Gates Primary Reading Tests and the Metropolitan Achievement Tests. The pupils who used the synthetic method also scored much higher on the Durrell test for hearing sounds in words (6).

The results of this early study indicated that a synthetic method could be used successfully along with a basal-reading program and serve as a valuable supplement in developing reading skills.

In the 1959 report the writer suggested that a follow-up study should be made at the end of three years or more of instruction to determine whether the differences found after one year of instruction still persisted. The writer also wished to determine the long-range effects of intensive phonics instruction given in first grade. The remainder of this report will present the findings of the testing program for these pupils that was carried out at the end of Grade 6.

Beginning with Grade 2 the Lippincott phonics program was discontinued, and all pupils in the study received reading instruction by the basal-reader approach. During the remaining five years, phonics instruction was given according to the teacher's manuals accompanying the basal-reading series. This report, therefore, is an attempt to measure the long-range effects of an intensive synthetic phonics program in first grade.

In May, 1962, as the pupils were nearing the end of Grade 6, the Gates Reading Survey, Form 2, was administered. In addition, two tests in spelling were given: one was a twenty-word spelling test of a random sample drawn from spelling word lists for sixth, seventh, eighth, and ninth grades; the other was a list of twenty nonsense words that contained syllables that were phonetic. The latter test afforded the pupils an opportunity to apply their knowledge of sounding.

The writer was able to locate 95 pupils of the 136 who made up the original experimental group, and 90 pupils of the 139 who were in the original control group. These two groups were found to be equal on the basis of intelligence as measured by the California Test of Mental Maturity, which was given in first grade, and on socioeconomic status as measured by the Warner Index of Status Characteristics. The t ratios indicated no significant differences between the two groups on these two factors.

The results of the Gates Reading Survey, which was administered in May, 1962, are presented in Table 1. The differences in the means were all favorable to the experimental group; however, only the differences on the vocabulary test were sufficiently high to reject the null hypothesis at the 5 per cent level. The t ratio on vocabulary indicates a difference that is significant in favor of the experimental group.

In addition to tabulating the data on the total number of pupils in the experimental and the control groups, it was thought desirable to compare the reading achievement of the pupils at three different levels

TABLE 1

*Mean Scores on the Gates Reading Survey Given in May, 1962,
for an Experimental Group and a Control Group*

| Test Section | Experimental Group* | | Control Group† | | | Proba- bility Level |
	Mean Score	Standard Deviation	Mean Score	Standard Deviation	t	
Vocabulary	7.27	1.86	6.67	1.7	2.31	.02‡
Comprehension	7.42	1.97	7.01	1.86	1.50	.13
Speed	8.50	2.32	8.33	2.16	1.00	.32

* Experimental group of ninety-five pupils.
† Control group of ninety pupils.
‡ Significant at the 5 per cent level of confidence.

of intelligence. For this purpose, the pupils in the experimental and the control groups were divided into the lowest 25 per cent, the middle 50 per cent, and the upper 25 per cent. The pupils in the experimental and the control groups at these three levels were found to be about equal in intelligence. The *t* ratios indicated no differences that could be considered statistically significant.

The results of the testing program for the lowest 25 per cent are presented in Table 2. For the pupils at this level, the differences in the means favored the experimental group but not enough to reject the null hypothesis at the 5 per cent level of confidence; however, the *t* ratio of 1.8 closely approximated this level.

Table 3 presents the results for the middle 50 per cent of each group. For this middle 50 per cent, the differences in the means on all three tests were favorable to the experimental group. The *t* ratios were high

TABLE 2

*Mean Scores on the Gates Reading Survey Given in May, 1962,
for the Lowest 25 Per Cent of the Pupils in the
Experimental Group and the Control Group*

| Test Section | Experimental Group* | | Control Group† | | | Proba- bility Level |
	Mean Score	Standard Deviation	Mean Score	Standard Deviation	t	
Vocabulary	6.24	1.40	5.62	1.04	1.8	.07
Comprehension	5.97	1.46	5.89	1.33	.15	.88
Speed	7.16	2.25	7.08	1.49	.15	.88

* Experimental group of twenty-six pupils.
† Control group of twenty-four pupils.

TABLE 3

*Mean Scores on the Gates Reading Survey Given in May, 1962,
for the Middle 50 Per Cent of the Pupils in the
Experimental Group and the Control Group*

| Test Section | Experimental Group* | | Control Group† | | | Proba- |
	Mean Score	Standard Deviation	Mean Score	Standard Deviation	t	bility Level
Vocabulary	7.53	1.83	6.5	1.36	3.0	.003‡
Comprehension	7.6	1.97	6.62	1.41	2.7	.007‡
Speed	8.95	2.15	7.93	1.83	2.4	.016§

* Experimental group of forty-three pupils.
† Control group of forty-three pupils.
‡ Significant at the 1 per cent level of confidence.
§ Significant at the 5 per cent level of confidence.

enough to reject the null hypothesis at a point well beyond the 1 per cent level of confidence. The pupils in this intelligence category apparently benefited more from synthetic phonics than the pupils in the other two categories did. This result is similar to the result obtained at the end of the first grade.

The results for the upper 25 per cent are shown in Table 4. At this level, the differences were slightly in favor of the control group; however, the *t* ratios were too low to be considered significant. This result is similar to that found at the end of the first grade: that children of high intelligence learned equally well by both methods.

The results of the two tests in spelling are given in Table 5. The scores indicate a significant difference in the means in favor of the ex-

TABLE 4

*Mean Scores on the Gates Reading Survey Given in May, 1962,
for the Upper 25 Per Cent of the Pupils in the
Experimental Group and the Control Group*

| Test Section | Experimental Group* | | Control Group† | | | Proba- |
	Mean Score	Standard Deviation	Mean Score	Standard Deviation	t	bility Level
Vocabulary	7.83	1.57	8.135	1.77	.69	.49
Comprehension	8.525	1.5	8.98	1.56	1.00	.32
Speed	9.25	2.17	10.01	2.05	1.10	.27

* Experimental group of twenty-six pupils.
† Control group of twenty-three pupils.

TABLE 5

*Mean Scores on Two Spelling Tests Given in May, 1962,
for an Experimental Group and a Control Group*

Tests	Experimental Group* Mean Score	Standard Deviation	Control Group† Mean Score	Standard Deviation	t	Proba- bility Level
Twenty-word spell- ing test	12.84	3.5	11.1	3.72	3.12	‡
Test of twenty nonsense words	16.7	3.24	14.9	3.7	3.33	‡

* Experimental group of ninety-five pupils.
† Control group of ninety pupils.
‡ Significant at the 1 per cent level of confidence.

perimental method. The *t* ratios are well above the result necessary to reject the null hypothesis at the 1 per cent level of confidence. The pupils who received phonics instruction by the synthetic method in first grade made a much higher score on the two spelling tests given at the end of Grade 6.

This follow-up study was made to determine the long-range effects of two methods of teaching phonics. The experimenter wished to determine whether the differences favorable to synthetic phonics found at the end of first grade would persist over a period of several years. From an analysis of the data collected at the end of Grade 6, several conclusions seem justified.

The differences in reading performance between the two groups under study were favorable to the synthetic method which used the Lippincott phonics program. After the comparisons that involved all the pupils in each group, the pupils were divided into three categories on the basis of intelligence. It was found that pupils in the middle 50 per cent of the intelligence range received greater benefit from synthetic phonics than the pupils in the highest and the lowest 25 per cent. For the upper 25 per cent of the pupils, the two phonic methods produced almost identical results. For the lowest 25 per cent of the pupils, the results slightly favored the pupils who used the synthetic phonics program.

The differences favoring the synthetic method that were found at the end of the first grade persisted through Grade 6. The results were similar at all three levels of intelligence. These data suggest that in differentiating phonics instruction more attention should be given to the pupils' intelligence.

Pupils taught by the synthetic method scored much higher on tests of spelling ability at the end of Grade 6 than pupils taught by the analytic method. Differences were high enough to be significant at the 1 per cent level of confidence.

In the study reported here, it should be noted that the synthetic and the analytic methods were compared in reading programs that were considered balanced in that attention was given to all the important skills in reading. In some earlier studies that compared these two methods, synthetic phonics was placed at a disadvantage by the fact that it was usually the major activity in the reading program. Proponents of some of these early synthetic phonics programs believed that phonics instruction should constitute the reading program. The lack of attention to other important reading skills caused many critics to condemn synthetic phonics when they should have been critical of reading programs that were imbalanced.

I found no evidence that synthetic phonics as used in this study represented an overemphasis. The nine difficulties listed as typical of synthetic phonics programs of an earlier era were not found to be characteristic of synthetic phonics as used in this study. The test results—which favored the synthetic method on vocabulary, comprehension, speed, and spelling—tend to support this viewpoint.

The results of this study, and of others that have been reported recently, lead me to believe that authors of basal readers should take a more realistic position on the issue of phonics. Recent research has indicated that synthetic phonics is highly beneficial for the average and below average pupil when this instruction is a part of a comprehensive, well-balanced reading program. Synthetic phonics is not incompatible with the word method, since both can be used from the beginning of the first grade for pupils who have developed the necessary readiness skills for beginning reading.

Progress in improving reading programs is likely to be retarded unless educators try to compromise the two extreme positions taken by the adherents of these two approaches to the teaching of phonics. Proponents of synthetic methods should refrain from developing reading programs that place undue stress on phonics to the neglect of other important skills in reading. The authors of basal-reader programs should recognize that many pupils have difficulty in learning to read and that synthetic phonics might make a valuable contribution in this area.

The reading progress of many children would be enchanced by a realistic reappraisal of the phonics controversy.

REFERENCES

1. William S. Gray. *On Their Own in Reading*, pp. 26–28. Chicago: Scott, Foresman and Company, 1948.
2. Emmett Albert Betts, *Foundations of Reading Instruction*, p. 623. New York: American Book Company, 1954.
3. David E. Bear. "Phonics for First Grade: A Comparison of Two Methods," *Elementary School Journal*, LIX (April, 1959), 394–402.
4. Julie Hay and Charles E. Wingo. *Reading with Phonics*. Teacher's Edition. New York: J. B. Lippincott Company, 1954.
5. Mabel O'Donnell. *Guidebooks for the First Grade Basal Readers*. Evanston, Illinois: Row, Peterson and Company, 1954.
6. Donald D. Durrell. *Improving Reading Instruction*, pp. 104–107. New York: World Book Company, 1956.

FOR FURTHER READING

Bailey, Mildred H., "The Utility of Phonic Generalizations in Grades One Through Six," *The Reading Teacher* 20 (February 1967) 413–418.

Bear, David E., "Phonics for First Grade: A Comparison of Two Methods," *Elementary School Journal* 59 (April 1959) 394–402.

Bleismer, Emery P., and Betty Y. Yarborough, "A Comparison of Ten Different Beginning Reading Programs in First Grade," *Phi Delta Kappan* 46 (June 1965) 500–504.

Bloomer, Richard H., "An Investigation of an Experimental First Grade Phonics Program," *Journal of Educational Research* 53 (January 1960) 188–193.

Burmeister, Lou E., "Usefulness of Phonic Generalizations," *The Reading Teacher* 21 (January 1968) 349–356, 360.

Chall, Jeanne, *Learning to Read: The Great Debate* (New York: McGraw-Hill Book Company, 1967).

Clymer, Theodore, "The Utility of Phonic Generalizations in the Primary Grades," *The Reading Teacher* 16 (January 1963) 252–258.

Gagon, Glen S., "Modern Research and Word Perception," *Education* 86 (April 1966) 464–472.

Gurren, Louise, and Ann Hughes, "Intensive Phonics vs. Gradual

Phonics in Beginning Reading: A Review," *Journal of Educational Research* 58 (April 1965) 339–347.

Heilman, Arthur W., *Phonics in Proper Perspective* (Columbus, Ohio: Charles E. Merrill Books, Inc., 1964).

Mills, Robert E., "An Evaluation of Techniques for Teaching Word Recognition," *Elementary School Journal* 56 (January 1956) 221–225.

Morrone, Victor, "A Critical Analysis of Scientific Research in Phonics" unpublished doctoral dissertation (Pittsburgh: University of Pittsburgh, 1958).

Smith, Nila B., "What Research Tells Us About Word Recognition," *Elementary School Journal* 55 (April 1955) 440–446.

Spache, George D., and Mary E. Baggett, "What Do Teachers Know About Phonics and Syllabification?," *The Reading Teacher* 19 (November 1965) 96–99.

Winkley, Carol K., "Which Accent Generalizations Are Worth Teaching?" *The Reading Teacher* 20 (December 1966) 219–224, 253.

Are Fast Readers the Best Readers?—
A Second Report*

J. HARLAN SHORES

The past few years has seen an increased amount of attention directed toward rate of reading, the focus of this correlation study. Claims that all pupils should read all material more rapidly cannot be justified; it seems clear that pupils need to learn to adapt their rate to suit the purpose for which they are reading. The rate of reading detailed material must be slower than reading for enjoyment in nontechnical, easy material. The goal is not to see how fast the pupils can read but rather to provide them with techniques for reading most efficiently. With such ideas in mind, teachers and administrators must evaluate "speed reading programs" (whether machine-oriented or not). As has often been said, one must always consider speed in terms of comprehension.

In this report, Shores suggests that the question posed in the title is more complex than might first appear. This report and its findings have important implications for the teaching of reading in the content fields. Two other reports by Shores (on science) and one by Troxel (on mathematics) cited in "For Further Reading" are pertinent to this topic, as well as the studies on the legibility of print, another facet related to speed of reading. Also see Schiller's research on reading-study skills in Chapter 4.

Whether fast readers are the best readers depends in large part upon what is meant by reading rate; that is, upon how rate is measured. Reading rate is ordinarily measured as an original reading time (*i.e.,* the words read per minute during a single reading and not including the time taken to answer comprehension questions), or it is measured as a total reading time including both the time for a single original reading and the time taken to answer comprehension questions. Most

* From *Elementary English* 38 (April 1961) 236–245. Reprinted with the permission of the National Council of Teachers of English and J. Harlan Shores, Professor of Elementary Education, University of Illinois, Urbana.

rate measures either do not permit rereading or discourage this practice even though some reading, such as keeping a long series of ideas in mind in proper sequence or following precise directions, obviously requires rereading even by proficient readers.

It is at once apparent that a single rapid reading for superficial comprehension is a different measure from one that also includes time to answer questions. The question-answering task is often as time-consuming as is the actual reading. It is also apparent that neither of these tests is the same as a measure of the amount of time taken to read and use these materials for whatever comprehension purpose the reader has in mind.

The fact that experiments with reading speed have differed in what is measured as reading rate probably accounts in large part for the somewhat conflicting findings. Realizing that some readers go through the materials once rapidly and then reread all or part of the material for the specific purposes set by the comprehension questions, an adequate measure of reading rate must provide three scores—an original reading rate, a time for reading the questions, rereading the materials, and answering the questions; and a total time which is the sum of the previous two.

The question then, "Are fast readers the good readers?" needs to be broken down into several questions. Defining a "good reader" as one who comprehends well, we need to ask, "Are good readers those who read rapidly during an initial reading?" Do the good readers read rapidly when dealing with the study-type comprehension questions and when rereading to answer the questions? Are the good readers those who take less time in total and read, reread, and answer questions? A single answer is not adequate for these three questions and they in turn give rise to others. Are the fast readers the good readers on each of these measures regardless of the difficulty of the material and the purpose for reading? It is to these questions that this article is directed.

In the January, 1950, issue of *Elementary English* this author and Kenneth L. Husbands reported an investigation concerned with the relationship between reading speed and comprehension (5). The general conclusion of this study was that there is no relationship between reading speed and comprehension when the task is difficult. The fast reader was not the best reader when he was reading biological science material in order to solve a problem. In fact, under these conditions the efficient and able reader slowed his rate to that of the inefficient reader.

STUDENT AND ADULT POPULATIONS

The present study, like the earlier one, was conducted with sixth-grade students. However, in the current study data were also collected from a group of able adult readers, and more adequate instrumentation was employed throughout.

All forty-six sixth graders of a K-12 consolidated school on the Southeastern coast of the United States comprised the student population. Even though the "tourist trade" was the largest industry, each of the children included was a permanent resident of the county. It is apparent from Table 1 that the children were of average age in grade and were somewhat above average in intelligence and reading achievement. In terms of their mental ability the group may have been slightly underachieving. Table 1 also indicates that the two sixth-grade groups reading for different purposes were closely equivalent in chronological age, mental age, and measures of general reading abilities.

The adult group was taken from several advanced undergraduate and graduate university-level courses dealing with the teaching of reading. A few of these were juniors and seniors in the program preparatory to teaching in the elementary grades. The majority were experienced teachers and administrators working toward graduate degrees.

TESTS USED

With the sixth-grade students four reading rate measures provided ten rate scores, and five comprehension measures provided eleven comprehension scores. The Iowa Silent Reading Tests (2) gave one rate score based on a portion of original reading time. Three tests developed by the author, each measuring an aspect of the reading of science materials, provided three rate scores each—a measure of original reading time, a measure of rereading and question-answering time, and a measure of total reading time.

Each of the rate tests provided one or more measures of comprehension and the California Achievement Tests (7) provided additional comprehension measures. Whenever sub-tests of the Iowa and California tests were measuring in the same area these scores were combined for a more adequate measure. Thus the following scores were available from these two reading tests: California comprehension,

TABLE 1

Equivalence of Groups Reading for Main Ideas and for Ideas in Sequence Expressed in Raw Scores

Measure	Group A (Main Ideas)		Group B (Sequence)		Group A plus B	
	Mean	SD	Mean	SD	Mean	SD
C.A. (months)	137.48	4.28	135.83	6.51	136.65	5.41
M.A. (months)	151.57	26.88	147.61	22.92	149.59	24.78
California Reading*						
Comprehension	29.26	6.80	27.87	6.11	28.57	6.43
Total Score	104.43	14.97	103.65	15.19	104.04	14.92
Iowa Silent Reading**						
Comprehension	69.87	22.88	71.13	21.73	70.50	22.07
Rate	26.70	8.23	26.57	10.16	26.63	9.14
Total Score	122.26	35.23	124.91	36.16	123.58	35.32
Combined Scores—						
California plus Iowa						
Comprehension	99.13	28.53	99.00	26.22	99.07	27.09
Vocabulary	100.43	16.85	103.00	16.67	101.72	16.62

* Ernest W. Tiegs and Willis W. Clark, *California Reading Test*, Los Angeles; California Test Bureau, 1950.
** H. A. Greene and V. H. Kelley, *Iowa Silent Reading Tests*, Yonkers on Hudson, N.Y.; World Book Co., 1956.

Iowa comprehension, combined comprehension, combined vocabulary, combined directed reading, combined references, combined interpretation, Iowa rate (California does not provide a rate score), California total score, and Iowa total score.

Mental ages were derived from the California Test of Mental Maturity, Non-Language Section (6), and the Sequential Tests of Educational Progress (4) were used to measure achievement in science.

After the standardized tests were administered, three unpublished tests developed by the author of this study were used. One of these, called *Reading for Problem Solving in Science,* is a forty-item test measuring ability to do directed reading for the solution of problems in science. The comprehension reliability of this test with the Kuder Richardson formula is .83. The rate reliability with the split-half method and the Spearman-Brown correction was .56 for original reading time, .43 for question answering time, and .39 for total time.

This was followed by the Directed Reading of Science Materials Tests administered in twenty successive sessions during which the 23 pupils in each sixth-grade group read a science passage of from 200 to 400 words that had been drawn from *Our Wonderful World* (8) and was at that time unfamiliar to them. Group A was instructed to read each passage for the main idea while Group B was instructed to read the same passage to keep the ideas of the passage in mind in their proper sequence. Different passages were employed for the different "tests." There was a total of twenty questions to be answered by those reading for main ideas and eighty questions for those reading for ideas in sequence. Three rate scores (original reading time, rereading and question-answering time, and total time) were taken for each of the twenty "tests." The split-half reliabilities of these tests of rate and comprehension are shown in Table 2 (1).

Fifty-one advanced undergraduate and graduate students read five of the same twenty selections from the *Directed Reading of Science Materials Tests* read by the sixth graders. Twenty-eight read for Purpose A (main ideas) and twenty-three read the same five selections for Purpose B (to keep ideas in mind in sequence). The adults were checked on comprehension and speed for each passage in the same manner as the sixth graders. The difference in the treatment was that the adults responded to all five passages at a single sitting whereas the children responded to only one passage at a sitting.

The adult population was deliberately chosen as a group of able readers. Most of the group were practicing elementary school teachers. A few were administrators and a few were advanced students (juniors

TABLE 2

Reliability of Scores on Directed Reading of Science Tests

Measure	Mean	Standard Deviation	Coefficient of Reliability*
Type A—			
Main Idea			
Comprehension	11.70	4.29	.80
Original Rate	443.74	126.99	.97
Question Rate	119.22	40.62	.82
Total Rate	567.35	138.48	.95
Type B—			
Ideas in Sequence			
Comprehension	36.34	10.73	.90
Original Rate	462.57	159.42	.96
Question Rate	449.87	177.68	.93
Total Rate	916.78	293.54	.98

* The split-half method and the Spearman-Brown correction were used with all scores.

and seniors) in a program preparatory to teaching. It may be that success in a field requiring much reading is better evidence of ability to do work-type reading than is any test now available. At any rate successful teachers and good students in teacher education programs probably can offer evidence of adequate reading skills.

As further proof of reading ability the adults scored well on the *Directed Reading of Science Materials Tests*. Their average accuracy level was 92 per cent when reading for main ideas, as contrasted with 56 per cent for sixth graders. When reading for the more difficult task of getting ideas in sequence the adult average accuracy level was 80 per cent whereas the sixth grade level was only 42 per cent. On the test of *Reading for Problem Solving in Science* the average adult accuracy level was 90 per cent and the average sixth grade level was only 63 per cent.

It is apparent then that the adult group used in this study are quite effective readers. It is then altogether likely that the relationships between speed and comprehension scores exhibited by this group more nearly represent the kind of relationships that are optimum than do those of sixth-grade students.

Early in the plans for the study serious consideration was given to the question of whether it would be appropriate to use the same measures and materials with able adult readers as are used with sixth-grade students. It is likely that literature or even "story type" material from science or the social studies that would be suitable and interesting to sixth-grade students would have little appeal for educated adults. However, the descriptive science materials used were thought to be suited to adults and of interest to them. This premise was strengthened by the fact that most of the adults indicated on an anonymous questionnaire that the materials were interesting. There is little question but that the materials made realistic adult demands upon the reading skills.

STATISTICAL METHOD

In order to substantiate that the two sixth-grade groups were not significantly different from one another in chronological age, mental age, science achievement, and general reading ability, the t test of significance of difference between means was used (1). The values of t ranged from .004 to .222 indicating that the slight differences between the two groups in these characteristics could easily be explained by chance factors.

Analysis of the data was made with product moment correlations (1) between the various rate and comprehension scores. These correlations for the sixth-grade population are set forth in Table 3. For the adult population the correlations between rate and comprehension are given in Table 4.

Comparisons between sixth-grade and adult populations were based upon the rate and comprehension correlations and upon mean comprehension and rate scores.

FINDINGS—SIXTH-GRADE STUDENTS

Fast readers are the best readers when rate is measured by the Iowa Silent Reading Test. In Table 3 the correlations between Iowa rate and the various comprehensions range from .39 to .82 with an average correlation of .58, significant at the one per cent level. The Iowa rate score does not correlate as strongly with the tests of science comprehension as with most of the Iowa and California tests of comprehension.

On the Reading for Problem Solving in Science Test, fast readers are not the best readers. With this type of reading there is little relationship between rate of initial reading and various measures of compre-

TABLE 3
Coefficients of Correlation Between Measures of Sixth-Grade Reading Rate and Comprehension*

	Calif. Total	Iowa Total	Calif. Comprehension	Iowa Comprehension	Combined Comprehension	Combined Directions	Combined Interpretation	Combined References	Rdg. Problem Solving Sci.	Directed Rdg. Sci.—Main Ideas	Directed Rdg. Sci.—Sequence	Average Correlations[1]
Rate Measures												
Iowa Rate	.56	.82	.50	.71	.70	.54	.66	.41	.38	.46	.39	.58
Reading Problem Solving Science												
Orig. Rate	.26	.27	.09	.21	.19	.16	.29	−.09	.20	.19	.19	.18
Ques. Rate	.01	.23	.02	.28	.23	.24	.12	.23	−.28	−.22	.16	.09
Total Rate	.18	.37	.10	.37	.33	.32	.30	.16	−.09	.31	.16	.25
Directed Reading Science (Main Ideas)												
Orig. Rate	.50	.62	.31	.61	.57	.62	.49	.30	−.03	.29		.45
Ques. Rate	−.06	.20	−.10	.19	.13	.04	.17	.08	.07	.07		.08
Total Rate	.41	.57	.10	.57	.52	.52	.45	.30	−.03	.26		.39
Directed Reading Science (Sequence)												
Orig. Rate	.58	.68	.45	.55	.56	.27	.72	.19	.39		.06	.47
Ques. Rate	−.02	.16	−.12	.10	.05	−.15	.23	−.09	−.13		−.46	.05
Total Rate	.29	.47	.16	.36	.34	.07	.52	.04	.13		−.25	.22

* The signs of all correlations have been converted to a common base. No sign indicates a positive relationship between speed of reading and comprehension.
[1] Average correlations were calculated in terms of Z equivalents.

TABLE 4
Coefficients of Correlation Between
Measures of Adult Reading Rate and Comprehension*

	Comprehension Measures		
Rate Measures	Directed Rdg. Sci. Main Ideas	Directed Rdg. Sci. Sequence	Reading for Problem Solving in Science
Directed Reading of Science Main Ideas[1]			
Orig. Rate	.03		
Ques. Rate	.10		
Total Rate	.07		
Directed Reading of Science Sequence[2]			
Orig. Rate		.04	
Ques. Rate		−.13	
Total Rate		−.09	
Reading for Problem Solving in Science[3]			
Orig. Rate			.26
Ques. Rate			.14
Total Rate			.23

* The sign of all correlations have been changed. No sign indicates a positive correlation between speed of reading and comprehension.
[1] N equals 28
[2] N equals 23
[3] N equals 19

hension. The highest correlation (See Table 3) was .29 with combined interpretation and the lowest was −.09 with combined references. Although most of these show a low positive relationship between rate of reading and comprehension, all of them are low enough to be explained by chance factors.

Those who read rapidly during a single reading of the Directed Reading of Science Materials Tests also comprehend well on tests of general reading abilities. These correlations (See Table 3) were generally significant ones for both the group reading for the main idea and for the group reading for a sequence of ideas. There are, however, notable exceptions for each group. The rapid readers for main ideas are not those who comprehend well when Reading for Problem Solving in Science where a low negative correlation was found. It is also interesting to note that the correlation between speed of reading science materials and comprehension in general reading abilities as measured by the Iowa and California tests is higher than is the correlation between speed and comprehension when reading the science materials for main ideas (.29).

Exceptions to the generality that those who read rapidly during a single reading of science materials for the purpose of keeping a series of ideas in mind in proper sequence are also those who comprehend well on tests of general reading abilities are found with two of the general reading abilities. Positive correlations but low enough to be explained by chance factors are found with the factors of use of references and following directions. Thus those who read science materials rapidly for sequence are not necessarily those who use references and follow directions well. It is rather strange to find a positive correlation at all between any measure of rate of reading and these somewhat meticulous types of reading comprehension, and, at least for use of references, the correlations with rate do tend to be generally low. However, comprehension of combined directions correlates well with original rate of reading on the Iowa test and on the Directed Reading of Science Tests for main ideas.

It is also interesting to note that the fast readers are not the best readers when both speed and comprehension are measured on the Directed Reading of Science Tests for sequence of ideas. This correlation (.06) is so low that one can say that there is no relationship between rate and comprehension for this relatively difficult reading task.

For both Directed Reading of Science Tests the correlations between original reading rate and the various comprehension measures average in the upper forties (significant at the five per cent level). The average correlation between original reading rate on the Reading for Problem Solving in Science Test and the various measures of comprehension was positive but low (.18) enough to be possibly explained by chance factors.

In view of the generally strong correlations between each of the measures of initial reading time and most of the various measures of general reading comprehension, it is interesting to note that this same result is not found between comprehension scores and time taken to reread and answer questions. Invariably the correlations are low or negative between comprehension and rate of question answering, which includes rereading. In other words those who read general reading test materials rapidly on a first reading also read well, but those who reread and answer questions rapidly are not necessarily those who read well. These correlations between comprehension and rereading and question-answering time ranged from $+.24$ to $-.28$ with average correlations for the three measures (See Table 3) of $+.09$, $+.08$, and $-.05$.

The total rate score is a combination of the original reading rate and the question-answering rate, and it really is not as meaningful as is either of the two scores from which it was derived. However, the correlations between the various comprehension measures and the total rate scores were as high as $+.57$ between the Iowa comprehension test and the Purpose A (main ideas) total rate scores and as low as $-.25$ between comprehension and total rate on the Purpose B (sequence) test. The average correlation was not significant at the five per cent level with any of the three tests deriving a total rate score.

FINDINGS—ADULTS AND CHILDREN COMPARED

The reader will recall that while the correlations between rates of original reading and comprehension of general reading abilities in the sixth-grade group were generally high, this was not true between rate and comprehension with the measures of the reading of science. While data for adults was not available regarding general reading abilities, it was possible to relate speed and comprehension measures for each of the three measures of the reading of science materials. Each of these correlations (See Table 4) was low—generally somewhat lower than it was with the children. Fast readers, even among adults, are not the best readers when reading scientific materials to solve a problem, to get the main idea, or to keep a series of ideas in mind in sequence.

A case was made earlier for regarding the fifty-one adult readers as a select group of fairly efficient readers on the basis of their professional and academic accomplishments as well as on the basis of their comprehension scores on the Directed Reading of Science and Reading for Problem Solving in Science Tests. How then do these relatively efficient readers differ from the sixth graders? It would seem that the efficient reader would adjust his rate downward, shift gears so to speak, when he was dealing with either more difficult materials or a more demanding purpose. Did the adults slow down for the more demanding tasks? Did the children?

Comparing the average comprehension score of the sixth-graders with that of the adults (See Table 5) the children scored 8.35 to the adults 15.91 (52 per cent as well) on the Purpose B (sequence) task. On the other hand the children scored 2.78 to the adults 4.60 (60 per cent as well) on the Purpose A task, and did 70 per cent as well on the RPSS (Reading for Problem Solving in Science) Test. Using these relative comprehension percentages as an index of difficulty the Purpose B task was most difficult, then Purpose A, and the RPSS Test was the least difficult.

Looking at the Original Rate—Words Per Minute column of Table 5, it is apparent that both groups slowed their rate somewhat for the more demanding task. The adults read the relatively easy RPSS Test at 291

TABLE 5
*Mean Comprehension Scores and Reading Rates
for Adult and Sixth Grade Testees**

Group	Compre-hension	Original Rate	Original Rate—WPM	Question Rate	Total Rate
Adult—Purpose A	4.60	73.28	213.15	32.25	105.53
Sixth—Purpose A	2.78	113.04	138.00	37.21	150.25
Adult—Purpose B	15.91	85.56	182.35	126.13	211.69
Sixth—Purpose B	8.35	114.17	136.62	128.30	242.47
Adult—Reading for Prob. Solv. Sci.	35.89	60.63	291.48	207.74	268.37
Sixth—Reading for Prob. Solv. Sci.	25.10	115.58	152.85	267.54	383.13

* Except for Original Rate—WPM (words per minute) the rate scores are in terms of number of five second intervals. Adult and sixth-grade scores are based upon the five passages read by both age groups.

words per minute. They slowed for Purpose A to 213 w.p.m., and for the more difficult Purpose B they read at only 182 w.p.m. The sixth graders also slowed somewhat as the materials became more demanding. They read the relatively easy RPSS Test at 153 w.p.m., for Purpose A at 138 w.p.m. and for the more difficult Purpose B at 137 w.p.m. But note the difference. Where the adults slowed 78 words per minute between RPSS Test materials and Purpose A and slowed another 31 words per minute between Purpose A and Purpose B, the children slowed only 14 w.p.m. between RPSS and Purpose A and only 1 w.p.m. between Purpose A and Purpose B. Even taking into account the fact that the children were reading more slowly and therefore each word per minute slower is a larger percentage of their actual rate, it is readily apparent that the adults are adjusting their rate to the difficulty of the task much more than are the children.

One way of noting this flexibility of rate on the part of the adults is that they read for Purpose A only 73 per cent as rapidly as they read the RPSS Test, and they read for Purpose B only 86 per cent as rapidly as they read for Purpose A. The children, on the other hand, read for Purpose A 86 per cent as rapidly as they read the RPSS Test, and they read for Purpose B 99 per cent as rapidly as they read for Purpose A.

Another way of noting the increased flexibility of reading rate among the adults is by comparing the average reading time for adults and sixth-graders on each of the three reading tasks. The children read the relatively easy RPSS Test materials only 52 per cent as rapidly as did adults. However, they read for the more difficult Purpose A at 65 per cent of the adult rate and for the most demanding Purpose B, they are reading at 75 per cent of the adult rate. It is likely that this trend to read relatively more rapidly as the task becomes more demanding should be reversed for most efficient sixth-grade reading.

This pattern of less difference between child and adult rates with relatively difficult materials than with relatively easy materials is even more obvious with rereading and question answering time than it is with rate of original reading. The children answered the relatively easy RPSS Test questions 78 per cent as rapidly as did the adults, but they answered the more difficult Purpose A materials at 87 per cent of the adult rate and they went through the most difficult Purpose B materials at 98 per cent of the adult rate. The adults are markedly adjusting their rate to the requirements of the task—slowing down and rereading when it is needed—whereas the children are making relatively minor rate adjustments as the reading demands increase.

CONCLUSIONS

1. Fast readers are the good readers when reading some kinds of materials for some purposes. When reading other kinds of materials for other purposes there is no relationship between speed of reading and ability to comprehend. In general the fast readers are the good readers on the reading tasks presented in the standardized tests of general reading ability. There is no relationship between speed of reading and comprehension for either sixth-grade children or well-educated adults when reading scientific materials for the purpose of solving a problem, getting the main idea, or for keeping a series of ideas in mind in sequence.

2. When either adults or sixth-grade children read the same materials for two different purposes and when the purpose for reading is set for the reader in advance of the reading, the purpose for reading influences the speed with which the reading is done. This finding is supported in Roossinck's study (3) of the reading of scientists and sixth-grade children.

3. There is no relationship for either adults or sixth-grade students between comprehension and rate of the work study reading involved in responding to the comprehension questions. In other words those who work rapidly on the rereading and question answering are not necessarily the best readers.

4. Efficient adult readers are much more flexible in adjusting reading rate to the demands of the task than are sixth-grade students. In comparison to the adults, the children read relatively more rapidly as the task becomes more demanding with a consequent loss in relative comprehension. The efficient adult slows his rate and rereads as necessary in keeping with the demands of the task. Sixth-grade students need to develop this type of rate flexibility.

5. Inasmuch as there are different relationships between rate and comprehension when rate is measured as an original reading time and when rate is measured to include rereading and question-answering time, it is important to define what is meant by reading rate. This finding also suggests that authorities in the field of reading would do well to attempt to standardize a practice for measuring reading rate. Since rereading and reorganizing what is read is both necessary and time consuming when reading for some purposes, the most meaningful measure of rate would be one which offered both an original reading time and a time for rereading and answering questions. The total time, which is a sum of these two, destroys some of the specificity of the composite parts and is useful only as an indication of the total amount of time taken to complete a work-study reading task.

REFERENCES

This study was conducted with the assistance of a research fund provided by Spencer Press, publishers of *Our Wonderful World, Childrens Hour,* and *The American Peoples Encyclopedia.*

1. Downie, N. M. and R. W. Heath, *Basic Statistical Methods.* New York: Harper and Brothers, 1959.

2. Greene, H. A. and V. H. Kelley, *Iowa Silent Reading Tests.* Yonkers-on-Hudson, N.Y.: World Book Co., 1956.

3. Roossinck, Esther P., *Purposeful Reading of Science Materials by Scientists and Children.* Doctor's Thesis. University of Illinois, 1960.

4. *Sequential Tests of Educational Progress.* Cooperative Test Division, Educational Testing Service, Princeton, N.J., 1957.

5. Shores, J. Harlan and Kenneth L. Husbands, "Are Fast Readers the Best Readers?" *Elementary English,* 27 (January 1950), 52–57.

6. Sullivan, Elizabeth R., Willis W. Clark, and Ernest W. Tiegs, *California Test of Mental Maturity, Non-Language Section.* Los Angeles: California Test Bureau, 1951.

7. Tiegs, Ernest W., and Willis W. Clark, *California Achievement Tests.* Los Angeles: California Test Bureau, 1950.

8. Zim, Herbert S., Editor-in-Chief, *Our Wonderful World.* Chicago, Ill.: Spencer Press, 1961.

FOR FURTHER READING

McNamara, Walter G., Donald G. Paterson, and Miles A. Tinker, "The Influence of Size of Type on Speed of Reading in the Primary Grades," *The Sight Saving Review* 23 (Spring 1953) 28–33.

Shores, J. Harlan, "Reading of Science for Two Separate Purposes as Perceived by Sixth Grade Students and Able Adult Readers," *Elementary English* 37 (November 1960) 461–468.

———, "Reading Science Materials for Two Distinct Purposes," *Elementary English* 38 (December 1960) 546–552, 565.

Taylor, S. E., "Eye Movements in Reading: Facts and Fallacies," *American Educational Research Journal* 2 (October 1965) 187–202.

Tinker, Miles A., "The Ten More Important Legibility Studies—An

Annotated Bibliography," *The Reading Teacher* 20 (October 1966) 46–48, 53.

————, "Experimental Studies on the Legibility of Print: An Annotated Bibliography," *Reading Research Quarterly* 1 (Summer 1966) 67–118.

Troxel, Vernon, "The Effects of Purpose on the Reading of Expository Mathematical Materials in Grade Eight," *Journal of Educational Research* 55 (February 1962) 221–227.

The Joplin Plan: An Evaluation*

WILLIAM R. POWELL

Various grouping arrangements have been tried in an effort to improve reading achievement. One of these is the Joplin plan, in which pupils are heterogeneously assigned to grade levels for the major part of the school day but homogeneously grouped according to reading achievement for reading instruction. Powell examines the results of a Joplin plan in an experimental study with a follow-up, ex post facto.

Care was taken in this study to see that the control and experimental groups came from similar populations. Schools were chosen on the basis of availability but they proved to be similar in regard to socio-economic levels, rates of promotion, attendance, percent of transfers, class size, time spent on reading, and level of experience and training of teachers. The tests utilized as measuring instruments were standardized. Similar results might not have been achieved had the variable of the methods of teaching reading used in the two programs been controlled, or had the study been concerned with other than lower socio-economic groups.

For other studies arriving at confirming or conflicting findings, see "For Further Reading." The Newport "score" article attempts to summarize the data on Joplin research to date. Some references are also given describing the use of the Joplin plan for arithmetic instruction. (See Davis and Tracy, Provus, Wallen and Vowles.) For related studies in this volume, see DiLorenzo and Halliwell's study of special teachers (Chapter 6); Adams' study of combination classes (Chapter 7); and Balow and Curtin's study of ability grouping (Chapter 7). See also, of course, Chapter 7, which is devoted to "Administration of the Curriculum."

School personnel have long attempted to meet children's needs through various organizational patterns. In 1847, John Philbrick organized the first graded elementary school in Quincy, Massachusetts.

* From *Elementary School Journal* 64 (April 1964) 387–392. Reprinted with the permission of The University of Chicago © 1964 and William R. Powell, Associate Professor of Education and Director, Center for Reading Research and Instruction, University of Illinois, Urbana.

Since then public schools have experimented with various plans for grouping in attempts to improve instruction. Shane has listed thirty-two types of grouping plans that have been used in classrooms in the United States (1).

The Joplin plan is one such plan. Basically it is a device for grouping children in the intermediate grades homogeneously on an interclass basis. The plan embodies the following successive steps: measuring the achievement and needs of children in the intermediate grades, organizing the children into relatively homogeneous groups independent of their grade classification, scheduling reading classes at the same hour during the day, and dispersing pupils to reading classes where the instruction is adapted to their needs (2).

NATION-WIDE ATTENTION

Although the Joplin plan is not new, few educators or laymen had heard about it before 1957. In 1954 Floyd described the plan in a professional journal (3). In 1957 the *Saturday Evening Post* described the plan for a lay audience (4), and in 1958 the *Reader's Digest* (4) reprinted a condensed version of the *Post* article. These publications gave the Joplin plan national recognition as well as its current name. The Joplin plan was then news. But there was still no objective proof for the results claimed by the proponents of this organizational design. About all it had to offer was sudden popularity.

In the month that the *Post* article appeared, the USSR launched Sputnik, the first space satellite. Sputnik had an immediate effect on education in the United States. Suddenly critics cried out that something was amiss in the schools, and the charges sent educators scurrying for panaceas. New methods and new teaching techniques were quickly adopted. Many plans that had not been validated rose to prominence. It was in this climate that some school systems adopted the Joplin plan to solve their reading problems.

There is still no empirical data to support claims for the superiority of this grouping plan. According to Morgan and Stucker (5), many school systems that use this plan report superior results in the middle grades, although there appears to be no published statistical research to validate the statements.

An evaluation of the Joplin plan seemed timely and necessary. There is a perennial interest in patterns of grouping pupils for instructional purposes. The opinions and claims of teachers who have used the

Joplin plan are overwhelmingly favorable in spite of the lack of significant investigations of the plan.

The purpose of the study was to compare the reading achievement of intermediate-grade pupils who were taught reading under two different patterns of organization: the Joplin plan and the self-contained classroom. Ten hypotheses were proposed stating that there were no significant differences between the two groups in reading achievement for boys and girls, for boys only, for girls only, for high reading achievers, for low reading achievers, in spelling, in arithmetic, in social studies, in science, and in study skills.

SAMPLE AND PROCEDURE

Two public elementary schools in Indianapolis, Indiana were selected for this study. School A has had the Joplin plan since January, 1958. At the time of this evaluation, the plan had been operating there for about three and a half years. School B had self-contained classrooms.

Two groups of fourth-, fifth-, and sixth-grade pupils of School A and School B were included in this study. The pupils had been enrolled continuously in their respective schools since entering the fourth grade. The pupils in School A were given reading instruction under the organizational design of the Joplin plan; the pupils in School B were given instruction in reading in their self-contained classroom by their regular homeroom teacher. There were 164 pupils from School A and 207 pupils from School B.

School A and School B had a common boundary line. The socioeconomic level of the two school populations, as measured by the Minnesota Scale of Paternal Occupations, was not significantly different. About 70 per cent of the pupils in each of the two schools were classified in Class 5, the semi-skilled group, and Class 6, the slightly skilled group. Chi-square was applied to the two distributions and found to be 9.48. This value gives a probability of about .15, and the null hypothesis of no difference was sustained.

The two schools had about the same rates of promotion and attendance and about the same per cent of transfer pupils. Class size and time spent in reading in the two schools were approximately equal. The two school environments were similar. The schools were also compared on the basis of the availability of materials, the extent of recreational reading by the pupils, and the extent of library participation by the pupils.

At the onset of the experimental program, the pupils in the two schools were approximately equal in reading achievement and in mental ability. The two groups were not far from the average city norms for these variables.

The teachers in School A and School B had about the same level of experience and training. The two schools had the same proportions of experienced and inexperienced teachers. The teaching staffs for the grades used in this study were compared on their understanding of reading problems. The test, The Elementary Grades: Teaching Tasks in Reading, was administered to all teachers of the classes used in this study. When a t test was applied to the means obtained from the teachers' scores, a t ratio of .98 was obtained. The null hypothesis of no difference was sustained.

The Henmon-Nelson Tests of Mental Ability: Revised Edition, Form B, were used to measure the mental ability of all the pupils included in the study. The Developmental Reading Tests, Intermediate Grades, Form IR–A, by Bond, Clymer, and Hoyt were used to measure the reading achievement of the pupils in the intermediate grades. The Stanford Achievement Tests, Elementary and Intermediate Battery, Forms K and KM, were used to measure the achievement of the pupils in the content areas: spelling, arithmetic, social studies, science, and study skills.

At the end of October, 1961, the Henmon-Nelson Tests of Mental Ability and the Developmental Reading Tests were administered to all the pupils in their own classrooms by the investigator. In November, 1961, the Stanford Achievement Tests were administered to the pupils by their respective classroom teachers under ordinary classroom conditions. All tests were scored by, or under the direct supervision of, the investigator.

Coefficients of correlation were computed between the intelligence, mental age, chronological age, reading, spelling, and arithmetic scores to determine which variable had the greatest effect on reading achievement.

Means and standard deviations were computed for each of the ten distributions used in this study. A series of critical ratios were calculated for each of the ten hypotheses on mental age and achievement, using successively reading achievement for boys and girls, achievement for boys only, for girls only, for high achievers in reading, for low achievers in reading, spelling, arithmetic, social studies, science, and study skills.

High achieving pupils were defined as the upper third of the distribution in reading achievement. Low achieving pupils were defined as the lower third of the distribution in reading achievement.

In every instance the criterion of classification was between School A and School B. The 1 per cent level of significance was used for rejecting the null hypothesis; the 5 per cent level represented regions of doubt.

FINDINGS

There were no significant differences between the test performance of the pupils in School A and School B in reading achievement.

There were no significant differences between the test performance of the boys or the girls in School A and School B in reading achievement.

There was a possible difference between the test performance of the superior readers of School A and School B in reading achievement. This difference would be at approximately the 5 per cent level of confidence and would favor the superior readers of School B.

In reading achievement there were no significant differences between the test performance of the inferior readers of School A and those of School B.

In spelling achievement there were no significant differences between the test performance of the pupils in School A and School B.

In arithmetic there were no significant differences between the test performance of the pupils in School A and School B.

In social studies achievement there were no significant differences between the test performance of the pupils in Grades 5 and 6 in School A and School B. The tests used to measure achievement in social studies, science, and study skills were not administered to the pupils in Grade 4.

In science achievement there were significant differences between the test performance of the pupils in Grades 5 and 6 of School A and School B. The difference was significant at the 1 per cent level of confidence in favor of the pupils in School B.

In study skills there were no significant differences between the test performance of the pupils in Grades 5 and 6 of School A and School B.

CONCLUSIONS

In this study definite attempts were made to equate the two schools that used different patterns of organization for reading instruction.

The statistical treatment of the data collected indicated that the same results could be obtained with other random samples. The two schools were compared on important variables known to have an effect on reading achievement. The only limitation of this study was the degree to which these factors were comparable in the two schools.

In the light of the evidence obtained, the following conclusions were drawn:

1. The Joplin plan of organization for reading instruction produced no significant differences in reading achievement when reading achievement under that plan was compared with reading achievement in a comparable self-contained classroom situation. This finding applied to the reading achievement of the entire group, to boys separately, to girls separately, to high reading achievers, and to low reading achievers. There was some evidence in the study to suggest that the self-contained classroom possibly produced higher reading achievement for the superior readers than the Joplin plan did.

2. The Joplin plan of reading instruction did not produce any significant differences in performance in the content areas when achievement in those areas was compared with achievement in a self-contained classroom. Any difference that might favor the pupils in School B in science achievement could be attributed to the amount of time and the emphasis given science instruction in that school, not to the organizational design.

3. The Joplin plan of reading instruction as used in this study did encourage wider reading of recreational materials among elementary-school pupils. This effect may not be inherent in the Joplin plan. The finding may indicate that pupils will read more and more varied materials if periods for recreational reading are provided, if recreational reading is encouraged by the classroom teacher, and if the necessary reading materials are in the classroom.

4. An experimental program, such as the Joplin plan, can produce higher teacher interest and enthusiasm for the teaching of reading or possibly any content area. However, the type of organization and the teacher's enthusiasm may be less important than the type of learning activities that take place in a classroom. The results of this study suggest that it takes more than physical grouping arrangements to affect reading achievement.

5. To produce a significant difference in the amount of reading the pupils do, the materials for recreational reading must be in the classroom. This is true even if a public library is near, or even next to, a public school. The easier the access to reading material, the more pupils will read.

6. Regardless of school organization, reading performance for pupils in intermediate grades was not commensurate with their ability or grade level. In both schools, pupil performance upon entering the intermedi-

ate grades was approximately normal as indicated by standardized measures. However, during the intermediate grades pupil performance in both schools did not keep pace with the normal grade placement. With the large number of pupils included in this study, it would appear that a decrease in pupil performance would not happen by chance; there must be a reason for this drop in performance. No hypothesis was suggested for the decrease, but it is noteworthy that the decrease is statistically significant.

7. The consistency of the critical ratios in favor of School B, even though School A had a greater volume of pupil reading and greater teacher interest, implies that the Joplin plan, when considered in totality, was less effective than the self-contained classroom approach.

RECOMMENDATIONS

On the basis of the evidence produced by this study, the following recommendations for further investigation and discussion are made:

Studies similar to the present one should be conducted using samples from various populations, especially socioeconomic levels other than the one used in this study.

Studies similar to the present one should be conducted, but another definition of superior and inferior readers should be used.

Experiments should be undertaken to test the effect of accessibility of reading materials on the amount of reading accomplished. Studies should be made comparing the amount of reading children do when they have a classroom collection with the amount they do when they must rely on collections in public libraries near the school.

Studies should be undertaken to determine the validity of the type of instruction actually given to pupils in the intermediate grades.

Studies should be initiated to discover whether there is a significant decrease in reading performance in the intermediate grades and if there is a significant decrease to discover the reasons for it.

REFERENCES

1. Harold G. Shane. "Grouping in the Elementary School," *Phi Delta Kappan*, XLI (April, 1960), 313–319.

2. William S. Gray. "The Teaching of Reading" in *Encyclopedia of Educational Research,* p. 1118. New York: Macmillan Company, 1960 (third edition).

3. Cecil Floyd. "Meeting Children's Reading Needs in the Middle Grades: A Preliminary Report," *Elementary School Journal,* LV (October, 1954), 99–103.

4. Roul Tunley. "Johnny *Can* Read in Joplin," *Saturday Evening Post,* CCXXX (October, 1957), 27+; also in the *Reader's Digest,* LXXII (January, 1958), 41–44.

5. Elmer F. Morgan, Jr., and Gerald R. Stucker. "The Joplin Plan vs. a Traditional Method," *Journal of Educational Psychology,* LI (April, 1960), 69–73.

FOR FURTHER READING

Carson, Roy M., and Jack M. Thompson, "The Joplin Plan and Traditional Reading Groups," *Elementary School Journal* 65 (October 1964) 38–43.

Cushenbery, Donald G., "Two Methods of Grouping for Reading Instruction," *Elementary School Journal* 66 (February 1966) 267–271.

Davis, O. L., and Neal H. Tracy, "Arithmetic Achievement and Instructional Grouping," *Arithmetic Teacher* 10 (January 1963) 12–17.

Green, D. R., and H. W. Riley, "Interclass Grouping for Reading Instruction in the Middle Grades," *Journal of Experimental Education* 31 (March 1963) 273–278.

Justman, Joseph, "Reading and Class Homogeneity," *The Reading Teacher* 21 (January 1968) 314–316, 334.

Kierstead, Reginald, "A Comparison and Evaluation of Two Methods of Organization for the Teaching of Reading," *Journal of Educational Research* 56 (February 1963) 317–321.

Moorhouse, William F., "Interclass Grouping for Reading Instruction," *Elementary School Journal* 64 (February 1964) 280–286.

Newport, John F., "The Joplin Plan: The Score," *The Reading Teacher* 21 (November 1967) 158–162.

Provus, Malcolm M., "Ability Grouping in Arithmetic," *Elementary School Journal* 60 (November 1960) 391–398.

Ramsey, Wallace, "Evalation of a Joplin Plan Grouping for Reading Instruction," *Journal of Educational Research* 55 (August 1956) 567–572.

Russell, David H., "Inter-Class Grouping for Reading Instruction in the Intermediate Grades," *Journal of Educational Research* 39 (February 1946) 462–470.

Spache, George, *Classroom Organization for Reading,* Annotated Bibliography Series (Newark, Delaware: International Reading Association, 1965).

Wallen, Norman E., and Robert O. Vowles, "The Effect of Intraclass Grouping on Arithmetic Achievement in the Sixth Grade," *Journal of Educational Psychology* 51 (June 1960) 159–163.

Standardized Reading Tests and Informal Reading Inventories*

ROBERT A. McCRACKEN

There are a number of techniques which teachers use in evaluating pupil progress or status in reading. Among these are teacher observation with scales or checklists, special textbooks and teacher-made tests, and standardized tests. Each procedure possesses strengths and weaknesses; too often teachers use only standardized achievement tests, unaware of their values and limitations. McCracken in this ex post facto study points up the need for knowledge about measurement instruments. The major thesis of McCracken's study is important, although it is recognized that it has shortcomings, particularly his use of nonrandom sampling with pupils of above average intelligence, which prevents wide generalizations. When teachers misinterpret standardized test reading scores, many pupils may not receive appropriate reading instruction. They may be placed in readers and content textbooks too difficult for them. Sipay's article (cited in "For Further Reading") supports this viewpoint.

Since informal reading inventory procedures are not described, an article describing the procedures used by McCracken is cited in "For Further Reading." Also see Johnson and Kress for a detailed and comprehensive description of informal reading inventory. Other articles in the section critically analyze various types of reading tests. One source rich with ideas is that edited by Barrett, and the book by Austin *et al.* is a comprehensive view of reading evaluation.

Another study dealing with measurement of instruction in this volume has been reported by Nelson and Mason (Chapter 6). Finally, the reader is referred to Buros' *Mental Measurement Yearbooks*.

The use of an informal reading inventory as part of classroom teaching procedures has been recommended. It is being utilized by many school systems. The standardized group reading test may mislead a

* From the February 1962 issue of *Education*, copyright 1962, by the Bobbs-Merrill Company, Inc., Indianapolis, Indiana. By permission of the publisher and Robert A. McCracken, Professor of Education, Western Washington State College, Bellingham.

teacher in determining the instructional reading level of a child. Standardized group reading tests do not yield sufficient information for the diagnosis of reading needs.

PURPOSE

The purpose of this study was to compare the grade level ratings of a group of sixth-grade children on the *Iowa Test of Basic Skills*, Form I, with ratings obtained on an informal reading inventory. This study was not conducted to suggest one standardized test as inadequate. The standardized reading test used in this study is part of the school testing program, and was selected because it is an excellent test.

THE SUBJECTS

Fifty-six pupils were studied. There were thirty-seven girls and nineteen boys. They comprised two sixth-grade classes housed in the same elementary school in a small city system. The median chronological age was 11 years and 2 months. Six months previously in the fifth grade the *California Test of Maturity,* Elementary S-Form was given. The median I.Q. for fifty-four of the fifty-six pupils was 115 with a range of 82 to 148.

THE TESTING

The tests were administered within a period of three weeks. The two sixth-grade classes took the *Iowa Test of Basic Skills,* Form I. The scores of the reading comprehension and vocabulary are used in this study. An informal reading inventory was administered to all pupils. Three reading-level ratings were made from the informal testing:

1. *Immediate instructional reading level*—The book level at which the pupil showed the first signs of needing reading instruction.
2. *Maximum instructional reading level*—The highest book level at which a teacher might instruct a pupil without encountering pupil frustration to the degree that instruction is impossible.
3. *Word recognition instructional level*—The lowest book level at which the pupil could not pronounce 90% of the vocabulary listed in the back of the basal reader. The words were presented in isolation. The book level

immediately above the 90% pronouncing level was used regardless of the percentage of the break-down below ninety.

THE RESULTS

Tables 1 and 2 summarize the test results.

The median Iowa reading comprehension grade level rating was 6.5; the median informal immediate instructional level was 4th reader; and the median informal maximum instructional level was 6th reader.

The average difference between the Iowa reading comprehension grade levels and the informal immediate instructional reading levels

TABLE 1

| | Reading Comprehension Achievement | | |
Grade level	Iowa	Informal minimum	Inventory maximum
10	1	0	0
9	3	0	0
8	8	0	1
7	10	1	7
6	14	11	28
5	15	13	5
4	5	15	7
3	0	14	6
2	0	2	2

TABLE 2

| | Reading Vocabulary Achievement | |
Grade level	Iowa	Informal Inventory
10	1	1
9	2	1
8	9	3
7	14	13
6	11	12
5	13	14
4	5	8
3	1	3
2	0	1

was 2.3 years. The average difference between the Iowa reading comprehension grade levels and the informal maximum instructional levels was 1.3 years. The difference between the median and the average was caused by one-half of the pupils scoring a maximum instructional level of sixth reader, with almost all the rest below.

The median Iowa vocabulary grade level score was 6.6. The median informal word recognition instructional level was 6th reader. The average difference between these was 1.0 year.

The Iowa test rated most of the children higher in both comprehension and vocabulary than the informal inventory. No pupil achieved an immediate instructional reading level higher than his Iowa comprehension grade level. Four pupils achieved 0 to 1 year better on the Iowa comprehension than their informal minimum instructional level; twelve pupils achieved 1 to 2 years better; twenty-eight pupils achieved 2 to 3 years better; nine pupils achieved 3 to 4 years better; and three pupils achieved 4 to 5 years better.

Five children achieved maximum instructional reading levels higher than their Iowa comprehension ratings. The differences were less than one year. Sixteen pupils achieved 0 to 1 year better on the Iowa comprehension than their informal maximum instructional level; twenty pupils achieved 1 to 2 years better; thirteen pupils achieved 2 to 3 years better; and two pupils achieved 3 to 4 years better.

Six children achieved informal word recognition levels higher than their Iowa vocabulary grade level, four by less than one year, and two by one year. Twenty-two pupils achieved 0 to 1 year better on the Iowa vocabulary than their informal vocabulary level; eighteen pupils achieved 1 to 2 years better; nine pupils achieved 2 to 3 years better; and 1 pupil achieved 3 to 4 years better.

The correlation between the Iowa reading comprehension and the immediate instructional reading levels was 0.78; the correlation between the Iowa reading comprehension and maximum instructional reading levels was 0.74; and the correlation between the Iowa vocabulary and the informal word recognition levels was 0.78. The scattergrams for these correlations showed a spread within each vertical and horizontal array of at least three years, very often four years, and sometimes five years.

DISCUSSION

The Iowa test and the informal reading inventory do not purport to measure identical skills. Comprehension of silent reading is part of informal reading inventory, but the child's total reading performance in oral and silent reading is evaluated. The Iowa vocabulary test measures word understanding; the informal word recognition test measures pronouncing.

On the Iowa test more than half of these pupils achieved grade level or above in reading comprehension. 36 of 56 pupils achieved scores of 6.0 or better, and 22 achieved scores of 7.0 or better. The informal maximum instructional levels approach these same distributions. 36 of 56 pupils achieved scores of 6th reader or better, and 8 pupils achieved scores of 7th reader or better. However, the informal intermediate instructional levels indicate only 11 pupils achieving 6th reader level, one 7th reader level, and none higher.

The *California Test of Mental Maturity* scores tend to agree with the Iowa scores, suggesting that the pupils are underachieving slightly. The informal reading scores indicate that many pupils are underachieving. It seems that group standardized reading testing permitted these children to reread and deduce correct answers by intelligent selection. Such testing obscures the need for reading instruction. Possibly these children comprehend because they are intelligent, rather than because they read well.

The standardized test scores would place 63% (35 pupils) of the children at a level of frustration if their scores were used to determine the book level needed for reading instruction. It would place 93% (52 pupils) of the children in a book which is too hard for pupil and teacher comfort.

Part of this misplacement could be eliminated by reinterpreting the standardized test scores. If all children were instructed in books at a level two years below their standardized test scores 21% (12 pupils) would be in books too hard for comfort. Of these twelve children, only 4% (2 pupils) would be at frustration level. 7% (4 pupils) would be reading books which were too easy.

Average and above-average standardized reading scores may lull teachers and administrators into false complacency, with the result that many able students never receive adequate reading instruction. These students underachieve throughout school. The informal reading inventory indicated a need for reading instruction for all of these children. The standardized test results could be interpreted to mean that instruction was not necessary for the upper 40%.

Using these standardized reading scores to determine the level of a basic text would place most of these children at frustration level. A frequent complaint of teachers is, "He can read (meaning that the test results say so) but he does not read his text adequately."

The problem is that the pupil cannot read the book. Regular practice at frustration level leads the pupil to think that reading is opening a book, mumbling to himself, while hoping that the teacher will not discover that he does not comprehend the material. For the pupil the connotations of comprehension, communication, and pleasure are divorced from the word *read*.

This discussion should not obscure the relatively high correlation between the Iowa and the informal scores. Teachers must learn to interpret these test scores since the standardized score tends to assign a higher grade level than the informal reading inventory.

In this study the standardized test grade levels were approximately two years higher than the instructional book level scores as measured by an informal reading inventory. It is possible to obtain reasonably good instructional grouping for reading by realizing that the standardized test score and the basal reader book level are not synonymous.

If a conclusion can be drawn from this study, it is that great care must be exercised when interpreting the scores of standardized reading tests, particularly when using the standardized test to establish teaching levels or instructional groups.

SUMMARY

Fifty-six sixth-grade pupils were tested using a standardized reading test and an informal reading inventory. The standardized reading comprehension and vocabulary scores were predominantly higher than the informal reading inventory instructional ratings.

FOR FURTHER READING

Austin, Mary C., Clifford L. Bush, and M. H. Huebner, *Reading Evaluation* (New York: The Ronald Press Company, 1961).

Barrett, Thomas, editor, *The Evaluation of Children's Reading Achievement*, Perspectives in Reading, No. 8 (Newark, Delaware: International Reading Association, 1967).

Bremer, Neville, "Do Readiness Tests Predict Success in Reading?" *Elementary School Journal* 59 (January 1959) 222–224.

Hayward, Priscilla, "Evaluating Diagnostic Reading Tests," *The Reading Teacher* 21 (March 1968) 523–528.

Johnson, Marjorie S., and Roy A. Kress, "Individual Reading Inventories," from *Sociological and Psychological Factors in Reading*, 21st Annual Reading Institute, Temple University, 1964, pp. 48–60.

McCracken, Robert A., "The Development and Validation of the Standard Reading Inventory for the Individual Appraisal of Reading Performance in Grades One Through Six," *Improvement of Reading Through Classroom Practice*, International Reading Association Conference Proceedings, Vol. 9, pp. 310–313 (Newark, Delaware: International Reading Association, 1964).

——, "The Oral Reading Performance of a Second Grade Class Using an Informal Reading Test," *Journal of Educational Research* 55 (November 1961) 113–117.

——, *Standard Reading Inventory* (Bellingham, Washington: Pioneer Printing Co., 1967).

Mitchell, Blythe, "The Metropolitan Readiness Tests as Predictors of First Grade Achievement," *Educational and Psychological Measurement* 22 (Winter 1962) 765–772.

Robinson, H. Alan, and Earl Hanson, "Reliability of Measures of Reading Achievement," *The Reading Teacher* 21 (January 1968) 307–313, 323.

Sipay, Edward R., "A Comparison of Standardized Scores and Functional Reading Levels," *The Reading Teacher* 17 (January 1964) 265–268.

Trella, Thaddeus M., "What Do Diagnostic Reading Tests Diagnose?" *Elementary English* 43 (April 1966) 370–372.

3

LANGUAGE ARTS

This chapter considers aspects of the language arts other than reading. Reading was discussed in a separate chapter only because it is such a major part of the language arts. However, the writers recognize the need for interrelating the various areas labeled "language arts" and recognize that their separation nullifies many of the communication values good teachers seek. Learning can be facilitated when teachers and pupils take an exploratory approach to the study of language and its uses. The reports in this chapter raise some significant issues for those who are concerned with the language development of children.

Specifically, this chapter includes research reports on the following topics: an historical overview, listening, literature, written expression, linguistics, spelling, and handwriting.

Another research included in the book which is related to this chapter includes: Schenke's study of information sources used by children (Chapter 6).

Three of the research reports for this chapter are of an experimental nature (Lundsteen, May and Tabachink, Hodges). An historical study (Mackintosh) opens the chapter and two other descriptive studies are included (Homze and Malmstrom). One study is of the ex post facto nature (Enstrom). One focuses on the kindergarten level, and another on the fifth grade; but the remainder cover the entire elementary school period. Space prohibits presentation of studies representing some areas of concern to language arts teachers, such as language difficulties among children, vocabulary development, language activities for low and high achievers, speech, and evaluation.

Some major resources which are directed specifically at language arts which the reader will find helpful include:

Research in the Teaching of English (Champaign, Illinois: National Council of Teachers of English, Spring 1967–present). This bulletin, published each Spring and Fall, contains detailed research reports. Also featured are reviews of books and researches, and bibliographies of research. The same organization publishes *Elementary English,* which gives some attention to research articles.

Shane, Harold G., *Research Helps in Teaching the Language Arts* (Washington, D.C.: Association for Supervision and Curriculum Development, National Education Association, 1955). This report is based upon questions which teachers asked and related research findings. It provides ready access to a substantial body of the research literature bearing on the teaching of the language arts.

————, and June Grant Mulry, *Improving Language Arts Instruction Through Research* (Washington, D.C.: Association for Supervision and Curriculum Development, National Education Association, 1963). This report is based upon the needs expressed by teachers in various areas of the language arts. It includes a thorough survey of research studies and reports and provides a valuable reference for language arts in the period 1955–1962.

Sherwin, J. Stephen, *Four Problems in Teaching English: A Critique of Research,* (Champaign, Illinois: National Council of Teachers of English, 1969). These critiques consider four problems: relationship of Latin to English mastery; the problem of spelling; increasing skill in writing; and to diagram or not to diagram.

In addition to *Research in the Teaching of English* and *Elementary English,* mentioned above, the National Council of Teachers of English (508 S. Sixth Street, Champaign, Illinois), the professional organization for persons concerned with language arts instruction at any educational level, provides an annual list of resources for the teaching of English.

A listing of resources (journals, annual lists, key bibliographies, and research summaries) is given below for the benefit of those who are specifically interested in research in the area of the language arts:

American Educational Research Association, "Language Arts and Fine Arts" (see sections on Listening; Speaking; Composition, Handwriting, and Spelling; Literature), *Review of Educational Research,* 31 (April 1961), 34 (April 1964), 37 (April 1967).

Blount, Nathan S., "Bibliography of Research in the Teaching of English: 1966," *Research in the Teaching of English,* Vol. 1, No. 1 (Spring 1967), pp. 98–125 (Champaign, Illinois: National Council of Teachers of English).

Burns, Paul C., "Research in Language Arts That Should Make a Difference," *Elementary English* 41 (March 1964) 279–284, 288.

———, and Vernon E. Troxel, "A Year of Research in Language Arts Instruction: 1960," *Elementary English* 38 (October 1961) 384–388.

———, "Another Year of Research in Language Arts Instruction: 1961," *Elementary English* 39 (October 1962) 549–555, 557.

Early, Margaret, "A Summary of Investigations Relating to the English Language Arts in Elementary Education—1961," *Elementary English* 39 (April 1962) 336–348, 366.

Harris, Chester W., editor, *Encyclopedia of Educational Research,* 3rd edition (New York: The Macmillan Company, 1960), Ernest Horn, "Spelling," pp. 1337–1354; Theodore Harris, "Handwriting," pp. 616–624; John Searles and G. Robert Carlson, "English," pp. 454–470.

Hunnicutt, C. W., and William J. Iverson, *Research in the Three R's* (New York: Harper and Brothers, 1958), Chapter 9, "Handwriting"; Chapter 10, "Spelling"; Chapter 11, "Grammar and Composition."

Lamana, Peter A., "A Summary of Research on Spelling as Related to Other Areas of the Language Arts," *The Journal of the Reading Specialist* 6 (October 1966) 32–39.

Language and Language Behavior Abstracts, edited at the University of Michigan Center for Research on Language Behavior in collaboration with Le Bureau pour l'Enseignment de la Langue et de la Civilisation Françaises a l'Etranger), Vol. 1, No. 1 (New York: Appleton-Century-Crofts, January 1967).

Petty, Walter T., "A Summary of Investigations Relating to the English Language Arts in Elementary Education: 1962," *Elementary English* 40 (February 1963) 150–164, 201.

———, and Paul C. Burns, "A Summary of Investigations Relating to the English Language Arts in Elementary Education: 1963," *Elementary English* 41 (February 1964) 119–137; for 1964, *Elementary English* 42 (April 1965) 411–430; for 1965, *Elementary English* 43 (March 1966) 252–277; for 1966, *Elementary English* 44 (April and May 1967) 392–401, 492–517.

———, Curtis P. Herold, and Earline Stoll, *The State of Knowledge About the Teaching of Vocabulary* (Champaign, Illinois: National Council of Teachers of English, 1968).

Sheldon, William D., and Donald R. Lashinger, "A Summary of Research Studies Relating to Language Arts in Elementary Education," *Elementary English* 45 (October 1968) 794–817 and (November 1968) 906–926.

Staiger, Ralph C., "Language Arts Research: 1962," *Elementary English* 40 (April 1963) 362–369, 378.

———, "Language Arts Research: 1964," *Elementary English* 42 (May 1965) 513–526.

———, "Language Arts Research: 1966" *Elementary English* 44 (October 1967) 617–638.

It will be obvious to the critical reader that there is still much research that needs to be undertaken in this important area of the school program. The following references provide a beginning for some profitable areas for research:

Dale, Edgar, "Vocabulary Measurement: Techniques and Major Findings," *Elementary English* 42 (December 1965) 895–901, 948.

Enstrom, E. A., "Reading–Handwriting Research," *The Reading Teacher* 21 (March 1968) 544–546.

Horn, Ernest, "Questions for Research on Handwriting," *Elementary School Journal* 62 (March 1962) 305–312.

Petty, Walter T., "Listening: Directions for Research," *Elementary English* 39 (October 1962) 574–577.

———, "Research Needs in Oral Language," *Elementary English* 44 (March 1967) 262–264.

Wyatt, Nita M., "Research in Creative Writing," *Educational Leadership* 19 (February 1962) 307–310.

Yee, Albert H., "The Generalization Controversy on Spelling Instruction," *Elementary English* 43 (February 1966) 154–161, 166.

Language Arts Curriculum:
Fifty-Year Highlights of the Elementary Program*

HELEN K. MACKINTOSH

Knowledge of the past is important in gaining a perspective on and an overall view of current educational programs. As philosophies, societal demands, information, tools, and educational values change, modifications in programs occur. Some periods emphasize the child; others, teacher preparation; some stress repetitive drill while others focus upon functional opportunities for expression. Mackintosh describes the multifaceted development of the language arts curriculum from 1910 to 1960. Few persons are more competent to evaluate the significant events of the past 50 years in the language arts.

Consider her basic hypotheses in writing this report. Note the sources and facts used to support her ideas and the appropriateness of the interpretations from the data. Several bibliographic references are offered in "For Further Reading" on a topic having current impact on the language arts program, namely linguistics. This volume contains three other historical overviews (Smith, Chapter 2; Wade, Chapter 4; and Craig, Chapter 6) and cites several others.

Fifty years is a long time when one is actually living it, but a relatively short time when it is put in the perspective of history and of education in the United States of America. The decades from 1910–1960 reflect many changes and many developments characteristic of a society in a country that fought three wars, experienced a major depression, and moved from an agricultural and industrial age to the atomic era. At the same time it must be clear that these exciting fifty years depend in a number of respects upon the events, educationally speaking, of the 1890's and the first decade of the Twentieth Century.

In a bulletin issued in 1949, Harlan Shores (1) reviewed research on elementary school curriculum covering the period of 1890–1949. He

* From *Elementary English* 40 (January 1963) 5–14. Reprinted with the permission of the National Council of Teachers of English and Helen K. Mackintosh, retired from U. S. Office of Education, Washington, D.C.

pointed out that in the 1890's, "Teachers tended to be impartial umpires between pupils and textbook in the recitation process." As a reaction against such practices, John Dewey and his disciples, in a sense paralleling the emphasis of G. Stanley Hall on the value of studying children's interests, were the godfathers of the experience curriculum. Over the period 1910–1960, such a curriculum was developed in forward-looking elementary schools.

If the definition is accepted that the curriculum is the sum total of experiences provided the child by the school, it is evident that regardless of what exists on paper, the nature and quality of the child's education depends primarily upon the breadth of vision and experience of his teacher. During the years 1910–1960 it is evident that there were many influences at work in the field of the language arts that touched the supervisor and, ultimately, the classroom teacher.

Research and experimental studies, the growth of professional organizations and of professional magazines; the publication of professional books, especially yearbooks of the National Society for the Study of Education; the increasing importance of libraries and of the production of more and more books for children; the pronouncements of groups such as the National Council of Teachers of English through its commissions and committees; and the emphasis on the production of curriculum guides by State departments of education, and by city and county school systems, made a contribution to the nature and scope of children's experiences in the language arts.

PERIOD OF 1910–1920

One of the early courses of study published in 1909 came from the city of Boston. (2) This course of study gave two-thirds of the time in English to reading and literature, except in grades one and two, where half of the time was given to oral and written English. The purpose set forth was to unify the work in English throughout the grades in the fields of spelling, handwriting, spoken and written English, reading, literature, dictionary work, technicalities (grammar), and dictation. Some of the suggestions offered are as sound today as they were in 1909. For example, "In conversational exercises involving questions, pupils should not be required to answer in complete sentences. Such use of language is unnatural, unusual in life, and peculiar to the schoolroom." And another statement reads, "There should be in every school some uniform method of correcting compositions to make the work most successful." The majority of the work in spelling was to be written rather than oral, and not only textbooks, but supplementary books, the school library, poems and prose were to be used in the program.

It is of interest to note that in this bulletin of 102 pages, 43 pages are devoted to various aspects of English. An inspection of time allotments, which provided 1,500 minutes per week in grades one through eight, reflects this same strong emphasis on English, even though all the subject areas (with some slight variations in label) that are part of the typical elementary school program were included in the child's school day in Boston in 1909. However, in large black type, attention is called to the fact that within the 1,500-minute time allotment, 240 minutes in the eighth grade should be devoted to independent study by each pupil, "neither assisted by nor interrupted by the teacher."

States as well as cities were producing general curriculum guides for teachers with emphasis on English. In 1910 Alabama (3) published such a course of study for teachers in that state. Some of the statements that seem to reflect the purpose and suggested use include ones such as the following: "These manuals should be carefully studied every day by all teachers who desire to become more efficient in their work. They constitute the basis of work in many teachers' institutes." Any interested teacher was invited to send for a copy of the manual and to include seven cents for postage. Some of the words and phrases that reflect the character of the material, largely written by a number of specialists, include, "the school as a socializing agency," and "thought-getting and thought-giving, the basis of the course of study." Listed were The Alabama Teachers' and Pupils' Reading Circle, School Improvement Associations, and Educational Journals as aids to the teacher.

Courses of study from Baltimore County, Maryland, (4) appeared first in 1909 and were revised in 1915. It is interesting to read statements such as the following: "The modern course of study makes it imperative for the teacher to have a broader view of the topic to be treated than that given in the text and supplementary books to which the pupils have access . . . will be subject to revision from time to time as experience shows its points of strength and weakness."

Reading, stories, and poems are given an important place in the work of first and second grades. Dramatization is mentioned. In grades one through four the course of study is outlined in respect to reading and literature, and language. In grades five through eight "grammar" is added to language. Throughout the publication the suggestions are specific for each grade.

Some of the pertinent statements found throughout the course of study seem to express the philosophy of those who prepared it. For example:

> "Language is learned largely by imitation; the child absorbs from all about him—his home, his classmates, his teachers, his books." (Grade One.)
>
> "Teachers should exercise discrimination and judgment in selection of subjects suited to children." (Grade Two.)
>
> "The reading should never become a mere rote or mechanical exercise." (Grade Three.)
>
> "Abundant knowledge, purposeful arrangement, spontaneity, a characteristic style, free use of related knowledge, expression of personal experience, judgment or preference sought as essentials." (Grade Four.)
>
> " 'Interest and delight must accompany all work done in literature.' " (Quoted from Percival Chubb.) (Grade Five.)
>
> "It is well to postpone the systematic treatment of formal grammar until the seventh year in school." (Grade Five.)

In the sixth grade teachers were urged to use all subject areas as a basis for teaching language. The seventh grade outline mentions voluntary and pleasure reading as recommended, as does the eighth grade. At this point spelling is discussed from the standpoint of selecting words from the daily lessons in other fields, as appropriate in grades 5, 6, 7, and 8.

Certainly most of the statements or points of view quoted would be equally sound today in a discussion of the content of the language arts and the philosophy that is represented in methods of teaching.

The 1915 revision of the 1909 course of study (5) carried the names of Lida Lee Tall and Isobel Davidson, names that would be known to persons of a certain vintage even today. The authors pointed out that in making the revision great care had been taken to secure unity from grade to grade; that outside specialists had been consulted; and that some "new departures" were incorporated. Among these were the use of "silent and oral reading," the school library, how to study, scientific testing, and use of standardized spelling scales.

It was in this decade that yearbooks of the National Society for the Study of Education dealt with problems in spelling and handwriting—time allotments, word selection, and methods of teaching.

In her book, *American Reading Instructions,* (6) Nila B. Smith traces the development of the teaching of reading in the United States. On page 149 she mentions the Reading-Literature series by Margaret Free and Harriette Treadwell as appearing first in 1910; and the Elson

Readers appearing from 1909 through 1914. The former series emphasized myths, some stories by American authors and with perhaps less than a fourth of the space devoted to stories of child life, and of nature. The latter series was designed to present a broader reading program with cultural emphases covering science, transportation, and communication, history, biography, citizenship, industry, invention, adventure, humor, travel, and world friendship.

Rather than attempt to trace the developments in reading as Dr. Smith viewed them, in terms of the decades, a brief summary is offered here. Books such as Huey's (7) led to interest in scientific investigation, which in turn influenced the development of standardized tests. . . . Seat work came into being. . . . There was recognition of the fact that reading must meet the practical needs of life. . . . Remedial reading was born. . . . Names such as those of Willis F. Uhl, Mary E. Pennell, and Alice M. Cusack appeared as the authors of books. . . . During the 1920's teachers' manuals came into general use, accompanied by supplementary material. . . . There was a trend toward the use of factual and informational material as appropriate for silent reading exercises. . . . In using these, teachers came to give an emphasis to speed of reading. . . . The Picture-Story Reading Lessons by Courtis and Smith emphasized reading as a tool in a reading program that was aimed at self-directed child activity. . . . At this point literary appreciation was somewhat overshadowed. . . . For the first time ability grouping was recommended. . . . Integration, both the term and the practice, was about to be adopted. . . . There was evidence of teachers' concern with child development. . . . At this point the Twenty-fourth Yearbook of the National Society for the Study of Education, Part I, was published in 1925. . . . The objectives set up in this volume have continued to influence the nature and quality of reading instruction even down to the present time. . . . Many professional books were published, courses of study increased in number, with greater emphasis given to literature again. . . . Optional procedures were suggested for the teacher's use. . . . Pre-primers appeared. . . . Dr. Florence Bamberger, in a significant experimental study, discovered that a book bound in a cover of highly saturated blue had greatest appeal for children and thereby established a new style for use of gay colors, with blue in the lead. . . . More attention was given to the physical features of the book, to the development of basic vacabulary lists. . . . There were more attempts at integration of reading with other subjects. . . . There were discussions of the place and use of phonics. . . .

In 1934 when Dr. Smith's book was published, reading was recognized as a tool. . . . However, the importance of children's interests was clearly recognized. . . . The ongoing importance of reading in the total program of the school was clearly determined.

It is significant to note that the year 1918 marks the beginning of the annual celebration of Book Week, which annually has an important place in every local community, as well as nationally. To trace the developments and contributions of this movement would be a story in itself.

1920-1930

Although the importance of this ten-year period might well include description and analysis of courses of study and curriculum guides, there are a number of "firsts" that should receive attention in these particular years. Of comparable value to curriculum workers, and to classroom teachers, are publications and new developments or modifications in philosophy, materials, and methods. Referred to earlier was the *Twenty-Fourth Yearbook*. (8) The influence of the pronouncements in this volume tied together much of the thinking that had been expressed by individuals in books or articles. But in the Yearbook a committee gave prestige to the objectives and to the nature and content of reading experiences.

Published in 1921 were two experimental studies that revived an emphasis on the importance of children's reactions to books, stories, and poems, and their voluntary choices of such materials. Dunn (9) studied children's interests in grades one, two, and three, in selections which possessed such qualities as good story, action, humor, repetition, and others. Jordan (10) studied library withdrawals made by children over a period of several weeks' time, sitting unobtrusively in the children's section where he could observe, as well as listen to comments made. Authors of literary readers made use of the findings of such studies as these, in selecting material of known interest to children.

An important "first" was the establishment in 1921 of the Newbery Medal Award by Frederick G. Melcher, publisher and editor, for the most distinguished contribution to American literature for children. The first book to be so distinguished was *The Story of Mankind* by William Hendrick Van Loon. The American Library Association, through a committee established for that purpose, makes the selection annually. In 1951 the chairman of this committee commented, "Looking back over the nominations of other years, we see issuing trends, new currents of thought, and reflection of national interest of people who work with books." (11)

Sterling Andus Leonard published a book (12) in 1922 which exerted strong influence over a period of years in the field of teaching literature especially, but in other aspects of reading as well. He helped readers to distinguish between and among purposes for reading. Too, he offered guidelines in methods of teaching that were developed in keeping with the belief that teachers must begin with children where they are, not where the teacher wishes them to be.

It was during the early 1920's that manuscript writing was imported from England to displace cursive writing, at least in grades one and two, and the early part of three, of the elementary school. Although at present, the majority of schools introduce cursive writing at some time during the third grade, the manuscript form is usually retained for use in those situations where it is appropriate, such as labeling, or the making of titles, or the preparation of written material for display purposes.

Although it cannot be labeled as a "first" in the strict sense of the word, the publication in 1923 of the story of an experiment by Ellsworth Collings (13) beginning in 1917, offered some specific help for teachers in knowing just how one can provide children with real experiences that are nevertheless genuine learning situations. This experiment carried on in a rural school reports in detail how children and teacher worked together. Oral and written expression were highly functional as described in this volume.

But the most important event between 1920 and 1930, from the point of view of the National Council of Teachers of English, was the establishment of *The Elementary English Review* by C. C. Certain, of Detroit, who throughout his lifetime continued the publication of this magazine for the guidance of elementary teachers. After Mr. Certain's death the magazine became the official organ of the National Council of Teachers of English in the elementary school field. Although the content includes research studies, the descriptive articles written by teachers themselves represent concrete help for both those who are experienced and those who are beginners. Today *Elementary English,* as the title now reads, keeps teachers up-to-date with respect to books for children, audio-visual aids, free and inexpensive materials, and any growing edges in language arts of value to the elementary school program.

The first issue of the magazine, Vol. I, No. 1, appeared in March 1924. The advisory board included names familiar to many Council members: Sterling A. Leonard, Orton Lowe, Florence Bamberger, R. L. Lyman, W. W. Hatfield, Patty Smith Hill, and Walter Barnes.

In describing the purpose and need for such a publication, the following statements were included: "A new magazine to fill a long-felt need in a field not previously served by professional journals. . . . The *Review* is devoted exclusively to teaching of English in elementary schools with emphasis upon social well-being of children." Listed are (1) study of literature; (2) silent and oral reading; (3) dramatics, composition, grammar, spelling; (4) standard tests; (5) scientific procedures for experimental teaching; and (6) more effective organization of Elementary Teachers of English.

It should be a matter of interest for present-day teachers to take a look at the titles of the articles that appeared in the first issue of *The Elementary English Review* and to compare them with the issue for November 1960.

Teaching Literature for a Fuller Experience
Stage Craft for the Elementary School Teacher
Silent Reading in the Elementary Grades
The Creation of Dr. Doolittle, by Hugh Lofting
A Spelling Procedure with Social Values
Intelligence and Problems of Instruction in English
Fun for Children
Practical Exercises for Classroom Use
Classroom Observations
Reviews and Abstracts
Shop Talk

1930–1940

A significant development in the early 1930's was the organization of the National Conference on Research in Elementary School English on February 23, 1932, in Washington, D.C. Later the words "Elementary English" were dropped from the name, but many of the continuing contributions of this organization have been focused on the elementary field. Today it is one of the organizations with which the NCTE actively cooperates.

Of interest to those concerned with the problems of helping children to develop legible handwriting were the experiments reported in 1932 on the use of the typewriter (14) in elementary schools. Although there has been no wholesale invasion of elementary school classrooms by the typewriter, further studies have been made and are being made. A recent study indicates that an extensive bibliography is available. For children with handwriting problems that are difficult to solve, the use of a typewriter may be a real motivation for written expression.

In 1935 our own Wilbur Hatfield edited for the Council a volume (15) which had been several years in the making with participation of many members of the organization. The use of the word "Experience" in the title signaled the fact that the thesis to be discussed was a more realistic approach to teaching and learning. Since this publication should be well known to Council members, no further discussion is needed at this time.

It was in 1937 that the Association for Childhood Education International issued its first *Bibliography of Books for Children* (16) with classification of titles in terms of children's interests, with brief annotations, and with a suggestion of the age range to which each book would appeal. Interestingly enough, the NCTE published its first book list in this same year, under the title *Reading for Fun.*

In the same year Frederick Melcher established the Randolph Caldecott Medal for the artist who had contributed the most distinguished picture book for American children during that year and annually thereafter. The first award was made in 1938 to Dorothy P. Lathrop for the book, *Animals of the Bible.*

In 1938 the Office of Education made an important contribution to the curriculum field in the publication of a survey of courses of study. (17) As the title indicates, the materials represent courses published during 1935 and 1936. The author classified 1, 262 pieces of material as deserving the label "curriculum." Dr. Leary reported that 88 per cent of courses were organized by subjects, and 53 per cent of all courses, whether organized by subject or otherwise, included units of work. One section of the survey made a general statement concerning the character of the courses in English. There was no mention of literature in the elementary school.

The author pointed out that the Minneapolis, Minnesota, course of study for elementary and junior high schools included activities shown by investigation to be those of major importance in everyday life: (1) conversation (including telephoning); (2) discussion; (3) explanation, description, directions; (4) storytelling and dramatization; (5) short talks and reports (including announcements); (6) meetings; (7) note taking; and (8) letter writing. Other cities and counties are listed as following a similar practice.

Courses in handwriting received mention in terms of the suggestions for diagnostic and remedial work, some consideration of lefthandedness, functional teaching, and suggestions for correlating handwriting with other school activities. More of the groups that had prepared courses were reported as favoring cursive rather than manuscript writing at this time.

In *reading* there were a number of trends indicated: (1) provision for wide reading experience; (2) organization of reading in large areas of interest; (3) building a background of experience before introducing first-grade children to reading; (4) recognition of the importance of reading readiness in all years beyond the first, extending into high school. Approximately half of the courses made some provision for individual needs of pupils.

As for *spelling*, there was some provision for correcting cases of spelling disability; there was a trend toward functional spelling, with emphasis on the importance of seeing words in context.

It was in 1939 that the Council, through a committee chaired by Angela Broening, issued a report (18) designed to show to what extent *The Experience Curriculum* of 1935 had made an impact on the teaching of English in the United States. The Committee studied the questions of thousands of persons interested in the problems of teaching and learning English. In the summary it was stated that flexibility in experience-centered units was an outstanding characteristic of current practice as evidenced by wide differences in method. All that was good in traditional methods had been absorbed into the experience curriculum.

Significant for elementary school teachers at the end of the 1930's was the publication of the handbook (19) for use of middle grade children. This book was designed to give children answers to their questions on form and usage largely by means of illustrations. It was to be a reference book and not a text.

Since the study by Dr. Leary summarized, in a sense, certain characteristics of curriculum in this period, only brief attention can be given to individual courses. However, Pasadena (20) made use of the term "language arts" in the title of its course, stressed need for understanding what reading readiness means, distinguished between learning to read and reading to learn, and provided suggestive criteria for evaluation. One quotation from the bulletin indicates the spirit of the publication—"Purposeful, persistent and properly directed practice is important for effective skill learning. Insight into pertinent relationships and meanings involved in a total situation is essential to any effective functional learning." This point of view may well be used to summarize many of the developments in this period.

1940–1950

Perhaps the most significant contribution to the curriculum in the field of English occurred in 1945 when the Executive Commitee established a Commission on the English Curriculum, with Dr. Dora V. Smith, of the University of Minnesota, as Director. Three volumes have been published, another has been completed, and another is in process. For purposes of this paper it is sufficient to mention the volume (21) for the elementary school. This volume was the cooperative product of a committee of elementary school persons who viewed elementary language arts as consisting of listening, speaking, reading, and writing interwoven into the total curriculum, with emphasis on the child development point of view.

In a Directory of the Council in the 1940's there appears mention of the Committee on Elementary School Reading List, established for the following purpose: "To prepare, with the aid of committee representatives from the American Library Association, classified and annotated book lists for elementary school pupils." Lists and supplements have been published and revised from time to time. *Adventuring with Books*, the current book list, is one in which the would-be purchaser may find titles, annotations, publishers, prices, and suggested age levels for each book.

It is sometimes difficult to place a new development as to time. This is true of the studies dealing with research in reading published by Traxler. The first of these, says the author, covered a period of ten years, beginning in the 1930's, but including part of 1940. The second covered the period 1940–44. The third (22) was concerned with research published from 1945 to 1952; and the most recent volume was available in May 1960. In each of these studies, the author provides an overview of the period which the study covers; discusses in summary form the outstanding developments; and provides a selected, carefully annotated bibliography. Each issue presents an accurate and comprehensive picture of the highlights in reading research for the period covered.

This was the period, too, when the *Forty-eighth Yearbook, Part II*, (23) was devoted to reading in the elementary school. As the foreword indicates, the volume was designed to realize ". . . the primary objective of providing an authoritative interpretation of the significance of new knowledge and of emerging problems in the field of reading." Dr. William S. Gray served as chairman of the committee. A quick glance through the table of contents brings to the eye such headings as child development, literature and personal reading, evaluation of pupil growth, in-service growth of teachers, and interpreting reading to the public.

Although the published bulletin (24) did not appear until 1952, a survey of courses of study made by Merritt and Harap covered the period 1948–50. Previously, Dr. Harap had reported such studies in professional magazines. Of a total of 543 guides reviewed in this bulletin, 82 were in English, 38 of them for the elementary school, and 28 of these using a combination of reading, writing, listening, and speaking. The authors noted the increase in number of language arts courses; commented on a trend toward sequential development; noted that 5 of the 82 courses were for grades 1–12. Of the 543 guides, 51 per cent contained suggestions for adjusting teaching to individual differences, especially in reading.

In a comparable study covering the years 1951–53, these same authors noted 112 teaching guides in language arts, 52 of these for the elementary school.

During the ten-year span of the 1940's, there are perhaps fewer new developments because of the fact that during the war-time years, professional groups did not have an opportunity to meet, but shared ideas in their publications.

1950–1960

In this period there are many new developments brought about by the entry of the whole world into the space age. Teachers, children, and parents are confused by some of the proposals made to take steps backward rather than forward in the development of curriculum. But some of the contributions made in the early 1950's should be enumerated. The International Reading Association became an entity during these years, having been formed through cooperation of existing groups. Through the *Reading Teacher* and annual conferences, this organization has made an important contribution to the language arts.

In 1953 the National Education Association, through its member departments of classroom teachers and the research groups, began the production of a series (25) of thin pamphlets, each easily read at one sitting, and directed to the teacher. The first of these was devoted to reading. Others in the series that related to language arts were on spelling, handwriting, and teaching composition. Each bulletin includes careful documentation.

In 1953 the Association for Supervision and Curriculum Development issued a bulletin (26) dealing with research in the language arts, a publication again written to the classroom teacher. At present, even more than in the past, there is a continuing need for the translation and interpretation of research in the language arts in order to make an improvement in classroom practices.

It was in 1954 that *Language Arts for Today's Children* (27) was published in the late fall.

In 1957 Dr. Pooley's volume on grammar (28) made its appearance. In the chapter devoted to the elementary school, he points out that all the evidence is against the teaching of grammar at that level. He says, "If there were any demonstrable evidence that the teaching of grammar in the grades up to and including six resulted in superior writing and speaking on the part of the children, such instruction might be justified." Dr. Pooley gives a birds-eye glimpse of linguistics in his discussion of new views on English grammar. Linguistics represents one of the growing edges for elementary school language arts.

Mention should be made especially of the studies conducted by Paul Witty and his associates of children's looking, listening, and reading habits. Each year beginning in 1951 and continuing yearly (29) these educators have made studies in the Chicago area of children's use of TV, and for a number of these years have also made studies of radio and the comics. It is stated that TV represents children's strongest interest, although whether in spite of it or because of it, librarians report that children are reading more books. Schools have the responsibility to capitalize on the wholesome interests developed from this source of stimulation, and to guide children by means of the language arts program.

Another contribution that should not be overlooked is in the form of compilations of research studies (30) made by the National Conference on Research and the Research Committee of the National Council of Teachers of English. The first appeared in the 1957 issue of *Elementary English,* reporting 289 studies under way in 1956. In the 1959 compilation, 284 research studies are reported for 1958. No breakdown is given with respect to those studies that are in the elementary school field.

We are now in the era of the ballpoint pen and of the teaching machine. It is the period of controversy with respect to philosophy, content of learning, and methods of teaching. At every turn there is need to support one's opinion or judgment with research. And, as this discussion has indicated, research is perhaps the most important earmark of the period 1950 to 1960. In view of the fact that some may feel that child growth and development as an influence has not been stressed sufficiently, it is important to reaffirm that this emphasis has probably contributed more than any single factor to the basic philosophy of the total elementary school program, and thereby to language arts as well. But, this movement has been present throughout the Twentieth Century. Whether it is the battle of the alphabet versus readiness, or creativity versus academic achievement, or individualized reading versus the three-group method, or the array of proposals for reorganizing the school or the class, there is never a dull moment in teaching, and especially in the field of the language arts. As Mrs. Partington might have said, "New names and new nostrums everywhere!"

REFERENCES

1. Harlan Shores, *A Critical Review of the Research on Elementary School Curriculum, 1890–1949*. College of Education, Bureau of Research and Service, University of Illinois Bulletin, Vol. 47, No. 8, September, 1949, Urbana, 1949. 29 pp.

2. Boston, Massachusetts. *A Provisional Course of Study for the Elementary Schools*. Boston, Printing Department, 1909. 102 pp.

3. Alabama *State Manual of the Course of Study for the Public Elementary Schools of Alabama*. The Department of Education, Montgomery, Alabama: Brown Printing Co., 1910. 255 pp.

4. *Outline Course of Study for the Public Elementary Schools of Baltimore County, Maryland*. Grades I–VIII, Towson, Md., Democrat and Journal Printers, September, 1909. 345 pp.

5. *Course of Study*—Public Schools, Baltimore County, Md. Grades I–VIII. September, 1915. Baltimore: William and Wilkins Co., $1.50 ppd. 653 pp.

6. Nila Banton Smith, *American Reading Instruction*. New York: Silver, Burdett and Company, 1934. 287 pp.

7. Edward Burk Huey, *The Psychology and Pedagogy of Reading*, New York: The Macmillan Company, 1908. 469 pp.

8. *The Twenty-Fourth Yearbook of the National Society for the Study of Education, Part I.* Bloomington, Illinois: Public School Publishing Company, 1925. 335 pp.

9. Fannie W. Dunn, *Interest Factors in Primary Reading Material.* New York: Teachers College, Columbia Univ. Contributions to Education, No. 113, 1921. 70 pp.

10. A. M. Jordan, *Children's Interests in Reading.* New York: Teachers College, Columbia Univ. Contributions to Education, No. 107, 1921. 143 pp.

11. Mary Peters, "The Newbery-Caldecott Awards—The Effect on Children's Literature." *Chicago Schools Journal,* January–February 1952. pp. 101–105.

12. Sterling A. Leonard, *Essential Principles of Teaching Reading and Literature.* Philadelphia: J. B. Lippincott Co., 1922. 437 pp.

13. Ellsworth Collings, *An Experiment with a Project Curriculum.* New York: The Macmillan Company, 1923. 346 pp.

14. B. D. Wood and F. N. Freeman, *Experimental Study of the Educational Influences of the Typewriter in the Elementary School Classroom.* New York: The Macmillan Company, 1932. 214 pp.

15. W. Wilbur Hatfield, *An Experience Curriculum in English.* New York: D. Appleton, 1935. 323 pp.

16. Association for Childhood Education International, *Bibliography of Books for Children.* Washington, D.C.: The Association, 1937. 76 pp.

17. Bernice Leary, *A Survey of Courses of Study and Other Curriculum Materials Published Since 1934.* Bulletin 1937, No. 31. U.S. Washington, D.C.: Department of the Interior, Office of Education. 185 pp.

18. Angela M. Broening, *Conducting Experiences in English.* A Report of a Committee of the National Council of Teachers of English. Based on Contributions of 274 Cooperating Teachers of English. New York: D. Appleton-Century, 1939. 394 pp.

19. Delia Kibbe, Lou L. LaBrant and Robert C. Pooley, *Handbook of English for Boys and Girls.* Chicago: Scott, Foresman and Company, 1939. 128 pp.

20. Pasadena, California. *Language Arts in the Elementary School Curriculum.* Pasadena, 1936. 187 pp.

21. The Commission on the English Curriculum of the NCTE. *Language Arts for Today's Children.* New York: Appleton-Century-Crofts, Inc., 1954. 431 pp.

22. Arthur E. Traxler and Agatha Townsend, *Eight More Years of Research in Reading*—Summary and Bibliography. Educational Records Bulletin, No. 64. New York 32. Educational Records Bureau, 21 Audubon Avenue, January 1955. 283 pp.

23. The Forty-eighth Yearbook of the National Society for the Study of

Education, Part II, *Reading in the Elementary School*. Chicago: The University of Chicago Press, 1949. 343 pp.

24. Eleanor Merritt and Henry Harap, *Trends in Production of Teaching Guides—A Survey of Courses of Study Published in 1948 Through 1950*. Nashville, Tennessee: George Peabody College for Teachers, 1952. 31 pp.

25. Arthur I. Gates, *What Research Says to the Teacher. Teaching Reading*. Washington, D.C. The National Education Association, 1953. 29 pp.

26. Harold G. Shane, *Research Helps in Teaching the Language Arts*. Washington: The Association, 1953. 80 pp.

27. Ibid.

28. Robert C. Pooley, *Teaching English Grammar*. New York: Appleton-Century-Crofts, Inc., 1957. 207 pp. (p. 126).

29. Paul Witty and others, "A Tenth Yearly Study and Comments on a Decade of Televiewing." *Elementary English*, Vol. 38, No. 8, December 1959. pp. 581–586.

30. Ralph C. Staiger, "Language Arts Research, 1958." *Elementary English*, 36 (November 1959), 502–510.

FOR FURTHER READING

Allen, Harold B., *Readings in Applied English Linguistics* (New York: Appleton-Century-Crofts, 1964).

Hall, Robert A., *Introductory Linguistics* (Philadelphia: Chilton Book Company, 1965).

Lamb, Pose, *Linguistics in Proper Perspective* (Columbus, Ohio: Charles E. Merrill Co., Inc., 1967).

Lefevre, Carl A., *Linguistics, English, and Language Arts* (Boston: Allyn and Bacon, Inc., 1969).

Marchwardt, Albert H., *Linguistics and Teaching of English* (Bloomington: Indiana University Press, 1966).

Ornstein, Jacob, and William A. Gage, *The ABC's of Languages and Linguistics* (Philadelphia: Chilton Book Company, 1965).

Critical Listening: An Experiment*

SARA W. LUNDSTEEN

Some crucial language skills have been woefully ignored or received only incidental instruction—listening is one of these. This report concerns an experimental study of how effective a series of direct lessons were in teaching some critical listening skills to intermediate grade pupils. Note the clear statement of the problem, its rationale, and the control of the variables. The design fits the research question and the materials (teaching lessons and listening test) are described and verified. The sample selected is stated to be of the middle to high socio-economic level, which should be recalled in interpreting the data. The author conducted a follow-up study, cited in "For Further Reading," to check the permanency and transfer of gains made in an earlier study on listening.

Reports by Canfield, Pratt, and Wilt in "For Further Reading" all treat different aspects of listening instruction. The Nelson and Mason study (Chapter 6), which treats critical thinking in the area of science, is also relevant. Many bibliographic references are provided by Duker and Witty and Sizemore (see "For Further Reading") for those interested in pursuing the topic of listening.

There is growing recognition of the importance of listening ability in the lives of children and adults. A number of studies—including investigations by Duker, Russell, and Witty—offer evidence on the significant role that listening plays in our daily lives (1–3).

The authors of some studies suggest that listening ability and critical listening ability are identifiable factors, separate from general verbal intelligence, vocabulary, and reading abilities (4–7). Correlational and factor analytic studies suggest that there may be a constellation of interrelated listening abilities and that critical listening may be included in the constellation (8).

* From *Elementary School Journal* 66 (March 1966) 311–315. Reprinted with the permission of the University of Chicago Press © 1966 and Sara W. Lundsteen, Associate Professor of Education, University of Texas, Austin.

The purpose of this study was to explore critical listening abilities as part of general listening ability, a part that could be tested and improved by well-planned instructional procedures and materials. In effect, the purpose was to identify, define, teach, and test certain abilities in critical listening. For the study the researcher used verbal materials especially prepared for upper grades of the elementary school. The abilities chosen for investigation were detection of the speaker's purpose, analysis and judgment of propaganda, and analysis and judgment of arguments.

Critical listening was defined as a fourfold process that included examining spoken materials in the light of related objective evidence, comparing the ideas under evaluation with some criteria, making a judgment on the ideas, and acting on the judgment made. The main hypothesis follows: There is an ability or a group of abilities in critical listening that can be taught and tested, and test results will show that an experimental group that was taught these abilities will make significantly greater gains in critical listening than a similar control group that had regular instruction in English but no instruction in critical listening.

Although the primary purpose of the investigation was to examine growth in certain critical listening abilities, the procedures used provided the opportunity to investigate differences in performance at the two grade levels under study and differences in the listening abilities of boys and girls. The procedures also provided an opportunity to investigate the relationships of three variables: interest, transfer to other in-school and out-of-school activities, and the suitability of the lessons on critical listening for the grade levels chosen.

DESIGN

A repeated-measurements design was used. Teachers who had volunteered the use of their classes for the study were randomly assigned to experimental and control groups. The interval between pre- and post-testing for the experimental and the control groups was nine weeks.

The sample, which was made up of twelve classes in a Texas city, included six fifth-grade classes and six sixth-grade classes. The experimental group had three fifth-grade classes and three sixth-grade classes. The control group likewise had three fifth-grade classes and three sixth-grade classes. In all, 287 pupils and twelve teachers took part. The experimental group had 146 pupils and six teachers. The control group had six teachers and 141 pupils.

Scores from measures of reading, mental ability, critical thinking, and general and critical listening ability were collected. On none of these measures was there any significant difference between the control group and the experimental group. The mean score for the sample on the California Test of Mental Maturity, Form E, was 123; the reading grade average for the Stanford Achievement Test, Form N, was seventh grade. Some pupils were described by the teachers, who knew the parents' occupations, as coming from low socioeconomic homes. But in general the pupils came from families from middle to high socio-economic level.

TEACHING MATERIALS

The control group followed the usual curriculum. The experimental group was given a series of eighteen lessons. These lessons were derived from a survey of related literature and two years' empirical observation of pilot classes. The lessons were collected in a 142-page teacher's guide.

Each week for nine weeks the teachers of the experimental group taught two lessons. Each lesson lasted forty minutes. The first lesson of the week developed concepts in critical listening; the second lesson enriched the learnings and provided additional practice on the concepts.

The theoretical structure of the lessons used concepts of programmed learning. The content involved a framework of related concepts for critical listening, presented to the pupils in a carefully planned sequence. The program provided branching for the teacher in the form of extra examples to be used as needed. Ideas were also borrowed from the concept of discovery in learning.

The pupils were presented with many illustrations of a certain concept important to critical listening. The children were expected to develop concepts from these concrete instances. For example, after examining advertising propaganda where the technique of "glad words" was used to sell a product, pupils were asked to name the trick.

The teachers were instructed to analyze the examples with the class and to elicit other examples from the pupils to illustrate the concept further. Guided by prompts and questions in the lesson, the pupils made charts that listed standards for judging.

The content of the lessons included three major areas, or abilities: detection of the speaker's purpose, analysis and judgment of propaganda, and analysis and judgment of arguments. The first three weeks were spent on introducing the unit and on developing abilities in detecting the speaker's purpose. The speaker's purpose included being funny, giving facts, or persuading. The next three weeks were spent on the study of propaganda. The pupils analyzed it and judged it according to the standards they themselves had evolved. The last three weeks were devoted to the study of arguments, weak and strong. During the lessons the pupils discovered such fallacies as false cause, improper use of expert opinion, circular thinking, and appeal to ignorance.

TEST OF CRITICAL LISTENING

Because no available test at the elementary-school level measured the abilities taught in the lessons the experimenter constructed an instrument, which was taped. It was made up of seventy-nine items. The items were grouped to follow the three main divisions of the lessons: detection of the speaker's purpose, analysis and judgment of propaganda, and analysis and judgment of arguments. The pupils were required to analyze the test selections, to select a judgment according to a given standard, and to select a reason for the judgment. The test itself and examples from the test are given elsewhere (8, 9).

How effective were the lessons designed to improve critical listening? Measures of critical listening ability showed a difference between the experimental group and the control group significant at the .01 level in favor of the experimental group, the group that had special lessons on critical listening (calculated $F = 76.91$). The statistic chosen was a simple one-way analysis of variance.

EVALUATION OF THE LESSONS

Questions on the transfer of learning in critical listening to other activities and questions on the suitability of the lessons were answered from data collected on weekly check sheets. These check sheets were filled in and turned in anonymously by the six teachers and the 146 pupils in the experimental group. On the check sheets teachers and pupils consistently reported examples of transfer from the lessons on critical listening to other in-school and out-of-school activities such as reading and interpersonal relations. During the study more than a thousand check sheets were turned in. Ninety per cent of these indicated that the lessons were suitable, well paced, and properly sequenced.

The differences between fifth- and sixth-grade test-score averages on critical listening were significant at the .01 level, in favor of the sixth grade. Test norms generally indicate progressive increase from grade to grade. There was no significant difference between the performance of the boys and the performance of the girls on the pretest. But the scores of the girls in the experimental group showed a significant difference between the results of the pretest and the results of the posttest. The difference was significant at the .05 level.

EVALUATION OF THE LISTENING TEST

An evaluation was made of the reliability and the validity of the test used to measure critical listening. Since the distribution of scores on the test of critical listening was normal, item analysis and indices of discrimination and difficulty were used to evaluate the test. The test and re-test method produced a reliability coefficient of .72 based on the results for a hundred pupils.

To evaluate the validity of the content of the test, five judges, who included university professors and a curriculum consultant, were asked to read the test critically. The judges generally agreed to the validity of the content of the test and the scoring key. After their evaluation, any item that they found questionable was revised or discarded.

The experimenter then used a factor analysis based on intercorrelations of sixteen test variables. The instrument appeared to yield four components of critical listening ability. On the basis of logical analysis of the content of the test items, these factors were labeled *general analysis and inference, value judgment regarding propaganda, factual judgment of arguments,* and *reasons for selecting a certain judgment of arguments.* In effect, there appeared to be differences between the two types of judgment: value judgment of good and bad propaganda and factual judgment of arguments. The evidence appears to support the theory that a critical listening process and critical listening abilities do exist.

The relationships between the critical listening scores and the scores on other measures used to describe the sample are positive and substantial. The results, which ranged from .26 to .64, are close to those that other investigators have found at the high-school level and at the elementary-school level (7, 10). The coefficients of correlation between total pretest scores of critical listening and other test scores obtained in the present study follow:

Pratt's (11) test of general listening .... .64
Hendrickson's (12) test of critical thinking .... .52
The Stanford Achievement Test, Form N, total reading .... .47
The California Test of Mental Maturity, Form E,
    Total: Verbal and Non-verbal .... .39
    Verbal .... .43
    Non-verbal .... .26

The results suggest the possibility of an independent ability or abilities of critical listening. This ability appears to be positively related to, but not congruent with, other verbal and thinking abilities, such as the variables just cited.

IMPLICATIONS

Several implications for theory and practice emerge from this study. The content, the concepts, the processes, and the abilities in critical listening appear to be amenable to empirical analysis and can be improved by practice as described in this study. The materials used in the study may make a contribution to curriculum procedures. Lessons and tests similar to those used in this study may yield other useful data on the improvement of critical listening abilities.

REFERENCES

1. Sam Duker. "Listening and Reading," *Elementary School Journal*, LXV (March, 1965), 321–29.
2. David H. Russell. "A Conspectus of Recent Research on Listening Abilities," *Elementary English*, XLI (March, 1964), 262–67.
3. Paul A. Witty. "A 1964 Study of TV: Comparisons and Comments," *Elementary English*, XLII (February, 1965), 134–41.
4. John G. Caffrey. "Auding Ability as a Function of Certain Psychometric Variables." Unpublished doctoral dissertation. Berkeley, California: University of California, 1953.

5. Donald Spearritt. "A Factorial Analysis of Listening Comprehension." Unpublished doctoral dissertation. Cambridge, Massachusetts: Harvard University, 1961.

6. William C. Wilson. "Some Inter-relationships of Verbal and Musical Listening Abilities in Elementary School Children." Unpublished doctoral dissertation. Berkeley, California: University of California, 1960.

7. Thomas Gerard Devine. "The Development and Evaluation of a Series of Recordings for Teaching Certain Critical Listening Abilities." Unpublished doctoral dissertation. Boston, Massachusetts: Boston University, 1961.

8. Sara W. Lundsteen. "Teaching Abilities in Critical Listening in the Fifth and Sixth Grades." Unpublished doctoral dissertation. Berkeley, California: University of California, 1963.

9. Sara W. Lundsteen. "Teaching and Testing Critical Listening in the Fifth and Sixth Grades," *Elementary English*, XLI (November, 1964), 743–47.

10. Gus P. Plessas. "Auding and Intelligence," *California Journal of Educational Research*, XIV (March, 1963), 90–94.

11. Lloyd Edward Pratt. "The Experimental Evaluation of a Program for the Improvement of Listening in the Elementary School." Unpublished doctoral dissertation. Iowa City, Iowa: State University of Iowa, 1953.

12. Dale Hendrickson. "Some Correlates in Critical Thinking of Fifth-Grade Children." Unpublished doctoral dissertation. Berkeley, California: University of California, 1960.

FOR FURTHER READING

Canfield, G. Robert, "How Useful Are Lessons on Listening?" *Elementary School Journal* 62 (December 1961) 145–151.

Duker, Sam, *A Bibliography on Listening* (Brooklyn, New York: Office of Testing and Research, Brooklyn College, 1961).

———, "Master's Theses on Listening," *Journal of Communication* 12 (December 1962) 234–242.

———, "Doctoral Dissertations on Listening," *Journal of Communication* 13 (June 1963) 106–117.

———, *Listening Bibliography* (New York: Scarecrow Press, Inc., 1964).

Hollow, Sister M. K., "Listening Comprehension at the Intermediate Grade Level," *Elementary School Journal* 56 (December 1955) 158–161.

Keller, Paul W., "Major Findings in Listening in the Past Ten Years," *Journal of Communication* 10 (March 1960) 29–38.

Lundsteen, Sara, "Critical Listening: Permanency and Transfer of Gains Made During an Experiment in the Fifth and Sixth Grades," *California Journal of Educational Research* 16 (November 1965) 210–216.

Pratt, Edward, "Experimental Evaluation of a Program for the Improvement of Listening," *Elementary School Journal* 56 (March 1956) 315–320.

Russell, David H., and Elizabeth Russell, *Listening Aids Through The Grades* (New York: Bureau of Publications, Teachers' College, Columbia University, 1952).

Taylor, Stanford E., "Listening," *What Research Says to the Teacher,* No. 29 (Washington, D.C.: National Education Association, April 1964).

Wilt, Miriam, "A Study of Teacher Awareness of Listening as a Factor in Elementary Education," *Journal of Educational Research* 43 (April 1950) 626–636.

Witty, Paul A., and Robert A. Sizemore, "Studies in Listening I," *Elementary English* 35 (December 1958) 538–552.

————, "Studies in Listening II," *Elementary English* 36 (January 1959) 59–70 and 37 (February 1959) 130–140.

————, "Studies in Listening: A Postscript," *Elementary English* 36 (May 1959) 297–301.

LITERATURE

Interpersonal Relations in Children's Literature, 1920–60*

ALMA HOMZE

This descriptive study was selected for the research techniques used as well as to represent the area of children's literature. The writer feels that if children's reading materials provide "backgrounds and behaviors with which a child identifies and from which he learns new ideas, attitudes, and behaviors," it is well to know the content of children's books. With increased publication of children's books and establishment of more library facilities at the elementary school level, an examination of trends in book content—particularly when it covers a span of years and is directed toward such an important area of concern as interpersonal relations—is highly pertinent.

A related study in this volume includes Rogers and Long's study of social sensitivity, Chapter 4. A study by Gast cited in "For Further Reading," dealing with minority groups in literature, is particularly timely.

Investigations of children's reading materials have been primarily concerned with vocabulary or sentence structure and length. However, of particular value are the few content analyses of books which describe characters as real people in real situations. Those books provide backgrounds and behaviors with which a child identifies and from which he learns new ideas, attitudes, and behaviors. Understanding the contents of children's books is, then, a prerequisite to understanding children's behavior.

* From *Elementary English* 43 (January 1966) 26–28, 52. Reprinted with the permission of the National Council of Teachers of English and Alma Homze, Assistant Professor of Education, Teachers College, University of Nebraska, Lincoln.

THE PROBLEM

To answer the question, "What is in a child's book?" the writer examined 780 samples of children's realistic trade books published from 1920 to 1960. The specific objectives of the investigation were to identify behaviors, backgrounds, and themes of the books and discern changes in those contents from the 1920–1940 period to the 1945–1960 period.

The nine categories of interpersonal behavior developed and defined were: Gives Direction, Accepts Direction, Rejects Direction, Joint Action, Supporting Action, Nonsupporting Action, Friendly Action, and Competitive Action. Those behaviors were analyzed in terms of who instigated the behavior and who received it, or the adult-child, child-adult, and child-child relationships. Background items investigated were the geographical area, rural-urban setting, and specific place of interaction, and the number, age, sex, familial relationship, occupation, socio-economic level, and ethnic group of the characters. General themes of the books were categorized under three headings: stories of families, stories of groups of children, and stories of individual children.

PROCEDURES

A list of realistic children's books was compiled from issues of *The Book Review Digest* published at five-year intervals. The list was submitted to three judges who selected the books which best portrayed characters performing believable behaviors. Seventy-eight books received 100 percent agreement to be included in the study.

The book analysis was based on samples found by dividing each book into ten equal sections, locating the first complete verbal interaction between two or more characters within each section, and analyzing each sample for the presence of the behavior and background items. Totals for each item present were computed for each year, and average percentages for the 1920–1940 and 1945–1960 period were calculated. Tables were developed which presented the results in five-year intervals, averages for the two periods, *t* scores, and levels of statistical significance.

Reliability of the system of analyses was examined by two independent judges who duplicated the process with ten books randomly selected from those in the study. There was a mean agreement between the investigator and the two judges of 93.60 percent for the behavior items, 95.73 percent for the background items, and 91.03 percent for the themes.

THE FINDINGS

The research revealed that adult characters give a decreasing number of friendly expressions and critical overtures, accept and reject fewer directions, and engage in fewer joint activities with child characters. Such changes in behavior implies that the influence of adults is being removed from the life of children. Children's books leave the impression that behaviors of adults and children do not overlap and that adults are not concerned about the growing independence of child characters. Parents, librarians, authors, publishers, and guidance workers must balance the growing gap in the relationship among book adults and children by writing and selecting books which present adult characters who do express love but also criticism, who enjoy working with children, and who exhibit mature judgment in balancing a child's independence with a social consciousness.

As the adult characters retreat from the child's world in books, the children become more openly critical, more candid in complying with or refusing directions, and less affectionate in their relationships with adult characters. Such behavior reinforces the independence of the child characters and their increasing disdain for and rejection of adult authority. To help child readers develop good relationships with adults, writers need to present child characters who have a respect for the wisdom, mature opinion, and experience of adults. At the same time, adults should be portrayed with exemplary characters and personalities that encourage imitation.

The decreasingly effective adult characters in these books gives readers the impression that this is a "child's world" without adult supervision or guidance. This "child's world" is further emphasized by the behaviors of the child characters. These fictitious models for real children are paragons of self-sufficiency. They direct activities, express little verbal support, openly criticize, and engage in more joint and more competitive interactions with each other. This behavior, increasingly independent of adult guidance, presents to readers tenuous relationships among child characters and questionable models for behavior. In selecting books for children's reading, parents and librarians need to include stories of child characters who can work cooperatively while they are affectionate and kind to each other.

The geographical locations described in children's books are more urbanized and extend throughout the United States. With the diversity of backgrounds, readers are better able to understand how lives of book characters are affected by their environment. However, a decreasing number of interactions in homes and recreation areas and an increasing number of interactions in streets may indicate to readers that one should meet friends in unsupervised areas. In writing books for children, authors may wish to describe homes as pleasant and desirable settings which offer privacy to children as well as to adults.

Even though locations described in books are more heterogeneous, the ages of the characters are more homogeneous. The numbers of interactions with adult relatives, friends, and teachers diminish while the numbers of situations with child relatives, friends, and other children increase. Again, the predominantly child-oriented world in these books provides many models of the reader's age but few mature, appealing adults through which a child reader could learn of adult behaviors. To complement the child characters, writers and publishers should include in children's books adult characters, especially parents, from whom readers can select desirable adult values.

Although the number of managers, clerks, and service workers is increasing, there is a variety of middle class occupations with meager or no representation in children's books. Since child readers meet few welders, carpenters, electricians, or plumbers in books, they can glean few conceptions of the influence of certain occupations on the lives of people and can develop little understanding of the values of being a waitress, hairdresser, gardener, or garbage man. Greater varieties of occupations in children's books would aid children in understanding and selecting their own occupations. It is suggested that writers be encouraged to extend the occupational groups described in children's literature and to emphasize the importance of all occupations to society.

That child characters are predominantly American middle class Caucasians serves to reinforce the image that children's books present not only a child's world, but a *particular* child's world. Although descriptions of various ethnic groups and upper and lower socioeconomic levels are increasing, the child characters have remarkably similar backgrounds. They are from white-collar families who have a vacation at grandma's farm every summer. If children's books are to extend the reader's insight, writers and publishers must portray a variety of characters which include various racial, national, religious, and vocational backgrounds.

CONCLUSIONS

As specific behaviors and backgrounds in the books examined have changed from the 1920–1940 to the 1945–1960 period, so the general themes of the books have also changed. There is an increasing emphasis on themes of problems and adjustments of individual child characters. Such books provide readers with a great variety of solutions to their own problems However, the decreasing number of stories of family life and of groups of children emphasizes the alienation of the child from his family and the independence of the children.

Writers could serve the organization of the family, the growth of democratic groups, and the development of mature solutions to behavioral problems by depicting wiser adults who actively participate in their children's lives, groups of children engaged in cooperative activities, and child characters who consider alternatives and future consequences of behavior as well as immediate independent goals.

While there is an increasing emphasis in children's books on the activities of child characters, there is a corresponding de-emphasis on the sensitivities of childhood. As the children in books direct their lives and amuse themselves with more and more material possessions, they seldom are described as discovering the pleasures of wild life, art and music, or even reading. Authors need to present characters who respond to beauty as well as to activity.

SUMMARY

"What is in a child's book?" This investigation revealed that realistic children's books depict a "child's world" in which adult characters are given decreasing importance. The child's world described in these books is a homogeneous one; it is a world of middle-class American children who direct their own lives without parents and solve their own problems without counselors. In writing books for readers, selecting books for publication, purchasing books for distribution, or enjoying books with children, authors, publishers, teachers, and parents can enrich children's reading by creating admirable adult characters, describing many types of characters with a variety of backgrounds, and stressing the relationship of the individual to his family, his peer group, and, ultimately, his society.

FOR FURTHER READING

Arbuthnot, May Hill, *Children and Books,* 3rd edition (Chicago: Scott, Foresman & Company, 1964).

Capps, Dan, "Kindergarten Children's Spontaneous Response to Story-books Read by Teachers," *Journal of Educational Research* 52 (October 1958) 75.

Erdmann, Naomi B., "Evaluating a Summer Library Program," *Elementary English* 43 (April 1966) 400–401.

Gast, David K., "Minority Americans in Children's Literature," *Elementary English* 44 (January 1967) 12–23.

Huck, Charlotte, and Doris Young, *Children's Literature in the Elementary School,* 2nd edition (New York: Holt, Rinehart & Winston, Inc., 1968).

Irwin, Martha E., "Evaluating Elementary Literature Programs," *Elementary English* 40 (December 1963) 846–849.

Young, Doris, "Evaluation of Children's Responses to Literature," *Library Quarterly* 37 (January 1967) 100–109.

Zimet, Sara F., "Children's Interest and Story Preferences: A Critical Review of the Literature," *Elementary School Journal* 67 (December 1966) 122–130.

WRITTEN EXPRESSION

*Three Stimuli for Creative Writing**

FRANK B. MAY and H. ROBERT TABACHNICK

This experimental study was selected because it deals with one aspect of promoting creativity. Creativity's humanizing qualities seem urgently needed in a society that threatens to become increasingly depersonalized and its potential value as a problem solving technique seems equally valuable to the individual and society. But some pertinent issues come to mind: What classroom atmosphere is needed to foster creativity? Why are the language arts peculiarly well suited to creative endeavors? What is the role of creative expression throughout the elementary school curriculum? For creative writing, which is more effective, direct or indirect instruction? What specific types of experiences generate in children a genuine desire to write quality compositions, help them become aware of their world and describe it precisely, enable them to use words that make characters and events real and vivid and eventually to write imaginative prose or a poem? Which techniques are effective with what types of children? Too little is known about the area of creative writing. Some teachers achieve good results with certain techniques; others are just as successful with others.

This study exemplifies the finest procedure in its reporting of previous studies, the operational questions asked, and the clear discussion of procedures and treatment. While scoring scales are available for evaluating imaginative stories (see Carlson in "For Further Reading"), judgment of creative writing is difficult at best, since it is virtually impossible to make objective the effect a writer's product has on an individual reader, which is what the elusive factor of "quality" becomes in the final analysis. Several references and research studies are cited in "For Further Reading" to provide a beginning for readers interested in this area of study. For those interested in "practical writing," Braddock, Burrows, Hunt, Meckel, Miller, and Strickland will be particularly helpful.

* From *Elementary School Journal* 67 (November 1966) 88–94. Reprinted with permission of the University of Chicago Press © 1966; Frank B. May, Associate Professor of Education, Washington State University, Pullman; and B. Robert Tabachnick, Associate Professor of Education, University of Wisconsin, Madison.

Teachers have invented an infinite number of gimmicks to stimulate children to write creatively. Yet teachers have no reliable way of selecting a motivating device—of answering with confidence such questions as, "Will this music stimulate creative writing more effectively than some other music? Will this picture (film, topic) be more effective than that one?"

The purpose of our study, which was partially funded by the United States Office of Education, was to examine the effects of various types of motivating stimuli on the quality of the creative writing of elementary-school children. We asked ourselves: "What are the basic characteristics of effective motivating stimuli for use in elementary-school creative writing programs?"

The Education Index lists articles which argue for this device or that device as a promising stimulus for creative writing. Little research has been done, however, to test whether a particular device actually results in any qualitative difference in children's writing. Nor have there been many studies in which the responses to one stimulus were compared with the response to another stimulus.

Torrance has found that prestige may be an effective motivation (1). Children seem to be more productive of ideas, he found, when their ideas are considered valuable by their teachers and their peers. Witty and Martin found that a film motivated children to write stories of high quality (2). Getzels and Jackson's differentiation between "high IQ" groups and "high-creativity" groups depended partially on stories induced by pictorial stimuli (3). None of these studies, however, were comparative ones.

Carlson did a comparative study which indicates that it might be possible to classify stimuli according to their relative effectiveness in encouraging creative writing of high quality (4). She found that an experimental group wrote more original stories in four of eight situations. The situations involved writing compositions based on gross stimuli such as toys, books, pictures, and records. Carlson's study, however, did not clearly delineate the precise differences among stimuli. Berry found no difference between the quality of children's creative writing induced by a film and that induced without benefit of the film (5). Both Wyatt (6) and Edmund (7) discovered that children wrote stories of higher quality when the stories were based on imaginary experiences rather than on actual experiences. Sofell found that a topic a child chose was more motivating than a topic suggested by the teacher (8).

None of the studies cited here was concerned with the specific characteristics that distinguish one stimulus from another. Yet there is evidence that creative people may be attracted to particular types of stimuli. MacKinnon's study of creative writers, architects, and engineers suggests that creative people are challenged by complex, unfinished, and unordered stimuli (9). Barron's study of Air Force captains demonstrated that creative people tend to like and construct things that are not simply ordered (10). Stein and Meer used Rorschach ink blots to measure creative thinking abilities and found a significant coefficient of correlation between Rorschach data and supervisory judgments of creativity (11).

The studies by Stein and Meer, MacKinnon, and Barron, indicate that an unorganized stimulus would be an appropriate device for inducing creative writing. Drews, however, found that highly creative adolescents like to make original interpretations of common phenomena (12). Furthermore, although the Rorschach ink blot test is often used to measure creativity, the Thematic Apperception Test can also be used for this purpose. While the Rorschach test requires the creative individual to synthesize an unorganized stimulus in an uncommon way, the Thematic Apperception Test requires him to make an original interpretation of an organized, common stimulus. Moreover, the investigations of creative thinking by Guilford and his associates have led them to use such terms as *spontaneous flexibility, adaptive flexibility*, and *redefinition* to define creative thinking (13). The words imply that creativity involves an ability to restructure common stimuli in order to produce something new.

Research indicates, then, that although creativity may be stimulated by an unorganized stimulus, it may also be stimulated by an organized stimulus. There is also some indication that choice may be an important stimulus. Research does not indicate, however, the relative effectiveness of these three types of stimuli in promoting either creative thinking in general or creative writing in particular.

Our initial investigation of this problem was limited to pictorial stimuli. Answers to the following questions were sought: Which type of picture stimulus—organized, unorganized, or a choice between the two—results in the greatest degree of creativity in children's written stories? Are similar results obtained with children at different age levels? Do boys respond differently than girls to the three stimulus conditions?

Two populations were used as subjects: 309 sixth-grade children and 294 third-grade children. All of them attended public schools in a medium-sized city on the Wisconsin shore of Lake Michigan, a city economically diversified and offering a normal range of socioeconomic classes.

The three stimulus conditions for the study were developed in the following way. First, an artist drew a simple line drawing of a tree, a hill, a person, and an object in the air near the person. Although the scene as a whole was ambiguous, the object was "probably" a flying bird. This drawing represented the organized stimulus. Next, the artist rearranged the lines and shapes in the original drawing to produce a non-objective drawing or design. This represented the unorganized stimulus. The third stimulus was a choice between the organized stimulus and the unorganized stimulus.

The third-graders and the sixth-graders were randomly assigned to one of the three stimulus conditions. Each child received a mimeographed sheet that had on it the organized (representational) drawing or the unorganized (non-objective) drawing or both drawings. The stimuli were administered by the regular classroom teachers, who participated in a short training session and received a standardized administration guide.

In each class each child received one of the three different stimuli. The teacher directed those who had a sheet with one picture on it to write a story that the picture made them think about. If they found two pictures on their sheet, children were directed to check their choice and then write about it. After forty minutes, the teacher collected the papers of the no-choice groups. The choice group was given an extra five minutes to compensate for the time taken to choose between the two pictures. All the stories were typed, with spelling and gross grammatical errors corrected.

Judges rated each composition. All stories written about the organized stimulus were judged independently by six judges. This set of judges was composed of three graduate students in English and three graduate students in education. Each judge read the stories in a different order. All stories written about the unorganized stimulus were judged independently by another set of six judges, consisting, again, of three graduate students in English and three graduate students in education. Of the twelve judges, five were men and seven were women. Each story was classified by each judge as either "creative" or "non-creative." The judges were instructed to "make a decision that *in general* or *as a whole* the story is creative or that *in general* or *as a whole* it is not creative."

Gross judgments were used rather than ratings based on uniform criteria, such as those developed by Yamamoto and Torrance (14), because of the major differences in the stimuli, which would lead to drastically different types of stories. Scaled ratings were not used, since investigators of creativity (15) have found that dichotomous classifications are as effective as weighted scores; the high coefficient of correlation between the unweighted and the weighted scores makes the latter measurement uneconomical.

Following the first wave of judgments, the judges who classified the stories about the unorganized stimulus classified the stories about the organized stimulus, and vice versa. Thus, each story was judged independently by twelve people. From these judgments a score ranging from 0 to 12 was derived for each story. A score of 5 indicated that five of the twelve judges considered the story "creative" and seven of the judges considered it "non-creative." Papers by third-graders and papers by sixth-graders were judged independently; the judges were informed about the grade level of the subjects, but not about the stimuli presented to them.

To estimate the inter-judge reliability, twenty compositions were selected randomly at the conclusion of all judging, and the judges were asked to classify them again. The agreement between first and second judgments was an average of 80 per cent.

We are including here two stories written by sixth-grade children. The first story was considered creative by eleven of the twelve judges. The second story was considered creative by none of the judges. The first story received a score of 11; the second, a score of 0.

The "creative" story:

"Jack, wake up," called his mother. Jack dove under his blankets. But after a few moments of darkness he raised his head from beneath the blankets. To his horror it was 20 to nine. He sprang out of bed and into his clothes and hustled down stairs. Jack grabbed the piece of toast his mother had set out for him and hurried on to school. On the way it seemed strange and quiet. Then the terrible truth struck him. He had forgotten to set the clock back one hour for daylight saving time. Now he was one hour early for school with nothing to do. Jack kicked a can as hard as he could. To his amazement the can said "Ouch!" He had nothing to do so he investigated further. He slowly lifted up the can and out jumped a leprechaun. Jack had heard of leprechauns in Ireland, but surely not here! The leprechaun whose name was Peter told Jack that he was on a goodwill mission here and wanted to help people. "Could you help me?" said Jack. He told Peter the predicament that he was in. At once the leprechaun sent Jack back through time. Jack found himself back in bed. "Jack, wake up." Jack looked up at the clock to find it only 20 to eight. Down at breakfast he looked out the window to see a tin can with a dent in it. He winked at the tin can and it winked back.

The "non-creative" story:

> This is a story about a boy who, at the end of the year, got his report card. This boy was very happy because he got five A's and the rest B's.
>
> When the boy got home he told his mother the good news. When his father got home he told him. His father said that for having improved so much he could stay up until 8:30 p.m.
>
> The next morning, as he was going out to play, the phone rang. His mother answered the phone. On the phone was the boy's teacher. His teacher said that the boy's report card got mixed up, that the boy had the wrong card. So the boy's mother, Mrs. Jones, brought out the boy's report card. The boy's teacher gave Mrs. Jones his report card.
>
> When the father came home they told him. Then they opened up the pamphlet and read his grades. They were A's and B's. That night he got 50¢ for every A and 25¢ for every B.

Differences in the mean creativity scores achieved by each group were compared by using a two-way analysis of variance. Table 1 shows the mean scores on the third-graders' creative compositions. None of the differences among or between means is significant. Each of the three stimulus conditions produced approximately similar results, with the performance of the third-grade boys not unlike the performance of the third-grade girls.

TABLE 1
Mean Scores on Creative Compositions by 270 Third-Grade Children*

| | | Stimuli | | |
Group	Organized	Unorganized	Choice	Total
Boys	2.80	3.18	2.96	2.98
Girls	3.47	3.31	2.84	3.21
Total	3.13	3.24	2.90	3.09

* Cells were equalized by random exclusion of subjects.

Table 2 shows the mean scores on the sixth-graders' creative compositions. The mean differences among the three stimuli (total scores of boys and girls combined) are not significant at the .05 level of confidence. However, when we examine Table 2 closely we find that the profile of the boys' performance is completely unlike the profile of the girls' performance. The boys achieved their highest mean score when they were presented with the non-objective drawing (unorganized stimulus); they received their lowest mean score when they wrote about the representational drawing (organized stimulus). The girls

TABLE 2

*Mean Scores on Creative Compositions by 258 Sixth-Grade Children**

		Stimuli		
Group	Organized	Unorganized	Choice	Total
Boys	2.07	4.09	3.12	3.09
Girls	4.09	3.16	4.30	3.85
Total	3.08	3.63	3.71	3.47

* Cells were equalized by random exclusion of subjects.

achieved their highest mean scores when they wrote about the representational drawing and when they were permitted to choose; they received their lowest mean score when they wrote about the non-objective drawing. The probability that such differences might occur by chance is less than one in a hundred. Although the over-all performance of the girls was significantly better than that of the boys ($p < .05$), the boys performed significantly better than the girls when responding to the unorganized stimulus.

The term *unorganized stimulus* may be misleading. The non-objective drawing is organized in such a way as to relate its lines and shapes to one another. Had these elements been scattered randomly about a page, or separated so that no element touched or overlapped any other, they might have stimulated responses quite different from those recorded—whether better or poorer we have no way of knowing. The word *organization,* as it is used here, refers to the explicitness and the completeness with which a drawing tells a story. The representational (organized) drawing is deliberately less explicit than it might be so that the children can use their imaginations to fill in the gaps. Is the running figure a boy or a girl? Is the figure running away from or after the bird or something else? The non-objective drawing is freer of story content than the other drawing, and it is this lack of content that we designate *unorganized.*

The three questions on which the study was based can be answered more precisely if we change the order in which they are asked. First: Do older and younger children respond in similar ways to the three stimuli? The performance of the third-graders differs markedly from that of the sixth-graders. The third-grade boys and the third-grade girls were like one another in their writing performance; none of the stimulus conditions produced stories that were judged as a group to be either more creative or less creative than those produced under the other stimulus conditions. The three stimulus conditions did produce quite different patterns of response for the sixth-grade boys as compared with the patterns of response for the sixth-grade girls.

This finding brings us to the next question: Do boys respond differently from girls to the three stimulus conditions? The third-grade boys did not differ from the third-grade girls in their responses. The sixth-grade boys did differ from the sixth-grade girls in their responses.

The answer to the final question—Which type of stimulus results in the greatest degree of creativity in children's writing?—depends on the subgroup. As we have already noted, the third-graders responded similarly to all three stimuli. The sixth-grade boys received their highest scores when writing about the non-objective drawing, although this stimulus produced the poorest result from the sixth-grade girls. The sixth-grade girls received their highest scores when writing about the picture of their choice (the third stimulus condition) or about the representational drawing. The scores of the boys writing under the stimulus of the representational drawing were the lowest received by any of the subgroups. It was also observed that while the sixth-grade boys were somewhat more likely than the sixth-grade girls to choose, under the third stimulus condition, to write about the unorganized stimulus, boys as well as girls chose overwhelmingly to write about the representational drawing, 73 per cent of the boys and 81 per cent of the girls choosing to do so.

This study provides evidence of the importance of recognizing differences in motivational patterns that may exist in a classroom, especially differences between the patterns of boys and girls. The results reported here also suggest ways of accommodating these differences. When pictures or drawings are used to stimulate creative writing, it is often difficult to find pictures that leave something of the story for children's imaginations to supply. In trying to catch the interest of children, teachers frequently offer a choice of pictures about different subjects. The pictures are often alike, however, in their lack of ambiguity. It may be useful to offer pictures that differ in form as well as in subject, pictures that are either highly abstract renderings of some subject or totally non-objective. A non-objective picture provides more opportunity for choice of ideas for writing than a representational picture does, and a non-objective picture may intrigue some of the boys who are not interested in the more explicit pictures.

A more experimental approach would be to mix the stimuli—to use an organized stimulus on one occasion, an unorganized stimulus on another occasion, and a choice on another. At any rate, it is doubtful that an organized stimulus alone or a choice among organized stimuli will allow adequately for individual variations in motivation pattern. A more effective approach would probably be to shift between organized and unorganized stimuli or to provide a choice between organized and unorganized stimuli.

REFERENCES

1. Paul E. Torrance. "Creative Thinking through the Language Arts," *Educational Leadership, 18* (October, 1960), 13–18.
2. Paul Witty and William Martin. "An Analysis of Children's Compositions Written in Response to a Film," *Elementary English, 34* (March, 1957), 158–63.
3. J. W. Getzels and P. W. Jackson. "The Study of Giftedness: A Multidimensional Approach," *The Gifted Student.* Cooperative Research Monograph No. 2. U.S. Dept. of Health, Education, and Welfare. Washington, D.C.: U.S. Government Printing Office, 1960.
4. Ruth K. Carlson. "Recent Research in Originality," *Elementary English, 40* (October, 1963), 583–89.
5. Eloise Berry. "Film and Creative Expression," *Elementary English, 35* (October, 1958), 383–86.
6. Nita M. Wyatt. "A Study of the Relationship of Extensive Reading to Certain Writing Skills of a Selected Group of Sixth-Grade Children," *University of Kansas Bulletin of Education, 16* (November, 1961), 13–18.
7. Neal R. Edmund. "Writing in the Intermediate Grades," *Elementary English, 36* (November, 1959), 491–501.
8. C. Sofell. "A Comparison of the Use of Imposed with Self-chosen Subjects in a Creative Writing Program." Master's thesis. Pittsburgh: University of Pittsburgh, 1929. Summarized by Edmund in *Elementary English, 36* (November, 1959), 495.
9. Donald W. MacKinnon. "What Makes a Person Creative?" *Saturday Review, 45* (February 10, 1962), 15–17, 69.
10. Frank Barron. "Originality in Relation to Personality and Intellect," *Journal of Personality, 25* (December, 1957), 730–42.
11. Morris I. Stein and Bernard Meer. "Perceptual Organization in a Study of Creativity," *Journal of Psychology, 37* (January, 1954), 39–43.
12. Elizabeth M. Drews. "The Four Faces of Able Adolescents," *Saturday Review, 46* (January 19, 1963), 68–71.
13. J. P. Guilford, R. C. Wilson, and P. R. Christensen. "A Factor-analytic Study of Creative Thinking, II: Administration of Tests and Analysis

of Results," *Reports from the Psychological Laboratory*, No. 8, University of Southern California, July, 1952.

14. Kaoru Yamamoto and Paul E. Torrance. *Scoring Manual for Evaluation of Imaginative Stories*. Minneapolis: Bureau of Educational Research, College of Education, University of Minnesota, January, 1961.

15. Robert C. Wilson, J. P. Guilford, and P. R. Christensen. "The Measurement of Individual Differences of Originality," *Psychological Bulletin*, *50* (September, 1953), 362–70.

FOR FURTHER READING

Applegate, Mauree, *Winged Writing* (Evanston, Ill.: Row, Peterson, 1961).

———, *Freeing Children to Write* (Evanston, Ill.: Row, Peterson, 1961).

Braddock, Richard, Richard Lloyd-Jones, and Lowell Schoer, *Research in Written Composition* (Champaign, Ill.: National Council of Teachers of English, 1963).

Burrows, Alvina T., "Teaching Composition," *What Research Says to the Teacher*, No. 18 (Washington, D.C.: National Education Association, 1959).

———, *et al.*, *They All Want to Write*, 3rd edition (Englewood Cliffs, N.J.: Prentice-Hall, Inc., 1964).

Carlson, Ruth Kearney, "An Originality Story Scale," *The Elementary School Journal* 65 (April 1965) 366–374.

———, *Sparkling Words* (San Francisco: Harr Wagner Publishing Co., 1965).

Edmund, Neal R., "A Study of the Relationship Between Prior Experiences and the Quality of Creative Writing Done by Fifth Grade Children," *Elementary English* 35 (April 1958) 248–249.

Hunt, Kellogg W., "Recent Measures in Syntactic Development," *Elementary English* 43 (November 1966) 732–739.

Meckel, Henry C., "Research on Teaching Composition and Literature," in N. L. Gage, editor, *Handbook on Research on Teaching* (Chicago: Rand McNally & Co., 1963), Chap. 18, pp. 966–1066.

Miller, B. D., and J. W. Ney, "Oral Drills and Writing Improvement in the Fourth Grade," *Journal of Experimental Education* 36 (Fall 1967) 93–99.

Oftedal, Laura, "Picture Writing: A New Tool in Creative Expression," *Elementary School Journal* 49 (September 1948) 37–46.

Parks, Margaret B., "Composition in Primary Grades," *Elementary English* 36 (February 1959) 107–121.

Petty, Walter T., and Mary E. Bowen, *Slithery Snakes and Other Aids to Children's Writing* (New York: Appleton-Century-Crofts, 1967).

Sharples, Derek, "The Content of Creative Writing," *Elementary School Journal* 68 (May 1968) 419–426.

Strickland, Ruth G., "Evaluating Children's Compositions," *Elementary English* 37 (May 1960) 321–330.

Taylor, Winifred F., and Kenneth C. Holdt, "The Effect of Praise Upon the Quality and Quantity of Creative Writing," *Journal of Educational Research* 60 (October 1966) 80–83.

Linguistic Atlas Findings Versus
Textbook Pronouncements on Current American Usage*

JEAN MALMSTROM

This descriptive study (based on a previous major survey that sought reliable data about linguistic patterns) has been selected to represent one of the most vexing problems confronting the language teacher, namely usage. "Usage" refers to the established oral language habits of an individual. Since a linguistically sound attitude toward usage is a goal of the modern English program, it is important to know the viewpoint of a descriptive linguist. (Also see Shane in "For Further Reading.")

In brief, this article reports findings of a five-year study which compared information about certain items of usage from the *Linguistic Atlas of the United States and Canada* with that from current textbooks. Quantitative aspects are reported and the bases for the analyses are clearly delineated. It seems clear that the basic assumption of this qualified investigator is that textbooks should reflect a current view of language based on recent research findings. The study may therefore be helpful in clarifying usage standards for today's language. Particularly today, concern for the poorly languaged child may demand a newer orientation toward language, shifting from emphasis upon prescription ("Here is your rule. Obey it.") to description ("This is what users of English do when they speak and write."). The emphasis upon formal and literary standards may give way to standards that consider cultural levels and functional and regional varieties of speech. Obviously standards for pronunciation and usage differ widely within the United States and any textbook which holds to a single undeviating standard of usage without regard to the features mentioned above may produce only frustration. Related is the Loban study of problems in oral English (cited in "For Further Reading"), a longitudinal study in which the subjects are stratified by social class, thereby making intracultural comparisons possible.

Other reports cited in "For Further Reading" by Cameron, Lefcourt, McDavid, and Womack deal with aspects of this topic. A somewhat similar analysis for speech and listening has been reported by Brown.

* From *English Journal* 48 (April 1959), 191–198. Reprinted with the permission of the National Council of Teachers of English and Jean Malmstrom, Professor of English, Western Michigan University, Kalamazoo.

A linguistic atlas is one tangible result of applying the principles and methods of descriptive linguistics to the language behavior of a specific geographic area. A linguistic atlas usually consists of maps that show graphically the dialects of the region being studied. A linguist engaged in the preparation of a linguistic atlas is called a linguistic geographer, or a dialect geographer, or a dialectologist. In his vocabulary, the word "dialect" has no connotations of slovenliness or ignorance. "Dialect" means simply "a variety of a language, regional or social, set off (more or less sharply) from other varieties by (more or less clear) features of pronounciation, grammar or vocabulary." (1) The word "dialect" is thus a neutral, precise, convenient, and scientific term used to describe a particular kind of language.

Linguistic geography is founded upon the key principles of descriptive linguistics. These are:

1. A language is a structural system, a set of behavioral habits by which the inhabitants of a particular community interact; as such it is an integral part of this community's total cultural pattern of behavior.

2. The facts of a language, like those of other behavior, can be objectively observed and described, and then scientifically analyzed to yield a consistent and complete theory by which the observed facts can be classified, and the non-observed facts can be predicted.

3. Speech is primary in the approach to the study of a language; in the development of the child and of the race, speech precedes writing. Writing is secondary; it represents speech by graphic symbols, and does so imperfectly. That is, writing cannot indicate completely and precisely the language's intricate patterns of pitch, stress, and juncture; it cannot reveal gesture or facial expression, nor other communicative elements inherent in the primary speech situation.

Information for a linguistic atlas is usually collected by means of face-to-face interviews between trained fieldworkers and representative natives of communities within the area being studied. These communities are chosen to give a fine-meshed cross-section of the area's composition—historical, cultural, economic, and geographic. The individual informants are selected to represent the community's different classes—in terms of age, education, and social and economic status. Interviews are permissive and open-ended, running anywhere from four to twenty hours. The fieldworker has a questionnaire containing specific usages that will reveal the characteristic pronunciation, grammar, and vocabulary of the region, but he listens to catch many of these forms in the normal flow of conversation rather than by direct questions, hoping thus to avoid any self-conscious or artificial usage. Each informant's responses are recorded on separate sets of work-sheets, in a finely graded phonetic alphabet, and when all the inter-views are finished, the lingistic geographer possesses a body of first-hand facts about the language which he can present on maps to make a linguistic atlas.

OUR LINGUISTIC ATLAS

The Linguistic Atlas of the United States and Canada was originally a project of the American Council of Learned Societies, and is his-torically connected with the National Council of Teachers of English. Between 1911 and 1917, the Council sponsored studies which revealed that memorizing conjugations and declensions or reciting "rules of grammar" did not improve students' ability to read, write, and speak their language. The profession was deeply concerned about improving English teaching. In the 1920's the great tradition of European lin-guistic geography spurred American linguists to give serious considera-tion to a Linguistic Atlas of the United States. In 1929, the National Council of Teachers of English bore the expense of a meeting in Cleve-land at which the definite proposal for the Atlas was formulated. The Council deemed the Atlas project on present-day American English closely relevant to its concern with the improvement of English teach-ing.

Field work for the Atlas began in New England in 1931. It has been subsequently carried on by correlated but independent regional atlases in the eastern and northern parts of the country and on the Pacific Coast. Records are complete for the Atlantic Seaboard from the north-eastern boundary of Maine to the northeastern tip of Florida, and also in the North Central States of Wisconsin, Michigan, Illinois, Indiana, Kentucky, and Ohio, and in the Upper Midwest States of Minnesota, Iowa, North and South Dakota, and Nebraska. Analysis of these com-pleted records has revealed three major dialect areas—Northern, Mid-land, and Southern—extending from east to west across at least the eastern half of the United States. The informants whose speech is reported in these completed records represent more than half of the total population of our country. Geographically, their residence covers one-third of the continental area of the United States. They represent discretely the highest, the middle, and the lowest levels of education within their respective communities. These levels may be thought of as corresponding roughly to a college education, a high-school education, and a common-school education or less. Usually these educational levels correlate fairly closely with social levels.

The Atlas therefore contrasts sharply with two other important and more familiar sources of information on usage: Leonard's *Current English Usage* and Fries's *American English Grammar*. Leonard gives opinions—expert opinions, it is true, but still only opinions—about current usage. Fries, on the other hand, deals solely with written materials in his grammar. These two sources are valuable indeed, but quite distinct from the Atlas in both purpose and result.

Like Leonard and Fries, the Atlas dialectologists did not attempt the impossible task of investigating all the items of current American usage. But for the items which are included in the Atlas, the information on the usage of the language is definitive. I have recently finished spending five years studying fifty-seven of these items to find out how this definitive Atlas information matches the statements which English teachers find in their textbooks. To cut the investigation to reasonable size, one representative grade was selected from each major level of English teaching for exhaustive analysis—grade 3 to represent lower elementary instruction, grade 6 for upper elementary, grade 8 for junior high school, grade 11 for senior high school, and grade 13 for college freshman instruction. For each of these grades I scanned the latest edition of all English language arts textbooks published between 1940 and 1955. There were more than two thousand of them, and of this group 312 were relevant to the study. That is, they contained statements concerning at least one of the fifty-seven selected usages. All these statements were copied, classified, and analyzed. The results throw new light on old controversy about usage.

From the evidence certain facts are immediately obvious. First, no textbook discusses all the fifty-seven items. Second, the lower the grade-level of the text, the greater the number of items omitted. Third, no two textbooks discuss identical sets of items. Fourth, the distinction between speech and writing is not strictly and consistently maintained in the textbooks. Fifth, textbook writers do not agree with each other on the meanings of the terms "colloquial," "standard," "nonstandard," "formal," "informal," and "vulgate."

ATLAS FINDINGS VS. TEXTBOOK STATEMENTS

A detailed comparison of the body of textbook statements with the Atlas findings reveals six fairly consistent patterns of divergence and congruence between them. These six patterns, in general, reflect (1) agreement between Atlas and textbooks on usages that agree with the received standard, and (2) great variety of disagreement on usages for which the Atlas shows divided usage, or educational, regional, or temporal variants. A few examples can illustrate each pattern.

Typical Pattern 1

In the first place, the Atlas reveals that cultured informants regularly use *sit* in a sentence like "Sit down." The linguistic geographer therefore terms this usage "standard." This finding agrees with the received standard regularly supported by the textbooks. But the Atlas shows also that, in large areas of the Atlantic Seaboard, *set* predominates in the speech of the high school graduates, and occurs with some frequency in the speech of the college graduates too. This same educational spread is only slightly less evident in the midwestern areas. The dialectologist terms such usage "popular," or characteristic of the middle level of education. This statement is an objective description of the facts of usage. In contrast, the 170 textbooks which discuss *sit* versus *set* express nine different viewpoints. Their usual procedure is to bracket *sit* and *set* together and call them a "troublesome," or "confusing," or "bothersome" pair of verbs. Students are then told that, in order to use these verbs "correctly," they must learn and compare their principal parts, their meanings, and their uses, and must know also that *sit* is intransitive while *set* is transitive. Strangely however, one of these textbooks, while insisting on the transitive nature of *set*, illustrates the principle with examples that contradict it, namely: "The lamp sets on the table" and "The vases set there too." Thirteen texts state that while *sit* is usually intransitive and *set* is usually transitive, certain "exceptions" or "idioms" that reverse this "rule" are acceptable. Examples of transitive *sit* are, for instance, "Sit the baby in a chair," "Sit yourself down," or "Sit a horse." Intransitive uses of *set* are, for instance, "Set out on a journey," or "The sun sets," as do concrete, jelly, plaster, and hens. Six other texts, however, state that, poultrymen to the contrary notwithstanding, the hen cannot set; she is a sitting hen. This kind of agreement on the received standard and disagreement on the popular usage is the mark of the first typical pattern of divergence and congruence between the Atlas and the textbooks.

Typical Pattern 2

Then we may consider *dove*, as alternate past tense for *dived*, in a sentence like "He dived in." The Atlas shows that cultured speakers in

Northern dialect areas, from New England to North Dakota, strongly prefer *dove*. In southern and western Pennsylvania, through the other regions of the Middle Atlantic States, and in the South Atlantic States to the Peedee River, cultured speakers strongly prefer *dived*. In north central and eastern Pennsylvania and in South Carolina and Georgia south of the Peedee, *dived* and *dove* both occur, with *dove* preferred by the more modern, younger, more educated speakers. Similar distribution is found in the North Central States where *dived* is used by a majority of only the most uneducated speakers in the more southern regions. These findings show that *dove* is a standard Northern form expanding southward. No textbook, however, mentions this regional distribution of *dove* in educated speech, although about one-third of the books discuss *dived* versus *dove*. Well over half of these books do not admit that *dove* is ever acceptable, and only a very small minority say without qualification that both *dived* and *dove* are standard. All this small minority are high school and college texts; elementary and junior high students find only *dived* judged acceptable in their textbooks. One of these offers the undocumented pronouncement that "expert swimmers usually say *dived*." In all, seventeen percent of the textbooks express twelve different opinions. These statements reflect the second pattern of divergence and congruence between the Atlas and the textbooks. It occurs typically when the Atlas shows an expanding usage which conflicts with the received standard.

Typical Pattern 3

A third pattern is observable with items like *he don't*, which also shows regional variations but which, unlike *dove*, is not expanding into neighboring regions. The Atlas shows that about seventy-five percent of the cultured informants in the Middle Atlantic States and about fifty percent of the same type in the South Atlantic States regularly say *he don't*. Only rarely in these areas do we find *he doesn't* along with *he don't* in educated speech. But in New England, the North Central States, and the Upper Midwest, where again many college graduates say *he don't*, we find *he doesn't* more often as a companion form. In fact, in these areas *he doesn't* becomes more frequent in ratio to better education and greater socioeconomic advantages. Thus, in the light of the Atlas, *he don't* is standard in Midland and Southern Atlantic Seaboard speech but not expanding northward or westward, since it is popular rather than standard in New England, the North Central States, and the Upper Midwest. More than half of the textbooks discuss *he don't*. Eighty-five percent of them say that since *don't* is a contraction for *do not*, it cannot be used for *doesn't*, which is a contraction for *does not*. Such statements assume obviously that the traditional "rules of agreement" have eternal verity; the Atlas denies this assumption. Further, they assume that language is logical; the Atlas disproves this assumption too. Smaller groups of textbooks assert variously that *he don't* is "nonstandard," or "vulgate," or "illiterate," or a "vulgarism," or "a common mistake of the older generations," or "as careless as going to a party with a soiled blouse or a dirty neck." Thus the textbook writers agree generally with each other but disagree with the Atlas.

When Fries examined the three thousand letters on which he based his *American English Grammar,* he found that no educated writer used *he don't*. This fact does not contradict the facts revealed by the Atlas. On the contrary, it serves to emphasize an intrinsic difference between speech and writing. The textbooks' comments on *he don't* show how easily their authors lose sight of this difference.

Typical Pattern 4

When we consider a usage like "It's me," we discover another typical pattern of divergence and congruence between the Atlas and the textbooks. The Atlas shows that an overwhelming majority of all informants in all areas say *it's me*. Moreover, an almost equally overwhelming majority are consistent in their use of the objective case in the third person, singular and plural. About sixty-six percent of the textbooks, 205 in all, comment on *it's me*. Their statements divide into five groups. The largest group—112 or about eighty-eight percent of the total—is the most prescriptive in tone and the farthest away from the Atlas facts, while the smallest group—six texts or about three percent of the 205 —agrees precisely with the Atlas. In other words, the largest group states without qualification that the nominative case must follow the verb *to be,* while the smallest group states that *it's me* is established American English usage. This kind of inverse correlation marks the fourth typical pattern. Since Fries found only one use of the predicative personal pronoun in his three thousand letters, we may conclude that *it's me* and *it's him, it's her,* or *it's them* occur almost always in speech not writing, and that consequently the Atlas evidence is completely authoritative. Again we can see that the textbooks do not keep speech and writing clearly separated.

Typical Pattern 5

Another pattern appears when the textbooks discuss an item on which the Atlas shows that standard usage is divided between different forms. For instance, in a sentence like "The broom is behind the door," the Atlas shows that both *back of* and *in back of* are standard alternates for the received standard *behind*. In other words, we have a case of divided usage. The textbooks, however, unanimously support the use of *behind* while about a fourth of them, adding comments about *back of* and *in back of,* express thirteen different points of view. For instance, twenty-five texts approve *back of* along with *behind;* ten condemn *back of* along with *in back of;* seven separate the three forms and call *behind* "formal," *back of* "informal," and *in back of* "vulgate"; one text states that *in back of* is "colloquial," while *behind* and *back of* are "formal." Here we can see vividly how loosely terms are used and how unpredictably they vary from textbook to textbook.

Typical Pattern 6

The sixth and last pattern appears when the Atlas shows that standard usage agrees with the received standard, which the textbooks unanimously support, but that several nonstandard variants are common also. For instance, Atlas and textbooks agree that *climbed* is the standard past participle of *climb*. When the textbooks warn their readers against nonstandard forms, however, they present a picture of uneducated usage that is inaccurate and incomplete in the light of the Atlas evidence. The only strong forms that the textbooks prohibit are *clum*—often spelled *c-l-u-m-b*—and *clom*—always spelled *c-l-o-m-b*. (The inclusion of that unpronounced *b* shows again the confusion between writing and speech.) The *Atlas* reveals, however, that *clim* is a much more common nonstandard variant in certain Northern dialect areas than either of the forms which the textbooks regularly mention.

In the light of all these facts, we reach the conclusion that, since the textbook writers as a group approach current American usage normatively, their statements are based on a premise that some arbitrary standard of "correctness" exists, that it can be discovered, and that it should be taught. This premise is usually unstated and often specifically denied, but nonetheless clearly evidenced by this study. We have already noted many examples of subjective and undocumented proscription. Very few textbooks published between 1940 and 1955 are entirely free from statements like "Never say *he don't*" or "Avoid *it's me*," for example. They are especially common in elementary and junior high texts. Of course, some textbook writers cite evidence to support their statements, but usually do so unscientifically. For instance, we often find published studies of usage excerpted without due regard for their total context or their original purposes. The work of Leonard, Marckwardt and Walcott, Pooley, and Fries, as well as the Atlas itself, all receive this kind of treatment. In like fashion, dictionaries are cited prescriptively with little or no recognition of the descriptive nature of lexicography or of the different definitions to be found in different dictionaries. We also find statements that "authorities agree" that certain controversial usages are "correct," but since these "authorities" are usually unspecified, too often we suspect that they are other textbook writers. My evidence shows that agreement among textbook writers on controversial usages is rare indeed.

Therefore, since the textbook writers as a group do not succeed in defining any consistent standard of "correctness" for the fifty-seven items herein discussed, their basic premise that such a standard exists comes into question. If it is an indefinable abstraction, it is of little practical value in teaching. Indeed, as we have seen, it can all too easily lead to contradictions and confusions.

Implications for Teaching

Descriptive linguistics, as exampled by the Atlas, suggests that we need a five-dimensional model for evaluating current American usage. The necessary five dimensions are social, situational, methodological, temporal, and regional. That is, we must keep in mind that either standard or nonstandard forms may be used in either formal or informal situations, transmitted by either speech or writing used by either young or old persons in either isolated rural areas or urban centers of culture, in the Northern, or the Midland, or the Southern dialect areas. Such evaluation is not simple.

While on the one hand, however, the Atlas cautions us to be careful and precise, on the other it comforts us. It shows that, whatever differences may distinguish dialects, likenesses far outnumber differences in current American English. Indeed, controversial usages demand attention mainly because they do not follow this normal tendency. In other words, typical intonation patterns, customary subject-verb-object word order, the inflectional -s which signals plural number or third person singular of the present tense, and the vast majority of vocabulary items belong without distinction to all dialects of American English. Consequently no functional block in communication normally obtrudes between native users of American English. If a teacher creates a psychological block by overemphasizing differences and underemphasizing likenesses, his pedagogical philosophy needs re-examination.

Thus from descriptive linguistics, as applied in the Atlas, we can learn not only specific facts about certain controversial usages, but much more importantly, an attitude toward the teaching of our language. From our Puritan forefathers we Americans have inherited the idea that things are either *right* or *wrong*, and as teachers we tend to see ourselves as the guardians of the right. The Atlas, however, by displaying the marvelous diversity of current American English, frees us from moral obligation to any one of the many American dialects. It suggests that we observe and discuss language behavior with the same objective interest that we use in talking about the other cultural mores of America. By giving more than lip-service to the concept of individual differences, we will expect and accept individual differences in language with the clear realization that each child speaks the dialect which he has heard spoken, and that he has heard much more speech outside the classroom than in it. Our function is not to make him ashamed of the dialect he has learned from his parents and his friends, but to add to it the standard dialect in order to increase his social and intellectual mobility. We do this job first, by teaching him to read and write the symbols by which language is recorded in books, and the spelling system by which they are arranged; and second, by encouraging him to use his new powers of reading and writing, along with his powers of speaking and listening, which he learned long before he entered our classrooms, to gather, consider, and express ideas that are important and new to him.

REFERENCE

1. Raven I. McDavid, Jr.'s definition in "The Dialects of American English," in W. Nelson Francis' *The Structure of American English* (New York: Ronald Press, 1958), p. 480.

FOR FURTHER READING

Brown, Kenneth, "Speech and Listening in Language Arts and Text-books: Parts I and II," *Elementary English* 44 (April, May 1967) 336–341, 461–465.

Bryant, Margaret M., *Current American Usage* (New York: Funk & Wagnalls, 1962).

Cameron, Jack R., "Tradition, Textbook, and Non-English Grammar," *Elementary English* 41 (February 1964) 145–148.

———, "The Sensitivity of Speakers of Standard English to Usage," *Research in the Teaching of English* 2 (Spring 1968) 24–31 (Champaign, Illinois: National Council of Teachers of English).

Cutright, Prudence, "A Comparison of Methods of Securing Correct Language," *Elementary School Journal* 34 (May 1934) 681–690.

De Boer, John J., "Grammar in Language Teaching," *Elementary English* 36 (October 1959) 413–421.

Greene, Harry A., "Direct versus Formal Methods in Elementary English," *Elementary English* 14 (May 1947) 273–285.

Groff, Patrick J., "Is Knowledge of Parts of Speech Necessary?" *English Journal* 5 (September 1961) 413–415.

Lefcourt, Ann, "Linguistics and Elementary School Textbooks," *Elementary English* 40 (October 1963) 598–601.

Loban, Walter D., *Problems in Oral English*, Research Report No. 5 (Champaign, Illinois: National Council of Teachers of English, 1966).

McDavid, Raven I., "American Social Dialects," *College English* 26 (January 1965) 254–260.

Mooney, P., "Generative Grammar in Grade Four," *Catholic School Journal* 66 (March 1966) 61–63.

Moyer, H. O., "Does Ear Training Help?", *Elementary English* 33 (April 1956) 216–219.

Shane, Harold G., *Linguistics and the Classroom Teacher* (Washington, D.C.: Association for Supervision and Curriculum Development, 1967).

Womack, Thurston, "Teachers' Attitude Toward Current Usage," *English Journal* 48 (April 1959) 186–190.

The Case for Teaching
Sound-to-Letter Correspondence in Spelling*

RICHARD E. HODGES

In spelling, various questions remain controversial. Certainly the issue of linguistically oriented versus a social-utility approach to spelling is not a particularly new one. Some (such as Horn, "Phonetics and Spelling" cited in "References") feel that pupils cannot deductively arrive at the spelling of most words since many common words do not conform in their spelling to any phonetic or orthographic rule. Others feel that there are patterns of regularity in spelling and that such linguistic clues should be emphasized by the teacher. Hodges analyzes both viewpoints and reports the findings of research on phoneme-grapheme correspondences completed in 1964 by a group study conducted at Stanford University under the direction of Dr. Paul R. Hanna and supported by the Cooperative Research Branch of the U.S. Office of Education.

As you study the report of this descriptive and experimental study, ask yourself: What insights were found into American-English orthography? What efforts were made to restrict subjective judgments along the way? As revealed by related articles by the Stanford team, cited in "For Further Reading," how do factors such as the position of a phoneme in a syllable, the syllabic stress, and "internal constraints" affect the spelling of a word? Can elementary school children be expected to spell linguistically regular words with the consistency suggested by computer findings? What research studies have explored children's spelling achievement under a linguistically-oriented program? (See Soloman and MacNeill's article cited in "For Further Reading." Also see Reid's study for an evaluation of five methods of teaching spelling to second and third graders.)

A wide variety of items appear in the bibilography "For Further Reading" to suggest the broad scope of possibilities for research in the area of spelling.

* From *Elementary School Journal* 66 (March 1966) 327–336. Reprinted with permission of the University of Chicago Press © 1966 and Richard E. Hodges, Associate Professor of Education, University of Chicago.

In 1953, Paul R. Hanna of Stanford University and one of his doctoral students, James T. Moore, published in the *Elementary School Journal* a report of their study of American-English orthography (1). The results of this study indicated that there is a much closer relationship between the sounds of spoken American English and their representation in writing than is usually supposed (2). Later, other researchers in spelling curriculum and instruction, and textbook publishers, critically examined the rationale and the findings of Hanna and Moore. Some accepted the findings. Others saw basic weaknesses in the rationale and the design of the research and in the conclusions drawn from it.

In 1957, the *Elementary School Journal* published a critique of the Hanna-Moore study, a critique that stemmed from another analysis of American-English orthography conducted by Ernest Horn, of the State University of Iowa (3). Horn's study cast serious doubt on the findings of Hanna and Moore, or at least on their interpretations of the findings. Horn found less consistent relationships between spoken and written American English than those indicated by Hanna and Moore. A later article by Horn (4) elaborated further the weaknesses of the case for regularity in the orthography. In brief, the positions taken by Hanna and Moore and by Horn represent a major division between those who believe that American-English spelling has considerable regularity and those who contend that such regularities are contrived.

Recently this controversy has been kindled anew. Hanna recognized that his study was not a conclusive examination of sound-to-spelling relationships in American-English orthography and that his research did indeed have serious weaknesses. Accordingly, Hanna, in collaboration with E. Hugh Rudorf and the present writer, undertook a much more extensive examination of our writing system and the degree to which it reflects oral language. A report of this research (5), like the research it superseded, has generated further criticism of the case for teaching spelling on the basis of patterns of sound-to-letter correspondences.

What, then, are the issues on each side of the controversy, and how has this recent research attempted to provide definitive insights into the nature of American-English orthography?

THE HANNA-MOORE STUDY

The rationale of the Hanna-Moore research rested on certain assumptions. First, these researchers assumed that the child entering school is the master of a rather large vocabulary of spoken words and that he soon acquires an increasing repertoire of words used in reading. Therefore, spelling programs should seek to enable the child to associate his speaking vocabulary with his reading vocabulary and to reproduce these associations in their accepted written forms.

Second, Hanna and Moore assumed that the orthography of the American-English language is alphabetically based; that is, American-English spelling is a system in which graphemes (the letters of the alphabet and their combinations) are used in writing to represent phonemes (the constituent sounds of English speech). An alphabetic writing system is in contrast to other types of orthographies in which written symbols may represent syllables or words. Accordingly, the ability to spell depends to a large extent on the ability to associate the appropriate graphemes with the phonemes that comprise the words of American-English speech.

With these two basic assumptions in mind, Hanna and Moore intended to analyze an American-English spelling vocabulary of three thousand words that were believed to represent the spelling words most common in children's usage and those most often taught in the first eight grades. From this list Hanna and Moore wanted to determine the extent to which each phoneme in the words comprising the spelling vocabulary of the elementary-school child is represented consistently in writing by a specific letter or combination of letters. In sum, the investigators intended to assess whether there are consistent relationships between phonemes and graphemes so that a speller could, with some assurance, select the correct written symbol for a given speech sound he heard and said in a word.

Hanna and Moore derived a standard pronunciation system of forty phonemes (including eight diphthongs; for example, *uy* as in *buy*) of spoken American English that included vowels, single consonants, consonant blends, suffixes, and final blends. This system used the *Thorndike Century Senior Dictionary* (6) as an authority and included only the preferred pronunciations given in that reference. The effects of syllable stress or lack of syllable stress on the pronunciation of phonemes were not considered unless these stress factors actually produced a different phoneme.

Each of the three thousand words (most of which were monosyllabic because of the sources from which they were taken) was then broken down into its component phonemes. The number of occurrences of each phoneme was then tabulated according to its position in a word or syllable. The tabulation was to show:

1. The number of different spellings of each phoneme.
2. The frequency of these spellings in the list of three thousand words.
3. The per cent of phonemes in the three thousand words that were regularly spelled.

A *regular spelling* was defined as that letter or combination of letters that is most frequently used to represent a given phoneme. The less frequently used letter representations of a phoneme were classified as *irregular spellings*.

What were the more important findings of this research? Generally, the investigators found that:

1. About four-fifths of the phonemes in the list of three thousand words have regular spellings.
2. Approximately three-fourths of the vowel phonemes in the words that had been analyzed are spelled by regular letter representations about 57 per cent to 99 per cent of the time.
3. Seven of the vowel phonemes have quite inconsistent letter representations (the vowel sounds in such words as *about, he, book, food, verb, all,* and the *y* sound in *onion*).
4. Single consonant phonemes are represented by their regular spellings about 90 per cent of the time they occur (as are the beginning consonant phonemes of *bed, dog,* and *gas*).
5. Doubled consonant letters (as in *address*) occur less than 1 per cent of the time in the word list.
6. Two consonant phonemes (the initial sound in *jam* and *gem* and the final sound in *jazz* and *has*) are quite irregularly represented in writing.
7. The so-called suffixes *le* and *on* (as in *table* and *lemon*) are also spelled quite irregularly.
8. About 82 per cent of the consonant blends are spelled in only one way (as is the initial consonant blend in *black*).

From these findings Hanna and Moore concluded that elementary-school spelling programs could profitably be organized to help pupils take advantage of the alphabetic nature of the American-English orthography (1). These programs, the researchers suggested, should capitalize on the regularity of the sound-to-letter patterns in learning to spell. The recognition of their work is testified to, at least in part, by researchers who subsequently have sought to verify or to reject their findings and by the references made to their study in many of the current spelling textbooks.

THE HORN STUDY

The conclusions that Hanna and Moore drew from their study, how-ever, were subject to careful analysis, particularly by spelling authori-ties who maintained that the orthography is not a consistent reflection of American-English speech. The most forthright and the most sub-stantial critique of the Hanna-Moore research was made by Ernest Horn, an eminent spelling scholar. Horn pointed out critical elements in the rationale and the design of the Hanna-Moore research which suggested that their findings were suspect (3). The most telling criti-cisms follow:

1. A list of the three thousand most commonly used words in writing is an inconclusive sample. Research based on many more words is necessary to demonstrate the consistency, or lack of consistency, of American-English orthography.

2. There is more than one accepted pronunciation of words. For example, American-English pronunciation differs in formal and informal speech and by regional dialects.

3. The definition of *regularity* is obscured because the investigators did not account for the frequency of the sounds or for the number of exceptions to the "regular" spellings they identified. In short, regularity is not in-sured merely because a given spelling of a phoneme is the most frequent representation of that sound. The spelling of a phoneme should be highly predictable (have few exceptions) and should be generalizable to large numbers of words before the label of *regularity* can be applied.

To lend strength to these criticisms, Horn replicated the research of Hanna and Moore but made several adaptations. Horn analyzed a sample of ten thousand words. He also attempted to account for multiple pronunciations of these words by checking several dictio-naries. As a final authority, he used Kenyon and Knott's *A Pronouncing Dictionary of American English* (7). Further, he assigned any so-called silent letters in a word (for example, the letter *b* in *debt*) to some sound in the word, a procedure that Hanna and Moore did not use.

What were some of the principal findings of Horn's study? Generally, Horn concluded that Hanna and Moore were correct in their estimation that English speech sounds do have common spellings; however, their interpretations of the findings were misguided, if not somewhat naïve. The limitation of their sample, Horn noted, caused them to make generalizations that did not hold up when a larger sample of the language was examined. Horn reported that:

1. Over a third of the words in *A Pronouncing Dictionary of American English* have more than one accepted pronunciation.
2. Over half of the ten thousand words contain silent letters in which an arbitrary judgment must be made when assigning them to a particular sound in a word. Further, about a sixth of the words contain doubled letters, and typically only one of the letters is pronounced.
3. Not only do several letters often represent a given sound, but a given letter often represents several sounds.
4. Many words commonly used in writing are polysyllabic and therefore contain unstressed syllables. The concept of regularity breaks down in unstressed syllables particularly (3).

Consequently, Horn drew sharply different conclusions regarding the feasibility of constructing spelling programs that emphasized sound-to-letter patterns in American English. In a later statement (4), Horn proposed that spelling generalizations be taught only when they are extremely powerful (that is, when they apply to large numbers of words and have few exceptions), because generalizations can easily be misapplied as well as correctly applied. He further indicated that large numbers of common words do not conform to any orthographic rule and therefore cannot be learned by children through a process of associating speech sounds and written symbols. Finally, children should be helped to learn the ways in which sounds are represented in writing rather than their most common spellings.

Horn's basic views have been reiterated elsewhere by various critics of the Hanna-Moore study, but often with embellishments that directly concern spelling curriculum and instruction. A recent critique (8) of the Hanna-Moore research indicates that:

1. Subjectivity is involved in assigning "silent" letters to some phonemic value.
2. Dialect differences and variability of word pronunciation in different sentence contexts complicate associating written symbols with given speech sounds.
3. There is a danger in generalizing about sound-to-letter correspondences from a narrow sample of American English to a more comprehensive sample.
4. Many "function" words (for example, *says, the*) do not fit any orthographic rules yet need to be learned by children early in their school

career; these words weaken the case for teaching spelling on the basis of regular sound-to-letter correspondences.

5. It is necessary to consider the frequency of particular sounds in words.

6. A strong case could also be made for teaching spelling on the basis of inconsistencies in the language rather than supposed consistencies.

THE STANFORD SPELLING PROJECT

Regardless of the position one takes on the research by Hanna and Moore, it is clear that their study is quite important for at least one basic reason: it raises significant questions and foments critical analyses. The fact that the Hanna-Moore study still continues to generate interest is testimony that the area these researchers explored is an important one and that their general premises have substance.

Yet, even their proponents were not able justifiably to claim that Hanna and Moore had made a truly comprehensive analysis of American-English orthography. What was obviously needed was a definitive analysis of American-English orthography, one that would be comprehensive and would be designed to obviate the weaknesses that were evident in the earlier study by Hanna and Moore.

Therefore, in 1961 Hanna proposed to the Cooperative Research Branch of the United States Office of Education that such a study be undertaken. The purpose of the research would be to determine how consistently the phonemes of American English are represented by particular written symbols in the orthography in a sample that included far more than three thousand words or ten thousand words. Further, using linguistic concepts and computer technology, this research would attempt to explore the nature of the orthography in much greater detail than had previously been done. Thus, the research would be, in part, an attempt to go beyond this earlier work by considering additional elements of American-English orthography. This research proposal received the sponsorship of the United States Office of Education, and the research was carried out from January, 1963, to December, 1964.

More detailed results of this research are available elsewhere (5, 9, 10). In general, however, the data from this study indicate that the orthography does indeed reflect spoken language with considerable consistency, particularly when the several components of the phonology (the sound system) underlying the orthography are taken into account.

It is certainly true that most phonemes are represented graphically in more than one way. And it is also true that the fact that phonemes are represented in many ways in large numbers of different words makes it difficult to sort out measures of consistency. For these reasons it was decided to examine the relationships between phonemes and their written representations in their positions in syllables and also to take into account the stress given to these syllables.

Let us examine the rationale and the design of this research to illustrate how it proposed to overcome the basic weaknesses of the Hanna-Moore research and to indicate the depth to which this study plumbed the nature of American-English orthography.

The research team wished to examine as large a sample of American-English words as would be definitive and practical to analyze. Accordingly, the first twenty thousand words from *The Thorndike-Lorge Teachers Word Book of 30,000 Words* (11) were used. Certain words were eliminated including proper names, contracted word forms, hyphenated words, abbreviations, archaic and poetic words, foreign words, trade names, slang and dialectal words, and words listed as "rare" in standard dictionaries. The elimination of these words resulted in a basic list of 15,284 words. This list was then supplemented by an additional 2,026 words taken from *Webster's New Collegiate Dictionary* (12), which included words that had entered the lexicon in recent years, and additional words of standard usage that were not included in the basic list. In no case, however, were derived forms of base words added to the list lest the "deck be stacked" by increasing the frequencies of certain phoneme-grapheme correspondences that are consistently spelled in prefixes and suffixes. Accordingly, derivations were included only when affixes were uncommon or when they changed the pronunciation of the base form of the word.

The list of 17,310 words was felt to be extensive enough to insure that many polysyllabic words were included. Further, the extensiveness of the word list enabled the research team to analyze phoneme-grapheme correspondences at several levels of the phonology underlying the orthography. These levels were sound-to-letter correspondences wherever they occur in *words*, sound-to-letter correspondences as they occur in positions in syllables, and sound-to-letter correspondences as they occur in positions in stressed and unstressed syllables.

Careful attention was paid to the selection of graphemic symbols that represent speech sounds in American-English writing. It must be agreed that compiling such lists of letter representations is a subjective task; but not entirely so. The so-called silent letters often have historical antecedents (for example, the vestigial letter *k* in *knock* at one time represented a phoneme, the initial sound one hears in *kit*). Furthermore, letters do not have sounds; they represent them. Letters do have names, but we do not spell words in writing by saying the names of the letters; we say the names of the letters only when we wish to spell words orally. In addition, it might be argued that, pedagogically, it is more meaningful and simpler to indicate that the initial *n* sound is written *kn* in *knock* than to point out repeatedly the silent letters that permeate our writing system. In any case, all letters in a given word were assigned to some sound (for example, the ending *o* sound in *though* is spelled *ough*) after carefully examining several references that discussed American-English orthography (13–16) and by consulting with linguists and language arts specialists who advised the project team.

Similarly, the doubled letters that often represent consonant phonemes were assigned to single speech sounds whenever the dictionary pronunciation indicated that this was appropriate. Indeed, a case might be made for the reformulation of the teaching of syllabication in elementary school, since the standard practice of separating words such as *follow* and *fellow* between doubled letters is a typographer's rule, not a reflection of the way such words are pronounced.

An important, if not crucial, consideration is the pronunciation system used in research of this nature. Obviously, language is dynamic; sounds in words used in running speech vary among dialect groups as well as among individuals. But the spelling of such words is another matter. Each word to be spelled is isolated from its context for the purposes of spelling and writing, and words that are unfamiliar to the speller are often pronounced in isolation from the context in which they occur.

As an aid to spelling, the pronunciation system used to analyze the consistency of the orthography is better based on lexical (or dictionary) pronunciations than on pronunciation systems that describe words occurring in running speech. Furthermore, the minor variations in speech sounds that occur in spoken discourse are not phonemic, that is, the substitution of one minor sound change for another does not alter the meaning of a word. Fortunately, for those who speak American English, such minor changes in sound, or allophonic variations, are assimilated without awareness; otherwise, the cognitive load of remembering all such allophones from several dialects and in different sentence patterns would be prodigious.

Thus, on logical grounds (and practically, too, in order to maintain a consistent sound system throughout the analysis), a pronunciation system was employed that included thirty consonant phonemes and twenty-two vowel phonemes. Actually, this coding system reflects the conventional phonemic codes used by linguists. The additional sounds included in this pronunciation system included vowel sounds before *r* sounds and certain diphthongs.

The decision to use a standard pronunciation system is not meant to argue that dialect differences in American English are negligible in the task of learning to spell. However, admonitions concerning the role of dialect in spelling are based primarily on logical rather than empirical grounds. That is, no concerted study has been made of how dialect differences affect spelling standard English. It is hoped that the results of this research will provide bases for undertaking studies that will compare spellings of words in the standard orthography with spellings of those words by individuals in various dialect communities. The author is at present formulating such studies.

To recapitulate, a sizable list of words was analyzed. The research used a consistent pronunciation system and a carefully prepared lists of letter representations to determine the degree to which these two systems (speech and writing) are related at several levels of the phonology underlying the orthography. The results of these analyses clearly indicate that the orthography is alphabetically based: large numbers of consistent phoneme-grapheme correspondences occur at least 80 per cent of the time in some position in stressed and unstressed syllables (9).

What do these findings indicate for the spelling curriculum of the elementary school? They suggest that a mastery of American-English spelling might be made easier by a conscientious programming of spelling materials that capitalizes on consistent sound-to-spelling correspondences and on the "rules" for making correct associations between phonemes and graphemes.

But such spelling programs require careful preparation and testing. For this reason, the research was intended as an analysis of American-English orthography and was not a study in elementary-school spelling curriculum and instruction. In short, the research has laid the conditions for curriculum construction and experimentation.

Clearly, the frequency with which consistent sound-to-letter correspondences occur in spelling large numbers of words is an important factor to be considered. To assess this factor, the present author tabulated the frequencies and percentages of all phoneme-grapheme correspondences occurring in the list of 17,310 words as well as the frequencies and percentages of the distribution of phonemes as they occur throughout the word list (9).

The research team also wished to test the value of the observable consistent phoneme-grapheme relationships found in the word sample for spelling words in the conventional American-English orthography. Accordingly, a second major phase of the total research project was undertaken by E. Hugh Rudorf. This phase involved the development of a computer program by which the 17,310 words can be spelled on the basis of these phoneme-grapheme relationships (10). For each phoneme a set of rules for predicting its spelling was derived from an analysis of the data obtained in the first phase of the research. The rules indicated how a particular phoneme would be spelled under the various conditions of position and stress, and how a preceding or following phoneme in the same syllable or word as the phoneme in question might affect its spelling.

To accomplish this analysis, the computer was provided with an "oral vocabulary" of 17,310 words, the sets of rules, and a list of the graphemes that stand for phonemes in the orthography. The computer was programmed to spell these words on the basis of the rules given. The findings of this analysis indicate that about half of the 17,310 words can be spelled on the basis of sound-to-letter patterns and that additional thousands of words can be spelled correctly if such morphological factors as affixation and compounding are taken into account.

The findings support the contention that there are productive relationships between the American-English writing system and the sounds in words that this writing system represents. The fact that many words, including some frequently used words, do not conform to these alphabetic principles does not require that we ignore the basic alphabetic structure of our orthography in our efforts to help children efficiently and effectively master the complexities of American-English spelling. Obviously, the spelling of some words can most easily be mastered by visual memorization. Other words contain certain uncommon spellings that require the pupil's special attention; yet parts of these words usually contain highly regular sound-to-letter correspondences when their positions in syllables and syllable stress are considered. Plainly, learning to spell is a more complex process than simply learning to make correct associations among phonemes and graphemes (17, 18).

An ideal solution to many of the vagaries of American-English orthography is some system of spelling reform. It is quite unlikely, however, that the problems that impede the development and acceptance of a revised form of American-English orthography can be overcome at this time (19). Meanwhile, it would be unfortunate, and a disservice to elementary-school children who are learning to spell, to underscore the negative aspects of an orthography which, in the main, is based on a consistent, and a historically interesting, sound-to-letter system (20).

REFERENCES

1. Paul R. Hanna and James T. Moore, Jr. "Spelling—from Spoken Word to Written Symbol," *Elementary School Journal,* LIII (February, 1953), 329–37.

2. James T. Moore, Jr. "Phonetic Elements Appearing in a Three Thousand Word Spelling Vocabulary." Unpublished doctoral dissertation. Stanford, California: Stanford University, 1951.

3. Ernest Horn. "Phonetics and Spelling," *Elementary School Journal,* LVII (May, 1957), 424–32.

4. Ernest Horn. "Spelling," *Encyclopedia of Educational Research,* pp. 1337–54. Chester W. Harris (editor). New York: Macmillan, 1960.

5. Richard E. Hodges and E. Hugh Rudorf. "Searching Linguistics for Cues to the Teaching of Spelling," *Elementary English,* XLII (May, 1965), 527–33.

6. E. L. Thorndike. *Thorndike Century Senior Dictionary.* Chicago: Scott, Foresman and Company, 1941.

7. John S. Kenyon and Thomas A. Knott. *A Pronouncing Dictionary of American English.* Springfield, Massachusetts: G. and C. Merriam Company, 1953.

8. Walter T. Petty. "Research Critiques." Edited by Patrick Groff. *Elementary English,* XLII (May, 1965), 584–87.

9. Richard E. Hodges. "An Analysis of the Phonological Structure of American-English Orthography." Unpublished doctoral dissertation. Stanford, California: Stanford University, 1964.

10. E. Hugh Rudorf. "The Development of an Algorithm for American-English Spelling." Unpublished doctoral dissertation. Stanford, California: Stanford University, 1964.

11. E. L. Thorndike and Irving Lorge. *The Teacher's Word Book of 30,000 Words.* New York: Bureau of Publications, Teachers College, Columbia University, 1944.

12. *Webster's New Collegiate Dictionary.* Edited by John P. Bethel. Springfield, Massachusetts: G. and C. Merriam Company, 1961 (sixth edition).

13. Godfrey Dewey. *Relative Frequency of English Speech Sounds.* Cambridge, Massachusetts: Harvard University Press, 1923.

14. W. Nelson Francis. *The Structure of American English.* New York: Ronald Press Company, 1958.

15. Robert A. Hall, Jr. *Sound and Spelling in English.* Philadelphia: Chilton Company, 1961.

16. Axel Wijk. *Regularized English.* Stockholm: University of Stockholm, 1959.

17. Paul R. Hanna and Richard E. Hodges. "Spelling and Communications Theory: A Model and an Annotated Bibliography," *Elementary English,* XL (May, 1963), 483–505, 528.

18. Richard E. Hodges. "The Psychological Bases of Spelling," *Elementary English,* XLII (October, 1965), 629–35.

19. Richard E. Hodges. "A Short History of Spelling Reform in the United States," *Phi Delta Kappan,* XLV (April, 1964), 330–32.

20. A detailed summary of the Stanford Spelling Project is being prepared for publication by the United States Government Printing Office for the United States Office of Education, as Project 1991.

FOR FURTHER READING

Archer, Clifford P., "Saving Time in Spelling Instruction," *Journal of Educational Research* 20 (September 1929) 122–131.

———, "Shall We Teach Spelling by Rule," *The Elementary English Review* 7 (March 1930) 61–63.

Brody, David S., "A Comparative Study of Different Forms of Spelling Tests," *The Journal of Educational Psychology* 35 (March 1944) 129–144.

Fitzgerald, James A., "Spelling Words Difficult for Children in Grades II–VI," *Elementary School Journal* 53 (December 1952) 221–228.

Gates, Arthur I., "An Experimental Comparison of the Study-Test and Test-Study Methods in Spelling," *Journal of Educational Psychology* 22 (January 1931) 1–19.

———, *A List of Spelling Difficulties in 3876 Words* (New York: Columbia University, 1937).

Gilbert, Luther C., and Doris W. Gilbert, "The Improvement of Spelling Through Reading," *Journal of Educational Research* 37 (February 1944) 458–463.

Guiler, Walter S., "Validation of Testing Spelling," *Journal of Educational Research* 20 (October 1929) 181–189.

————, and Gilbert A. Lease, "An Experimental Study of Methods of Instruction in Spelling," *Elementary School Journal* 43 (September 1942) 234–238.

Hanna, Paul R., Jean S. Hanna, Richard E. Hodges, and E. Hugh Rudorf, "Linguistic Cues for Spelling Improvement," *Elementary English* 44 (December 1967) 862–865.

Hildreth, Gertrude, *Teaching Spelling* (New York: Holt, Rinehart & Winston, Inc., 1955).

Hodges, Richard E., "Phoneme-grapheme Correspondences in Monosyllabic Words," in J. Allen Figurel, editor, *Forging Ahead in Reading*, International Reading Association Conference Proceedings, No. 12 (Newark, Delaware: International Reading Association, 1968), pp. 56–67.

Horn, Ernest, "A Basic Writing Vocabulary," *University of Iowa Monographs in Education*, No. 4 (Iowa City: University of Iowa Press, 1925).

————, "Teaching Spelling," *What Research Says to the Teacher*, No. 3 (Washington, D.C.: National Education Association, January 1954).

Horn, Thomas D., "Effect of Corrected Tests in Learning to Spell," *Elementary School Journal* 47 (January 1947) 272–285.

————, "Research in Spelling," *Elementary English* 37 (March 1960) 174–177.

Knoell, Dorothy M., and Chester W. Harris, "A Factor Analysis of Spelling Ability," *Journal of Educational Research* 46 (October 1952) 95–111.

National Conference on Research in English, *Research on Handwriting and Spelling*, Thomas D. Horn, editor (Champaign, Illinois: National Council of Teachers of English, 1966).

Northby, Arwood S., "A Comparison of Five Types of Spelling Tests for Diagnostic Purposes," *Journal of Educational Research* 29 (January 1936) 339–346.

Osburn, Worth J., "Teaching Spelling by Teaching Syllables and Root Words," *Elementary School Journal* 45 (November 1954) 32–44.

Pavlak, Stephen E., "A Critical Analysis of Scientific Research in Spelling." Unpublished doctoral dissertation (Pittsburgh: University of Pittsburgh, 1956).

Personke, Carl, and Lester Knight, "Proofreading and Spelling: A Report and a Program," *Elementary English* 44 (November 1967) 768–774.

Reid, Hale C., "Evaluation of Five Methods of Teaching Spelling—2nd and 3rd Grades," *Instructor* 75 (March 1966) 77ff.

Rice, Joseph M., "The Futility of the Spelling Grind," *Forum* 23 (April and June 1897) 163–172, 409–419.

Russell, David H., "A Diagnostic Study of Spelling Readiness," *Journal of Educational Research* 37 (December 1943) 276–283.

———, "Second Study of the Characteristics of Good and Poor Spellers," *Journal of Educational Psychology* 46 (March 1955) 126–141.

Schoephoerster, Hugh, "Research into Variations of the Test-Study Plan of Teaching Spelling," *Elementary English* 39 (May 1962) 460–462.

Soloman, Gerbert, and Ian MacNeill, "Spelling Ability: A Comparison Between Computer Output Based on a Phonemic-Graphemic Algorithm and Actual Student Performance in Elementary Grades," *Research in Teaching of English* 1 (Fall 1967) 157–175.

Weller, Louise, and M. E. Broom, "A Study of the Validity of Six Types of Spelling Scales," *School and Society* 40 (July 21, 1934) 103–104.

The Relative Efficiency of the Various Approaches to Writing with the Left Hand*

E.A. ENSTROM

The left-handed writer—a topic that has been selected to represent the broad spectrum of studies done in the field of handwriting—has been studied intensively by Enstrom. The typical classroom has at least one and possibly two or three left-handed children. Our systems of handwriting have been developed for the majority who are right-handed. Improper left-handed writing habits can impede the speed and quality of a child's handwriting. This need not happen if teachers follow the provisions suggested by Enstrom's ex post facto research.

Particular strengths of this report include: a review of the literature from 1847 to 1962; a clear statement of purpose; a good design for a study of this type; clear presentation of the data, helped considerably by diagrams; and well-substantiated conclusions. The subjects (chosen by an unspecified method) were not aware that the testing concerned left-handedness and therefore they probably reacted normally in the test situations. While the technical descriptions of different hand positions must be read carefully, the conclusions are clearly presented. A wide variety of references in "For Further Reading" suggest the broad range of possibilities for research in the area of handwriting.

A previous report, taken from an unpublished dissertation by the writer, (1) covered the extent of the use of the left hand in handwriting. It was found that 11 per cent of pupils in grades one through six preferred the left hand. Among boys, 12.5 per cent used the left hand, and among girls, 9.7 per cent. This second report will deal with the relative efficiency of the various approaches to writing with the left hand.

* From *Journal of Educational Research* 55 (August 1962) 573–577. Reprinted with permission of *The Journal of Educational Research*, and E. A. Enstrom, Director of Research, Peterson System of Directed Handwriting, Inc., Greensburg, Pennsylvania.

THE LITERATURE

In a study of 108 references dating from 1847 to the present, the writer found no mention of left-handedness until the year 1915. These references included (1) handwriting instruction books for pupils and adults, (2) teachers' manuals in handwriting, (3) books devoted exclusively to handwriting, and (4) courses of study dealing with handwriting.

From the first mentioning of the problem in 1915, (2) there has been a gradual increase in reference to left-handedness. The literature, to the present, revealed six different approaches to the problem. The suggested slope of letters varied from the more easily read forward slant, to vertical, and to questionable backhand. Yet, with all of the disagreement and dearth of understanding, there were no research attempts to find better answers to the problem confronting the teacher of this segment of the school population. West (3) even recommended such a study as early as 1927, but the suggestion went unheeded.

TECHNIQUES ACTUALLY USED BY LEFT-HANDED WRITERS

The writer began his search for methods actually used by children in classrooms with the aid of a camera and sketch pad. Careful notes were taken of likenesses and differences among the techniques employed by these writers. Grades five through eight were selected for this phase of the study. It was felt that in these more advanced grades, habits would be well set, resulting in techniques of writing that were established sufficiently to permit comparative evaluation.

The two-year study of this phase of the problem revealed that more classifiable methods and variations were in use than were listed in the literature. Instead of six approaches, the writer found 15 different techniques that could be classified and that were used frequently enough to be tested for relative efficiency.

The classroom observer will discover that there are two general groups attempting to write with the left hand; those who keep the writing hand below the writing line (Group I in the writer's study) and those who approach from the left side of the paper and more or less "hook" the wrist while writing (Group II). A careful look will reveal many differences among pupils found in each group.

GROUP I

Writing-hand-below-the-writing-line adjustments. All these adjustments are relatively smear-free.

I-C   Paper is not turned enough to be the reverse of right-handed placement. Angle between the arm axis and paper ruling is less than 90°. Writing slope varies but is downward (usually very irregular).

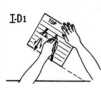

I-D1   Reverse of right-handed position. Arm axis is 90° with paper ruling. Downward strokes are directed toward elbow, "into the sleeve." Writing slope approaches vertical and is usually somewhat irregular.

I-D2   Reverse of right-handed position. Arm axis is 90° with paper ruling. Slant strokes are directed downward and outward (leftward). Slant is generally forward and uniform.

I-E   Paper is turned more to the right (clockwise) than the reverse of right-handed placement. Arm axis angle with paper ruling is greater than 90°. Slant motion is a sideward (leftward) push of the writing arm. Slant is uniformly forward.

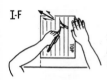

I-F   Extreme turning of the paper. Paper ruling is 90° (plus or minus 5°) with the front edge of the desk. Slant motion is a sideward (leftward and upward) push of the writing arm. Slant is generally forward and uniform.

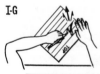

I-G   Very extreme turning of the paper. Paper ruling is greater than the 90° (above). Angle between top of paper and the front edge of the desk is usually between 50° and 30°. Slant is a sideward (upward) push of the writing arm. Slant is generally forward and uniform.

GROUP II

Writing-hand-above-the-writing-line adjustments. Inherent smearing possibility exists with all these writing techniques.

Adjustments numbered II-A. Paper is turned leftward as for right-handed placement. These are the three basic hooked wrist techniques.

II-Aa

II-Ab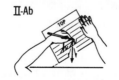

II-Ac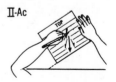

| Wrist is turned on edge enough to permit maximum flexing. | Wrist is somewhat flattened. Less flexing —more finger movement. | Wrist is flat. Practically no flexing—all finger or whole arm movement, or mixture of two. |

Adjustments numbered II-B. Same as II-A except that the paper ruling is generally parallel with the lower edge of the desk (plus or minus 5°).

II-Ba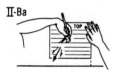

II-Bb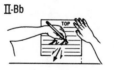

II-Bc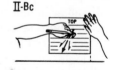

| Wrist is turned on edge enough to permit maximum flexing. | Wrist is somewhat flattened. Less flexing —more finger movement. | Wrist is flat. Practically no flexing—all finger or whole arm movement, or mixture of two. |

Adjustments numbered II-D. Same as II-A but paper is turned rightward (clockwise) as for "correct" left-handed placement, yet wrist is still hooked.

II-Da

II-Db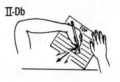

II-Dc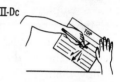

| Wrist is turned on edge enough to permit maximum flexing. | Wrist is somewhat flattened. Less flexing —more finger movement. | Wrist is flat. Practically no flexing—all finger or whole arm movement, or mixture of two. |

In Group I, there were six different classifiable variations taken into account, (1) the relationship between the lower edge of the paper and the front edge of the desk, (2) the angle formed between the arm axis and the paper ruling, and (3) the direction of the movement which determined leverage (or lack thereof) and slope (slant, or lack thereof) in the written product. For details of Group I techniques, with variations, see the plate entitled "Group I."

Group II, consisting of the loosely termed "hookers," included nine classifiable techniques. Variations were found (1) in the placing of the paper in relation to the front edge of the desk (which also affects body posture), and (2) the extent to which the wrist is turned on edge and "flexed" during the writing process. Some writers keep the wrist on edge sufficiently to facilitate a hinge action at the joint as the basic movement supporting the writing. Others keep the wrist flat (probably the result of teacher instruction directed to right-handed writers) that permitted only poor wrist movement. Still others may be classified as being approximately half-way between these two extremes. Descriptions of each of these adjustments are found on the plate entitled "Group II." (4)

A comparison of the frequency of the use of techniques showed that certain adjustments held preference by pupils in both Groups I and II. In Group I, the most frequently used technique, it was later found, held high advantage in both speed and quality. In Group II, a less desirable technique was used more frequently. With advancing grades, however, it was found that this less desirable method tended to convert into the most desirable approach for this often condemned group.

EVALUATION OF THE ADJUSTMENTS

The criteria used as a basis for the evaluation of the various techniques employed were (1) the quality of the handwriting product, (2) the rate of writing, (3) ability to produce neat, smear-free papers, and (4) healthful body posture considerations. In addition to the study of the quality of papers produced and the time required in writing them, notes regarding smearing tendency and possible health hazards were made during the initial study and classification of all left-handed writers.

Every precaution was taken in the evaluation phase of the work to make sure that each pupil was actually using his classified technique. Testing for speed was done by using the best combined recommendations for such testing. Whole classes were tested and left-handed writers were not aware that the testing concerned them. Quality scores were obtained through the use of the Ayres Scale (5) with trained experts rating the scrambled papers five separate times. The average of the five ratings was used as the final quality score with special precautions taken for any rare discrepancies. None of the persons scaling the papers had information as to which of the fifteen techniques was used by the writer of any given page. Two different samples were used in the quality testing: (1) The rate test where the pupils were instructed to write "as well as you can, as fast as you can," and (2) an additional sample where the pupils were merely asked to write as well as they could. Favorable comparison here showed that the original instructions had been followed.

SCOPE OF THE STUDY

At first it was thought that the study would be sufficient in scope if 400 left-handed writers were classified and evaluated for efficiency. However, upon breaking down the four grades into a possible fifteen different adjustments in each, it was thought advisable to extend the study by at least 200 more cases. After this had been done, it was then further decided that, to remove all possible doubt regarding findings, 500 additional cases would be studied, tested, compared, and included. After the elimination of any cases that would possibly interfere with valid findings (pupils using two different techniques, handicapped pupils unable to follow testing instructions, etc), 1,103 usable left-handed writers were included in the final evaluation. This proved more than ample in securing the desired information.

It should also be mentioned that the findings were obtained from schools where handwriting is generally well taught through a program of in-service help consisting of workshops, class visitations and demonstrations by resource personnel available at scheduled intervals during the school term. (6) The chief objective of the study was to find the efficiency potential of each adjustment in use.

FINDINGS: RELATIVE EFFICIENCY OF VARIOUS TECHNIQUES

In Group I, the I-E adjustment (not taught in the area prior to the testing, but discovered by pupils in the group) also rated highest in quality and in rate of all six Group I techniques. In each grade, pupils using this approach ranked much higher than the quality norms set for the grade. The same was true for speed scores in all grades except eighth, where the rate finding was the same as the norm. (The exceedingly high quality here apparently slowed the speed to some extent.)

The I-D_2 adjustment (taught in the area) was next in frequency of use, was above grade standard in quality, but below rate standards in grades five and seven, almost at the rate standard in grade six, and above in grade eight. The general picture here, while good, was not as favorable as in I-E.

The I-F technique (not taught, but discovered by pupils) fluctuated more in findings than the two previous adjustments. It was above quality standards in grades five, six and seven; below in eight. It was below rate standards in grades five and six; above in seven and eight.

The frequently recommended (in the literature) I-D_1 technique (pulling the arm "into the sleeve") was at quality standard in grade five, but well below standard in grades six, seven, and eight. In rate, grade five was slightly below standard, grade six further below, but grades seven and eight were above. This speed, however, resulted in the previously mentioned very low quality scores for these two grades. In spite of its frequent recommendation, there is nothing to suggest that this adjustment should be taught to left-handed pupils as a means of solving their writing problems.

The other two adjustments in Group I (I-C and I-G) were so poor (or fluctuated so much) as to warrant no consideration at all.

In Group II, only one approach can be recommended, and then with some reservations. This more desirable "hooked" technique was used by 20 percent of pupils in this classification. This approach is II-Aa, and showed very high quality with above standard rate in all grades except grade five. However, there are two inherent drawbacks to this solution: (1) The side of the hand does not move readily across the page, particularly if the hand tends to perspire. (2) Since the hand, vigorously flexing, moves through the work written, there is always danger of smearing—again, more so if the hand perspires. All other Group II approaches were either low in speed and quality, fluctuated greatly, or presented possible health hazards (stooped shoulders, twisted backs, etc.), so cannot be considered desirable.

CONCLUSIONS: ADJUSTMENTS HOLDING
THE GREATEST PROMISE FOR SUCCESS

In Group I, half of the six adjustments can be considered generally good in four efficiency considerations: (1) quality, (2) rate, (3) freedom from smearing, and (4) posture. Of the remaining, one adjustment (I-G) is erratic because of too few cases; another, the frequently recommended I-D$_1$ approach is very low in quality, and still another, the I-C, is very low in both quality and rate.

The best Group I adjustments, in order of desirability, are:

I-E

I-D2

I-F

These three success-producing techniques make up approximately 69 per cent of Group I writers.

In Group II, only one adjustment out of nine can be considered good, and then with reservations. It is:

II-Aa

While this adjustment, used by only 20 per cent of the group, ranks high in both quality and rate, inherent weaknesses exist and, under less than favorable conditions, can be very handicapping. These weaknesses, as mentioned, are the difficulty of sliding the side of the hand forward in carrying the writing across the page, and smearing tendencies under conditions that cause hand perspiration.

The remaining 80 per cent of Group II writers use modifications in the adjustment that cannot be recommended, either from (1) the efficiency standpoint in quality, rate, or even greater tendency to smear, or (2) from physical health considerations. They seem to have little to recommend them.

It can be concluded that Group I techniques are best, all things considered, and should be taught at beginning stages in writing. Adjustment II-Aa is the most desirable of the "hooked" group and all advanced grade hookers who are unable, or do not desire, to make major changes should be helped to modify their approach to conform most nearly with this more desirable technique.

REFERENCES

1. Enstrom, E. A., *The Extent of the Use of the Left Hand in Handwriting and the Determination of the Relative Efficiency of the Various Hand-Wrist-Arm-Paper Adjustments,* unpublished Ph.D. dissertation: University of Pittsburgh, 1957. Dr. Herbert T. Olander was advisor.

2. Zaner, C. P., *Zaner Method Writing, Arm Movement, Teacher's Manual No. 4, 5,* Columbus, O.: Zaner and Bloser Co., 1915, p. 14.

3. West, Paul V., *Changing Practice in Handwriting Instruction,* Bloomington, Ill.: Public School Publishing Co., 1927, 55–56, 133.

4. In addition, a more detailed description of each adjustment is found in the original dissertation for those who wish to delve into the problem even further. See 1., above: 24–26, 45–60.

5. Ayres, Leonard P., *Measuring Scale for Handwriting, Gettysburg Edition,* Princeton, N.J.: Cooperative Test Division of Educational Testing Service.

6. The Peterson System of Directed Handwriting, Greensburg, Pa.

FOR FURTHER READING

Andersen, Dan W., "Handwriting Research: Movement and Quality," *Elementary English* 42 (January 1965) 45–53.

——, "Handwriting Research: Style and Practice," *Elementary English* 42 (February 1965) 115–125.

——, "What Makes Writing Legible," *Elementary School Journal* 69 (April 1969) 364–369.

Bell, Hugh M., "The Comparative Legibility of Typewriting, Manuscript and Cursive Script: I. Easy Prose, Letters and Syllables," *Journal of Psychology* 8 (October 1939) 295–309; "II. Difficult Prose and Eyemovement Photography," *ibid.* 8 (October 1939) 311–330.

Burns, Paul C., *Improving Handwriting Instruction in Elementary Schools,* revised edition (Minneapolis, Minnesota: Burgess Publishing Co., 1968).

Committee on Research in Basic Skills, *Ten Years of Research in Handwriting*, 1949–1959 (Madison: Department of Education, University of Wisconsin).

Dougherty, Mary L., "History of the Teaching of Handwriting in America," *Elementary School Journal* 18 (December 1917) 280–286.

Enstrom, E. A., "Research in Handwriting," *Elementary English* 41 (December 1964) 873–876.

Erlebacker, Adrienne, and Virgil E. Herrick, "Quality of Handwriting Today and Yesterday," *Elementary School Journal* 62 (November 1961) 89–93.

Feldt, Leonard S., "The Reliability of Measures of Handwriting Quality," *Journal of Educational Psychology* 53 (December 1962) 288–292.

Freeman, Frank N., "An Analytical Scale for Judging Handwriting," *Elementary School Journal* 15 (April 1915) 432–441.

———, "An Evaluation of Manuscript Writing," *Elementary School Journal* 46 (March 1946) 375–380.

———, "Teaching Handwriting," *What Research Says to the Teacher*, No. 4 (Washington, D.C.: National Education Association, 1954).

———, "A New Handwriting Scale," *Elementary School Journal* 60 (January 1959) 218–221.

Gates, Arthur I., and Helen Brown, "Experimental Comparisons of Print, Script and Cursive Writing," *Journal of Educational Research* 20 (June 1929) 1–14.

Goetsch, Walter R., "The Effect of Early Handwriting Instruction," *Elementary School Journal* 36 (December 1935) 290–298.

Groff, Patrick J., "From Manuscript to Cursive—Why?", *Elementary School Journal* 61 (November 1960) 97–101.

Harris, Theodore L., and G. L. Rarick, "Problems of Pressure in Handwriting," *Journal of Experimental Education* 26 (December 1957) 151–178.

Herrick, Virgil E., *Comparison of Practices in Handwriting Advocated by Nineteen Commercial Systems of Handwriting Instruction* (Madison: Committee on Research in Basic Skills, University of Wisconsin, 1960).

———, "Handwriting and Children's Writing," *Elementary English* 37 (April 1960) 248–258.

Hildreth, Gertrude, "Manuscript Writing After Sixty Years," *Elementary English* 37 (January 1960) 4–13.

Lewis, Edward R., and Hilda P. Lewis, "An Analysis of Errors in the Formation of Manuscript Letters by First Grade Pupils," *American Educational Research Journal* 1 (January 1965) 25–36.

Newland, T. Ernest, "An Analytical Study of the Development of Illegibilities in Handwriting from Lower Grades to Adulthood," *Journal of Educational Research* 26 (December 1932) 249–258.

Noble, J. Kendrick, Jr., "Handwriting Programs in Today's Schools," *Elementary English* 40 (May 1963) 506–512.

Otto, Wayne, and G. Lawrence Rarick, "Effect of Time of Transition from Manuscript to Cursive Writing Upon Subsequent Performance in Handwriting, Spelling, and Reading," *Journal of Educational Research* 62 (January 1969) 211–216.

Petty, Walter T., "Handwriting and Spelling: Their Current Status in the Language Arts Curriculum," *Elementary English* 41 (December 1964) 839–845, 959.

Polkinghorne, Ada R., "Current Practices in Teaching Handwriting," *Elementary School Journal* 47 (December 1946) 218–224.

Quant, Leslie, "Factors Affecting the Legibility of Handwriting," *Journal of Experimental Education* 14 (June 1946) 297–316.

Templin, Elaine M., "How Important is Handwriting Today?" *Elementary School Journal* 61 (December 1960) 158–164.

Tenwolde, H., "Comparison of Handwriting of Pupils in Certain Elementary School Grades Now and Yesterday," *Journal of Applied Psychology* 18 (July 1943) 437–442.

4

SOCIAL STUDIES

The writers assume social studies to include not only content—drawn from history, geography, political science, economics, sociology, anthropology, psychology, and philosophy—but study skills, the social development of the child, including the development of values, and effective human relations. Also evident in this chapter is their opinion that process goals (attitudes, values, self-concepts, study and thinking skills) are fully as important as content goals (facts, concepts, and generalizations) in social studies instruction; and that learning by experiencing is as important as learning by reading, viewing a film, or listening to a lecture.

In this chapter the selected research treats the following topics: historical overview and projections, human relations, the development of social sensitivity, content, study skills, current events, and map learnings. A concern for history is reflected in the Wade study, for geography in that by McAulay, for economics in Smith, for sociology in Joyce and Weinberg, for anthropology in Clark and Clark, for psychology in both Rogers and Long and Clark and Clark, and for philosophy in the Rogers and Long study.

Social studies is a major concern in many articles outside this chapter. These related studies include: Homze, "Interpersonal Relations in Children's Literature, 1920–1960," Chapter 3; Schenke, "Information Sources Children Use," Chapter 6; and Schwartz, "An Investigation of the Effects of a Seventh and Eighth Grade Core Program," Chapter 7.

The research in this chapter includes two experimental studies (Schiller and McAulay); two action studies (Joyce and Weinberg, and Smith); one survey (Rogers and Long); one ex post facto (Clark and Clark); and one combined historical and survey (Wade). They distribute themselves one each to K–1–2, 2–4–6, 3–5, 4, 6, 7, and one K–12.

A listing of sources follows for the benefit of those wishing to pursue further some aspect of social studies research:

Social Education, the official journal of the National Council for the Social Studies, 1201 Sixteenth St., N.W., Washington, D.C. 20036 (eight issues per year). The reader particularly interested in the area of social studies should give thought to a membership in this council, which will entitle him to receive *Social Education* and the yearbooks and supplementary bulletins of the Council and to attend the annual meetings.

The Social Studies, published by McKinley Publishing Co., 112 S. New Broadway, Brooklawn, New Jersey 08030 (seven issues per year).

Yearbooks of the National Council for the Social Studies; for example: Michaelis, John U., editor, *Social Studies in Elementary Schools;* 32nd Yearbook (Washington, D.C.: National Council for the Social Studies, 1962).

Several specific references include:

American Council of Learned Societies and National Council for the Social Studies, *The Social Studies and the Social Sciences* (New York: Harcourt, Brace & World, Inc., 1962).

Berelson, Bernard, and Gary A. Steiner, editors, *Human Behavior: An Inventory of Scientific Findings* (New York: Harcourt, Brace & World, Inc., 1964).

Brodbeck, May (editor), *Readings In The Philosophy of The Social Sciences* (New York: The Macmillan Company, 1968).

Clements, H. Millard, William R. Fielder, and Robert B. Tabachnick, *Social Study: Inquiry in Elementary Classrooms* (Indianapolis: The Bobbs-Merrill Co., Inc., 1966).

Cox, C. Benjamin, William D. Johnson, and Roland F. Payette, "Review of Research in Social Studies: 1967" *Social Education* 32 (October 1968) 557–571.

Davis, O. L., Jr., "Organized Knowledge Influencing Curriculum Decisions: Social Studies," *Review of Educational Research* 33 (June 1963) 248–249.

Douglas, Malcolm P., *Social Studies: From Theory to Practice in Elementary Education* (Philadelphia: J. B. Lippincott Co., 1967).

Dunfee, Maxine, and Helen Sagl, *Social Studies Through Problem Solving* (New York: Holt, Rinehart & Winston, Inc., 1966).

Estvan, Frank J., *Social Studies in a Changing World* (New York: Harcourt, Brace & World, Inc., 1968).

Feldman, Martin, and Eli Seifman, *The Social Studies: Structures, Models, and Strategies* (Englewood Cliffs, N.J.: Prentice-Hall, Inc., 1969).

Fenton, Edwin, *The New Social Studies* (New York: Holt, Rinehart & Winston, Inc., 1967).

Gibson, John S., *New Frontiers in the Social Studies: Goals for Students, Means for Teachers* (New York: Citation Press, 1967).

———, *New Frontiers in the Social Studies: Action and Analysis* (New York: Citation Press, 1967).

Girault, Emily S. and C. Benjamin Cox, "Review of Research in Social Studies: 1966" *Social Education* 31 (May 1967) 388–396, 404.

Gross, Richard E., and William V. Badger, "Social Studies," in Chester W. Harris, editor, *Encyclopedia of Educational Research* (New York: The Macmillan Company, 1960), pp. 1296–1319.

Gross, Richard E., Walter E. McPhie, and Jack R. Fraenkel, *Teaching The Social Studies: What, Why, and How* (Scranton, Pa.: International Textbook Company, 1969).

Hanna, Lavone A., Gladys L. Potter, and Neva Hagaman, *Unit Teaching in the Elementary School,* revised edition (New York: Holt, Rinehart & Winston, Inc., 1963).

Harrison, Sylvia E., and Robert J. Soloman, "Review of Research in the Teaching of Social Studies 1960–1963," *Social Education* 28 (May 1964), 277–292.

Henry, Nelson B., editor, *Social Studies in the Elementary School* (Chicago: University of Chicago Press, 1957).

Herman, Wayne L. (editor), *Current Research in Elementary School Social Studies* (New York: The Macmillan Company, 1969).

Jarolimek, John, *Guidelines for Elementary Social Studies* (Washington, D.C.: Association for Supervision and Curriculum Development, N.E.A., 1967).

———, *Social Studies in Elementary Education,* 3rd edition (New York: The Macmillan Company, 1967).

Kenworthy, Leonard S., *Social Studies for the Seventies* (Waltham, Mass.: Blaisdell Publishing Co., 1969).

Massialas, Byron G., and Frederick R. Smith, editors, *New Challenges in the Social Studies* (Belmont, California: Wadsworth Publishing Co., Inc., 1965).

McClendon, Jonathon C., "Teaching the Social Studies," *What Re-*

search Says to the Teacher, No. 20 (Washington, D.C.: National Education Association, 1960).

McPhie, Walter E., *Dissertations in Social Studies Education: A Comprehensive Guide,* Research Bulletin No. 2 (Washington, D.C.: National Council for the Social Studies, 1964).

Metcalf, Lawrence E., "Research on Teaching the Social Studies," in N. L. Gage, editor, *Handbook of Research on Teaching* (Chicago: Rand McNally & Co., 1963, pp. 929–965).

Michaelis, John U., *Social Studies for Children in a Democracy,* 4th edition (Englewood Cliffs, N.J.: Prentice-Hall, Inc., 1968).

———, and A. Montgomery Johnston, *The Social Sciences: Foundations of the Social Studies* (Boston: Allyn and Bacon, Inc., 1965).

National Council for the Social Studies, "The Role of the Social Studies," *Social Education* 26 (October 1962) 315–318, 327.

Preston, Ralph C., *Teaching Social Studies in the Elementary School* (New York: Holt, Rinehart & Winston, Inc., 1968).

Price, Roy Arthur, *Needed Research in the Teaching of the Social Studies,* Research Bulletin No. 1 (Washington, D.C.: National Education Association, 1964).

Ragan, William Burke, and John D. McAulay, *Social Studies for Today's Children* (New York: Appleton-Century-Crofts, 1964).

Roberts, J., "Curriculum Development and Experimentation: Social Studies K–12," *Review of Educational Research* 36 (June 1966) 356–357.

Rogers, Vincent R., editor, *A Sourcebook for Social Studies* (New York: The Macmillan Company, 1969).

Servey, Richard E., *Social Studies Instruction in the Elementary School* (San Francisco: Chandler Publishing Co., 1967).

Timothy, Sister Mary, "Research: Impact Upon the Curriculum in Social Studies," *National Catholic Education Association Bulletin* 63 (August 1966) 383–390.

Wesley, Edgar Bruce, and William H. Cartwright, *Teaching Social Studies in Elementary Schools,* 3rd edition (Boston: D. C. Heath & Co., 1968).

Ferment in the Social Studies:
What Are the Directions of Change? *

BERNICE STILES WADE

Based on a broad survey of all state departments of education and selected local school systems, a comparison of curriculum guides from 1930–1950 with those of 1958–1963, and a survey of current national and regional projects, the researcher has drawn up a report on history, status, and trends in the teaching of the social studies. She presents an exciting story of curriculum redesigning which has characterized other subject areas and which is now upsetting traditions in the social studies. The reader may find it interesting to compare the historical reports on reading by Smith (Chapter 2), on language arts by Mackintosh (Chapter 3), and on science by Craig (Chapter 6). Other accounts of history and trends in the social studies can be found in the list "For Further Reading."

This report lacks some of the details of procedure and data which might be desired, but these can be found in the original dissertation at the University of North Carolina.

Curriculum workers are well aware that the social studies program for the public schools is today experiencing the widespread ferment which just a short time ago was characteristic of the programs in mathematics, science and modern foreign languages. The demand for a new social studies program is coming now from every part of the nation and from every national professional organization related to the field.

A study made in 1963 not only revealed the extent of the present ferment and the multitude of curricular efforts to update the program which are already under way, but also the fact that there is considerable agreement about what broad changes are needed and why. These conclusions were drawn from: (1) an analysis of professional literature published from January, 1958 to June, 1963; (2) an examina-

* Article not previously published. Printed with permission of the author, an Associate Professor at North Carolina College, Durham.

tion of major national and regional curriculum projects; and (3) a study of the status of the social studies programs in the fifty state departments of education and in selected local school units.

AREAS OF AGREEMENT

Both educators and social scientists, speaking through the above sources, base their arguments for a new social studies program upon the following premises:

1. That the recent scientific and technological advances have put a new burden on the schools, and on the social studies in particular:
   (a) The citizens of tomorrow, who must have the knowledge and skills needed to understand and help solve the socioeconomic problems of a world community as well as those of their own community, must work from a broader and deeper base of knowledge;
   (b) Tomorrow's citizens must be prepared for the uncertainties of rapid changes, which necessitate a reorientation of method, content materials and teacher education;
2. That the dramatic developments within the social and behavioral sciences make it imperative to close the gap between research findings in the academic fields and related subjects as taught in school;
3. That a more acceptable framework, grades kindergarten to twelve, is necessary for relating the information from *all* the social sciences to the goals for the social studies, and for readily incorporating the vital new knowledge as it appears;
4. That not only the new evidence concerning early readiness for learning, but also the longer period of preparation needed today for the specialist in any field, makes imperative a reconsideration of what can and should be taught at different age levels;
5. That the "explosion of knowledge" in all areas makes it necessary to restudy what knowledges and skills are of most worth, and what organizational patterns and methods of instruction are most suited to teaching them;
6. That the current social studies program common for grades one through twelve is repetitious, lacking in unity, and outdated, being designed for another generation with different individual and societal needs.

RECOMMENDED CHANGES

Educators and social scientists quite generally advocated the following changes for the new social studies program:

Objectives

No one advocated changing the basic objectives related to developing the kinds of citizens needed in the American democratic society. However, there was general agreement among the educators and social scientists, speaking as individuals or as participants in the various study groups, that these basic objectives could best be achieved through attention to the content of the social sciences and to the methods of inquiry used by social scientists.

Content and Organization

1. Establishment of a new unifying structure replacing the present historical framework that would permit both an earlier introduction and a more extended treatment of all the social sciences.
2. Development of a program strong in content, required from grades one through twelve, based upon the structure of the social sciences but not neglectful of contributions made by research in learning and growth patterns.
3. Selective content in terms of eras and areas, permitting thoroughness rather than coverage. This format was called "judicious sampling" by some and "postholing" by others.
4. Content to be selected by educators and social scientists working together:
    (a) social scientists to identify the key ideas from each discipline;
    (b) curriculum specialists to translate them into a spiraling pattern appropriate to the varying levels of maturity.

Specific content changes frequently suggested fell into seven general groups:

1. World understandings developed at every grade level through greater attention to:
    (a) global geography,
    (b) the non-Western world,
    (c) the new nations,
    (d) map studies,
    (e) culture concepts,
    (f) current world affairs.
2. Attention to patriotism and Americanism at every grade level, with a study of the major ideologies at the upper grade levels.
3. Opening the "closed" ethical and controversial areas.

4. A planned and systematic study of economics through the grades, particularly as it relates to the American free enterprise system.

5. A primary grade program that is realistic in terms of the needs and interests of the child today.

6. The omission of content presently included in the social studies program that is unrelated to the social sciences.

7. A reorganization of courses for grades seven through twelve which permits a "back-to-back" or two-year sequence in successive grades to provide greater depth study with less repetition of the two areas assigned to these grades: (a) U.S. history, geography, government and problems, and (b) world history, geography and cultures. (This change was less frequently mentioned but received increasing comment in the latter part of the period studied.)

Methodology

1. The unit for correlating and integrating content from the various social sciences as well as from other curriculum areas, particularly for the elementary school.

2. An inquiry-centered approach, variously termed problem solving, critical thinking, reflective thinking, and so on.

3. A familiarity and experience with the research methods of the several social sciences.

SUMMARY: ANALYSIS OF STATE AND LOCAL SOCIAL STUDIES PROGRAMS

1. *The fifty state departments of education are updating the social studies*

The persons responsible for designing the curriculum at state and local levels are actively working on the problem, as the following tabulation indicates:

(a) Of the 39 state departments of education that prepare curriculum guides or courses of study, 36 recently have been or now are engaged in revision of their guides. The other 3 are involved in preparing special materials for the social studies, although not revising their guides.

29 are revising from kindergarten or grade one to grade twelve

5 are revising from grades seven to twelve

2 are revising the elementary bulletin
6 are preparing their first social studies guide

(b) The eleven state departments of education which do not prepare curriculum guides or courses of study are actively concerned with updating the program in one of the following ways:

Reviewing and/or revising scope and sequence bulletins, minimum standards or a state framework of courses
Preparing new supplementary materials in the field to update the program
Assisting local school units which are re-examining the curriculum

2. *Social scientists and educators are working together to design the new state programs*

Scholars from the social sciences are increasingly being included in the major revision studies throughout the nation.

(a) Consultants to the guides revised in the 1958–1960 period were largely social studies educators.
(b) Consultants to almost all the revision studies since 1961 have also included social scientists.

3. *The old historical framework is being replaced*

The frameworks upon which many of the new programs are built represent the first major attempts to derive content from all the social science disciplines. In some cases it represents greater integration of the social sciences; in others it has resulted in less unity and more emphasis on the individual disciplines.

4. *The old sequence pattern is being broken*

The pattern of sequence which has prevailed for many years, largely recommended by a national committee in 1916 (1), has been broken in the new programs developed by the state departments of education. Because many of the revision studies were incomplete when the study was closed (June, 1963), the extent and directions of change could not be fully evaluated. Reports indicate that major changes over previous programs may be expected in a number of states, notably:

Louisiana, Colorado, New Hampshire, New York, Wisconsin and Wyoming.

(a) *Primary grades, Kindergarten through grade three.* In ten of the twelve new state programs for the primary grades the expanding-horizon concept (home, neighborhood, community) was broadened considerably. Conscious efforts were made to expand the horizon and add depth. For example:

   (1) The early development of basic concepts from the social sciences;
   (2) Opportunities for extending topics to a state, national and world setting
   (3) Specified map study skills
   (4) Comparative studies of here and now with the far away in space and time
   (5) Current events

(b) *Grades four through twelve*

   (1) 12 states revised programs, grades four through six
   (2) 17 states revised programs, grades seven through nine
   (3) 15 states revised programs, grades ten through twelve

Table 1 illustrates the following changes appearing in the programs for grades four through twelve:

   (1) The sequence pattern has been broken at grades four, six, nine and twelve
   (2) Though the study of the U.S. remains at grades five, eight and eleven, a new emphasis is given at each grade
   (3) There is a small beginning of the "back-to-back" approach (a two-year sequence of a related area)

The curriculum guides and questionnaire responses from 57 local school units showed that the changes being recommended at state levels were being implemented at the local levels in a variety of unique ways.

5. *Some changes in objectives are appearing*

There were fewer changes in the objectives for the new programs than in the content. The broad objectives related to perpetuating a democratic society through the development of an informed and responsible citizenry were similar in all the new guides and also common to the former programs. The objective varied only in the degree of increased emphasis on patriotism and dedication to preserving the democratic way of life.

Some of the specific knowledge, understandings, attitudes, values, beliefs and skills that were considered necessary for developing the kinds of citizens needed in today's democratic society were not common to the earlier objectives. These reflect:

(a) the new viewpoint of the several social sciences;

(b) the methodology of the social scientists;

(c) the common concerns for the rapidly changing world scene. For example:

> No longer can the education of individuals be directed toward adjustment of the *status quo*. It must be directed toward understanding change, evaluating changes, directing change, and making the necessary personal adjustment to change. (2)

(d) the general belief that tomorrow's citizens must work from a broader base of knowledge in solving the human problems of a world society, engendered by recent technological advances.

6. *Some changes in methodology are appearing*

(a) Some form of grouping into basic or terminal programs for slow learners and specialized courses for the superior students was common to all new secondary guides and to many of the junior high programs.

(b) Team teaching was recommended in a few instances, but in most cases was suggested for study by the local unit, particularly at the senior high level.

(c) Teaching the skills and providing opportunities for individual research was encouraged. (3)

(d) Teaching to develop skills in problem solving, critical thinking, decision making and self-direction was recommended. (3)

(e) Television was mentioned frequently for study by the local unit as a source of possible advantages.

(f) Selecting fewer issues and teaching in depth ("postholing") was often considered a desirable replacement for past efforts to cover the area and time span assigned to a course.

(g) Wider use of resources (library resources, community facilities and audio-visual teaching aids).

TABLE 1
Common Social Studies Sequence Patterns of the Two Periods, 1930–1950 and 1958–1963

	Common Sequence (1930–1950)	Common Sequence (1958–1963)	Exceptions (1958–1963)
Fourth Grade	Type Communities Around the World	The State (in a regional setting)	3—combined study of state with type communities in state, U.S. and world; 2—retained old topic
Fifth Grade	U.S. History and Geography	U.S. History and Geography (Canada included in 7; attention specified to social, economic and cultural aspects in 7; emphasis to Colonial period)	None
Sixth Grade	Old World Backgrounds and Geography of Eastern Hemisphere	Western Hemisphere other than U.S., or Latin America only.	3—retained old topic though modified to emphasize culture areas 1—U.S. History following U.S. Geography in grade 5
Seventh Grade	Geography (Diversity in areas of world to be studied)	Geography of Non-Western World (99—Geography of Eastern Hemisphere; 4—Geography of World with emphasis on non-Western nations)	1—Geography Western Hemisphere; 1—U.S. History (Emphasis 1776 through Reconstruction) 2—combined Geography of World with 1 semester state study
Eighth Grade	U.S. History	U.S. History and/or Geography and/or Government (7 combined study of state; focus on early American history, prior to or including Civil War period)	None

TABLE 1 (Cont'd.)

Ninth Grade	Civics	A World Study (World Geography in 7; World Geography and 1 semester U.S. Government in 1; World Cultures or World Civilizations in 3; Part of 2-year sequence)	2—State History and Geography and Government 1—Local Community 1—U.S. History and Basic American Institutions (Part of 2-year sequence)
Tenth Grade	World History	World History or World Civilizations (Greater attention to non-Western World, new nations and modern times)	1—U.S. History and Government, 2-year sequence
Eleventh Grade	U.S. History and Government	U.S. History and Government (Emphasis from post-Civil War to present; American institutions, conflicting ideologies and economic systems) 3—part of 2-year sequence, grades eleven and twelve	None
Twelfth Grade	Problems of Democracy	8—Problems or 8—U.S. Government and/or a single social science	1—World Culture

SUMMARY: ANALYSIS OF MAJOR NATIONAL AND REGIONAL SOCIAL STUDIES PROJECTS

1. *The projects' proposed programs are radical departures from:*

(a) the prevailing social studies programs in the public schools;

(b) the new programs of the various state departments of education;

(c) the programs being developed by any of the other new project groups.

The programs are similar only in that they are content-strong and built upon broad generalizations from the social sciences. The content, emphases and sequence to develop the "big ideas" differ greatly from project to project.

2. *The projects represent a tremendous manpower base and often have substantial financial support*

Scholars from some or all of the following fields are helping to design the variety of new social studies programs for the schools: archaeology, anthropology, economics, education (representing public schools and colleges of education), ethnology, geography, history, philosophy, political science, social psychology and sociology.

The two projects cited below are among the largest new projects that illustrate the above findings:

(a) THE ESI–ACLS PROJECT. (Educational Services, Incorporated and the American Council of Learned Societies Social Studies Curriculum Project: Curriculum Development Program in the Humanities and Social Sciences), which based its program upon a structure of generalizations, "takes the nature of society, its structure and its changes over time, as the main focus." (4) The sequence begins with a study of relatively simple (primitive) societies in the primary grades and advances to the beginnings of urban life and the earliest civilizations in the middle grades and to the larger communities of modern society in the ninth grade. The programs for grades ten, eleven and twelve are presently under construction. (In terms of scope, financial backing and numbers of scholars actively at work, this is the largest project under way.)

(b) THE GCSSP. (Greater Cleveland Social Studies Program). A highly structured program which develops sequential generalizations from philosophy and logic as well as from each of the seven social sciences, GCSSP is built upon a greatly modified expanding-horizon sequence for grades kindergarten through three. A chronological approach from ancient to modern times is the theme for grades four through eight and is repeated for grades nine through twelve. (5)

The present study supports the conclusion that the social studies program is moving from one era to another that is radically different and as yet uncharted. Although the ferment is widespread and new proposals are legion, coming from scholars in all the related disciplines, from all the national professional organizations concerned with the field and from almost all the state departments of education, there are some indications of the directions the new program will take.

Because every recommendation and proposal reported in the sources investigated in the study have placed greater attention on the subject matter and the methods of inquiry of each of the social sciences, the new social studies emerging from this period of unprecedented unrest in the field will:

(1) be a unified, highly structured, content-strong program, built upon a framework adequate for deriving more content from all the social sciences;

(2) begin earlier and be required longer;

(3) be taught from an inquiry-centered approach, utilizing the methodology of the social sciences;

(4) be directed toward more of the world at every grade level, and

(5) try to build more understanding of and appreciation for the American democratic society and its economic system.

REFERENCES

1. National Education Association. *The Social Studies in Secondary Education,* A Report of the Committee on Social Studies of the Committee on the Reorganization of Secondary Education, Department of the Interior, Bureau of Education, No. 28, Washington: Government Printing Office, 1916.

2. Illinois Department of Education. *Teaching Social Studies K–9,* Springfield, Illinois: Department of Education, 1963, Page 5.

3. These were found in some of the guides of the 1950's but were common to all new guides of the 1960's.

4. American Council of Learned Societies and Educational Services Incorporated. *A Preliminary and Tentative Outline of a Program of Curriculum Development and Tentative Outline of a Program of Curriculum Development in the Social Studies and Humanities*, Cambridge, Massachusetts, February 15, 1963, Part I, Page 5.

5. Educational Research Council on Greater Cleveland. *Preliminary Greater Cleveland Social Studies Project K–12 Curriculum Chart*, Cleveland, Ohio, 1962.

FOR FURTHER READING

Bruns, Richard F., and Alexander Frazier, "A Survey of Elementary School Social Studies Programs," *Social Education* 21 (May 1957) 202–204.

Cuomo, A. N., "What Problems Do Teachers Have in Teaching Social Studies?", *New York Society Experimental Study Education Yearbook*, 1963, 162–164.

Duffey, Robert V., "Practices Reported by Teachers in Elementary School Social Studies," *Report to the General Research Board* (College Park, Md.: University of Maryland, 1967).

Ediger, Marlow, "Social Studies Then and Now: 1890's, 1960's," *School and Community* 51 (November 1964) 20.

Harap, Henry, and Eleanor Merritt, "Trends in the Production of Curriculum Guides," *Educational Leadership* 13 (October 1955) 35–39.

Wilkinson, Rachel D., "Social Studies in the Elementary School," *Education* 84 (January 1964) 280–285.

Emotional Factors in Racial Identification and Preference of Negro Children*

KENNETH B. CLARK and MAMIE P. CLARK

There is much evidence of an increased necessity and desire in our nation and in the world to attack and solve problems of human relations, particularly those related to racial groups. The writers of this anthology believe that it is the responsibility of the social studies to teach effective human relations and particularly to teach individuals and minorities, as a basis for mutual respect, self-understanding and self-acceptance. This responsibility has not always been demonstrated in the textbooks and other materials placed in the hands of school children. This report was included because it deals with human relations in general, with the attitudes of Negroes toward themselves in particular, and also with the study and measurement of attitudes.

This is an ex post facto paper which is soundly based on previous research of the authors and of others. Considering the problems of using individual interviews as the data gathering device, a very good sample of 160 children was selected representing various ages, geographic origins, and skin colorings. A careful analysis and discussion of the data is followed by comparisons with data drawn from spontaneous comments by the children and from clinical experience.

Other related selections in this volume include Homze's study of interpersonal relations in children's literature (Chapter 3), Rogers and Long's study of social sensitivity (Chapter 4), and Stright's study of attitudes (Chapter 5). Particular attention is called to the books by Noar and by Havighurst and Neugarten in "For Further Reading."

THE PROBLEM

It has been shown (1) that at each age level from three years through seven years, Negro children have a well developed knowledge of the

* From *Journal of Negro Education* 19 (Summer 1950) 341–350. Reprinted with permission of the publisher and Kenneth B. Clark, President, Metropolitan Applied Research Center, and Professor, The City University of New York, and Mamie P. Clark, Executive Director of the Northside Center for Child Development, New York City.

concept of racial differences between "white" and "colored" as this is indicated by the characteristic of skin color—and that this knowledge develops more definitely from year to year to the point of absolute stability at the age of seven. It was further shown that the dynamics of self-identification in medium and dark-skinned children is somewhat different and more stable than in light-skinned children. There were no significant differences between Northern and Southern children in the awareness of racial differences.

Previous studies have shown that the majority of these subjects prefer a *white* skin color and reject a brown skin color. This preference was found to decrease gradually from four through seven years. This tendency to prefer a white skin color was most pronounced in children of light skin color and least so in dark children. Northern children had a more definite preference for white skin color than children in Southern communities.

The specific problem of this study is a further analysis of the dynamics of racial attitudes in Negro children.

This paper presents results from one of the several techniques devised and used by the authors to investigate the development of racial identification and preference in Negro children. Results presented here are from the Coloring test and from spontaneous remarks of the children as they responded to other experimental techniques. A few excerpts from presently observed clinical cases are also appended.

PROCEDURE

In addition to the Doll and Line Drawing techniques described in the previously published material, the five-, six-, and seven-year-old subjects were given a Coloring test.

This test consisted of a sheet of paper on which there were outline drawings of a leaf, an apple, an orange, a mouse, a boy, and a girl. A box of crayons, including the usual assortment and brown, black, white, and tan, was given to the child. Each child was asked first to color the objects and the mouse in order to determine whether there was a stable concept of the relationship of color to object. If the child passed this portion of the test he was then told: "color this little boy (or girl) the color that you are. This is _____ (child's name), color him (or her) the color you are." After this request was complied with the child was then told: "Now this is a little girl, (or boy). (2) Color her (or him) the color you like little boys (or girls) to be."

There was a total of 160 subjects whose responses on the Coloring test were stable enough to analyze. The following tabulation shows the number of subjects according to age, region in which they lived, and skin color:

	5 year	6 year	7 year	Totals
Southern				
Light	0	3	1	4
Medium	3	14	19	36
Dark	3	13	10	26
Northern:				
Light	11	7	7	25
Medium	15	18	13	46
Dark	6	8	9	23
Totals	38	63	59	160

RESULTS

Identification Based upon Coloring Test

The results of the Coloring test reveal an extensive pattern of the basic dynamics which formed the context of the racial preferences and identification of these children. In the main the responses fell into the following categories: reality responses, phantasy responses, and irrelevant or escape responses. Reality responses were those in which the children colored the outline drawing of a child with a color reasonably related to their own skin color. Phantasy responses were those in which the child colored his representation in a color markedly different (*i.e.*, very much lighter, white, yellow, etc.) from his own skin color. Irrelevant or escape responses were those in which a child who had colored the leaf, apple, orange, and mouse in realistic and relevant colors, colored his own representation or preference in a bizarre fashion (*i.e.*, purple, red, green, etc.).

A qualitative observation of the responses of these children as they worked indicated that in general they colored themselves with painstaking care, as compared to the matter-of-fact manner in which they colored the leaf, apple, orange, and mouse. This was true except in those cases which were classified as escape responses; where the child engaged in marked random scribbling when asked to color himself.

In general, with the exception of escape responses, the children tended to color themselves with a noticeably lighter color than their own and applied much less pressure than when coloring the objects and the mouse.

The results in Table 1 support the previous finding that the majority of these children were able to make identifications based on the reality of their own skin color. The higher percentage of reality identifications found in the coloring technique, 88 per cent, as compared with 66 per cent found when using the doll technique, reflects that: (1) in the Coloring test it was considered a reality response for a very light-skin child to color himself as white; and (2) three- and four-year olds were not used in the Coloring test.

TABLE 1
*Identification of all Subjects
on Coloring Test*

	Number	Per Cent
Reality response	141	88
Phantasy response	8	5
Irrelevant response	11	7

Table 2 strongly supports previously published results with the line-drawing and doll techniques. There is a general increase, with age, in the per cent of subjects who make correct racial identification in terms of their own skin color. Phantasy responses decrease with age. Irrelevant or escape responses decrease sharply with age, disappearing at the seven year level.

TABLE 2
*Identification of Subjects at Each Age
Level on Coloring Test*

	5 Year		6 Year		7 Year	
	No.	%	No.	%	No.	%
Reality response	30	80	54	86	57	97
Phantasy response	2	5	4	6	2	3
Irrelevant response	6	15	5	8	–	–

Table 3 further substantiates the previous finding that some of the factors and dynamics involved in racial identification are substantially the same for the dark and medium children, in contrast to dynamics for the light children.

TABLE 3
Identification of Subjects in Light, Medium, and Dark Skin Color Groups on Coloring Test

| | Light | | Medium | | Dark | |
	No.	%	No.	%	No.	%
Reality response	29	100	70	85	42	86
Phantasy response	—	—	3	4	5	10
Irrelevant response	—	—	9	11	2	4

It can be seen from Table 3 that 15 per cent of the medium children and 14 per cent of the dark children made phantasy responses (colored themselves white or yellow) or gave irrelevant or escapist responses (colored themselves in a bizarre color such as green, red, etc.). The 100 per cent reality responses of the light children represent the authors' decision to classify their coloring of themselves as white or yellow as a reality response—since such a response appears to be an indication of the child's concept of reality, based upon a concrete perceptual fact. Of these 29 light-colored children, 10 colored themselves light brown, indicating a growing awareness of social reality which is in contrast to perceptual reality.

That there are no significant differences between Northern and Southern children in self-identification, confirms previous findings.

TABLE 4
Identification of Subjects in Northern (Mixed Schools) and Southern (Segregated Schools) Groups on Coloring Test

| | North | | South | |
	No.	%	No.	%
Reality response	81	86	60	91
Phantasy response	7	8	4	6
Irrelevant response	6	6	2	3

Color Preference Based Upon Coloring Test Results

Table 5 indicates that 48 per cent of the subjects colored their preferences in brown, 36 per cent of them colored their preferences in white, and 16 per cent used a bizarre or irrelevant color. When all of the children refusing to use the color brown or black are considered, it is sig-

TABLE 5
Color Preference of all Subjects on Coloring Test

	Number	%
Brown or black	77	48
White or yellow	58	36 ⎱ 52%
Irrelevant color	25	16 ⎰

nificant that 52 per cent of this total group rejects the color brown. Only 5 of the 77 children who colored their preference brown or black used the black crayon. These results tend to support previous results, although the trend was seen more definitely with the Dolls test.

Table 6 again substantiates the previous finding that the rejection of brown color decreases with age. At the seven year level, for the first time with any of the techniques used, the majority (65%) of the children indicate their preference for brown color. However, even at age seven a sizable percentage (35%) of the group rejects the brown or black color by coloring their preference white or making an escapist response to the test.

Table 7 indicates that for the light and medium children the percentage of preference for the brown color and rejection of this color is

TABLE 6
Color Preferences of Subject at Each Age Level on Coloring Test

	5 year		6 year		7 year	
	No.	%	No.	%	No.	%
Brown	14	37	25	40	38	65
White	11	29 ⎱ 63	32	50 ⎱ 60	15	25 ⎱ 35
Irrelevant color	13	34 ⎰	6	10 ⎰	6	10 ⎰

TABLE 7
*Color Preferences of Light, Medium, and Dark Skin
Color Groups on Coloring Test*

	Light		Medium		Dark	
	No.	%	No.	%	No.	%
Brown	15	52	42	51	20	41
White	11	38 ⎱ 48	26	32 ⎱ 49	21	43 ⎱ 59
Irrelevant color	3	10 ⎰	14	17 ⎰	8	16 ⎰

about the same. Both groups are equally divided in preferring and rejecting the brown color. On the other hand, only 41 per cent of the dark children prefer brown while 43 per cent prefer white and 16 per cent escape the issue by making bizarre responses. Altogether 59 per cent of the dark children rejected brown. This finding is at variance with the results from the Dolls test which showed the darker children showing less preference for the white and a higher preference for the brown doll compared to the light children. This discrepancy might be explained by the fact that the Coloring test appears to be a more sensitive method for bringing out some of the subtleties, complexities and conflicts involved in the pattern of children's attitudes toward skin color. The fact that 16 per cent of the dark children and 17 per cent of the medium children make irrelevant responses to the request for coloring their preference would seem to suggest a conflict in this area which this method is capable of detecting and which these results reflect.

Table 8 indicates a significant difference between Northern and Southern children in their skin color preferences. A substantial majority of the Southern children (70%) color their preference brown while only 36 per cent of the Northern children indicate a preference for brown. On the other hand 44 per cent of the Northern children color their preference white while only 25 per cent of the Southern children do so. It is significant to note from Table 8 that additional evidence of greater emotional conflict in the Northern children is suggested by the fact that 20 per cent of these children made an irrelevant response (colored their preference in a bizarre color). Only 5 per cent of the Southern children colored their preference in a bizarre color.

It cannot be argued that the greater tendency of the Northern subjects to color their preferences white was merely a reflection of the fact that there were 25 light children found in the Northern sample and only 4 light children in the Southern sample.

TABLE 8
Color Preferences of Subjects in Northern (Mixed Schools) and Southern (Segregated Schools) Group on Coloring Test

| | North | | South | |
	No.	%	No.	%
Brown	34	36	46	70
White	41	44	17	25
Irrelevant color	19	20	3	5

The evidence against this assumption is found in the following Table 9 which compares the preferences of Northern and Southern 6 and 7-year-old dark and medium children only.

TABLE 9
Preference of Northern and Southern Medium and Dark Children
(6 and 7 Years Old) (Medium and Dark Combined)

	6 Year				7 Year			
	North (N = 26)		South (N = 27)		North (N = 22)		South (N = 29)	
	No.	%	No.	%	No.	%	No.	%
Brown	4	15	18	67	13	60	23	80
White	20	77	8	30	4	18	5	17
Irrelevant	2	8	1	3	5	22	1	3

It is clear from the results in Table 9 that the greater tendency of Northern children to prefer white or give an irrelevant or escapist response, compared to Southern children, is a consistent fact even when only the medium and dark children are compared. A substantial majority of the Northern dark and medium 6-year-old children (77%) color their preferences *white*—while 67 per cent of the Southern dark and medium children of this age color their preference *brown.*

Eighty per cent of these Southern 7-year-olds color their preference brown compared to 60 per cent of the Northern dark and medium 7-year-olds who color their preference brown. While there is a substantial increase in indicated preference for brown from 6- to 7-year-old Northern children it should be pointed out that even at the 7-year level 40 per cent of the Northern children are still indicating a preference for white or giving an escapist response to the request for a preference coloring. This fact is considered further indication of a greater degree of emotional conflict centering around racial or skin color preference in the Northern children.

Spontaneous Comments

Southern children have nearly three times as many spontaneous explanations of their choices of brown or white in the preference series as do Northern children; 54 such comments come from Southern children and 20 from Northern. This might be considered as being indicative of the greater preoccupation of these Southern children with racial matters, or a greater spontaneity on their part in reference to this subject, or an attempt on the part of the Northern children to have as little contact with a probably disturbing or painful area as possible—to repress their anxiety and to say as little as possible. Some evidence in support of this latter hypothesis is the fact that for the most part only the Northern children refused to continue in the experiment when they were confronted with the task of identifying with a brown-skin color after they had already negated the brown and indicated a preference for white.

In classifying the types of spontaneous responses made by those children who explained their choices, the following categories emerged:

(1) Explanation in terms of color as the definite and deciding factor.
(2) Explanation in terms of ugly or pretty.
(3) Explanation in terms of dirty or clean.
(4) Evasive explanation.
(5) Explanations with the use of the epithet "nigger."

Fifty-three per cent of the explanations of the Southern children were in terms of the skin color or race of the dolls which they chose. Thirty-two per cent were explained in terms of the ugliness of the colored doll and the prettiness of the white doll (an occasional child chose the brown doll in terms of its prettiness.) Nine per cent of the children sought explanations, the function of which seemed evasive, 4 per cent made their explanations in terms of the brown doll or themselves being a "nigger" and only 2 per cent in terms of "dirty" or "clean."

For the Northern children, the picture is somewhat different. Forty-five of these Northern children who explained their choice explained

TABLE 10
Types of Explanations Offered for Preference Choices

| | North (N = 20) | | South (N = 54) | |
	No.	%	No.	%
Color				
Bk—Wh	9	45	29	53
Ugly—Pretty	2	10	17	32
Dirty—Clean	1	5	1	2
Evasive	8	40	5	9
"Nigger"	—	—	2	4

them in the simple, definite terms of color differences between the dolls. However, whereas only 9 per cent of the explanations of the Southern children were evasive, 40 per cent of the explanations of the Northern children can be classified as being evasive or in terms of trivial and irrelevant factors. This finding tends further to support the assumption that the Northern group (even at this age) generally tends to repress or attempt to escape from the apparently painful fact of the meaning of color differences in American society.

Ten per cent of these Northern children explained their choices in terms of "ugly" or "pretty." Again this explanation was in terms of the brown doll being "ugly" and the white doll being "pretty." Only one of the Northern children explained his choice in terms of "dirty" or "clean." It may be of significance to point out that whereas two of the Southern children explained their choices with use of the term "nigger" to designate the rejected brown doll, none of the Northern children used this epithet.

Some Examples of Spontaneous Comments of Children

1. Explanations of Rejection of Brown Doll:

South

"because him foot ugly"
"looks bad all over"
"looks bad cause it don't look pretty"
"cause its brown—I would like to be brown"
"cause him black—cause his cheeks are colored—it's ugly"
"cause he is a nigger"

North

"I don't like brown"
"cause it looks like a Negro"
"I look brown cause I got a suntan"
"cause it hasn't got any eyelashes"

2. Explanations of Choice of White Doll:

South

"cause he's not colored like these—
      they are the best looking cause
      they're white"
"cause its the prettiest one"
"cause she's got red on her cheeks"
"cause it got pretty hands, eyes, and eyebrows"

North

"cause its got blue eyes—cause its got pretty eyes"
"cause its white—it's pretty"
"my teeth are pretty—they're white—
    my mother is white too"
"I'm a high yellow gal"
"cause that the good one"
"cause his feet, hands, ears, elbows, knees,
    and hair are clean"

Some Data From Clinical Experience (3)

Although data from clinical experience are not conclusive in themselves they strongly support the results and conclusions presented in this and other papers.

It appears that where the child brings up the subject of race at all, his expressions are indicative of negative attitudes toward the Negro race. Following are some samples of the spontaneous expressions of children using identical families of white and brown dolls in free play.

P. Age 9, Medium brown

(Selects only white family of dolls)
"Who likes black men" . . . "My mother is pinky white like" . . . I would never marry a black man" . . . "Lets get her a man with white skin" . . . "No ladies don't mingle with white men but lets us get a man with *light* skin."

T. Age 6, Light brown

(Separates white from colored dolls—pairs off white with colored—they fight—always the white doll wins. When replacing dolls separates white from colored in same box.) "The white and the black should not be in one box."

R. Age 11, Medium brown

(Played taking dolls to doctor—used only white dolls—gave brown dolls to therapist saying she didn't like colored children.) Therapist asked which doll was herself and R. replied "none—I am the mother of them all." When therapist asked which doll she preferred the most, R said, "no preferences."

S. Age 9, Medium brown

(Noted two sets of dolls, selected only colored dolls to play with.) Asked therapist if he were white or colored—when therapist answered white said, "that's good—white people treat you better. I don't like colored."

SUMMARY

Significance of Results from Coloring Test

The data here strongly support the conclusions drawn from the line-drawing and doll techniques concerning the dynamics of racial identification and preference in Negro children.

The Coloring test offers a greater choice of responses to be made than either the line-drawing or doll technique. Thus the tendency of these Negro children to reject the brown color is expressed not only in coloring their preferences white but also in making irrelevant or escapist responses. The latter form of expressing rejection of the brown color points to an emotional conflict centering around some children's evaluation of their own skin color and particularly in their skin color preferences.

This escapist response (in coloring preferences) is most marked in children living in the North and most marked in five year olds but is found in some children in both North and South, at all ages, and through all skin color groups.

The clear-cut rejection of brown as a skin color preference (coloring one's preference white) is most marked in the dark children, but appears to a considerable extent in all skin-color groups and throughout all age levels.

The above is further significant when it is seen that in making self-identifications on the Coloring test only 5 per cent of the children color themselves white (as compared to 36 per cent preferring white) and only 7 per cent color themselves in an escapist manner (as compared with 16 per cent coloring their preferences in an escapist manner). Moreover, in identifying themselves the escapist response of using a bizarre color had disappeared by the age of seven.

These data suggest that by the age of seven the Negro child cannot escape realistic self-identification, but many of them indicate a clear-cut preference for white and some of them evidence emotional conflict (bizarre responses) when requested to indicate a color preference.

It appears from the data that coincident with the awareness of racial differences and racial identity there is also the awareness and acceptance of the existing cultural attitudes and values attached to race. It is clear that the Negro child by the age of five is aware of the fact that to be colored in contemporary American society is a mark of inferior status.

The discrepancy between identifying one's own color and indicating one's color preference is too great to be ignored. The negation of the color, brown, exists in the same complexity of attitudes in which there also exists knowledge of the fact that the child himself must be identified with that which he rejects. This apparently introduces a fundamental conflict at the very foundations of the ego structure. Many of these children attempt to resolve this profound conflict either through wishful thinking or phantasy—expressing itself in a desire to escape a situation which focuses the conflict for them. By the seven-year level the Negro child seems to be developing some stabilizing ideas which might help to resolve the basic conflict between his racial self-image and the negative social evaluation of his skin color. The early age at which this conflict exists and for which stabilizing mechanisms appear in an attempt to resolve them seems a significant finding not only for scientists interested in the problem of personality development but social scientists interested in racial problems and techniques for racial adjustment.

These results seem most significant from the point of view of what is involved in the development of a positive, constructive program for more wholesome education of Negro children in the realities of race in the American culture. They would seem to point strongly to the need for a definite mental hygiene and educational program that would relieve children of the tremendous burden of feelings of inadequacy and inferiority which seem to become integrated into the very structure of the personality as it is developing.

REFERENCES

1. Horowitz, R. E. Racial Aspects of Self-identification in Nursery School Children, *Journal Psychology*. 8: 91–99, 1939.

   Clark, K. B. and Clark, M. P. Skin Color as a Factor in Racial Identification of Negro Preschool Children, *Journal Social Psychology*. 11: 159–69, 1940.

   Clark, K. B. and Clark, M. P. Segregation as a Factor in the Racial Identification of Negro Preschool Children: a preliminary report. *Journal Experimental Education*. 11: 161–63, 1939.

   Clark, K. B. and Clark, M. P. The Development of Consciousness of Self and the Emergence of Racial Identification in Negro Preschool Children. *Journal Social Psychology*. 10: 591–99, 1939.

   Newcomb, T. M. and Hartley, E. L., *Readings in Social Psychology*, New York, Henry Holt and Company, 1947, pp. 169–78. (Clark, K. B. and M. P., "Racial Identification and Preference in Negro Children").

2. Each subject was given a picture of the opposite sex. Study made possible by fellowship grant from the Julius Rosenwald Fund, 1940–41.

3. Some cases in psychiatric treatment at Northside Center for Child Development.

FOR FURTHER READING

Amidon, Edmund, and Carl B. Hoffman, "Can Teachers Help the Socially Rejected?," *Elementary School Journal* 66 (December 1965) 149–154.

deCharms, Richard, and Virginia Carpenter, "Measuring Motivation in Culturally Disadvantaged School Children," *Journal of Experimental Education* 37 (Fall 1968) 31–41.

Deutsch, Martin, Irwin Katz, and Arthur Jensen, editors, *Race, and Psychological Development* (New York: Holt, Rinehart, & Winston, Inc., 1968).

Grambs, Jean Dresden, *Intergroup Education* (Englewood Cliffs, N.J.: Prentice-Hall, Inc., 1968).

Havighurst, Robert J., and Bernice L. Neugarten, *Society and Education,* 3rd edition (Boston: Allyn and Bacon, Inc., 1967).

Hines, Paul D., and Leslie Wood, *A Guide to Human Rights Education* (Washington, D.C.: National Council for the Social Studies, 1969).

Klausner, S. J., "Social Class and Self-Concept," *Journal of Social Psychology* 51 (November 1953) 201–205.

Lane, Howard, and Mary Beauchamp, *Human Relations in Teaching* (Englewood Cliffs, N.J.: Prentice-Hall, Inc., 1955).

Levine, Daniel U., Sharon Albers, and Robert H. Krieger, "The Community Context of School Desegregation in a Mid-Western City," *Elementary School Journal* 67 (December 1966) 113–121.

National Council for the Social Studies, *Social Education* 33 (April 1969). This entire issue (15 articles) is devoted to Black Americans and Social Studies and Minority Groups in American Society.

Noar, Gertrude, *Teaching and Learning the Democratic Way* (Englewood Cliffs, N.J.: Prentice-Hall, Inc., 1963).

Spencer, Thomas E., "On the Place of the Negro in American History," *The Social Studies* 60 (April 1969) 150–158.

Wax, Harold D., "The Negro in Early America," *The Social Studies* 60 (March 1969) 109–119.

An Exploratory Study of the Development
of Social Sensitivity in Elementary School Children*

VINCENT R. ROGERS and ELIZABETH LONG

The position is taken throughout this volume that schools have a major responsibility for process goals—particularly the development of attitudes or values in children. Sensitivity or altruism is only one of many areas of attitudes for which schools should assume such responsibility.

Although the United States has long prided itself on its altruism, population growth, an expanding world, urbanization, mobility, automation, mass media, and a narrowing of the roles of the home and community may have led to decreasing sensitivity. This study is significant not only for suggesting that the school has an important responsibility for developing social sensitivity in children but for describing a useful test ("Who shall we help?") for measuring sensitivity.

This research may be classed as a survey. Further researches should be done to sample segments of the population other than the middle-class, suburban group.

The reader's attention is called to the references listed by the researchers as well as those in "For Further Reading." In this volume there are a number of studies reflecting concern for values and suggesting ways to develop them in schools. These include: Homze's analysis of interpersonal relations in children's literature (Chapter 3), Clark and Clark's study of racial identity (Chapter 4), and Stright's study of attitudes (Chapter 5).

It is perhaps ironic that our social scientists have concentrated for so many years on a study of the most negative types of human beings. As Pitirim Sorokin (9) puts it, we have been cultivating "an ever increasing study of crime and criminals; of insanity and the insane; of sex perversion and perverts; of hypocrisy and hypocrites. . . . The criminal has been researched incomparably more than the saint or altruist.

* From *Journal of Educational Research* 59 (May–June 1966) 392–394. Reprinted with permission of *The Journal of Educational Research,* and Vincent R. Rogers, University of Connecticut, Storrs.

The result is that our social scientists know little about positive types of persons, their conduct and relationships."

Given an increasingly complex impersonal world, the need to develop the "positive type," i.e., the individual who feels a genuine sympathy and concern for other human beings seems exceedingly important. While the amount of attention and financial support given to the study of "negative types" is comparatively huge, the establishment in California of a Center for the Study of Righteous Human Behavior indicates an increasing interest in the altruistic personality, as does the continued support of Sorokin's Harvard Research Center in Creative Altruism.

While there is considerable research dealing with the growth of feelings of sympathy and concern among pre-school children (2, 4, 5, 6) and among college students (1, 3, 7), little information is available concerning the growth of such feelings in elementary school children (8, 10). Research dealing with adult feelings of sympathy and concern for human beings *wherever* they may live (9) seems to indicate that many adult Americans are relatively unconcerned about human misery, tragedy, etc., that occurs any considerable physical distance from them. While we may get relatively excited about a local tragedy, for example, an earthquake in Iran seems to arouse little personal sympathy among us. The purpose of this study then is to measure the extent to which children in grades two, four and six demonstrate feelings of sympathy and concern for people in a series of physical locations progressing from near to far. We are interested in learning more about children's willingness to go out from themselves—to be altruistic—to offer help to people in distress wherever they may be.

PROCEDURES

The population studied consisted of 188 children attending an elementary school located in a largely middleclass suburb of Minneapolis. Fifty-six second graders, 64 fourth graders and 68 sixth graders were included in the study.

A 27-item paired comparisons "Who Shall We Help?" test was constructed. Children were asked to "contribute" $10.00 to people in need in various localities, categorized as either "near" (our state), "somewhat more distant" (our nation) and "far away" (the world). Children were asked to *imagine* that they had ten dollars to give away in each story. If they wished to help the people in the first part of the story, they were to write $10.00 in the "A" column. If they wished to help the people in the second story they were to write $10.00 in the "B" column. The children were told, for example, that many people in Minnesota were without homes because of a flood (Part A). A storm in India had also left many people homeless (Part B). They were then asked to decide to which group they would prefer to give their $10.00. There were three items in each category, i.e., local, national and international, and each item was compared with every other item on the test. In each case the child was asked to decide to whom he would prefer to give an imaginary ten dollars. One-half of the test was given one day and the second half the following day, each session requiring approximately thirty minutes.

All of the second-grade children were tested and then re-tested two weeks later in an effort to determine the reliability of the instrument. A high degree of consistency was found, indicating that the instrument is reasonably reliable. (See Table 1.) Approximately one week following the administration of the test, an informal discussion was held with the second graders to ascertain their reasons for giving away their money as they did; the fourth and sixth graders wrote a short paragraph in which they were asked to tell to whom they gave most of their money and why they did so. The children's responses indicated that they were, in fact, concerned about people and their problems rather than merely expressing an interest in the exotic. (See Tables 2 and 3.)

RESULTS AND DISCUSSION

Second-grade children demonstrated a significant concern for people in other parts of the world. When deciding between their state versus the world, they indicated that despite physical distance these people would need their financial help to a greater degree than would people near home. (See Table 4.)

TABLE 1
*Consistency of the Desires of Second-Grade
Children to Aid People on Re-test Following
Two Week Delay*

Identical Choices	539	87%
Different Choices	82	13%
Total	621	
Subjects	23	

TABLE 2

Distribution of Answers of Fourth-Grade Children to Questionnaire

	Reason	Number	Per Cent
Gave most to the State		0	0
Gave most to the Nation		6	10
Because we must keep our country strong	6		
Gave most to the World		58	90
Because they are poorer than the U.S.	48		
Because there are more people in the World	6		
Because we should not just think of our own country	3		
Because our country could make friends that way	1		
Subjects		64	100

TABLE 3

Distribution of Answers of Sixth-Grade Children to Questionnaire

	Reason	Number	Per Cent
Gave most to the State		2	3
Because our own state should be strong	2		
Gave most to the Nation		4	6
Because we must keep our country strong	4		
Gave most to the World		62	91
Because they are poorer than the U.S.	58		
Because our country could make friends that way	4		
Subjects		68	100

TABLE 4

Expressed Desires of Second-Grade Children to Aid People in Need

	Total	Number	Proportion	Critical Ratio
State vs. Nation	504	265–239	53–47	1.36
State vs. World	504	219–285	43–57	3.18**
Nation vs. World	504	210–294	42–58	3.63***

Children in grades four and six are even more emphatic in their expressed desires to aid people in need that are far from home. (See Tables 5 and 6.)

TABLE 5
Expressed Desires of Fourth-Grade Children to Aid People in Need

	Total	Number	Proportion	Critical Ratio
State vs. Nation	576	212–364	37–63	6.19***
State vs. World	576	150–426	26–74	11.43***
Nation vs. World	576	137–439	24–76	12.38***

TABLE 6
Expressed Desires of Sixth Grade Children to Aid People in Need

	Total	Number	Proportion	Critical Ratio
State vs. Nation	612	284–328	46–54	2.00*
State vs. World	612	136–476	22–78	14.00***
Nation vs. World	612	136–476	22–78	14.00***

Note: One asterisk (*) indicates significance at the five per cent level or greater, two asterisks (**) indicate significance at the one per cent level or greater, and three asterisks (***) indicate significance at the .001 level or greater. Whenever the difference in preferences is significant the preferred category is underlined.

The greatest growth in concern for people farther away seems to occur between grades two and four. There is apparently little change between grades four and six. (See Tables 7 and 8.)

Fourth- and sixth-grade children seemed eager to help other countries largely because they perceive the rest of the world as "poor." Similarly, they (as with the second graders) saw little existing need in either their home state or in the United States. Our country is perceived as "rich" by these suburban boys and girls.

We found results, then, most encouraging in the general sense, assuming that one agrees that the development of feelings of sympathy and concern for human beings everywhere is a desirable goal of social studies education. The study raises interesting questions, however, con-

TABLE 7

Expressed Desires of Second-Grade Children to Aid People in Need
vs. Expressed Desires of Fourth-Grade Children to Aid People in Need

	Second Grade Proportions	Fourth Grade Proportions	Critical Ratio
State vs. Nation	53–47	37–63	3.33***
State vs. World	43–57	26–74	5.66***
Nation vs. World	42–58	24–76	6.00***

TABLE 8

Expressed Desires of Fourth-Grade-Children to Aid People in Need
vs. Expressed Desires of Sixth-Grade Children to Aid People in Need

	Fourth Grade Proportions	Sixth Grade Proportions	Critical Ratio
State vs. Nation	37–63	46–54	3.13**
State vs. World	26–74	22–78	1.38
Nation vs. World	24–76	22–78	.69

Note: One asterisk (*) indicates significance at the five per cent level or greater, two asterisks (**) indicate significance at the one per cent level or greater, and three asterisks (***) indicate significance at the .001 level or greater. Whenever the difference in preferences is significant the preferred category is underlined.

cerning the possible continued growth (or lack of growth) of such feelings as children grow into adulthood.

SUMMARY

While there has been considerable research dealing with the "negative type" in our society, little has been done to investigate the growth of feelings of sympathy and concern in elementary-school children. More specifically, this study was concerned with the extent to which these children might demonstrate feelings of concern for people in far away places when forced to choose between helping "foreigners" and people closer to home. A "Who Shall We Help" test was constructed, which attempted to measure children's willingness to give such help. One hundred eighty-eight children were tested at grade levels two, four and six. The writers concluded that children at *all* of the grade levels tested expressed considerable concern for people in far off places with the greatest growth occurring between grades two and four. A great majority of children at all grade levels perceive the United States as "rich" and in little need of financial help. The other countries included on the test were largely perceived as "poor."

REFERENCES

1. Bender, L. E. and Hastorf, A. H. "On Measuring Generalized Empathic Ability (Social Sensitivity)," *Jrnl. of Abnormal and Social Psychology,* VIIIL:503–506, October, 1953.

2. Bridges, K. L. M. *The Social and Emotional Development of the Pre-School Child.* New York: Harcourt Brace, 1935.

3. Friedricks, Robert Winslow. "An Exploratory Study of Altruism," unpublished doctor's dissertation, The University of Wisconsin, Madison, 1957. 362 pages.

4. Isaacs, Susan. *Social Development in Young Children.* New York: Harcourt, Brace and Company, 1937. 480 pages.

5. Murphy, Lois B. *Social Behavior and Child Personality, An Exploratory Study of Some Roots of Sympathy.* New York: Columbia University Press, 1937. 344 pages.

6. Piaget, Jean. *The Moral Judgement of the Child.* New York: Harcourt, Brace and Company, 1932.

7. Rettig, Salomon. "An Exploratory Study of Altruism," unpublished doctor's dissertation, Ohio State University, Columbus, 1956.

8. Ruderman, Lilyan D. "An Exploration of Empathic Ability in Children and its Relationship to Several Variables," unpublished doctor's dissertation, Columbia University, New York, 1961.

9. Sorokin, Pitirim A. *Altruistic Love.* Boston: The Beacon Press, 1950. p. 5.

10. Wright, Beatrice A. "Altruism in Children and the Perceived Conduct of Others," *Jrnl. of Abnormal and Social Psychology,* XXXVII:218–233, 1942.

FOR FURTHER READING

Anderson, Richard C., "Learning in Discussions: A Resume of the Authoritarian-Democratic Studies," *Harvard Educational Review* 29 (Summer 1959) 201–215

Chesler, Mark, and Robert Fox, *Role-Playing Methods In The Classroom* (Chicago: Science Research Associates, 1965).

Crosby, Murial, *An Adventure in Human Relations* (Chicago: Follett, 1965).

Crystal, Josie, "Role-Playing in a Troubled Class," *The Elementary School Journal* 69 (January 1969) 169–179.

Damrin, Dora E., "The Russell Sage Social Relations Test: A Technique for Measuring Group Problem Solving Skills in Elementary School Children," *Journal of Experimental Education* 28 (September 1959) 85–99.

Davidson, H., and G. Lang, "Children's Perceptions of Their Teachers' Feelings Toward Them Related to Self-Perception, School Achievement, and Behavior," *Journal of Experimental Education* 29 (December 1960) 107–18.

Figert, Russell L. "An Elementary School Form of The Dogmatism Scale," *Journal of Experimental Education* 37 (Winter 1968), 19–23.

Harris, Larry A., "A Study of Altruism," *Elementary School Journal* 68 (December 1967) 135–41.

McAulay, John D., "Children's Reactions to November 22, 1963," *Pennsylvania School Journal* 113 (November 1964) 108–121.

Osborn, D. Keith and William Hale, "Television Violence," *Childhood Education* 45 (May 1969) 505–507.

Shaftel, Fannie R., *Role-Playing For Social Values* (Englewood Cliffs, N.J.: Prentice-Hall, Inc., 1967).

Thomas, R. Murray, "Personal Encounter for Social Understanding," *Education Leadership* 24 (November 1967) 497–500.

Using the Strategies of Sociology in Social Education*

BRUCE JOYCE and CARL WEINBERG

One hears much these days about the structure of knowledge and the disciplines but one sees very little curriculum research specifically related to the use of the structures of knowledge. In this action research, the authors identify key structural ideas, search for forms in which children can observe samples of these ideas, develop and test questions to help children find examples, and analyze the social studies curriculum for places to use such structures.

Perhaps not everyone will agree that this is a research study. However, the writers feel that the action study is an important kind of research in dealing with questions about what to teach and how to organize subject matter for the curriculum. Although the research is informal, a sample is used of 60 third graders and 120 fifth graders in groups of 10 to 15, within a normal intelligence range. The data are not reported statistically, but rather anecdotally. However, the findings here are perhaps as important as findings based upon precise data and sophisticated statistics. The procedures of this study can be used in other subject areas to improve curriculum selection.

This study is but one example of research dealing with content in the curriculum; the list "For Further Reading" includes others. Also related to this study is Wade's report on the history and trends in the social studies at the beginning of this chapter.

Recent attempts to use scholarly disciplines in the education of children have concentrated on the proposition that each discipline has a structure of ideas which directs its investigations and organizes its findings. Bruner (1) has summarized thinking about the role of scholarly structures in the education of young children by advancing the following hypotheses:

* From *Elementary School Journal* 64 (February 1964) 265–272. Reprinted with permission of the University of Chicago Press © 1964; Bruce Joyce, Teachers' College, Columbia University, New York; and Carl Weinberg, Associate Professor, The University of California at Los Angeles.

First, the major structural ideas of scholarly disciplines are essentially very simple.

Second, these ideas can be developed in a form that even young children can discover—in childish terms at first and later in progressively more sophisticated forms.

Third, structural ideas can be used as organizing themes in the curriculum; the ideas can be reiterated and rediscovered in more complex and more adequate terms.

Fourth, the child who is taught in such a way that he discovers the structural ideas in disciplines will be at an advantage for several reasons.

Structure facilitates memory; learning how things are related makes it easier to remember facts. Structure provides intellectual power by insuring greater comprehension of the area concerned. Structure facilitates transfer of learning to new situations and new problems. Structure is the language of the scholar. By learning structure the learner is brought closer to the leading edge of a discipline.

Schwab's analysis suggests that structural ideas should be regarded as tentative, changing expressions of relationships (2). Once upon a time knowledge was viewed as a "congeries of well-tested hypotheses" (2). Now Schwab points out, "The structure of a discipline consists, in part, of the body of imposed conceptions which define the subject-matter of that discipline and control its enquiries" (2: 4).

Structure is a network of hypothetical constructs, subject to constant modification, which direct the strategy of a discipline. As inquiry proceeds, new information is gathered, which is used in the development of new structures, which in turn become the principles of new inquiries. Schwab clearly implies that we should teach structures as strategies, as the ever changing guiding principles of the search for knowledge.

The structures of the social sciences may be useful in social education, as Bruner suggests. We have developed a process for translating the structures of a social science into a form that children can discover and use. In developing this process we made three assumptions.

First, structural ideas should be developed from the child's own observations, even as the scientist develops structural ideas from his observations. Thus, structural ideas should not be taught directly so much as constructed out of the child's experience. Approached in this way, structures can be learned as tentative and changing, as ideas to be revised as understanding deepens.

Second, since structures control inquiry within a discipline, it may be that they can be taught as principles of inquiry—as questions to be answered and as means of classifying information. Viewed as principles of search, structures can be learned as strategies that unfold with experience and analysis.

Third, the value of structural ideas in the education of young children remains to be tested empirically. A proposed process for making structures the basis of a curriculum area should include a program of research.

The social studies are most frequently defined as the study of human relationships. The content of sociology is human relationships and the products of human relationships. No discipline applies to the total spectrum of social studies topics more completely than sociology does. For example, the human group is ubiquitous in the social studies (3), and sociology has developed admirable tools for the analysis of groups.

We selected sociology, therefore, to illustrate a process through which the central ideas of social science can be translated into a form that can be discovered and used by young chlidren.

Our program of action consisted of the following steps:

1. The identification of several structural ideas of sociology, namely, those pertaining to the analysis of the human group.
2. A search for forms in which children could observe examples of these concepts.
3. The development of questions that would help children search for examples of the structural concepts.
4. A series of conversations in which we asked the children to examine the groups in which they live in terms of the questions developed in the preceding step. The conversations led to revision of the questions and the forms in which children could observe the concepts.
5. The analysis of the topics now taught in the social studies curriculum of the elementary school to determine where the structures of sociology could be introduced to children and where the structures of sociology would enhance the analysis of problems.

We selected and defined four concepts that are primary in the analysis of the human group. These four concepts are *norms, sanctions, values,* and *roles.*

All the topics we selected had content that is within children's firsthand experience. Actually, of course, the human group has observable forms in most topics in history, in the study of any nation, and in nearly every aspect of contemporary society (3). We restricted our study to content in the children's lives, so that we could test their reactions to our guiding questions without the necessity of teaching a lengthy unit of study.

We defined *norms* as rules that prescribe certain types of action and forbid other types. Norms appear in the family, in the school, in the community, and in peer groups, each of which is studied in the elementary school.

Observable forms of norms in the community include greeting neighbors, cutting lawns, and dressing up for church.

To help children find observable forms of norms, we developed guiding questions, of which the following are examples:

"What are some things that people on our street do all the time?"
"What do our neighbors expect of us? What do we expect of them?"

Observable forms of norms in school include doing homework, coming to class on time, not swearing, not pushing in line, not cheating. The guiding questions included:

> "What are some things that our teacher and our principal expect us to do and would not like if we didn't do?"
> "What are some of the things we expect everyone to do in school?"

Table 1 presents observable forms and guiding questions for norms in the family and the peer group.

Table 2 presents observable forms and guiding questions for the concepts *sanctions, values,* and *roles* in relation to the topic *Community.* We defined *sanctions* as penalties for unacceptable behavior or rewards for conforming to standards, *values* as objects of preference by a social group, and *roles* as normative patterns that are assigned to individuals. For the sake of brevity, we have not included observable forms and guiding questions for other topics for these concepts.

HOW DID CHILDREN RESPOND TO THE GUIDING QUESTIONS?

Our next step was to enter classrooms and hold conversations with children to determine whether our guiding questions would help them find observable forms of the basic concepts. We held conversations with groups of ten to fifteen children at a time. Each conversation lasted from thirty to forty-five minutes. Altogether we conversed with about sixty third-graders and about 120 fifth-graders who represented the total normal range of academic ability.

TABLE 1

Topics, Observable Forms, and Guiding Questions for Norms

Concepts	Topics	Observable Forms	Guiding Questions
Norms	Family	We clean our room. We love our parents, and our parents love us. We do not hurt our younger brothers and sisters.	When we are at home, what are some things our parents expect us to do and would not like if we did not do?
		Our parents feed, clothe, and take care of us.	What are some things we expect our parents to do and would not like if they did not do?
	Peer Group	We do not push or bully. We play fair in games We do not quit. We accept the vote of the group. We defend boys in our-group against outsiders. We join in games. (We do not refuse to play.)	What are some things we expect our friends to do that we would not like if they did not do? On the playground? In class? In games?

235

TABLE 2

Topics, Observable Forms, and Guiding Questions for Sanctions, Values, and Roles

Concepts	Topics	Observable Forms	Guiding Questions
Sanctions	Community	Smiles Frowns Telling our parents Pat on back Money rewards Not inviting us in Not talking to us Not letting their children play with us	What are some ways that people in our neighborhood can get others to do what they believe to be the right thing? When somebody always does things like walking on lawns, that others do not like, what can we do to get them to stop? When someone does the right thing, something we like, what can we do to show him we approve?
Values	Community	Cleanliness (cars, houses) Neatness (lawns, houses) Work Clothes Church-going Friendliness Participation	What kind of things do people we know want for themselves? What do we want for ourselves? What are some things we would like to be? What kind of people do we admire? What are the most popular people in the neighborhood like?
Roles	Community	Policeman Woman Doctor Builder Janitor Real estate salesman Old man	What value do we place on each job? What kinds of different jobs do people have? What do we call some of them? What makes them different from each other?

Nearly all the children were able to cite observable forms of the concepts. The following section contains the guiding questions on norms and some of the responses of the third-graders:

"What are some things that you expect each other to do all the time and you believe others expect of you?"

"You expect them to be quiet in class and do their work."

"You expect everyone to pay attention to the teacher."

"You expect everyone to keep busy, even after you're done."

"You're expected to know your work."

"Well, how about on the playground? What are some of the things you expect others to do? How do you expect them to behave?"

"Well, when you're playing, you expect them not to knock it [the ball] out of people's hands and not to come over and catch it if they're not in the game."

"You expect everybody to play safely, not to run or knock people down or anything like that."

The following section contains guiding questions on norms and some of the responses made by fifth-graders:

"What are some things that you expect everybody to do in this class, ways you expect each other to behave?"

"We expect everybody to do their work."

"We expect each other to work together and get along in what we're doing. You know, to co-operate."

"We expect everybody to put their hands up when they want to talk and not to talk without permission."

"What about on the playground? What are some ways that you expect each other to behave, things you think they should or even shouldn't do?"

"You expect them to want to play your game, and not quit or refuse to play and make it hard for you to have a game because you don't have enough for a team."

"You expect everyone to let you in their game, let you play with them, not in the middle, but when they start."

"Think of your home. What are some things you expect each other to do?"

"My mother expects me to make my bed. It's better to make my bed, or they don't give me my allowance."

The following excerpt, taken from group interviews with third-graders, indicates that these children were able to identify and talk about sanctions used on them and by them.

"What are some things we do to show others that we are not happy with what they do? For example, if somebody is not playing fair or is breaking up our game, how could we show them that we don't like it?"

"You could holler at him."

"You could just move away and not play with him."

"You could tell him that you'll never let him play in any of your games ever again."

"You could tell the teacher on him."

"What are some things that are done here in school when people don't do what they're expected to do?"

"Well, if you were the teacher, you could be very strict with him and tell him he'll get a bad grade if he doesn't do it."

"You could punish him."

"How could you punish him?"

"By putting him in a corner and maybe yelling out his name to do the right thing."

"How would this make him feel?"

"Embarrassed. It would make him feel ashamed."

"What about at home, what could your parents do to make sure you did the things they expected you to do?"

"They could send you to bed."

"Take away your allowance."

"They could spank you."

"They could tell you that they were very angry with you."

"What about some nice things? Are there some things you like that they might do to get you to do the things they expect you to do?"

"Oh, yes. They could buy you things, presents."

"They could give you money."

"They could let you go some place that you wanted to go, like a movie."

The following passages, taken from group interviews with fifth-graders, indicate their observations on sanctions:

"When somebody is not co-operating, say here in class or on the play-ground or maybe even in your home, what are some things you can do to show him that you don't like what he is doing?"

"I could say that I'll tell Mr. Smith if he doesn't co-operate."

"Well, your parents could hold something out, like a present or something, and not give it to you unless you co-operate."

"They might not let you do something you want to do but if you do it, then they will let you."

"My mom might give me a cookie if I go up and do my homework."

"Suppose you do something they like. How can they show you they approve?"

"They can say that they're proud of you and show that they like it. They can give you compliments."

"They could give you extra money, like if you go to the store for them."

"When you do something for somebody, you expect a thank-you."

Responses made by fifth-graders indicate that they are capable of thinking about values:

"What are the most popular boys and girls in the school like? Why are they so popular?"

"Usually the boys are good in sports."

"They're usually good in their work. They get good grades."

"Well, you have to be a good sport."

"What is a good sport? How can you tell one?"

"It's like when you lose or something; you don't holler or complain about it."

"Sometimes when you're out in baseball, there are some boys who say they weren't out, and they argue about it."

We did not attempt to quantify the responses to our questions or to judge their quality, since this phase of our investigation was to determine roughly whether children are able, with respect to human groups they know, to identify examples of concepts the scholar would use to describe these groups. Our guiding questions are a strategy that children might use to analyze groups from a sociological standpoint. These crude data appear to indicate that the guiding questions did lead children to observable forms of concepts.

Several other tasks seem advisable. First, to identify where and how teaching such strategies can be useful in the social studies curriculum. Next, to design and carry out research to discover the effect of teaching strategic questions to children and to identify and test means of leading children to progressively more sophisticated strategies and concepts.

HOW CAN STRATEGIC QUESTIONS BE USED IN THE SOCIAL STUDIES CURRICULUM?

As Joyce has pointed out, the selection of a topic only defines an area of content (3). The approach to the topic determines what content within the topic area is emphasized. The use of guiding questions such as those we have identified may lead the child to analyze social topics in terms analogous to those used by the scholar. If the child studies the Eskimo family, the Japanese family, and his own family by finding answers to the guiding questions we have spelled out, he is in a position to compare the families in terms of norms, values, and sanctions—categories the sociologist uses to analyze the family.

The guiding questions identified for concepts describing the human group should be applicable in many places in the elementary social studies curriculum. Topics such as the home, community helpers, the family, and the neighborhood include forms of the concepts. Studies of Indians, Eskimos, and family life in other lands would be enhanced by focusing on sociological concepts. Observable forms of sociological concepts can be found in the study of the state and the nation, elections, historic personalities and eras. The study of other cultures has long needed a more rigorous strategy.

In summary, the authors believe that the structures of the behavioral sciences can be identified, that observable forms of these major concepts can be found in topics throughout the elementary-school curriculum, and that guiding questions can be formed that will lead children to the structural ideas of the disciplines and provide a method by which children can analyze social topics with an organized strategy.

WHAT RESEARCH IS NEEDED?

Over a period of time, will the use of questions related to important concepts enable children to learn the structural ideas of a discipline? Will repeated emphasis on a strategy of guiding questions enable children to develop a strategy they can use independent of teacher direction? Will such a strategy limit or extend the range of content which children explore and the skill with which they organize and search evidence? We have embarked on several studies in which we hope to answer these questions in part, using the sociological concepts described here.

Further effort is needed to identify the structural ideas of the several sciences and translate them into strategic questions to be tried der research conditions. An attempt should be made, also, to whether to integrate the structures and strategies of the l sciences.

REFERENCES

1. Jerome S. Bruner. *The Process of Education.* Cambridge, Massachusetts: Harvard University Press, 1960.
2. Joseph J. Schwab. "The Concept of Structure in the Subject Fields." An address presented to the Twentieth Annual Meeting of the Council on Cooperation in Teacher Education of the American Council on Education, Washington, D.C., 1961.
3. Bruce R. Joyce. "Humanizing Social Studies Content," *Elementary School Journal,* LXIII (December, 1962), 125–31.

FOR FURTHER READING

Alilunas, Leo J., "An Analysis of Social Studies Content in the Middle Grades," *The Social Studies* 62 (November 1961) 210–218.

Arnsdorf, V. E., "An Investigation of the Teaching of Chronology in the Sixth Grade," *Journal of Experimental Education* 29 (March 1961) 307–313.

Bailey, W. C., and F. J. Clune, Jr., "Anthropology in Elementary Social Studies," *Instructor* 75 (November 1965) 48–50.

Brameld, Theodore, and E. B. Sullivan, "Anthropology and Education: Anthropology in the Curriculum," *Review of Education Research,* 31 (February 1961) 75–77.

Cordier, Ralph W., "The Study of History Through State and Local Resources" *The Social Studies* 60 (March 1969) 99–104.

Fraenkel, Jack R., "A Curriculum Model For The Social Studies" *Social Education* 33 (January 1969) 41–47.

Gill, Clark C., "Interpretations of Indefinite Expressions of Time," *Social Education* 26 (December 1962) 454–456.

———, "The Latin American Curriculum Project: Review and Preview" *The Social Studies* 60 (April 1969) 172–174.

Hellmann, Robert A., "Case for Anthropology in Public Schools Curricula," *Phi Delta Kappan* 44 (October 1962) 43–44.

Herman, Wayne L., Jr., James E. Potterfield, C. Mitchell Dayton, and Kathleen G. Amershek, "The Relationship of Teacher-centered Activities and Pupil-centered activities to Pupil Achievement and Interest in 18 Fifth-Grade Social Studies Classes," *American Educational Research Journal* 6 (March 1969) 227–239.

Hess, Robert D. and Judith V. Torney, *The Development of Political Attitudes In Children* (New York: Doubleday, 1968).

Jarolimek, John, "Curriculum Content and the Child in the Elementary School," *Social Education* 26 (February 1962) 58–62, 117–120.

———, "The Taxonomy: Guide to Differentiated Instruction," *Social Education* 26 (December 1962) 445–447.

Joyce, Bruce R., "Humanizing Social Studies Content," *Elementary School Journal* 63 (December 1962) 125–131.

Kaltsounis, Theodore, "A Study Concerning Third Graders' Knowledge of Social Studies Content Prior to Instruction," *Journal of Education Research* 57 (March 1964) 345–349.

McAulay, John D., "Social Studies in the Primary Grades," *Social Education* 18 (December 1954) 357–358.

National Council for the Social Studies, *Social Education* 32 (February 1969). This is a special issue on anthropology; the March 1968 issue contains five articles on anthropology in elementary schools.

Patrick, John J., "Implications of Political Socialization Research for the Reform of Civic Education" *Social Education* 33 (January 1969) 15–21.

Potterfield, James E., "An Analysis of Elementary Children's Ability to Learn Anthropological Content at Grades 4–5–6," *Journal of Educational Research* 61 (March 1968) 297–299.

Quintana, B., and P. Sexton, "Sociology, Anthropology, and Schools of Education: A Progress Report," *Journal of Educational Psychology* 35 (November 1961) 97–103.

Rosenstiel, A., "Anthropology and Childhood Education," *School and Society* 87 (November 21, 1959) 482–483.

Shunk, W. R., and B. Z. Goldstein, "Anthropology and Education: Anthropology's Contribution to Education," *Review of Educational Research* 34 (February 1964) 72–74.

Smith, Ronald O., and Charles F. Cardinell, "Challenging the Expanding-Environment Theory," *Social Education* 28 (March 1964) 141–143.

The Effects of the Functional Use of Certain Skills in Seventh Grade Social Studies*

SISTER PHILOMENE SCHILLER, S.L.

The topic of study skills could just as defensibly be included in the chapters on Reading, Language Arts, Mathematics, or Science as in this chapter because the responsibility for study skills lies with all school subjects. However, since the content of this selection is social studies, and since some people traditionally associate study skills with social studies, it has been included here. Acquisition of study skills is critical because they are essential to independent scholarship, which is becoming increasingly important. This study envisions these skills as being learned in a functional setting in units. The unit is perhaps our most important device for organizing the social studies program, although unfortunately many elementary school teachers do not utilize it.

This is an example of experimental research using a good size sample of 5 classrooms (150 students) in the experimental group and a similar size control group. The general intelligence level and the socioeconomic level are not stated, except that they are the same for both groups. The experimental program is described but nothing of the program of skill instruction carried on by the control teachers is reported—perhaps due to lack of space.

Related to this study is the one by McAulay on map learnings (Chapter 4), and that by Carpenter comparing a reading method with an activity method in science (Chapter 6). The list "For Further Reading" reflects concern for other skills important in the social studies program, such as thinking skills and creativity.

Mastery of the skills to be used in the learning situation is a prerequisite of efficient study. Indispensable to achievement in the social studies is a command of certain specialized skills which will assist

* From *Journal of Educational Research* 57 (December 1963) 201–203. Reprinted with permission of the *Journal of Educational Research* and Sister Philomene Schiller, Professor of Education and Lecturer in Linguistics, Loretto Heights College, Denver, Colorado.

pupils in obtaining information. Experimental investigations have shown that the direct method of teaching these skills is more effective than the indirect procedure. However, no empirical data are available on the effects of the functional use of work-study skills on mastery of the skills. This investigation was undertaken to contribute to scientific knowledge on this problem in methodology.

The major purpose of this study was to determine experimentally the effects of the systematic and functional use of work-study skills on mastery of the skills and on achievement in the social studies. A related problem was to ascertain the effect of the experimental procedure on the achievement of pupils of three levels of mental ability.

SUBJECTS

The findings of this investigation are based on tests given to 288 seventh-grade pupils attending ten parochial schools in St. Louis, Missouri. The number of pupils who took all the tests was 296; 150 of this number were in the experimental group, and 146 were in the control group. The statistical technique used in this study was analysis of variance of the scores divided into three mental-ability groups. In the use of this technique, it is recommended that equal numbers be used in the groups being compared. Therefore, three equal-frequency subgroups of mental ability were formed in the control group; this process reduced the number of control subjects to 144. Forty-eight pupils constituted each of the three levels of intelligence. In the experimental section, 144 subjects were included; the number of cases in each of the mental-ability groups was 48. The pupils were eliminated at random by the use of the table of random sampling numbers.

The ten schools were representative of the parochial-school system. The five classes of the experimental group were comparable to the five classes of the control group in socio-economic background and in pupil-teacher ratio. The five teachers of the experimental group and the five teachers of the control subjects were similar in teaching proficiency and in teaching experience.

APPRAISAL INSTRUMENTS

Prior to the experiment, the subjects were administered an intelligence test and standardized tests in work-study skills, geography achievement, and history achievement. At the termination of the experiment, alternate forms of the standardized tests in work-study skills, geography, and history were given to all pupils.

The specific tests utilized were the following: the Kuhlmann-Anderson Test, G; the Iowa Every-Pupil Tests of Basic Skills, Test B, Work-Study Skills, Advanced Battery, Form L and Form M; the California Tests in Social and Related Sciences, Geography, Elementary Battery, Form AA and Form BB; and the California Tests in Social and Related Sciences, The American Heritage, Elementary Battery, Form AA and Form BB.

EXPERIMENTAL PROCEDURE

The instructional materials used in this experiment were skill outlines and social studies units. Skill outlines were prepared by the investigator to provide a detailed development of each of the five work-study skills employed in this investigation. Since no detailed social studies units were available for the teachers, the following units were prepared by the investigator: five units on the geography of the United States and three history units on the exploration and colonization of North America.

In the design of the experiment, the parallel-group technique was employed. For 14 weeks, the teachers of the experimental and the control classes followed the instructional procedures. During the first eight weeks, the geography units were taught; for the final six weeks, the teachers taught the history units. The amount of time devoted to the social studies in both the experimental and the control classes was a daily period of 45 minutes. The pupils of both groups had access to the following materials: globes, maps, dictionaries, and supplementary social studies books.

In the experimental group, the pupils used the work-study skills systematically and functionally in the social studies program. The skills employed were the following: selection of reference books, location of information through the use of the index, interpretation of maps, utilization of the dictionary, and comprehension of the data presented in graphs, charts, and tables. To ensure that the pupils understood the skills, the teachers of the experimental group used part of the social studies period during the course of the first and second geography units to teach the skills.

After the work-study skills had been taught, provision was made for the pupils to practice the skills during the process of acquiring information related to the social studies units. Definite opportunities for the use of the skills were listed in the margins of the geography and history units. Topics were suggested that required the pupils to read widely in supplementary books. In obtaining the collateral information, pupils had the opportunity to utilize the five work-study skills. Subsequently, in the presentation of the information to the class in the form of panel discussions and individual reports, the pupils listed the books consulted and referred to globes and maps to establish the specific locale of their reports.

In the control group, the pupils used the work-study skills as they were needed. The skill outlines were not utilized by the teachers of the control group, nor was a definite time set for teaching the skills in the social studies period. The teachers of both the control and the experimental classes taught the same geography and history units. However, in the units utilized by the control group, no suggestions for the application of the work-study skills to the content were listed. The teachers of the control pupils employed their regular methods of teaching geography and history.

In the statistical analysis of the data, the application of the critical-ratio technique to the scores on the initial tests demonstrated that the pupils of the experimental and control groups were comparable in all variables at the outset of the experiment. In the analysis of the final scores, the subjects were assigned to subgroups of superior, average, and limited mental ability on the basis of intelligence quotients derived from the Kuhlmann-Anderson Test. The analysis of variance was used in the statistical treatment of the final scores on the following tests: work-study skills, considered as a group; geography achievement; history achievement; and each of the work-study skills. With respect to each of these variables, the double-classification analysis of variance was employed to determine the following: 1) the significance of the difference between the means of the two groups when the scores were classified according to method; 2) the significance of the differences among the means of the three levels of intelligence; and 3) the interaction of method and mental ability.

FINDINGS

When the final test scores were analyzed statistically, the following results were obtained:

1. Pupils of the experimental group, who utilized the work-study skills systematically and functionally in the social studies, achieved significantly greater mastery of the skills than did pupils of the control group, who made incidental use of the skills. Evidence for this fact was provided by the F-ratio for method, 28.376, which was statistically significant at the .01 level in favor of the experimental group.

2. Statistically significant differences in acquisition of the work-study skills existed among pupils of superior, average, and limited intelligence. Irrespective of the method, intellectually superior pupils achieved a higher mean in the skills than did average subjects, and average subjects obtained a significantly higher mean than did pupils of limited ability. The F-ratio for intelligence, 91.563, was statistically significant at the .01 level. When the t-test was applied to the separate differences of the mean scores, the critical ratios of 7.36, 6.16, and 13.52 were obtained. These ratios were statistically significant at the .01 level.

3. Neither method indicated a significant difference in mastery of the work-study skills at any one mental-ability level. This fact was demonstrated by the non-significant F-ratio for interaction, .224.

4. Subjects of the experimental group, who used the skills systematically in the social studies, attained significantly greater gains in geography achievement than did pupils of the control group, who utilized them as the need arose. Evidence for this fact was provided by the F-ratio for method, 18.365, which was statistically significant at the .01 level in favor of the experimental group.

5. Statistically significant differences in achievement in geography existed among pupils of superior, average, and limited intelligence. Regardless of the method, superior pupils achieved a significantly higher mean on the geography test than did average subjects, and average subjects attained a higher mean score than did pupils of limited ability. The F-Ratio for intelligence, 70.215, was statistically significant at the .01 level. The application of the t-test to the separate differences of the means resulted in the critical ratios of 6.26, 5.59, and 11.85, which were statistically significant at the .01 level.

6. Neither method indicated a statistically significant difference in geography achievement at any one level of intelligence. Evidence for this fact fact was provided by the non-significant F-ratio for interaction, 1.359.

7. In the analysis of final history scores, the non-significant F-ratio for method, 2.844, demonstrated that no statistically significant difference existed between the final history means of the experimental and the control groups when the scores were classified according to method.

8. Statistically significant differences in achievement in history existed among pupils of superior, average, and limited mental ability. The

F-ratio for intelligence, 39.425, was statistically significant at the .01 level. When the t-test was applied to the separate differences of the mean scores, the critical ratios of 4.52, 4.36, and 8.88 were obtained. These ratios were statistically significant at the .01 level.

9. Neither method indicated a statistically significant difference in history achievement at any one mental-ability level. This fact was demonstrated by the non-significant F-ratio for interaction, 1.543.

10. Pupils of the experimental group achieved significantly greater mastery of each of the five skills than did pupils of the control group. The following F-ratios for method were statistically significant at the .01 level in favor of the experimental group: 25.381 for interpretation of maps, 6.889 for selection of reference books, 11.076 for use of the index, and 11.598 for utilization of the dictionary. In the analysis of scores on the test in comprehension of the data in graphs, charts, and tables, the F-ratio for method was 4.954. This F-ratio was statistically significant at the .05 level in favor of the experimental group.

11. With respect to mastery of each of the five skills, statistically significant differences existed among pupils of superior, average, and limited mental ability. The following F-ratios for intelligence were statistically significant at the .01 level: 32.435 for interpretation of maps, 25.520 for selection of reference books, 61.848 for use of the index, 36.905 for utilization of the dictionary, and 56.389 for comprehension of the data in graphs, charts, and tables. In the case of each of the five skills, the application of the t-test to the separate differences of the means revealed that all critical ratios were statistically significant at the .01 level.

12. In the case of each of the five skills, the non-significant F-ratio for interaction demonstrated that neither method operated significantly at any one level of intelligence. The following F-ratios for interaction were obtained: 1.335 for interpretation of maps, .367 for selection of reference books, 2.490 for use of the index, .099 for utilization of the dictionary, and 1.602 for comprehension of the data in graphs, charts, and tables.

CONCLUSION

This study demonstrated that the systematic and functional use of work-study skills in the social studies results in mastery of the skills and promotes a significant increase in geography achievement. A command of these skills will assist pupils in augmenting their store of information. This increase in knowledge will prepare them for participation in national and world affairs and will help them in making wise decisions pertaining to economic, social, and political problems.

REFERENCE

1. This study was directed by Marion U. Blanchard, Ph.D., Fordham University, New York, 1960.

FOR FURTHER READING

Bruner, Jerome S., "The Act of Discovery," *Harvard Educational Review* 31 (Winter 1961) 21–32.

Carpenter, Helen McCracken, editor, *Skill Development in the Social Studies*, 33rd Yearbook (Washington, D.C.: National Council for the Social Studies, N. E. A., 1963).

Collier, Malcolm, "A Question About Questions," *Social Education* 29 (December 1965) 555–556.

Cox, C. Benjamin, "An Inquiry into Inquiries," *Social Education* 29 (May 1965) 300–302.

Fair, Jean, and Fannie R. Shaftel, *Effective Thinking in the Social Studies*, 37th Yearbook (Washington, D.C.: National Council for the Social Studies, 1967).

Howell, Wallace J., "Work-Study Skills of Children in Grades IV to VIII," *Elementary School Journal* 50 (March 1950) 384–389.

Hyram, G. H., "Experiment in Developing Critical Thinking," *Journal of Experimental Education* 26 (December 1957) 125–132.

Kaplan, Abraham, *The Conduct of Inquiry* (San Francisco: Chandler Publishing Co., 1964).

Kemp, C. Gratton, "Critical Thinking: Open and Closed Minds," *The American Behavioral Scientist* 5 (January 1962) 10–15.

Kersh, Bert Y., and Merl C. Wittrock, "Learning by Discovery: An Interpretation of Recent Research," *Journal of Teacher Education* 13 (December 1962) 461–468.

Kliebard, Herbert, "In Search of Modes of Inquiry," *Social Education* 29 (December 1965) 556–558.

Lakey, Charles, "The Discovery Method in Social Studies," *Teacher and Curriculum* (New York: U.S. Commission for UNESCO, 1964).

Massialas, Byron C., *The Indiana Experiments in Inquiry: Social Studies*, Bulletin of School of Education, Vol. 39 (Bloomington, Indiana: University of Indiana, May 1963).

Nesbitt, William A., *Simulation Games for the Social Studies Classroom* (New York: Foreign Policy Association, 1968).

Rokeach, Milton, *The Open and Closed Mind* (New York: Basic Books, Inc., Publishers, 1960).

Sanders, Norris M., *Classroom Questions: What Kinds* (New York: Harper & Row, Publishers, 1966).

Schmuck, Richard, Mark Chesler, and Ronald Lippitt, *Problem Solving to Improve Classroom Learning* (Chicago: Science Research Associates, 1966).

Shaver, James P., "Educational Research and Instruction for Critical Thinking," *Social Education* 26 (January 1962) 13–16.

Stern, Carolyn, and Evan R. Keislar, "Acquisition of Problem Solving Strategies by Young Children, and its Relation to Mental Age," *American Educational Research Journal* 4 (January 1967) 1–12.

Taba, Hilda, Samuel Levine, and Freeman F. Elzey, *Thinking in Elementary School Children,* USOE Cooperative Research Project 1574 (San Francisco: San Francisco State College, 1964).

Current Events for the Elementary School*

LLOYD L. SMITH

This study was included because it deals with current events, an important part of a sound social studies program; the teaching of critical thinking, important in all subject areas; and the use of the classroom newspaper. Since social studies texts cannot hope to keep abreast of developments, they must be supplemented. Because much social studies material may be abstract, or remote in time or place, relevance must be introduced through current events. Children need to develop the attitudes and skills required to keep up—how to read a newspaper, how to listen to newscasts, how to think critically, how to analyze propaganda—and current events instruction is an ideal setting for developing such skills and attitudes.

This study is an example of an action research. The teacher tried out an element of content and technique for 30 minutes a week for a semester with no controls, using pre- and posttests plus observations of each class meeting. Such studies are important pilot researches for later ones using controls, representative samples, longer experimental periods, and more sophisticated data analyses.

Related to this study are those by Schiller on study skills (this chapter), and Lundsteen on critical listening (Chapter 3). Although there are many references (see "For Further Reading") on the need for and ideas about current events, this is an area in which research is needed.

"Under no circumstances may France any longer be considered among the leading nations of the world. She might wish to be looked upon in such a way, but anyone who has read widely in the last few years knows that it just isn't so. One must say that the French no longer belong in a Summit Conference."

"Didn't Russia supply equipment and money for the new Aswan Dam? That means that they will get more help from Egypt. Russia is trying to get them in with its other satellites."

* From *Social Education* 25 (February 1961) 75–78. Reprinted with permission of The National Council for the Social Studies and Lloyd L. Smith, Professor of Education, University of Iowa, Iowa City.

Comments of the type just quoted, coming occasionally with fervor and always with conviction, characterized the critical inquiry exercised by several students of the sixth grade at the University Experimental School at the State University of Iowa during the 1959–60 school year. They were involved in a year-long investigation carried on to assess the apparent values and problems attendant to a directed program of teaching current events at the elementary school level. As students in earlier grades, they had upon occasion discussed major news items as they arose spontaneously within the classroom and had upon other occasions utilized news clippings from newspapers and news magazines as part of the routine of sharing time. However, as a class they had not studied from current events materials common to all in a structured discussion setting each week; neither had they carried the responsibility of preparing and presenting to the other class members background material for understanding current happenings which have rather obvious and immediate effects upon the thinking of all informed citizens.

Are sixth graders mature enough to consider with profit the events which are of such complexity as to tax the thinking power of even the most informed and experienced news analysts and commentators? Or, on the other hand, is a program of current events at the elementary level so restricted to simple features—names, places, and actual behavior of people—that such a study can be little more than another cataloging of information in a program already overburdened with discrete information? These questions formed the basis for the investigation.

That current events are being considered in elementary school classes, even in classes much younger than sixth grade, is an obvious fact that may be determined by recognizing the sale of weekly current events publications for elementary schools. Apart from sheer incidence, however, there remains the question of whether such study is an effective use of school time in terms of affording to the student an opportunity to deepen his understanding of the world around him, the people whose actions have large-scale ramifications, and, moreover, the sources of power which today build the world in which he shall live as an adult in a few short years. If the elementary school student can take these complex ideas and use them as part of his power knowledge in acquiring new insights in future study, the school thus has an undeniable responsibility to teach current events; if the child becomes confused in a welter of words because of the complexity of the modern world's contradictory and puzzling events, then clearly the optimum time for teaching lies later in school life than the elementary school. This is not to deny that current events study, like other school subjects, requires a developmental program of teaching; it is simply to say that the subject is best approached initially in such a way that the student had ready evidence that he is making progress—that because of instruction, he now knows more and understands the subject better than he did a week, a month, or a year ago. This quality of sensing one's progress has often been noted as a possible reason for the relative lack of interest held for social studies by elementary children. (1)

THE TYPE OF INSTRUCTION

The experimental program at the University School was purposely kept simple in design. The attempt was to avoid the glamorous yet time-consuming activities which may themselves become the focus of instruction in favor of an approach which utilized practically all of its instructional time allotment in a directed discussion of current events. The salient features of the approach were these:

1. Instructional time in the class schedule was kept at one 30-minute period weekly. The pupils' preparation for the discussion period came from free time during the school day, or from out-of-school study time.

2. A weekly elementary news publication was used as common material for the discussion. The publication utilized was chosen because all articles in it were reports of current events, contrary to the multi-function of many other weekly publications intended for elementary schools. Because reading proficiency in the class was generally above grade level, little difficulty was anticipated with the reading vocabulary of this publication described by its publishers as intended for use with sixth- or seventh-grade classes.

3. The pupils' preparation for the discussion was carried out prior to the current events period. It usually consisted of reading with care two selected articles in the current issue. Having concentrated their efforts upon two major articles (usually selected by the teacher upon the arrival of the publication each week), the pupils were then free to read the remainder of the publication. Encouragement was given to pupils indicating a desire to find additional information about the topics to be considered from the school library or from material at home, but no assignments of this type were given.

4. Procedures for conducting the lessons were changed occasionally as the need for variety was discerned. In order of the frequency of their use, these three basic approaches were used:

a. *The teacher-led discussion.* For this methodology approach, the teacher read carefully the issue of the weekly news magazine to be used, selected one or two feature articles to be discussed, and prepared thought-provoking questions which would serve as the framework for discussion. The concern was mainly with the selection of questions which called for comparisons, the drawing of inferences, and the formation of conclusions. Naturally, certain questions were designed to clarify the facts as they had been presented in the publication, but the focal point was upon higher thought processes.

b. *The student panel presentation.* Upon a few occasions, variety in presentation was achieved by making a selected group of students responsible for a featured article. It was the students' responsibility to prepare and present background information for the area of news being featured and to interpret for the remainder of the class the article in question. The portion of the class not participating directly listened to the presentation and directed questions to panel members at the conclusion of the presentation. The teacher's role in this type of approach was that of selecting students to serve on the various groups and assisting in finding additional information.

c. *Individual student outlining.* Under the outlining arrangement, three students were assigned to each of the featured articles. After careful reading, one pupil wrote on the blackboard a concise statement concerning the purpose of the article; that is, what it attempted to offer to the reader. A second student placed on the blackboard a summary (usually three or four sentences) of the contents of the article; a third student wrote a single-statement conclusion to be drawn from reading and thinking about the article. These brief outlines, placed on the blackboard in advance of the lesson, served as the controlling elements for a teacher-led discussion.

Once again the simplicity of the approaches used should be stressed. There was no attempt to rewrite the news in a student newspaper or to tape-record news interviews as they might be appropriate, or to assign regular news listening and watching in out-of-school hours. All of these activities might well contribute to current events learning, but are tremendously time-consuming. The central reasoning was that if sixth-grade students can study current events with profit and enjoyment within economical time requirements, we are on safe ground to begin experimentation directed toward finding the value of various types of embellishments for current events teaching. On the other hand, if sixth-grade students must be fed current events only through attractive and time-consuming motivational activities, this might be taken as evidence supporting the postponement of formal instruction until added mental maturity has been gained.

EVALUATION PROCEDURES

Historically, it has been difficult to evaluate programs of current events instruction because of the ever-changing nature of the subject matter. Tests cannot be subjected to trial-and-revision procedures used in more stable areas because the material at each testing period must be essentially different from that of its predecessors. Anticipating this restriction in ability to test the values of the instructional periods with the class in question, it was decided to test through written examinations if possible, but to rely primarily upon observational evidence gathered during the lessons themselves. Each of the lessons was observed by at least one observer who recorded the proceedings in one of two ways: (1) a near-verbatim record of questions and discussion (including replication of student outlines when used), or (2) use of the *Discussion Response Scale,* an instrument constructed expressly for use with the current events discussion. The *Scale,* reduced in size in order to conserve space, is reproduced below.

DISCUSSION RESPONSE SCALE

	Quality		
Type of Response	*1*	*2*	*3*
1. Statement of Fact			
a. New material			
1. Personal Experience			
2. Gained from reading or other means			
b. Personal opinion of fact			
c. Reiteration of previous idea(s)			
2. Inferential Statements			
a. Relationship of two or more previously stated ideas			
b. Relationship of previously stated idea(s) and new idea(s)			
c. Introduction of two new ideas and relationship			
3. Statements of Conclusion			
a. Point of fact			
b. Course of action to be pursued with problem area			
c. Need for further discussion or information			
4. Interrogation			
a. Genuine answer-seeking question			
b. Comparison with previous statement			
c. Rhetorical question			

Thus the observer had two primary tasks: (1) to classify the type of response given by the student, and (2) to assign to it a quality rating. The following descriptions of quality ratings were discussed at length by both the author and the observer and accepted as adequate for the purposes at hand.

1. Unsure of exact facts being used; deviates considerably from the central topic of the discussion; incorrect relationships expressed; questions only to provoke or to draw favor or attention to self; responses have emotional or personal basis only; inferences improperly drawn because of assumption of unwarranted knowledge; conclusions totally impractical in light of existing circumstances; personal animosity toward another pupil apparent cause for comment.

2. Quality answer, yet less than complete; no new information given or evidenced, yet an accurate recapitulation of previous class comments or clarification of own previous comments; facts stated with reasonable accuracy (slight errors of time, place, or name allowable); questions of clarification or verification of another student's comment; inferences partially correct, even if not completely drawn; comments on topics bearing tangentially upon subjects of discussion; conclusions adequate, though not as broadly applicable as might be desired.

3. Accurate and complete statement of facts as presently known and as presented in new medium cited; placing a new, correct idea in the context of the discussion; commenting to the point of relationship of a new idea to previous discussion ideas; penetrating questions of general significance or of necessary detail; inferences illustrating high-level thinking; theoretical conclusions reasonable; conclusions regarding action practical in light of existing circumstances.

There are inevitable differences that arise between raters using a classification scheme such as required by the *Discussion Response Scale*. There are even conceivably some differences that would be apparent within a single rater's ratings for a given response if it were possible to repeat the rating process. The first source of unreliability was investigated through the use of two observers rating the same lesson on three occasions. It was found that although exact agreement certainly did not exist, the classification of response type as well as quality index agreed to an extent that indicated that as a general guide to student achievement, the *Scale* was useful. It was employed upon eight separate occasions by the same observer.

In consideration of the evidence gathered from the use of the *Scale* and its supplementation through the near-verbatim written accounts of other current events lessons with the class, the following conclusions were reached:

1. Sixth graders need not be confined to a simple discussion of facts in a teacher-directed discussion of current events. They can also be brought to the point of drawing proper inferences and sound conclusions about the events occurring at a national or international level. There is an obvious dependency upon the nature of the topic under discussion that conditions the type of response which may be elicited. For example, when discussing an area far removed from any direct experience (the new politics of France, for example), students apparently find some necessity for staying close to the facts as presented in the article studied. On the other hand, personal opinion and personal conclusions are likely to flow freely in a discussion of an event such as the visit of a foreign dignitary or a pending national election.

2. A significant proportion of sixth graders' responses in a current events discussion may be expected to be thoughtful and reflective. With practice, a class at this grade level can keep to the point without interjecting an over-abundance of non-significant personal references. Examination of tallies from the use of the *Scale* revealed that well over 80 per cent of the responses were classified in the upper two quality ratings. If sixth graders are brought to the point of feeling that what they have to say is respected and will be carefully considered by other class members, they will almost certainly exercise added care in framing statements of opinion and conclusion.

3. As in other fields of study, wide variations exist with regard to interest and ability in current events. Students who contribute much in one current events lesson tend also to contribute much in other current events lessons. By careful selection of featured events and pupil participants, a teacher may gain insight into an individual student's interests and abilities, and may even ignite a spark of interest that will in many instances continue to grow through subsequent lessons.

4. It is extremely difficult for a class of sixth graders, even a capable class, to sustain a high-level discussion without regular teacher comment between student responses. In the case of both the student panel presentations and the student outlines, all save the most outstanding students found it difficult to extemporize, a problem which is understandable in view of their relative lack of background information. While such administrative arrangements as panels and individual reports may be advantageous from the motivational standpoint, it is also true that the teacher needs at all times to remain close to the central focus of the activity currently taking place.

OBJECTIVE TESTING

An objective examination covering knowledge in th_ ~urrent events area and pupil attitudes toward the study of current events preceded the beginning of the instructional lessons. A comparable examination was administered after a semester of study. The testing results indicated the following:

1. Approximately equal success with the two tests of knowledge of current events.
2. Increased recognition expressed by the students of the importance of studying current events.
3. General student acceptance of the methodology employed as being interesting and profitable.
4. General student acceptance of the weekly news magazine being used as providing news coverage of high caliber written at an appropriate reading level.

Although not as extensive as might have been desired, the objective testing thus furnished information which supplemented the observational evidence referred to previously.

IMPLICATIONS

It is abundantly clear from the comments which have been presented throughout the preceding sections that our considered judgment is that we need to make greater use of current events in a total social studies program at the elementary school level. In fact, the program begun with the sixth grade is to be extended on a systematic basis into the fourth and fifth grades. Whether other schools should consider a strengthening of this facet of their social studies program is properly the concern of the local school system, and not the province of this report. However, the broader viewpoint from within which our opinion has been formulated may serve as a beginning point for the re-thinking of the issue of teaching current events at the elementary school level.

While current events form a very flimsy basis for an entire social studies program, it would at the same time appear that a study of contemporary affairs is imperative in today's social studies program.

The pace of the modern world is alarming; political events occur each day to modify what basic text material may say about a nation. Television, particularly, brings to the child of twentieth-century America many impressions that events are happening, but at best are only a compressed view requiring much insight for interpretation. The role that the school must play is that of providing time and background for the examination of the world as it changes. Admittedly, events in the future cannot be forecast accurately; this is, in fact, what makes the study of current events a fascinating one—new factors enter rapidly, making what might have been a logical prediction about the future very illogical in the light of the newer developments.

It will not be possible for any school system to outline completely what is to be studied in current events. It is possible, however, and probably commendable, for a local school system to establish basic instructional policies governing the work to be done. What types of news media are to be used? Upon what types of events will attention be centered? What types of thinking are to be fostered by work in the current events area?

The current events program, properly carried out, stands to provide that most important link between gaining new knowledge and the application of that knowledge to something which is immediately important. Within the program, too, can be developed the process of learning how to think critically and to judge realistically how the world works. For many years, current events appear to have been thought of as a part, but essentially an unplanned part, of a sound elementary school program in social studies. That day has passed; today current events understandings are a necessity for the intelligent and inquiring mind, no less so for children in elementary school than for students in secondary school and for adults.

REFERENCE

1. Among the most recent references drawing attention to this quality is the discussion by Professor Chase in Nelson B. Henry, editor, *Social Studies in the Elementary School*, The Fifty-sixth Yearbook of the National Society for the Study of Education, Part II. Chicago, Ill.: University of Chicago Press, 1957. p. 163 ff.

FOR FURTHER READING

Clark, Delbert, editor, *Current Affairs and Modern Education* (New York: The New York Times, 1950).

Gross, Richard E., *How to Handle Controversial Issues,* revised edition (Washington, D.C.: National Council for the Social Studies, 1958).

Kimball, Reginald S., "Researches in the Teaching of Contemporary Affairs and the Identification of Needed Research," in John C. Payne, editor, *The Teaching of Controversial Affairs,* 21st Yearbook (Washington, D.C.: National Council for the Social Studies, 1950).

Kinney, Lucien, and Katharine Dresden, editors, *Better Learning Through Current Materials* (Stanford, California: Stanford University Press, 1949).

Kravitz, Bernard, "Factors Related to Knowledge of Current Affairs in Grades 7 and 8," *Social Education* 26 (March 1962) 143–145.

McAulay, John D., "Current Affairs in the Social Studies," *Social Education* 23 (January 1959) 21–22.

——, "Controversial Issues in the Social Studies," *Education* 86 (September 1965) 27–30.

National Education Association, *Controversial Issues in the Classroom* (Washington, D.C.: National Education Association, 1961).

Map Learnings in the Fourth Grade*

J. D. McAULAY

This study was included not only because it deals with map skills, but also because it is yet another illustration of the use of units as an organizing structure for social studies learning. Maps are of increasing importance in this shrinking and mobile world of ours. They constitute a storehouse of knowledge which the student of social studies must develop the skills to tap.

McAulay's report serves as a good illustration of the controlled experimental method of research in which a serious attempt was made to insure similar control and experimental groups, to control as many factors as possible except one—extensive use of maps—and to carefully compare the resulting data by statistical means. It would be interesting to know how much time was spent per day on the social studies work; also to know something of the validity and reliability of the noncommercial tests used. It would be worthwhile to have this same experiment performed at other age or grade levels.

Schiller's research on study skills (earlier in this chapter) and Carpenter's comparing a reading method and an activity method in science (Chapter 6) are pertinent to the research in this study.

"Geography is in part the study of what man has done to his environment." (1) Skill in the proper use of maps is most essential to the understanding of man's adaptation to his physical environment. Generally the formal teaching of map skills begins in the fourth grade (2) and the pupil is initiated in the study of the globe. (3)

During October, November and December of 1963 a study was conducted in two fourth grades to determine: 1. Are fourth grade children sufficiently mature in ability and social experience to learn map skills early in the school year? 2. Can fourth grade children understand social studies content more effectively through the use of maps rather than through the use of reading materials? 3. Can particular map skills

* From *Journal of Geography* 63 (March 1964) 123–127. Reprinted with permission of the publisher and J. D. McAulay, Professor of Elementary Education, Pennsylvania State University, University Park.

be assimilated in conjunction and association with a social studies unit? 4. Have fourth grade children acquired map knowledge through travel and mass media?

STUDENTS, TEACHER AND OBJECTIVES

The children involved in the study came from the rural areas of central Pennsylvania. The two classrooms selected were situated some 15 miles apart, were within the same school district and thus used the same course and unit outlines. A unit on Pennsylvania was studied in both classrooms during the months of October and November. In classroom A the children were exposed to as many free and inexpensive materials, trade books, posters and illustrations concerning Pennsylvania as could be procured. A globe and a wall map of the Commonwealth were available in the classroom and were referred to occasionally. But generally no effort was made to teach the children about Pennsylvania from the map. In classroom B commercial maps were used extensively. The children were asked to work with desk-size-outline maps and to complete some 15 to 20 map projects. Some trade books, texts and free and inexpensive materials were available to this class but not in such abundance as in classroom A.

In classroom A of 38 children the scores from the Otis Mental Ability Alpha test ranged from 94 to 145 with a mean score of 114. In classroom B of 36 children the scores from the same test ranged from 93 to 138 with a mean score of 112. The chronological ages of the children in classroom A ranged from 8 years 9 months to 11 years 1 month with a mean age of 10 years 2 months. In classroom B the age range was from 8 years 11 months to 11 years 3 months with a mean age of 10 years 3 months. The teacher of classroom A had 21 years of experience in the classroom, 18 of them in the one school and 15 of these continual service in the fourth grade. The teacher of classroom B had 18 years of classroom teaching, 12 of them in the one school and eight of these in the fourth grade.

The unit on the Commonwealth of Pennsylvania, lasting three months and taught in both fourth grades contained the following objectives: (1) to secure an appreciation of the diversity of natural resources within the Commonwealth, (2) to understand the founding of Pennsylvania as a colony by William Penn and the contribution made by the state to the Revolutionary War and the War between the States, (3) to be able to locate and understand the importance of the principal centers of population within the Commonwealth and (4) to understand the interdependence and relationship of Pennsylvania with the neighboring states.

DIFFERENCES IN INSTRUCTION

In classroom A for each objective every child completed either a book report or a booklet; and as a group it completed a work project such as a mural, a diorama, a play, a series of posters or a display of artifacts. The children in classroom A constructed no maps. However, the wall map of Pennsylvania and the globe were used as references and teaching aids during the unit. For each objective in classroom B each child completed a series of maps and as a member of a committee helped to make one large map which was illustrated on butcher paper or helped construct a project involving map ideas. Projects were in three dimensions from salt and flour, built on the sand table, cut from plywood or constructed on cardboard.

Each child in both classroom A and classroom B kept a social studies workbook. (4) The children in classroom A used the notebook to collect individual book reports and work projects. Children in classroom B used the notebook to collect a dozen or more completed maps (5) of Pennsylvania as well as illustrations to explain particular maps.

The following items, themes and/or types of maps were completed by the children in classroom B during the development of the unit. Maps showed: (1) directions north, south, east and west in an outline of the county in which the school is located, (2) the states bordering the Commonwealth, (3) the principal rivers and water resources of the state, (4) industrial areas of the state, (5) principal topographical areas and sections of the state, (6) principal climatic areas of the state (based on average rainfall and average temperature per year), (7) lines of longitude and latitude within the state, (8) the principal Indian tribes in the territory William Penn settled, (9) the first settlements in the colony, (10) those areas of the Commonwealth pertinent to the Revolutionary War, (11) the battles and movements of troops within the state at the time of the War between the States and (12) areas within the state which were considered depressed.

By working on these maps the children were exposed to the following understandings:

1. A map can show the natural and cultural features of a particular area of the earth's surface.

2. The scale of miles on a map (or globe) helps to determine the distance of one place from another. The children learned that maps are drawn to different scales; the larger the scale used the larger each feature appears on the map.

3. Ten map symbols can be used to represent ten different things.

4. The children learned how high above sea level particular areas of the state are located. They learned that altitude refers to height of land measured from sea level.

5. They learned something of the general slope of the land and the general direction in which the rivers flow.

6. They learned that all places on an east-west line are directly east or west of one another and are the same distance north and south of the equator.

7. They were exposed to the meaning of latitude as the distance north or south of the equator, and to the idea that east-west lines on the maps are lines (or parallels) of latitude. They learned that all places in Pennsylvania are north of the equator and therefore in north latitude.

8. The children were taught to locate and place the Commonwealth in relation to the Tropic of Cancer and the Arctic Circle.

9. Finally they were taught the globe has imaginary lines running north and south through the poles and that all places in Pennsylvania located on a north-south line are exactly north or south of one another.

At the end of September 1962 a questionnaire was completed by the parent of each child involved in the study (Table 1). It shows that children in classroom A had received the greater opportunity to secure geographic understandings from the home and from the community. More than half the children in classroom A have a wall map of the earth in their homes; have traveled outside the state; visited another country or lived in another state. Children in classroom B where maps were used freely had little opportunity in the home for developing geographic understanding.

In late September before the unit on Pennsylvania was initiated the children in both classrooms A and B were given that section of the California test in Social Studies II, elementary Form A A related to geographic understandings. During the third week in December the same children were given Form B B of the same test.

Computing by *t test* the gain or loss of geographic learnings from the scores achieved on the California test in social and related sciences, for classroom A $t = .313$ indicating an insignificant gain in geographic

Table 1

Results of Questionnaire Concerning Child's Geographic Understandings Secured from the Home and the Community

Question	Classroom A			Classroom B		
	Yes	No	No ans.	Yes	No	No ans.
1. Do you have a TV set in your home?	35	1	0	36	2	0
2. Do you have a globe of the earth in your home?	17	19	0	7	31	0
3. Do you have a wall map of the earth in your home?	24	11	1	11	27	0
4. Have you travelled out of the State of Pennsylvania?	24	11	1	21	17	0
5. Have you travelled to another country?	14	22	0	4	32	2
6. Have you lived in another state?	18	18	0	4	34	0
7. Have you lived in another country?	4	32	0	1	35	2
8. How far do you live from school?	least distance ¼ mile greatest distance 8 miles mean distance 2 miles			least distance ¼ block greatest distance 20 miles mean distance 6 miles		

learnings during the eight weeks. In classroom B $t = 6.65$ indicating a very significant gain in the eight week period. The standard error of the difference in the classrooms at the end of eight weeks was 1.34. The probability of obtaining two means as different or more different, is less than one in one hundred.

At the conclusion of the three month period spent on the unit on Pennsylvania the children in both classrooms A and B were given three tests. Test one concerned geographic place information on Pennsylvania. Test two attempted to evaluate the child's general knowledge and acquaintance with the Commonwealth of Pennsylvania. Test three attempted to determine if a child could secure social studies information from a map.

From the scores secured the standard deviation for test one was 1.28 indicating that the probability of an equal or greater difference between the two classrooms is less than one in one hundred. The standard deviation for test two was 1.24 and for test three 1.37. The children in classroom B achieved scores on these tests significantly greater than did the children in classroom A.

Three graduate students in the Department of Geography at the Pennsylvania State University examined the notebooks at the conclusion of the unit kept by children in classroom B. The maps in the workbook were graded for accuracy of location, for correct use of map symbols and for indication of map skills. The scale of grading was one to four. The average grade received by the 36 children in classroom B on the first four maps completed was 1.7, the average grade received on the last 4 maps completed was 2.8. The children made considerable improvement during the unit on map work and map understanding.

CONCLUSIONS OF THE STUDY

1. Fourth grade children seem to be sufficiently mature and capable to learn and use map skills early in the school year.
2. It would seem that maps do help fourth grade children understand social studies content more efficiently and effectively. Maps properly used, can be a productive instrument in the understanding of the social studies.
3. It would seem that fourth grade children can acquire map skills and understandings in conjunction and integrated with an on-going social studies unit. It would not seem necessary to teach map skills and understandings as separate entities.

4. Children may have the opportunity to acquire some map knowledge through the home and community environment but such knowledge must still be directed and coordinated within the social studies program.

The reading and study of maps can be incorporated within the unit organization of the social studies. Such incorporation clarifies and expands the unit if the children are systematically taught how to use map symbols and interpret such symbols to secure particular information. Children enjoy map work and if suitable motivation is used the child can quickly assimilate and use map knowledge.

REFERENCES

1. Mayer, Martin, *Where, When, and Why Social Studies in American Schools,* Harper & Row, New York, 1963, p. 34.
2. Ruby M. Harris, *The Rand McNally Handbook of Map and Globe Usage,* 3rd ed., New York, 1960, p. 59.
3. Preston E. James (editor) *New Viewpoints in Geography,* 29th Yearbook of National Council for the Social Studies, Washington, 1959, p. 124.
4. Aquable Newsprint Pad #887. 12″ × 8″ (rough).
5. Nystrom series of Desk Maps No. D D 137.

FOR FURTHER READING

Davis, O. L., Jr., "Learning About Time Zones in Grades Four, Five, and Six," *Journal of Experimental Education* 31 (Summer 1963) 407–412.

Edwards, John Hayes, "How Well Are Intermediate Children Oriented in Space?," *Journal of Geography* 52 (April 1953) 133–143.

McAulay, J. D., "Second Grade Children's Growth in Comprehension of Geographic Understandings," *Journal of Geography* 65 (January 1966) 33–37.

Rushdoony, Haig A., "Achievement in Map-Reading: An Experimental Study," *Elementary School Journal* 64 (November 1963) 70–75.

5

ELEMENTARY SCHOOL MATHEMATICS

Since the launching of the first artificial satellite in 1957 there has been increased interest in arithmetic teaching. The tremendous zeal with which elementary school mathematics and the methods of teaching it have recently been studied has resulted in much criticism and many proposals for improving instruction. This part of the anthology includes research on the following topics: pre-first grade; Piagetian concepts; basic operations; verbal problem solving; newer topics; comparisons with foreign arithmetic achievement; arithmetic difficulties; and attitudes.

McAulay's study of map learnings (Chapter 4) is related to this area.

Three of the research reports for this part (Gray, Riedesel, D'Augustine) are of an experimental nature. Other types of studies include: descriptive (Coxford); survey (Bjonerud, Stright); case study (Ross); ex post facto (Kramer). The studies span pre-first grade through grade seven. Space prohibits presentation of studies to represent some areas of concern to teachers of elementary school mathematics, such as an historical overview; studies dealing with each specific operation; non-pencil-and-paper arithmetic; percentage; measurement; anxiety and mathematics learning; culturally disadvantaged students; the role of drill or practice; gifted students; grouping for instruction; personality characteristics; sex differences; teacher preparation; and evaluation.

For those interested in elementary school mathematics, the list of the publications of the National Council of Teachers of Mathematics would be of value. The *Yearbooks* are an outstanding source of ideas; and *The Arithmetic Teacher* (Washington, D.C.: National Council of

Teachers of Mathematics, N.E.A.), frequently offers research articles and provides a section specifically dealing with research in elementary school mathematics. NCTM began the publication in 1969 of *The Journal of Research in Mathematics Education*. This journal reports research studies and suggested problems for investigation, ways of conducting this research, and the implications of research results for teaching and curriculum development. Three other major resources which the reader should find useful are:

Glennon, Vincent J., *What Does Research Say About Arithmetic,* revised edition (Washington, D.C.: Association for Supervision and Curriculum Development, 1958). This report supplies a comprehensive survey of research studies and reports in relation to questions raised by teachers. It relates research findings to the day-to-day problems of instruction in the various areas of arithmetic. It is practical, yet offers a sound basis for curriculum planning and instruction.

———, and Leroy S. Callahan, *Elementary School Mathematics, A Guide to Current Research* (Washington, D.C.: Association for Supervision and Curriculum Development, 1968). This report brings up to date the above-mentioned source.

Ashlock, Robert B., and Wayne L. Herman, *Current Research in Elementary School Mathematics,* New York: The Macmillan Company, in press.

A rather comprehensive listing of resources is given below for the benefit of those who are particularly interested in research in the area of elementary school mathematics instruction:

American Educational Research Association, "Natural Science and Mathematics," *Review of Educational Research* (Washington, D.C.: National Education Association) 34 (June 1964) 273–285; 31 (June 1961) 248–259; 27 (October 1957) 329–342; 21 (October 1951) 290–304; 18 (October 1948) 337–349; 15 (October 1945) 276–278; 12 (October 1942) 386–404; 7 (December 1937) 545–557; 4 (April 1934) 140–143.

American Educational Research Association, *"Teaching Arithmetic," What Research Says to the Teacher,* No. 2 (Washington, D.C.: National Education Association, 1953 (Robert S. Morton); revised edition, 1962 (Herbert F. Spitzer).

Beatty, Leslie S., "Re-orienting to the Teaching of Arithmetic," *Childhood Education* 26 (February 1950) 272–278.

Brown, Kenneth, *Analysis of Research in Teaching of Mathematics:* 1955 and 1956, U.S. Department of Health, Education, and Welfare, Office of Education (Washington, D.C.: U.S. Government Printing Office, 1958).

———, and Theodore L. Abell, "Research on the Teaching of Arithmetic," *Childhood Education* 26 (February 1950) 272–278.

———, and J. J. Kensella, *Analysis of Research in Teaching of Mathematics:* 1957 and 1958, U.S. Department of Health, Education, and Welfare, Office of Education (Washington, D.C.: U.S. Government Printing Office, 1960).

———, *et al.*, *Analysis of Research in Teaching of Mathematics:* 1959 and 1960, U.S. Department of Health, Education, and Welfare, Office of Education (Washington, D.C.: U.S. Government Printing Office, 1963).

Brownell, William A., and Foster E. Grossnickle, "The Interpretation of Research," *Arithmetic in General Education,* 16th Yearbook (Washington, D.C.: The National Council of Teachers of Mathematics, 1941), pp. 304–317.

Burns, Paul C., "Arithmetic Research That Has Made a Difference," *Elementary School Journal* 65 (April 1965) 386–392.

———, and Donald J. Dessart, "A Summary of Investigations Relating to Mathematics in Elementary Education: 1964," *School Science and Mathematics* 66 (December 1966) 838–849.

Buswell, Guy T., "Arithmetic," *Encyclopedia of Educational Research,* 3rd edition (New York: The Macmillan Company, 1960), pp. 63–74. See 1941 edition for Guy M. Wilson, "Arithmetic."

———, and C. H. Judd, *Summary of Educational Investigation Relating to Arithmetic,* Supplementary Educational Monographs, No. 27 (Chicago: University of Chicago Press, 1925).

Dooley, Sister M. Constance, "The Relationship Between Arithmetic Research and the Content of Arithmetic Textbooks," *The Arithmetic Teacher* 7 (April 1960) 178–184.

———, "The Relation Between Arithmetic Research and the Content of Arithmetic Textbooks" (1900–1957), *Journal of Experimental Education* 29 (March 1961) 315–318.

The Elementary School Journal (Chicago: University of Chicago Press), "Summary of Arithmetic Investigations," 1926–1932; "Selected References on Elementary School Instruction—Arithmetic," 1933–1966.

Fehr, Howard F., "Present Research in the Teaching of Arithmetic," *Teachers College Record* 52 (October 1950) 11–23.

Gane, James T., "Research Should Guide Us," *The Arithmetic Teacher* 9 (December 1962) 441–445.

Gibb, E. Glenadine, "A Selected Bibliography of Research in the Teaching of Arithmetic," *The Arithmetic Teacher* 1 (April 1954) 20–22.

Hunnicutt, C. W., and William J. Iverson, editors, *Research in the Three R's* (New York: Harper and Bros., 1958), "The Third 'R'," pp. 347–429.

Monroe, Walter S., and May Englehart, *A Critical Summary of Research Relating to the Teaching of Arithmetic,* Bulletin No. 58 (Urbana, Illinois: University of Illinois Press, 1931).

National Council of Teachers of Mathematics, *Research in Mathematics Education* (Washington, D.C.: The Council, 1967).

Pikal, Frances, "Review of Research Related to Teaching of Arithmetic in the Upper Elementary Grades," *School Science and Mathematics* 57 (January 1957) 41–47.

Riedesel, C. Alan, *Guiding Discovery in Elementary School Mathematics* (New York: Appleton-Century-Crofts, 1967), "Research References," pp. 461–464.

———, and Marilyn N. Suydam, "Research on Mathematics Education, Grades K-8 for 1967," *The Arithmetic Teacher* 15 (October 1968) 531–544.

Scandura, Joseph M., "Research in Mathematics Education—An Overview and a Perspective," *Research in Mathematics Education,* (Washington, D.C.: National Council of Teachers of Mathematics, 1967), pp. 115–25.

Schaaf, William L., "Selected Annotated Bibliography," *Instruction in Arithmetic,* 25th Yearbook (Washington, D.C.: National Council of Teachers of Mathematics, 1960), p. 32–54.

Sherer, L., "Some Implications from Research in Arithmetic," *Childhood Education* 29 (March 1953) 320–324.

Stretch, Lorena B., "One Hundred Selected Research Studies," *Arithmetic in General Education,* 16th Yearbook (Washington, D.C.: National Council of Teachers of Mathematics, 1941), pp. 318–327.

Summers, Edward G., "A Bibliography of Doctoral Dissertations Completed in Elementary and Secondary Mathematics from 1918 to 1952," *School Science and Mathematics* 61 (May 1961) 323–335.

———, and James E. Stochl, "A Bibliography of Doctoral Dissertations Completed in Elementary and Secondary Mathematics from 1950 to 1960," *School Science and Mathematics* 61 (June 1961) 431–439.

————, "Elementary and Secondary Science and Mathematics Dissertations Reported in 1962," *School Science and Mathematics* 63 (December 1963) 733–738.

————, and Billie Hubrig, "Doctoral Dissertation Research in Mathematics Reported for 1963," *School Science and Mathematics* 65 (June 1965) 505–528.

Suydam, Marilyn N., "The Status of Research on Elementary School Mathematics," *The Arithmetic Teacher* 14 (December 1967) 684–689.

Van Engen, Henry, "A Selected List of References on Elementary School Arithmetic," *Mathematics Teacher* 43 (April 1950) 168–171.

Weaver, J. Fred, "A Bibliography of Selected Summaries and Critical Discussions of Research on Elementary School Mathematics," *The Arithmetic Teacher* 7 (November 1960) 364–366.

————, *The Arithmetic Teacher* (Washington, D.C.: National Council of Teachers of Mathematics), 4 (April 1957) 89–99; 5 (April 1958) 109–118; 6 (April 1959) 121–132; 7 (May 1960) 253–265; 8 (May and October 1961) 255–260, 301–306; 9 (May 1962) 287–290; 10 (May 1963) 297–300; 11 (April 1964) 273–275; 12 (May 1965) 382–387; 13 (May 1966) 414–427; 14 (October 1967) 509–517.

————, "Research on Mathematics Education, Grades K–8, for 1966," *The Arithmetic Teacher* 14 (October 1967) 509–517.

Wrightstone, J. Wayne, "Influence of Research on Instruction in Arithmetic," *The Mathematics Teacher* 45 (March 1952) 187–192.

There is still much research that needs to be undertaken in the area of elementary school mathematics. The following references provide some profitable ideas for research:

Fehr, Howard F., editor, *Needed Research in Mathematical Education* (New York: Teachers' College, Columbia University, 1966), 25 pp.

Glennon, Vincent J., "Research Needs in Elementary School Mathematics Education," *The Arithmetic Teacher* 13 (May 1966) 363–368.

Romberg, Thomas A., and M. Vere DeVault, "Mathematics Curriculum: Needed Research," College of Education, University of Georgia: *Journal of Research and Development in Education* 1 (Fall 1967) 95–112.

Weaver, J. Fred, "A Conference on Needed Research in Mathematical Education, *The Arithmetic Teacher* 13 (November 1966) 594–596.

For discussion of various aspects of research studies in elementary school mathematics (which are also applicable to research in general), see:

Riedesel, C. Alan, "Suggested Content for Research Articles Published in *The Arithmetic Teacher*," *The Arithmetic Teacher* 14 (November 1967) 581–583.

———, and Jack N. Sparks, "Designing Research Studies in Elementary School Mathematics Education," *The Arithmetic Teacher* 15 (January 1968) 60–63.

———, "Some Comments on Developing Proper Instrumentation for Research Studies in Mathematics," *The Arithmetic Teacher* 15 (February 1968) 165–168.

———, "Survey Research in Elementary School Mathematics," *The Arithmetic Teacher* 15 (March 1968) 260–263.

———, "Every Teacher Is a Researcher," *The Arithmetic Teacher* 15 (April 1968) 355–356.

Scannell, Dale P., "Obtaining Valid Research in Elementary School Mathematics," *The Arithmetic Teacher* 16 (April 1969) 292–295.

Arithmetic Concepts
Possessed by the Pre-School Child*

CORWIN E. BJONERUD

Bjonerud's survey is timely, since great attention is being focused upon the pre-school child. As a result of this and similar research in other areas (see Hillerich's study in Chapter 2; Inbody in Chapter 6; and Hampleman in Chapter 7) the content of beginning school years, grades 1 and 2 particularly, is being examined.

Other studies of the arithmetic concepts possessed by pre-school children are cited in "For Further Reading." These studies help build a foundation of facts upon which hypotheses can be constructed and open the door for more research in this area. The date of a study of this nature is an important consideration.

One important feature of survey research is that it deals with a sample which is representative of the entire group about which the investigator wishes to draw conclusions. Since the subjects of Bjonerud's study were pupils in a college demonstration school—assigned to it by the area in which they live—these children may perhaps be more exposed to an academic environment than most pre-kindergarten children. No validity or reliability data are provided for the test questions constructed and administered by the investigator. In terms of socio-economic considerations, the Dunkley study, cited in "For Further Reading," is especially timely.

The first half of the twentieth century has seen many studies made by educators to determine the most desirable time to start a planned sequential instructional program in arithmetic for the young child. These studies have presented findings that vary from initial instruction starting in the first grade to a recommendation that beginning formalized instruction be delayed until the seventh grade. However, these studies indicate that, in general, the young child benefits when systematic instruction starts during his first-grade experiences.

* From *The Arithmetic Teacher* 7 (November 1960) 347–350. Reprinted with permission of The National Council of Teachers of Mathematics and Corwin E. Bjonerud, Professor of Education, San Francisco State College, California.

It is interesting to note that previous studies of arithmetic and the young child were carried out after the child was well into or past his kindergarten year of public school. While formalized instruction in arithmetic is rarely started in kindergarten, an informal, incidental program in elementary number concepts is commonly taught. This leaves educators with unanswered questions regarding the extent of number knowledges and skills possessed by the preschool child at the start of kindergarten.

What do we know about five-year-olds? Actually, there is much to learn about these children as they come to us filled with enthusiasm about embarking on the great new experience of going to school. As public educators, we receive the child after he has had approximately five years of training and experience in the home. We accept the general fact that homes offer a great variety of backgrounds and meaningful experiences. We even go so far as to accept the wide differences among homes. We look at the five-year-old and say he is different from others in his peer group because of his family inheritance, his environment, number of siblings and their age relative to him, and the type of home life, travel, and personal experiences provided. We will go further and accept differences caused by a large number of less evident home experiences as well as by the partially understood pattern of child growth and development.

Accepting these differences, we have a tendency to overlook the specific differences in specific areas of knowledge. Are we guilty of taking the kindergarten child into our schools with only a vague notion of the number concepts that his previous five years have permitted him to acquire? In an attempt to answer this question, a study was made of the arithmetic concepts possessed by one hundred beginning kindergarten children in the Livonia, Michigan, public schools in the fall of 1957. The study was repeated again in February, 1960, with twenty-seven pupils, an entire midyear class of beginning kindergarten children, in the demonstration school on the campus of San Francisco State College in San Francisco, California. The children in the demonstration school are not a select group. Rather, they are all children of this age residing in an assigned attendance area determined by the San Francisco Unified School District.

The purpose of the study was to discover some of the specific number concepts possessed by the preschool child at the time of kindergarten entrance. In no way, whatsoever, has the study been conducted to permit interpretation as an inventory of a child's readiness for formal instruction in arithmetic. Instead, it is hoped that the findings may bring about a closer scrutiny of what is generally accepted by teachers as normal number knowledge at the beginning of the kindergarten year, with the result that the planned instruction may be based realistically on the knowledges and needs of the five-year-old.

Two tests were developed to aid in securing the needed data. The first test was an individual oral interview containing fifty-seven responses. Number knowledges tested included abstract counting by ones and tens, rational counting by ones and twos, number sequences, ordinal numbers, identification of number symbols, recognition of number quantities, ability to name and recognize common instruments of measurement, recognition of the coins and dollar bill in the United States monetary system, and the ability to combine smaller coins to total the value of larger coins and the dollar bill.

The second test constructed was a written picture-test containing forty-five responses. Arithmetical concepts that could be presented clearly in picture form were selected. These included premeasurement understandings, such as *largest, smallest, tallest, shortest, longest, under, inside, beside, nearest,* and *farthest;* recognition of simple geometric figures, such as *circle* and *square;* telling time to the full and half-hour; counting less than ten items and recognizing the written symbol for the total; reading the number words to ten and recognizing their written symbols; fractional parts of a whole, such as *one-half, one-third,* and *one-fourth;* fractional part of a group of items, such as *one-half;* simple addition combinations in oral problem situations; simple subtraction combinations in oral problems with the ability to recognize the result in the written symbol. Considerable effort was made to see that each item and picture were ones familiar to five-year-olds.

The data secured from both groups of children who were presented with the tests were strikingly similar. In generalizing the findings, both groups will be treated as one.

Considerable variance in ability to do rote counting by *one* was evidenced, but every child displayed some facility in this number knowledge. The mean for the entire group was approximately nineteen, while five children were able to count to one hundred or higher. The tabulation showed that four of these five children were boys, with one boy reaching the total of 112.

The majority of the children were unable to do rote counting by ten, but approximately 25 per cent exhibited some ability to perform this arithmetical skill. A few demonstrated their ability to do rote counting by ten to one hundred. Some individual comments made during this portion of the test were, "I thought there was only one way to count!" while another child promptly counted to sixty by fives.

As might be expected, there was a marked similarity between the ability of the children to do rational counting by one and rote counting by one. The mean, again for the entire group, was about nineteen. For some, as the higher numbers were reached, there was slight confusion of one-to-one correspondence. A few counted in blocks of sequence, jumping several decades and continuing without error.

Few children displayed an understanding of number sequences other than the sequence of numbers by one. Less than 10 per cent understood a sequence of odd numbers, but approximately 20 per cent succeeded when a sequence of even numbers less than ten was used. Only about 5 per cent were able to respond with an understanding of a number sequence by five when the total was no higher than the number twenty. Most of the incorrect responses given in the variety of sequences consisted of giving the next digit (e.g., 3, 5, 7, 8).

The results of the items concerned with ordinal numbers showed that more than half of the children had some understanding of this concept. Approximately 95 per cent understood the ordinal number *first*, while slightly more than 70 per cent knew *middle* and *last*. At least 50 per cent displayed a knowledge of the ordinal numbers *second* and *fourth*.

These beginning kindergarten children possessed considerable understanding of number selection skills and were able to recognize a quantity of items numbering less than four immediately. Some were able to recognize more than four items, but less than nine items. All of the children were able to select quantities of three or less. The majority of the children resorted to counting the objects one at a time, but a few were able to group items for quicker and more efficient recognition.

In situations where flash cards with a variety of pictured items were used, some rather enlightening ability to estimate was evidenced. Ninety-three per cent of the children immediately recognized two items when flashed, but this percentage dropped quite drastically after four items had been flashed. When eight items (the maximum number used) was flashed, the percentage of children responding accurately was 21 per cent. More than one-fourth of the children estimated by regrouping in the higher numbered items and then asked if they could check their answers by counting. Some actual responses were : "Let's see, two and two more, and two—that's six of them"; "Two and two, four. Two fours—there's eight." When asked to point out the picture containing the number of candles he would have on his birthday cake to show how old he was, one boy declared, "I'm 4½," and he immediately picked out the cards picturing four and five candles.

It was evident that a large percentage of beginning kindergarten children possess a high degree of understanding of terms describing premeasurement concepts and are able to recognize several common instruments used in measurement. Approximately 80 per cent or more of the children responded accurately to situations requiring an understanding of *largest, smallest, tallest, longest, most, inside, beside, closest, and farthest*. A smaller percentage, approxmiately 50 per cent, recognized situations describing the terms *shortest, few, underneath,* and *some*.

The response on the oral and written tests pointed out a high degree of ability to recognize common instruments used in measurement. When requested to name the instrument girls and boys would use to perform a specific job, 89 per cent were able to name the clock and 51 per cent could name the calendar. Approximately one-third were able to name accurately the yardstick, foot rule (ruler), scale and thermometer. Comments worth noting included those by one girl who said. "There are two kinds—weather and sick," when referring to the thermometer, and a boy who suggested his solution for finding out how cold it was by saying, "We could call someone up—the weatherman—or look at the television." Maybe our recent advances in technology have reduced some of our measurement instruments to obsolescence as far as common usage is concerned.

Data secured from the study revealed the ability of about 50 per cent of the five-year-olds tested to recognize time on the full hour when referring to a clock. Fewer possessed the ability to recognize time on the half-hour, as only about one-third of the children responded accurately to situations requiring this knowledge. It would appear that this skill is not beyond the ability of most of these five-year-olds if they are given the opportunity to use the clock in meaningful situations.

There was little verbal response or interest shown when a selection of coins and a dollar bill were displayed on the table. Some commented that it was "a lot of money," another said, "My brother has money," while still another merely stated he had a bank. When asked what they would or could do with the money, little enthusiasm was evoked, with the responses being almost entirely limited to the idea that it was something to play with or to put in one's bank. Eighty per cent of the children immediately recognized the penny, but only 38 per cent recognized a nickel. No particular pattern seemed to develop in the knowledge displayed according to the coins' values. The two extremes were mentioned previously, and they included the coins with the least value. While 39 per cent of the children knew there were five pennies in a nickel, only 15 per cent knew how many quarters, and but 10 per cent knew how many half dollars there are in a dollar.

It appears that the majority of preschool children possess the ability to recognize the geometric figures of a circle and a square. Ninety-one per cent of the boys and girls tested were able to respond readily and accurately to the illustration of a circle, while 76 per cent recognized the figure of a square. It is interesting to note that it was necessary for the child to possess a knowledge of the names of these two geometric figures in order to respond accurately to their pictured illustrations.

The results of the study seemed to bear out some understanding of simple fractional concepts when about 50 per cent of the children were able to recognize one-half of one item. Eighty-nine per cent recognized an item divided into thirds, and 66 per cent responded accurately to one-fourth of an item. Thirty-three per cent displayed the ability to select one-half of a group of items.

It is interesting to discover the high degree of skill evidenced in solving word problems that involve simple addition and subtraction facts. Almost 90 per cent of the children successfully solved addition combinations, while approximately 75 per cent accurately solved subtraction combinations. The children responded to these problems by marking a series of similar pictures. It appeared to be much more difficult for them to solve more complicated oral problems whose sums or differences exceeded five. To respond correctly, it was necessary for the child to solve the more difficult problems mentally and then indicate the answer on a written number symbol. The test was purposely constructed to contain the more difficult situations, and it was gratifying to note that as high as 35 per cent of the children were able to solve one of the problems successfully. The lowest response was 10 per cent on one problem, but the over-all average of success was 26 per cent of the group being studied.

What are some of the educational implications to be drawn from the responses of these 127 beginning kindergarten children. Certainly some thought should be given to possible adjustments in the presentation of arithmetical concepts in the kindergarten and the first grade. Specifically these might include:

1. A planned arithmetic-readiness program presented at the kindergarten level. This would require a systematic presentation to replace the incidental approach that is now generally employed. It appears that this type of instruction could begin no later than the second semester of the kindergarten year.

2. A program of arithmetic in the first grade that would reflect the readiness period carried out in the kindergarten. The readiness program would

be considerably shorter at the first grade level for most children, but could be extended for whatever period necessary for each child before the concepts developed in the usual first grade program are presented. This program would allow more time in the first grade for a broadened experience in arithmetic for most children.

3. An inventory of the child's number concepts should be made during the first part of the kindergarten year so that more emphasis in both the kindergarten and the first grade can be placed on developing number understandings for those children whose background experience have been more limited than those of the majority. This would appear to be a reasonable approach, inasmuch as the data received from this group of children seem to indicate that the ability of beginning kindergarten children to understand many basic arithmetical concepts is a reality.

FOR FURTHER READING

Brace, Alec, and Doyal L. Newson, "The Preschool Child's Concept of Number," *The Arithmetic Teacher* 12 (February 1965) 126–133.

Brownell, William C., *Arithmetic in Grades 1 and 2* (Durham, North Carolina: Duke University Press, 1941).

Buckingham, B. R., and Josephine MacLatchy, "The Number Abilities of Children When They Enter Grade One," *Research in Arithmetic*, 29th Yearbook of the National Society for the Study of Education, Part II (Bloomington: Public School Publishing Company, 1930), pp. 473–524.

Dunkley, M. E., "Some Number Concepts of Disadvantaged Children," *The Arithmetic Teacher* 12 (May 1965) 359–361.

Gunderson, Agnes G., and Ethel Gunderson, "What Numbers Mean to Young Children: Number Concepts Compared with a 1940 Study," *The Arithmetic Teacher* 6 (October 1959) 180–185.

Koenker, Robert H., "Arithmetic Readiness at the Kindergarten Level," *Journal of Educational Research* 42 (November 1948) 218–223.

MacLatchy, Josephine H., "The Pre-School Child's Familiarity with Measurement," *Education* 71 (April 1951) 479–482.

Suppes, Patrick, and Rose Ginsberg, "Experimental Studies of Mathematical Concept Formation in Young Children," *Science Education* 46 (April 1962) 230–240.

Williams, Alfred H., "Mathematical Concepts, Skills, and Abilities of Kindergarten Entrants," *The Arithmetic Teacher* 12 (April 1965) 261–268.

The Effects of Instruction
on the Stage of Placement of Children
in Piaget's Seriation Experiments*

ARTHUR F. COXFORD, JR.

This descriptive study is representative of studies which may be classified as "Piagetian." As suggested by the titles in "For Further Reading," Piaget has long been involved in studies dealing with the young
child's conception of number, space, and geometry, as well as areas
other than mathematics. Considerable attention has been directed
again lately toward his developmental psychology.

Coxford's study is a replica of a Piaget study, with an attempt to
note any changes in the pupil's levels of achievement ("advancement
from one stage to the next" to paraphrase Piaget). The writer explains
his instructional procedures and results in detail and the construction
of learning sequences for the various levels is well done. Further, the
researcher recognizes that his sample was small and that his results
can be generalized only to bright children. His work, however, could
be the basis of "examination of larger and more normal groups of
children."

Inbody's study of children's understanding of natural phenomena in
this volume (Chapter 6) is related to the Coxford study. Other studies
dealing with pre-first grade children in this volume are reported by
Hillerich, Chapter 2; and Bjonerud, Chapter 5.

In his book, *The Child's Conception of Number*, Jean Piaget (1)
stated that the concept of number has three basic aspects: cardinal
number, ordinal number, and unit. He has given criteria for determining
when a child understands each of the basic concepts. A child understands cardinal number when he is able to construct a one-to-one correspondence between two sets of objects and to conserve this correspondence when it is no longer perceptually obvious.

* From *The Arithmetic Teacher* 11 (January 1964) 4–9. Reprinted with permission of The National Council of Teachers of Mathematics and Arthur F. Coxford, Assistant Professor of Education, University of Michigan, Ann Arbor.

A child understands ordinal number when he is able to do four things. First, a child must be able to arrange in a sequence a set of objects which differ in some aspect. Piaget calls this act *seriation*. Second, he must be able to construct a one-to-one correspondence between two sequences of objects in which the elements of the sequences correspond because they have the same relative positions in the sequences. Such a one-to-one correspondence is called a *serial correspondence*. Third, he must be able to conserve a serial correspondence when it is no longer perceptible. Fourth, a child must be able to conserve an *ordinal correspondence* between two sequences of objects. The conservation of an ordinal correspondence is accomplished when a child can find an object in an unordered set (but a set which is capable of being ordered) which corresponds to a given object in an ordered set. The act of conserving an ordinal correspondence requires a child to arrange a sequence of objects and construct a serial correspondence between two sequences, either mentally or physically.

In both the concept of cardinal number and the concept of ordinal number the idea of unit is very important. A child cannot construct an accurate one-to-one correspondence between two sets of objects unless he perceives the elements of each set as equivalent units. A child cannot construct an accurate sequence unless he perceives each element of the set as a unit which can be put in a sequence because of some characteristic, such as length or width, which changes from element to element. Also units are important in coordinating ordinal and cardinal number, that is, in deducing the cardinal number of a set given its ordinal number.

Piaget concluded that the concepts of cardinal number, ordinal number, units, and number are interdependent and develop together. Number is not merely a property of a set of objects or merely a property of a sequence, but a property of both together.

PROBLEM

Piaget, in his experimental work, categorized the concept attainment of children by ages into three stages. The first stage is no understanding, and the third stage is complete understanding. The second stage is transitional, bridging the gap between the first and third. A primary question for those responsible for the education of children is this: Does instruction change the age at which children attain stages 2 and 3?

There were two purposes for the study reported here: (a) to replicate Piaget's experiments in seriation, serial correspondence, and ordinal correspondence, and (b) to ascertain the effect of instruction on advancing a child from one stage to the next.

PROCEDURE

The subjects for the experiment were 60 children from the Laboratory School of The University of Michigan enrolled during the 1962–63 school year. The children ranged in age from 3 years 6 months to 7 years 5 months. First, a pretest was given to place the 60 children in the three developmental stages. Twenty-seven of the children were tested as stage 1, 28 were tested as stage 2, and 5 were tested as stage 3. Instruction was then given to a group of 24 of the children for four weeks in 10- to 15-minute sessions. The total amount of instructional time was approximately 60 minutes. The 24 children chosen for instruction were matched by chronological age with a control group of 24 children also chosen from the 60 children. Finally, a posttest, which was identical with the pretest, was given to the 24 instructed children and the 24 control children in order to determine the developmental stages for a second time. The 12 children not chosen for instruction or for the control group were in stage 3 or were reluctant to leave their classroom with the experimenter. Hence they were omitted from further investigation.

PRETEST AND POSTTEST

Each child was interviewed individually in the pretest and posttest, and the responses made were recorded. The materials used in both tests were:

a) Ten cardboard balloons which ranged in size from a radius of 1½ cm. to 5 cm., with an average radius increment of 0.35 cm.

b) Ten cardboard sticks that ranged from a length of 10 cm to 21 cm., with an average length increment of 1.1 cm.

c) One 39 × 30 cm. picture of a balloon on a stick.

To indicate the relationship between the set of balloons and the set of sticks, the experimenter told a story about a backyard carnival in which the child was to sell balloons on a stick. Before the balloons could be sold, the child had to put the correct stick with each balloon. The experimenter emphasized that there was one and only one stick that went with each balloon and that the biggest stick went with the biggest balloon, etc. The picture of a balloon on a stick was shown to the child.

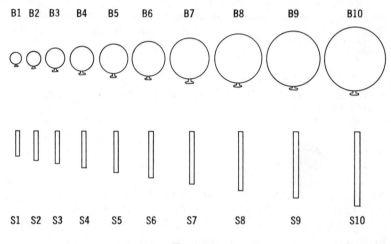

Figure 1

The balloons and sticks were randomly arranged in two separate groups for the first item on the test. The figure shows their correct arrangement upon completion of the test. The first item of the test was to put the sticks with the balloons.

a) "Arrange the balloons and the sticks so we can tell very easily which stick goes with each balloon." If the child did not arrange the balloons and sticks in sequences while putting them together, he was asked to do so.

When the sticks and balloons were arranged correctly, each stick was moved 10 cm. from the corresponding balloon to a position directly opposite that balloon. The experimenter pointed to balloon one (B1) and asked:

b) "Which stick goes with this balloon?" Then the same question was asked, pointing to B2, B3, etc., in order. The question was then repeated for B5, B9, B3, and B7.

c) The sticks were rearranged so stick one (S1) was opposite B2, S10 was opposite B9, and the other sticks evenly spaced between S1 and S10. The questions in *b* were asked again.

d) The sticks were rearranged in a row twice as long as the balloon row. The questions in *b* were asked again.

The sticks were disarranged and spread out before the child (the balloons were still in order). The child was asked:

e) "Which stick goes with this balloon (pointing to B6)?" Item *e* tests ordinal correspondence, for the child must reconstruct the sequence and the serial correspondence in order to answer correctly.

The children were placed in the three stage according to the following criteria:

Stage 1: No part of the test correctly done.
Stage 2: Item *a* correctly done, but mistakes made in items *b, c, d,* or *e*.
Stage 3: The complete test correctly done.

INSTRUCTION

Of the 24 children who were chosen for instruction, 12 were in stage 1 and 12 in stage 2. These children were instructed in groups of two for 10 to 15 minutes. Groups of two children were chosen to create a situation in which competition could be used in the instructional periods. Also each child was asked to check his partner's work, which allowed every child to be given extra instruction in each period. Furthermore, the children were more at ease in the presence of a classmate.

The materials for the instruction were made of cardboard and consisted of 8 right triangles, 8 trapezoids, 8 rectangles, 8 sticks, 8 houses, and 8 chimneys. In various combinations, these cardboard materials were used to build sailboats, lamps, houses, Christmas trees, and dishes. Each set of objects was constructed so that each object of a given set was of a different size.

Instruction for children in stage 1

The instruction for children in stage 1, outlined below, was based on the fact that these children could not put a set of objects in a sequence or construct a serial correspondence.

FIRST SESSION.   Each child was given three trapezoids differing greatly in size. The children played with the trapezoids, were asked to pile them up like dishes, and were asked to line them up like boats in a row.

SECOND SESSION.   The materials were five trapezoids for each child. The children were asked to pile up three trapezoids like dishes;

then they were given another trapezoid and asked to put it in the correct position in the pile of dishes. The children were given the fifth trapezoid and asked to make a Christmas tree with all five trapezoids.

THIRD SESSION. Five right triangles and five trapezoids were used by each child. The children were shown a picture of a sailboat and were asked to build sailboats from the right triangles and trapezoids. They were asked to put the sailboats in order from smallest to largest. They were asked questions such as: "Which boat is the smallest? The largest?" and "Which boats are larger than a certain one? Smaller than a certain one?"

FOURTH SESSION. Six houses, right triangles, and chimneys were given to each child. Essentially the same procedure was used as in the third session.

Instruction for children in stage 2

The instruction for the children in stage 2 was based on the fact that they made mistakes in items *b, c, d,* or *e* of the test. In each of the four instructional sessions, the children seriated the objects that they were given, constructed serial correspondences between the sets of objects, and checked their partner's arrangements.

The acts mentioned above were used to begin each session. The two children then played the game outlined below, as instructed by the experimenter. In each game, the basic pattern was the same. First, each child was given a set of objects; for example, one child was given a set of 7 right triangles and the other a set of 7 trapezoids. Then, alternately, each child chose one of his objects. This object was to be matched by the other child with the corresponding object from his set. Finally, the first child decided whether the match was correct. If not correct, he corrected it. Before playing each game, a serial correspondence between the sets of objects had been constructed by the children. Hence, the game emphasized the ordinal correspondence between the two sequences of objects.

FIRST SESSION. The materials were two sets of 7 boats and 7 sails. Game 1: The experimenter took the sails from each child and chose one of the sails from each set. He gave the chosen sails to the children and asked the children to put these sails with the correct boats. The children could see the remaining sails in each set. They were then asked to check their choices by putting the remaining sails with the appropriate boats.

SECOND SESSION. The children each used 8 boats and 8 sails. Game 2: One set of boats and sails was used for the game. Each child chose one set of objects which were exposed to the view of both children, but the objects were not in order. In turn each child chose one of his objects and asked the other child to put the correct object from his set with it. The children ended by putting the sailboats in a sequence.

THIRD SESSION.   Each child was given 8 houses, 8 roofs, and 8 chimneys. Game 3: Only one set of houses, roofs, and chimneys was used. Each child chose one set of the objects, i.e., houses, roofs, or chimneys. The remaining component of the complete house was in a sequence and exposed to the view of both children. In turn, each child chose one of his objects, and the other child matched it with the object of his which corresponded to it. Together they chose the third part of the complete house from the set in the sequence. The children finished by putting the complete houses in a sequence.

FOURTH SESSION.   Eight lampshades, 8 stems, and 8 bases were used by each child. Game 4: Each child and the experimenter were given one of the three parts of the lamp. The game proceeded as in Game 3.

RESULTS AND DISCUSSION

Table 1 summarizes the results of the pretest. The sixty children were classified according to developmental stage and chronological age. For example, the numbers 17, 8, and 2 in the column labeled *Stage 1* indicate that, of the 27 children who tested as stage 1, 17 were less than or equal to 57 months old; 8 were between 57 and 72 months old; and 2 were over 72 months old. The chronological age ranges in the vertical classification of Table 1 correspond to the stages predicted

TABLE 1

Number of Children in Each Stage Classified by Chronological Age

	Stage 1	*Stage 2*	*Stage 3*
A CA ≤ 57	17	3	0
B 57 < CA ≤ 72	8	15	1
C 72 < CA	2	10	4
	$N = 27$	$N = 28$	$N = 5$
	Mean CA = 56.2	Mean CA = 69.8	Mean CA = 77.6
	SD = 9.9	SD = 9.6	SD = 5.0

A & B & C vs. 1 & (2, 3); $\chi^2 = 20.40$, $p < 0.005$

by Piaget; for example, CA ≤ 57 is the age at which children were in stage 1 in Piagets' work.

The *chi-square test* value of 20.40 indicates that the developmental stage and chronological age of the 60 children in Table 1 are very probably not independent. That is, the developmental stage of the University Laboratory School children is most probably related to their chronological age. Also the mean chronological ages of 56.2 for stage 1, 69.8 for stage 2, and 77.6 for stage 3 were in the age range predicted by Piaget. Hence, the University Laboratory School children tested did, *on the average,* corroborate Piaget's predictions of chronological age and developmental stage.

However, tempering this conclusion is the fact that the children tested were very bright (see Table 2), and there were notable exceptions to Piaget's predictions. In particular, one child 83 months old was tested as stage 1 and after instruction was still in stage 1. Another child of 46 months was tested as stage 2 and after instruction was found to be in stage 3.

Table 2 summarizes the pretest and posttest data for the 24 experimental and 24 control children. The classifications *Exp. I, Control I,* etc., indicate respectively stage 1 youngsters who were instructed, stage 1 youngsters who were not instructed, etc. Table 2 is read verti-

TABLE 2
Summary of Pretest and Posttest Data

		Exp. I	Control I	Exp. II	Control II
Pretest stage	1	12	12	0	0
	2	0	0	12	12
	3	0	0	0	0
Posttest stage	1	10	9	0	0
	2	2	2	6	10
	3	0	1	6*	2
Mean CA		56.5	57.2	68.9	67.8
SD of CA		10.6	9.2	9.7	8.3
Mean MA		70.5	70.5	97.0	92.2
SD of MA		17.7	18.0	15.6	18.1
Mean IQ		120.2	119.5	135.9	135.4
		N = 9	N = 11	N = 11	N = 11

* $z = 1.85$; $p < 0.05$

cally; that is, the column labeled *Exp. I* indicates that, of 12 children who pretested as stage 1 and were given instruction, 10 posttested as stage 1 and 2 as stage 2. These children had a mean CA of 56.5 months with a standard deviation (SD) of 10.6 months, a mean MA of 70.5 months with a SD of 17.7 months, and a mean IQ of 120.2. The statement $N = 9$ indicates that the last three vertical categories in the *Exp. I* column were computed for 9 of the 12 children.

Of the children originally tested as stage 1 who were given instruction (*Exp. I*), some made gains in their tested stage. The same was true of some of the children tested as stage 1 who were not given instruction (*Control I*). The gains were not statistically significant.

However, the group of children tested as stage 2 who were given instruction (*Exp. II*) made significant gains over the group which was not instructed (*Control II*), as shown by the one-sided *z-test* of proportions. The value $z = 1.85$ was significant at the 5 percent level, which means that the decision to accept the hypothesis that instruction has an effect in advancing a child from stage 2 to stage 3 would be correct 95 percent of the time. The mean mental ages of 97.0 and 92.2 for *Exp. II* and *Control II* were tested with the *t-test* and were not found to be significantly different.

Of the children who were instructed and moved from stage 2 to stage 3, three were boys and three were girls. The youngest was a boy of 46 months and the oldest was a girl of 80 months. It appears, then, that there were factors other than age that made a child receptive to instruction. Moreover, in the uninstructed group, the two children who advanced from stage 2 to stage 3 were two of the youngest. Also there were children with higher IQ's and MA's in both groups who did not make gains.

Perhaps even more interesting than the results in Table 2 was the interest of the children. The children who were tested thoroughly enjoyed playing and working with the materials of the test and instruction. One kindergartner even went so far as to make a set of the test materials and pretend to test her classmates with them. The interest of the children in the materials implies that such materials could be used to promote enjoyable learning experiences for young children.

SUMMARY

The experiment replicated Piaget's experiments dealing with seriation, serial correspondence, and ordinal correspondence. A selected group of children was given instruction, and the results of the test and instruction were reported and discussed. The major conclusions drawn were: (a) the University Laboratory School children tested did, on the average, corroborate Piaget's predictions concerning stage placement and chronological age, and (b) children tested as stage 2 made significant gains in stage placement by means of instruction over comparable children who were not instructed. The general applicability of these conclusions is tempered by the fact that the sample was small and the children were exceptionally bright. Further research would include examination of larger and more normal groups of children.

REFERENCES

1. Jean Piaget, *The Child's Conception of Number*, translated by C. Gattegno and F. M. Hodgson (New York: The Humanities Press Inc., 1952).

FOR FURTHER READING

Brearley, Molly, and Elizabeth Hitchfield, *A Guide to Reading Piaget* (New York: Schocken Books, Inc., 1966).

Brownell, W., *The Development of Childrens' Number Ideas in the Primary Grades*, Supplementary Educational Monographs No. 35 (Chicago: The University of Chicago Press, 1928).

Elkind, D., "The Development of Quantitative Thinking: A Systematic Replication of Piaget's Studies," *Journal of Genetic Psychology* 98 (March 1961) 37–46.

Feigenbaum, Kenneth D., "Task Complexity and IQ as Variables in Piaget's Problem of Conservatism," *Child Development* 34 (June 1963) 423–432.

Piaget, Jean, *The Child's Conception of Number* (London: Routledge and Paul, 1952).

———, and B. Inhelder, *The Child's Conception of Space* (New York: Humanities Press, Inc., 1956).

———, B. Inhelder, and Z. Szeminska, *The Child's Conception of Geometry* (New York: Basic Books, Inc., Publishers, 1960).

An Experiment in Teaching of Introductory Multiplication*

ROLAND F. GRAY

This study dealing with introductory multiplication has been selected: (1) to represent the many studies which may be classified as "basic operations studies"; and (2) to serve as an excellent model of the type of controlled experimentation needed in educational research. In "For Further Reading" a number of other outstanding studies dealing with addition, subtraction, multiplication, and division are cited.

The theoretical background of this study is well developed and leads to the specific problem the researcher wished to investigate. The sampling is well done. One of the major strengths of the research is the control of the variables. The statistical design deserves the highest rating. Gray developed his own test instruments and presents reliability data for them. Some readers might wish that he had included more than one item on the tests that cover untaught procedures which can be interpreted as transfer. Features of "discovery" or "let the pupil find out for himself" may be noted in this study.

Recent changes in approaches to the teaching of introductory multiplication reflect current trends in arithmetic instruction which lay greater stress upon an early development of understandings of principles and properties central to mathematics as a whole. This is seen as a part of what may be termed the *modern mathematics* trend which is characterized by an increased concern for teaching arithmetic as a branch of mathematics. Central to this view seems to be an assumption that a recognizable structure underlies mathematics, much of which can be learned with initial instruction in the elementary school and which, when understood, can serve to render children more independent in their approaches to quantitative situations. (1) This influence

* From *The Arithmetic Teacher* 12 (March 1965) 199–203. Reprinted with the permission of The National Council of Teachers of Mathematics and Roland F. Gray, Associate Professor of Education, University of British Columbia, Vancouver, B.C., Canada.

is reflected in the newer approaches to the teaching of multiplication by the considerable attention given to developing an understanding of the operation and its special properties. (2) In the newer arithmetic programs, multiplication is introduced and explained in such terms as repeated additions, mappings, arrays, and Cartesian products. The commutative, associative, and distributive properties for multiplication are developed extensively.

Much of the content of these newer arithmetic programs is an outgrowth of the efforts of prominent mathematicians and educators working together in teams for the purpose of improving mathematics instruction. They have produced proposals which appear to be thoroughly and logically developed and which hold promise of improvement in instruction. However, thus far, much of what has been produced rests primarily on the opinions or judgments of these experts. There is very little data indeed from research studies upon which to base an evaluation of these professional judgments. There is a need, then, for carefully controlled experimental investigations of the effectiveness of programs based on these mathematical principles to promote pupil growth as measured by achievement and understanding. To provide data relevant to this need, the present experiment investigated the effectiveness of a program of instruction in introductory multiplication which was based on the development of an understanding of the distributive property.

METHODS AND PROCEDURES

This experiment was conducted in twenty-two third-grade classes in San Pablo and Vallejo, California, both communities within the San Francisco metropolitan area. A total of 480 children participated in all phases of the study. Careful attempts were made to assure that the subjects had had no previous formal instruction in multiplication, and that they had had no previous experience in any of the newer arithmetic programs.

Two sets of eighteen experimental lessons designated treatment one (T-1) and treatment two (T-2) were devised by the experimenter. Both sets of lessons were designed to introduce the multiplication combinations through those in which four is a factor. Procedures for carrying and multiplying with two-digit factors were not presented in any of the lessons. The T-1 lessons closely followed methods currently in use in the California State Series in which multiplication is explained in terms of repeated additions and as arrays of objects in rows and columns. The lessons also provided for practice or drill in memorization of the combinations, but made no mention of the distributive property or its applications. (3) The first five of the T-2 lessons were identical with the first five T-1 lessons to insure that both groups had the same basic understandings of multiplication through the combinations with two as a factor. The remaining thirteen T-2 lessons were designed to introduce and explain all additional multiplication combinations solely in terms of the distributive property for multiplication. For example, 4×4 was presented as $(4 \times 2) + (4 \times 2)$. Less time was provided for drill exercises since additional time was needed to demonstrate the distributive property. No attempt was made to have the T-2 subjects memorize the combinations. Both sets of lessons were limited to forty minutes each. The experimental period extended through eighteen school days. All students in both groups were told they were participating in an experiment.

Each of the twenty-two participating teachers held regular California teaching credentials. All held bachelor's degrees, and none held a master's degree. The teachers were divided into two groups on the basis of age, marital status, and years of experience. The treatments were then assigned at random within each group of teachers. This procedure was followed to provide a check on the effects of these teacher characteristics on pupil performance. All teachers met in a weekly consultative conference with the experimenter throughout the experimental period. The experimenter made periodic visits to the classrooms to assure that experimental procedures were carefully followed.

The randomization procedures produced experimental groups which did not differ significantly in age and in measures of arithmetic reasoning. The effects of intelligence as indicated by IQ measures and pre-experimental arithmetic achievement were controlled statistically.

Measures of pre-experimental multiplication achievement were obtained with an experimenter-made forty-item paper and pencil test. The criterion measures consisted of four additional experimenter-made paper and pencil tests, viz., a posttest of multiplication achievement, a posttest of transfer, a retention test of multiplication achievement, and a retention test of transfer. The two posttests were administered at the close of the experimental period. The two retention tests were administered at the end of a three-week retention period during which no multiplication or division was taught. Reliability was established by a test-retest technique, the results of which are presented in Table 1. An individual interview test, developed after Brownell's technique, (4) was administered to a random sample of 110 subjects for information on their understanding of the distributive property and the multiplication operation.

TABLE 1
Test-Retest Reliability Data of Experimenter-Made Tests

Test	r	Interval
Pretest of multiplication	.94	4 days
Posttest of multiplication	.93	4 days
Retention test of multiplication	.88	4 days
Posttest of transfer	.82	4 days
Retention test of transfer	.87	4 days

Analysis of covariance, *t* tests, and chi square tests were used where appropriate to test for significance of differences between the treatment groups. The decision rule established for this study was to reject a null hypothesis when the probability of a Type I error was .01 or less.

RESULTS

The findings of this study were obtained from two different sets of data: the objective-type paper and pencil tests and the interview tests.

Findings from the Paper and Pencil Tests

Score from the pretest of arithmetic achievement and IQ scores were used as covariants in an analysis of covariance with each of the four criterion measures. The adjusted means obtained by this procedure were tested for significance of differences between treatments. No statistically significant differences were found which were traceable to the teacher characteristics investigated. The data for tests of significance between means on the four criterion measures are presented in Table 2, and may be summarized as follows:

1. Differences of the posttest of multiplication achievement favored the T-2 group, but were not statistically significant.
2. Statistically significant differences favoring the T-2 group were found on the posttest of transfer ability, the retention test of multiplication achievement and the retention test of transfer.

TABLE 2

A Comparison of the Treatment Groups on the Criterion Measures

	T-1 group (N = 229)		T-2 group (N = 251)		
	Adj. mean	SD	Adj. mean	SD	t
Posttest of multiplication	26.1	7.63	27.8	7.64	2.30
Posttest transfer	9.1	6.14	11.2	6.51	3.09*
Retention test multiplication	25.9	8.52	29.9	8.53	5.09*
Retention test transfer	11.6	7.15	13.7	7.16	3.22*

* Significant at the .01 level.

Findings from the Interview Tests

The interview test, comprised of five items, was designed to indicate whether a subject was able to give a rational explanation of multiplication procedures, or whether he gave only rote answers or mechanical solutions to the test items. The interview also provided evidence on the number of subjects who appeared to have learned how to apply the distributive property to find products for both familiar and unfamiliar combinations. The difference in numbers of subjects in each of several response categories was tested for statistical significance by the chi square technique. Selected data are presented in Tables 3 and 4. The general findings are summarized below.

1. Significant differences were found favoring the T-2 group in number of subjects who gave correct responses to the one test item which required application of untaught procedures.
2. Significant differences were found favoring the T-2 group in the number of subjects who used the distributive property in finding answers for all items.
3. Eleven per cent of the T-1 subjects and 46 per cent of the T-2 subjects used the distributive property to find products to one or more test items.
4. Significant differences were found favoring the T-2 group in the number of subjects who gave rational explanations of procedures used on one test item. Differences favored the T-2 group on the other four items, but were not significant.
5. The T-2 subjects who used the distributive property to find products were significantly superior in IQ to those who relied on rote memory, counting, or repeated additions to find products.

TABLE 3
*Differences in Number of Subjects
Falling in Selected Response Categories on the Interview Test*

	T-1 group (N = 55)	T-2 group (N = 55)	χ^2
Number of subjects using the distributive property on one or more test items	6	25	15.76*
Number of subjects giving correct responses to test Item #5 requiring use of untaught procedures	11	28	11.88*
Number of subjects using the distributive property to find products to Item #5	0	16	18.72*
Number of subjects giving a rational explanation for procedure in Item #5	5	25	18.33*

* Significant at the .01 level.

TABLE 4
*Relationship Between Response Level on Interview Test and IQ and
Arithmetic Reasoning Score for the T-2 Subjects who used the
Distributive Property to Solve One or More Problems*

	Used distributive property (N = 25)		Did not use distributive property (N = 30)		
	Mean	SD	Mean	SD	t
IQ	112.00	13.29	97.00	12.00	4.39*
Arithmetic reasoning	14.79	1.67	13.11	2.41	2.82

* Significant at the .01 level.

CONCLUSIONS

Within the limitations of the sampling procedures employed the data presented above would appear to support the following conclusions.

1. A program of arithmetic instruction which introduces multiplication by a method stressing understanding of the distributive property produced results superior to methods currently in use.

2. Knowledge of the distributive property appears to enable children to proceed independently in the solution of untaught multiplication combinations.

3. Children appear not to develop an understanding of the distributive property unless it is specifically taught.

4. Insofar as the distributive property is an element of the structure of mathematics, the findings tend to support the assumption that teaching for an understanding of structure can produce superior results in terms of pupil growth.

REFERENCES

1. Cf. Dorothy M. Fraser, *Current Curriculum Studies in Academic Subjects* (Washington: The National Education Association, 1962), pp. 27–42. *The School Mathematics Study Group Newsletter No. 4* (March, 1960), pp. 3–5. Kenneth E. Brown, "The Drive to Improve School Mathematics," *The Revolution in School Mathematics* (Washington: The National Council of Teachers of Mathematics, 1961), pp. 15–29.

2. Cf. Robert L. Morton, *et al.*, *Modern Arithmetic through Discovery,* Grade Three, Teachers' Manual (Morristown, New Jersey: Silver Burdett Co., 1963). Robert E. Eicholtz, *et al.*, *Elementary School Mathematics,* Book Three, Teachers' Edition (Reading, Massachusetts: Addison-Wesley Publishing Co., Inc., 1963). Science Research Associates, *Greater Cleveland Mathematics Program,* Teachers' Guide for Third Grade (Chicago: Science Research Associates, 1962).

3. Leo J. Brueckner, *et al.*, *The New Discovering Numbers,* Grade Three Teachers' Manual, California State Series (Sacramento: California State Department of Education, 1957).

4. William A. Brownell and Doris V. Carper, *Learning the Multiplication Combinations,* Duke University Research Studies in Education, No. 7 (Durham, North Carolina: Duke University Press, 1943), pp. 49–53, 88–90, 121–122.

FOR FURTHER READING

Brownell, William A., "An Experiment on 'Borrowing' in Third Grade Arithmetic," *Journal of Educational Research* 41 (November 1947) 161–171.

Brueckner, Leo J., and Harvey O. Melbye, "Relative Difficulty of Types of Examples in Division with Two-Figure Divisors," *Journal of Educational Research* 33 (February 1940) 401–414.

Buckingham, B. L., "Upward Versus Downward Addition," *Journal of Educational Research* 16 (December 1927) 315–322.

Capps, Lelon R., "A Comparison of the Common Denominator and Inversion Method of Teaching Division of Fractions," *Journal of Educational Research* 56 (July–August 1963) 516–522.

Corle, Clyde C., "A Study of the Quantitative Values of Fifth and Sixth Grade Pupils," *The Arithmetic Teacher* 12 (November 1960) 333–340.

Dawson, Dan T., and Arden K. Ruddell, "An Experimental Approach to the Division Idea," *The Arithmetic Teacher* 2 (February 1955) 6–9.

Flournoy, Frances, "The Effectiveness of Instruction in Mental Arithmetic," *Elementary School Journal* 55 (November 1954) 148–153.

———, "Developing Ability in Mental Arithmetic," *The Arithmetic Teacher* 4 (October 1957) 147–150.

———, "Children's Success with Two Methods of Estimating the Quotient Figure," *The Arithmetic Teacher* 6 (March 1959) 100–104.

———, "A Consideration of Pupils' Success with Two Methods for Placing the Decimal Point in the Quotient," *School Science and Mathematics* 59 (June 1959) 445–455.

Gibb, E. Glenadine, "A Review of a Decade of Experimental Studies Which Compared Methods of Teaching Arithmetic," *Journal of Educational Research* 46 (April 1953) 603–608.

———, "Take-Away Is Not Enough," *The Arithmetic Teacher* 1 (April 1954) 7–10.

Hartung, Maurice L., "Estimating the Quotient in Division," *The Arithmetic Teacher* 4 (April 1957) 100–111.

Hightower, Howard W., "Effect of Instructional Procedures on Achievement in Fundamental Operations in Arithmetic," *Educational Administration and Supervision* 40 (October 1954) 336–348.

Howard, C. F., "Three Methods of Teaching Arithmetic," *California Journal of Education Research* 1 (January 1950) 25–29.

John, Lenore, "The Effect of Using the Long-Division Form in Teaching Division by One-Digit Numbers," *Elementary School Journal* 30 (May 1930) 675–692.

Johnson, John T., "Whither Research in Compound Subtraction?," *The Arithmetic Teacher* 5 (February 1958) 39–42.

Kenney, Russell A., and Jesse D. Stockton, "An Experimental Study in Teaching Percentage," *The Arithmetic Teacher* 5 (December 1958) 294–303.

Knipp, Minnie B., "An Investigation of Experimental Studies which Compare Methods of Teaching Arithmetic," *Journal of Experimental Education* 13 (September 1944) 23–30.

LeBaron, Walter A., "A Study of Teachers' Opinions in Methods of Teaching Arithmetic in the Elementary School," *Journal of Educational Research* 43 (September 1949) 1–9.

Miller, Jack W., "An Experimental Comparison of Two Approaches to Teaching Multiplication of Fractions," *Journal of Educational Research* 57 (May–June 1964) 468–471.

Morton, R. L., "Estimating Quotient Figures When Dividing by Two-Place Numbers," *Elementary School Journal* 48 (November 1947) 141–148.

Moser, H. D., "Two Procedures for Estimating Quotient Figures when Dividing by Two-Place Numbers," *Elementary School Journal* 49 (May 1949) 516–522.

Olander, Clarence E., "The Use of a Readiness Test in Teaching a Unit on Signed Numbers," *School Science and Mathematics* 57 (February 1957) 131–138.

Petty, Olan, "Non-Pencil-and-Paper Solution of Problems: An Experimental Study," *Arithmetic Teacher* 3 (December 1956) 229–235.

Scott, Lloyd, "Children's Concept of Scale and the Subtraction of Fractions," *The Arithmetic Teacher* 9 (March 1962) 115–118.

———, "A Study of Teaching Division Through the Use of Two Algorisms," *School Science and Mathematics* 63 (December 1963) 739–752.

Swenson, Esther J., "Difficulty Ratings of Addition Facts as Related to Learning Methods," *Journal of Educational Research* 38 (October 1944) 81–85.

Tredway, D. C., and G. E. Hollister, "An Experimental Study of Two Approaches to Teaching Percentages," *The Arithmetic Teacher* 10 (December 1963) 491–495.

Weaver, John F., "Whither Research on Compound Subtraction?," *The Arithmetic Teacher* 3 (February 1956) 17–20.

Wolf, William C., "Non-written Figuring: Its Role in the Elementary School Curriculum," *Educational Research Bulletin* 39 (November 9, 1960) 206–213.

Zweng, Marilyn J., "Division Problems and the Concept of Rate," *The Arithmetic Teacher* 11 (December 1964) 547–556.

Verbal Problem Solving:
*Suggestions for Improving Instruction**

C. ALAN RIEDESEL

This clearly written report provides many examples of the program used, and takes into consideration the range of arithmetic abilities found in most classrooms. It also deals with an important topic—the role assigned to word problems in the elementary mathematics programs. For too long verbal problems have been "taken for granted." Critical study of the procedures for teaching problem solving appears important. Word problems provide a means of bringing quantitative situations to the attention of pupils, showing that operations have significant applications and that arithmetic arises in life situations. With this in mind, teachers must consider a program for developing the greatest possible problem solving facility among their pupils. This study treats several specific procedures that might be considered in a well-rounded program of instruction.

While no hypotheses are given in the study, they are implied; necessary data on the researcher-made test are given; and the overall design is appropriate. However, some readers may question if too much personal judgment was permitted in the selection and separation of samples into experimental and control groups. The statement of results is exceptionally well reported and the suggestions made at end of the study should prove helpful to most readers.

The attention of the reader is called to the practice of accepting differences of significance at the .10 level—a considerably lower significance level than is customary in the behavioral sciences.

The verbal or word problem has long been an area of arithmetic instruction of great concern to teachers and the cause of much pupil anxiety. This situation has led to the formulation of many proposals for improving the teaching of verbal problem-solving ability. Interest in most of these proposals has waned quickly after teacher tryout or after

* From *The Arithmetic Teacher* 11 (May 1964) 312–316. Reprinted with permission of The National Council of Teachers of Mathematics and C. Alan Riedesel, Professor of Education, Pennsylvania State University, University Park.

studies to test their validity failed to produce clear-cut evidence of the worth of the proposals. The overall result has been that during instruction on verbal problems the major portion of instructional time is devoted to the solution of the same verbal problems by all the students in a class and by means of general or poorly defined procedures. In view of the range of arithmetical ability found in most classrooms, it is necessary to have many pupils attempting to solve problems that are too difficult, while other more able pupils must be concerned with the solution of problems that are too easy. When the above situation is coupled with the fact that pupils are not guided into using specific suggestions which are believed to make for improved word problem-solving ability, there is little wonder that this area of arithmetic remains a matter of concern to teachers.

In an attempt to provide material better suited to pupil ability, some teachers have resorted to use of textbooks from different grade levels, and some textbook writers have included a few difficult problems (usually indicated by a star or other symbol) in each set of word problems. A little investigation of the use of these two procedures shows that neither procedure is regarded with much enthusiasm by leaders in the field of arithmetic instruction.

The suggestions for improving verbal problem solving used in the study reported here attempt to provide (1) verbal problems of two levels of difficulty for use in the same classroom and (2) specific experience with highly recommended procedures for improving pupil achievement in the solution of verbal problems.

The following five procedures were selected for use in this study: (1) writing the number question or mathematical sentence, (2) using drawings and diagrams, (3) having pupils formulate problems, (4) presenting problems orally, and (5) using problems that do not contain numerals.

The purpose of this study was to compare the effectiveness of the use of specific verbal problem-solving procedures in connection with the provision of two levels of problem difficulty to the problem-solving program followed in typical textbook instruction.

A total of thirty arithmetic problem-solving lessons were prepared. Each of the thirty lessons was written at two levels of difficulty. The problems for pupils of above-average problem-solving ability were reproduced on yellow paper while the problems for pupils of below-average problem-solving ability were reproduced on white paper. The lessons made use of the five specific procedures referred to above. Following the problems for each lesson was a "How's Your P.Q.?" problem which was more difficult than the other problems in the lesson. These problems were for optional use. Copies of detailed answer sheets were provided so that each pupil was able to correct his own work. The lesson material for one day follows.

PROBLEM-SOLVING LESSON 21— USING DRAWINGS AND DIAGRAMS (WHITE PAPER)

Read the problem carefully and then use a drawing or diagram to help you solve it. Try to check your work by using another method of solution.

1. When he was practicing basketball, Bill made 3 of every 5 free throws he attempted. If he continues at that rate, how many will he make out of 25 shots?
2. The Dover basketball team is playing at Mt. Royal, which is 135 miles away. The game begins at 7:30 P.M. The team starts at 4 P.M. and plans to arrive ½ hour before game time. Will they arrive on time if they average 40 mi. per hr.?
3. Al bought 6 valentine cards marked "3 for 25¢." What was the cost of his purchase?
4. Lloyd needed to buy some fishhooks before going on a fishing trip with his father. If the fishhooks sell at 6 for 10¢, how much will 18 fishhooks cost?

How's Your P.Q. ???? (Lesson 21)

Claudia was getting dressed for a party when a thunderstorm caused the lights to go out. She knew that she had only three colors of socks— white, yellow, and blue—but wanted to be sure she had a matching pair. Her brother said, "Just take several, and then when we get in the car you can pick out a matching pair." What would be the least number of socks that she could take to be sure to get a pair that matched?

PROBLEM-SOLVING LESSON 21— USING DRAWINGS AND DIAGRAMS (YELLOW PAPER)

Read the problem carefully and then use a drawing or diagram to help you solve it. Try to check your work by using another method of solution.

1. A baseball diamond is 90 ft. by 90 ft. (See diagram.) If a player runs a race of 100 yards in 12 seconds, how long will it take him to run around all of the bases? Assume that he ran on the base lines.

2. Billy wishes to cut a board that is 16 ft. 3 in. long into 5 equal parts. Ignoring the saw cuts, how long will each part be?

3. A nickel (5¢) is made of both nickel and copper. For every pound of nickel in the mixture there are 3 pounds of copper. How many pounds of copper will be needed to make 24 lbs. of coins?

4. The Cardinals won 5 of the first 8 games that they played. At that rate how many games would they win out of 56 games?

How's Your P.Q. ???? (Lesson 21)

A train leaves Albertsville headed east for Bakersville every two hours. At exactly the same hour a train leaves Bakersville for Albertsville. The trip requires 12 hours. How many trains will be met by a train in going from Albertsville to Bakersville?

CORRECTION SHEET FOR LESSON 21—
USING DRAWINGS AND DIAGRAMS
(WHITE PAPER)

1. The following diagram can be used to find the number of free throws Bill will make out of 25.

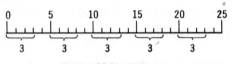

Total of 15 free throws

2. If the team wants to arrive ½ hour before game time, it must arrive by 7:00 P.M. This allows from 4 P.M. to 7 P.M., or 3 hours for travel. If the team travels at 40 miles per hour, the diagram at the top of page 305 shows that they will not arrive on time.

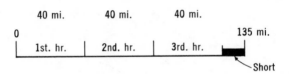

3. The drawing shows that if the cost of 3 cards is 25¢, then 6 cards will cost 50¢.

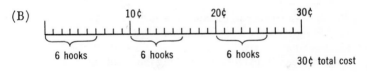

4. The problem can be diagramed in several ways; two of these ways are shown below:

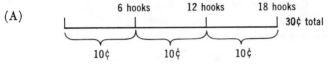

Lesson 21—"How's Your P.Q.?"

You can draw a picture of a number of socks. Note that any time you pick out four socks you must have 2 of the same color. *Answer:* 4.

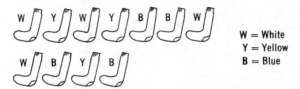

W = White
Y = Yellow
B = Blue

CORRECTION SHEET FOR LESSON 21—
USING DRAWINGS AND DIAGRAMS
(YELLOW PAPER)

1. First it is important to be sure we use the same units. Change the 90 ft. to 30 yards.

Checking the diagram we find that the total distance around the diamond is 120 yards. Thus, we know it will take longer than 12 seconds for the player to run around the diamond. We can find the length of time it takes by multiplying:

distance around the diamond—120

$$\frac{120}{100} \times 12$$

100 yards—100

$$\frac{6}{5} \times 12 = \frac{72}{5} = 14\frac{2}{5} \text{ sec. Ans.}$$

2. Visualize cutting this into five equal parts:

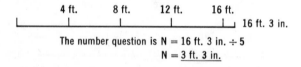

The number question is N = 16 ft. 3 in. ÷ 5

N = 3 ft. 3 in.

3. The diagram below provides aid in solving the problem:

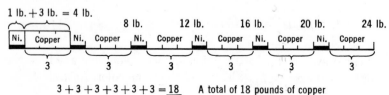

3 + 3 + 3 + 3 + 3 + 3 = 18   A total of 18 pounds of copper

4. The number line below can be used as an aid in solving the problem:

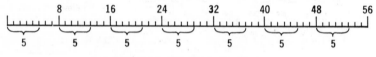

For a total of 35 wins in 56 games.

Lesson 21—"How's Your P.Q.?"

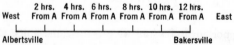

At any given hour there will be 7 trains on the track headed east (from Albertsville to Bakersville) and 7 trains headed west. A train going east will have met all these 7 trains by the time it is 6 hours out of Albertsville. During this time 3 other trains have left Bakersville; and by the time the eastbound train arrives at Bakersville, 2 other trains will have left and 1 will be departing. *Answer: 13.*

A forty-eight item, tape-recorded, problem-solving test was developed for the study. The problems were presented orally on tape and were also duplicated on the answer sheets. Analysis of the test revealed a mean item difficulty of .51, a mean index of item discrimination of .57, and a reliability of .90 as determined by the Spearman-Brown formula. The use of the Spearman-Brown formula was deemed appropriate since 95 per cent of the students finished each item on the test. This test and the problem-solving section of the Iowa Tests of Basic Skills were used as pretests and final tests to compare the gains of experimental and control groups.

The experimental and control groups were composed of sixth-grade classes from three Iowa cities. Eleven experimental and nine control classes took part in the study. Placement of the classes into experimental or control groups was made on the judgment of the curriculum supervisors, who attempted to distribute experience of the teachers, ability of the students, and teaching ability specifically in arithmetic between the experimental and control groups. A total of 505 sixth-grade children participated in the entire program.

The participating experimental and control teachers were oriented to the program by the writer. Illustrative lessons were provided as an aid to the introduction of each problem-solving procedure.

The tape-recorded test developed for the study and the problem-solving section of the Iowa Tests of Basic Skills were administered to the experimental and control classes. In determining the level of problem-solving materials to be used by a pupil in the experimental groups, the tape-recorded test score was used along with the judgment of the teacher. In the case of borderline students, the teachers were directed to allow such students to attempt some lessons at each level and, with the help of the teacher, to determine the groups with which they would receive maximum benefit.

During the course of the study the experimental classes worked three special problem-solving lessons a week. The problems presented in their textbooks were omitted unless they were an integral part of the introduction of a new topic. The control groups followed the regular problem-solving program presented in the textbooks. Actually the control classes worked a greater number of problems during the study than the experimental classes.

At the end of the ten-week period the posttests on both measures were administered. Questionnaires and essays were used to obtain the subjective judgment of the teachers and pupils concerning the materials.

The tests were corrected and the *t* statistic was used to compare the mean class gain scores between experimental and control groups. The 10 per cent level of significance was used.

Results showed:

1. The difference between mean gains on the tape-recorded test favored the experimental subjects and was significant beyond the .1 per cent level.
2. The difference between mean gains on the problem-solving section of the Iowa Tests of Basic Skills favored the experimental subjects and was significant between the 5 and 10 per cent levels.

From the analysis of the questionnaires and essays it can be concluded that:

1. The lessons are of benefit to above-average, average, and below-average problem solvers.
2. The materials are of appropriate difficulty and reading level.
3. The specific procedures are effective in improvement of pupil problem-solving achievement.
4. Children find such materials worthwhile and enjoyable.
5. Children are receptive to "How's Your P.Q.?" type problems.
6. Pupils enjoyed working problems taken from a variety of sources. The pupils in this study revealed a definite preference for problems from foreign and old United States textbooks.

On the basis of the work conducted with pupils and teachers in the course of this study, the following suggestions warrant consideration:

1. Teachers and others who prepare arithmetic materials will enhance the educational value of their teaching materials by developing problem-solving lessons of multilevel difficulty.
2. Greater use should be made of such specific procedures as writing the number question, use of drawings and diagrams, pupil formulation of problems, orally presented problems, and using problems without numerals.

3. Greater use should be made of the tape recorder in test presentation.
4. In preparing materials for increasing pupil interest in arithmetic, curriculum workers will find it profitable to include problems from foreign textbooks and from old United States textbooks.

FOR FURTHER READING

Balow, I. H., "Reading and Computation Ability as Determinants of Problem Solving," *The Arithmetic Teacher* 11 (January 1964) 18–22.

Chase, Clinton I., "The Position of Certain Variables in the Prediction of Problem-Solving in Arithmetic," *Journal of Educational Research* 54 (September 1960) 4–14.

Corle, Clyde G., "Thought Processes in Sixth Grade Problems," *Arithmetic Teacher* 5 (October 1958) 193–203.

Johnson, Harry C., "Problem Solving in Arithmetic: A Review of the Literature," *The Elementary School Journal* 44 (March and April 1944) 396–403, 476–482.

———, "The Effect of Instruction in Mathematical Vocabulary Upon Problem Solving in Arithmetic," *Journal of Educational Research* 38 (October 1944) 97–100.

Pace, Angela, "Understanding and the Ability to Solve Problems," *Arithmetic Teacher* 8 (May 1961) 226–233.

NEW CONTENT

*Topics in Geometry
and Point Set Topology—A Pilot Study**

CHARLES H. D'AUGUSTINE

The inclusion of geometry represents one of the most important of the many recent changes in the elementary school mathematics program. Geometry in former programs largely centered on measurements. The more recent emphasis is upon non-metric geometry, concerned with points, curves, and planes; their properties; and their relationships to each other. This experimental study was selected to represent this recent trend in geometry as well as the new topics in modern elementary mathematics—algebra, sets, logic, negative numbers, other numeration systems, probability, and statistics. References in "For Further Reading" reflect these topics. The introduction of newer content brings forth pertinent questions: What concepts are important and for what age and type of pupil? What teaching approaches are practical and sensible (meaningful and purposeful to the pupil), and will emphasize individual thinking and a spirit of inquiry?

Particular attention is called to these features of the report: the statement of the problem; construction and testing of the programmed technique which helped control the teacher variable; the test content; the consideration of intelligence, reading, and achievement in the pupils' success with the topics under study; and the interpretation and generalizations from the data. Since only one class composed the sample for this pilot study, the suggestions for further work noted in the last paragraph of the report seem appropriate.

Other areas of the curriculum also need answers about newer content. For example, see Wade's research in Chapter 4.

There is evidence that children develop certain ideas and concepts fundamental to geometry and topology long before they understand such concepts as one-to-one correspondence and number associated with a set. (1) Jean Piaget (2) discovered that even at the age of

* From *The Arithmetic Teacher* 11 (October 1964) 407–412. Reprinted with permission of The National Council of Teachers of Mathematics and Charles H. D'Augustine, Ohio University, Miami.

three years a child could distinguish a simple closed curve from a non-simple closed curve. Suppes and Hawley (3) working with primary school students, found that many of Euclid's concepts, which could be discovered by construction, were both teachable and stimulating.

Although there is some research supporting the hypothesis that geometrical and topological topics are teachable, there is a need for further definitive research which can answer the following questions:

1. Which geometrical topics are teachable at various grade levels?
2. To what extent are students stimulated by these topics?
3. At what level are certain topics learned with a high degree of efficiency in terms of time and expended effort?
4. Which of these topics are appropriate at various grade levels? (i.e., a subjective evaluation must be made of their place and of their value to the total school curriculum).

Several methods of evaluating the teachability of geometrical and topological topics are available to the experimenter. If the topic is one which is already within the experience of elementary school teachers, then one has only to design an experiment and find teachers who are willing to participate in the experiment. If this is not the case, then the experimenter must either give teachers extensive conceptual training or design an experiment independent of the teacher.

It was felt that some of the topics included in this experiment were beyond the experience of most elementary school teachers; therefore, the writer designed a programmed unit. (4) The programming technique gave the experimenter the advantage of greater flexibility in the selection of experimental subjects. Programmed materials also gave each child a more uniform experience with these topics, thus adding reliability to the measure of overall success with the experimental group.

DEVELOPMENT OF THE PROGRAMMED TEXT

A programmed text for a one-week unit was developed by the writer. The programmed text was to develop the concepts of points and sets of points, and by a logical sequential structure develop the properties of lines, line segments, collinearity, and broken lines. From these properties it was hoped to develop properties of simple closed curves, convexity and non-convexity, boundedness, interior and exterior regions.

By extension of these properties, the properties of various polygons (i.e., triangles, rectangles, quadrilaterals, squares, and parallelograms) could be developed.

A rough sequential learning program was drafted. In order to check the pedagogical and mathematical soundness of the rough draft program, the following sources were used: *A Contemporary Approach to Classical Geometry* by Walter Prenowitz, *Geometry for Primary Grades* by Newton Hawley and Patrick Suppes, SMSG *Geometry*, and articles by Jean Piaget.

These topics were pretested with a sixth-grade student classified by his teacher as an above-average arithmetic student. From these individual tutoring sessions, which were tape recorded and analyzed, a second draft of the program was formed. Five sixth-grade students participated in the testing of the second draft. Careful record was kept of those frames which led to answers deemed unacceptable. A third draft of the program, consisting of one hundred and sixty-nine frames, was then developed and given to a sixth-grade student classified by his teacher as being one of his "poorest" arithmetic students. An end-of-unit test was constructed and administered to this student. At this point the writer felt that the program was in a stage of development which would permit trial with a sixth-grade class.

THE CLASS

A sixth-grade class was selected at Leonard Wesson Elementary School, Tallahassee, Florida. Pupils had been randomly assigned to this class by the administration. The class consisted of thirteen boys and thirteen girls.

Students in this school represent a fairly stable school population. These students had pursued a conventional arithmetic program up to the time the pilot study began.

In the second month of the sixth year, a battery of California Test Bureau tests had been administered to all members of the class. Table 1 shows a frequency distribution of the results of these ability and achievement tests.

These features about the class should be noted:

1. The mean I.Q. was 99.4.
2. The mean reading achievement was at the 7.1 grade level.
3. The mean arithmetic achievement was at the 6.1 grade level.

TABLE 1
Ability and Achievement Levels of Pilot Study Class,
California Test Bureau Tests

Mental maturity		Reading level		Arithmetic	
Interval	Frequency	Interval	Frequency	Interval	Frequency
119–123	5	9.3–9.8	3	7.7–8.0	1
114–118	1	8.7–9.2	3	7.3–7.6	2
109–113	2	8.1–8.6	1	6.9–7.2	1
104–108	2	7.5–8.0	4	6.5–6.8	4
99–103	4	6.9–7.4	2	6.1–6.4	5
94–98	1	6.3–6.8	4	5.7–6.0	6
89–93	4	5.7–6.2	3	5.3–5.6	4
84–88	2	5.1–5.6	3	4.9–5.2	2
79–83	3	4.5–5.0	2	4.5–4.8	0
74–78	0	3.9–4.4	1	4.1–4.4	1
69–73	2				
Total = 26		Total = 26		Total = 26	
Mean = 99.4		Mean = 7.1		Mean = 6.1	
Std. Dev. = 16.1		Std. Dev. = 1.6		Std. Dev. = 0.8	

Thus, with the exception of being above average in reading, the class was average in achievement and intelligence when compared with the national norm.

PILOT STUDY ROUTINE

The twenty-six students were told that they were going to study topics in mathematics not ordinarily taught at the sixth-grade level. They were instructed in the use of a programmed text, as none had had previous experience with this type of instructional material. Mrs. Jones, the subjects' sixth-grade teacher, had allotted the writer an hour block of time each day for five consecutive days.

Since there were thirty-six words contained in the program which were not found in Edgar Dale's list of words common to sixth graders at the 80 percent level, the writer introduced a sufficient number of these words each day to insure that the students would have a sight, although not a conceptual control, when they encountered these words in the program. No attempt was made to develop conceptual understanding of these words outside the limit of the program.

Each student worked independently and at his own rate. He was required to read each frame and make certain types of responses on an answer sheet. These responses ranged from "fill-in" type questions to simple straight line constructions, or checking the congruency of a simple closed curve with a piece of acetate and a grease pencil. Some of the frames required the student to determine the "truth" or "falsity" of a given set of statements or to provide a counter example (via pictures) to establish the "falsity" of the statement.

As each student finished the programmed text, his completion time was recorded. The first student finished after 230 minutes. The last student finished after 288 minutes. One can note in Table 2 that the rate of completion was fairly uniform.

TABLE 2
Distribution of Completion Times for Programmed Text

Minute Intervals	229–234	235–240	241–246	247–252	253–258	259–264	265–270	271–276	277–282	283–288
Frequency	5	2	2	4	1	3	3	2	2	2

TEST CONTENT AND STRUCTURE

Upon the student's completion of the programmed text, he was administered a test, designed by the writer, on geometrical and topological concepts. This test consisted of sixty-three items. These items fell into two categories. There were items which related directly to the concepts taught in the program, and there were items which the writer felt might represent a student's ability to extend and generalize beyond the scope of the program. Each concept tested was included in at least two test items so as to give greater reliability to error analysis.

The first part of the test consisted of seventeen "true" or "false" statements.

Sample

(T) (F) Any three points in a line are collinear.

The second part of the test consisted of twenty-one completion type questions. Some of these questions had two or three parts.

Sample

The figure at the right is not a quadrilateral because . . .

(1) it is the join of more than _____.

(2) it can have more than _____ diagonals.

The conceptual extension part of the test was divided into two parts. The first part of the test consisted of five multiple-choice items, which had up to five correct answers.

Sample

Choose the correct names from the list and place them in the blanks below the figure.

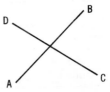

simple closed curve

parallelogram

square

rectangle

triangle

quadrilateral

The second part of the test consisted of four completion items.

Sample

Pretend that $\overline{AB}$ and $\overline{CD}$ are diagonals in an invisible quadrilateral.

(1) $\overline{AD}$ is congruent to $\overline{CB}$.

(2) $\overline{AC}$ is congruent to $\overline{DB}$.

This quadrilateral is called a _____.

ANALYSIS OF RESULTS

It was subjectively predetermined that a student scoring 46 to 63 would be viewed by the author as having had excellent success with all of the geometry and topology topics. A score of 35 to 45 was viewed as representing moderate success, while a score less than 35 was felt to represent, at most, limited success.

As can be noted in Table 3, nine students achieved excellent success, eight students moderate success, and nine students limited success.

An analysis was made of the role that intelligence, reading achievement, and computational arithmetic achievement played in a student's success with these topics as measured by the geometry and topology test.

In Table 4 it can be seen that students with at least average intelligence achieved moderate to excellent success with some or all of the topics tested.

In Table 5 it can be seen that achievement in reading appeared to play a significant role in a student's success with the geometry-topology test. This implied relationship may be due to the high correlation which exists between most intelligence test scores and reading achievement test scores.

TABLE 3
Distribution of Geometry-Topology Test Scores

Interval	14–17	18–21	22–25	26–29	30–33	34–37	38–41	42–45	46–49	50–53	54–57	58–61
Frequency	2	4	3	0	0	4	2	2	4	2	2	1

Mean: 36; range: 15–58.

TABLE 4
A Comparison of Levels of Success on the Geometry-Topology Test Scores and Intelligence Test Scores

Levels of success	Intelligence Quotient interval				
	69–89	90–99	100–109	110–119	120–123
Excellent			4	2	3
Moderate		2	4	1	1
Limited	7	2*			

* Both scores were 91.

TABLE 5
The Success with Geometry-Topology Topics Compared with Reading Achievement Grade Placement

Levels of success	Reading grade placement intervals					
	3.9–4.9	5.0–5.9	6.0–6.9	7.0–7.9	8.0–8.9	9.0–9.9
Excellent			1	2	1	5
Moderate			4	2	2	
Limited	3	5	1			

In Table 6 it can be seen that achievement in computational arithmetic did not appear to have had an influence on the student's success with the geometry-topology test. To determine if this was a valid conclusion, a Kendall Partial Rank Correlation was computed. Holding reading fixed, a Kendall Partial of −.045 was obtained between success on the geometry-topology test and computational arithmetic achievement. This was not significant at the .05 level.

TABLE 6

The Success with Geometry-Topology Topics Compared with Computational Arithmetic Achievement Grade Placement

	Arithmetic grade placement intervals			
Levels of success	3.9–4.9	5.0–5.9	6.0–6.9	7.0–7.9
Excellent		2	4	3
Moderate		5	3	
Limited	2	5	2	

ANALYSIS OF THE TEACHABILITY OF TOPICS

Test questions which related directly to topics taught via the program were categorized into general topics. Each of these categories was analyzed to determine the percentage of success each of the top seventeen students had with each category (see Table 7).

The writer feels that categories with rankings one through eight represent highly teachable topics.

It is possible to make certain statements regarding the success of this program in teaching certain topics and to extend these statements to inferences about the teachability of these topics at the sixth-grade level. However, this study has not determined the unteachability of those topics which met with limited success. This study has only shown that the limited success may be due to one or more of the following reasons:

1. There was faulty programming with relation to these topics.
2. There was pedagogical error in the approach taken in the structure of the program presentation.
3. New words should have been introduced in conceptual context.
4. Topics were not appropriate to this maturity level.
5. Topics would have been easier to grasp by other instructional techniques.

TABLE 7
Analysis of Categorical Success

Category	Number of questions in category	Number of correct responses	Number of correct responses possible	Percentage correct
1. Interior, exterior, and boundary points	2	33	34	97
2. Congruency	2	30	34	88
3. Simple closed curves	4	59	68	87
4. Properties and definition of triangle	3	43	51	84
5. Collinearity	3	42	51	82
6. Countable and uncountable sets of points	3	42	51	82
7. Properties of lines and line segments	6	79	102	77
8. Properties of broken lines	4	52	68	76
9. Properties and definition of rectangle	3	35	51	69
10. Property of convexity and non-convexity of simple closed curves	7	79	119	66
11. Property of square	1*	11	17	65
12. Properties and definition of parallelogram	5	54	85	64
13. Properties of diagonals	3	30	51	59
14. Properties and definition of quadrilateral	5	45	85	53

* One item was omitted because it failed to discriminate between the top and bottom 27%.

SUMMARY

The writer felt that there was a lack of definitive research on the teachability of topics relative to geometry and topology at the elementary school level. An investigation was conducted with one sixth-grade class at Leonard Wesson Elementary School, Tallahassee, Florida. The experimental design employed a programmed unit, developed by the writer, which attempted to teach such topics as properties of points, lines, simple closed curves, convex and non-convex regions, congruency, and polygons.

Each student worked independently and at his own rate. On completion of the program he was given a test on topics relating to geometry and topology.

On the basis of their test scores, students were classified into predetermined levels of success. Nine of the students were classified as having achieved excellent success, eight as having achieved moderate success, and nine as having achieved limited success. There appeared to be no relation between a student's ability to achieve with computational topics and his success with geometry and topology topics as taught in the program.

Test items were classified into concept categories, and an analysis of the top seventeen students' success with these topics was made. Topics classified as highly teachable on the basis of this analysis were:

1. interior, exterior and boundary points.
2. congruency.
3. simple closed curves.
4. properties and definition of triangle.
5. collinearity.
6. countable and uncountable sets of points.
7. properties of lines and line segments.
8. properties of broken lines.

No attempt was made to pass judgment on the unteachability of those topics which met with limited success.

The programmed unit employed in the experimental design proved to be a highly efficient experimental tool. Its limitation was that it did not give each student a wide variety of instructional techniques to aid in the student's mastery of the concepts explored. Thus, while it was possible to make subjective judgments with regard to positive success, it was not possible to draw any conclusions with regard to the unteach-ability of certain topics, because with other instructional techniques the students might have experienced success with the "limited success" topics.

Further research is needed, employing larger population samples, a broader scope of topics, many elementary school levels, and a variety of teaching techniques before it can be determined which topics are teachable, suitable, and efficiently learnable at various levels in the elementary school.

REFERENCES

1. Research funds for this investigation were provided by The Florida State University Research Council.

2. Jean Piaget *et al., The Child's Conception of Geometry* (New York: Basic Books, Inc., 1960), pp. 389–408.

3. Newton Hawley and Patrick Suppes, *Geometry for Primary Grades* (San Francisco: Holden-Day, Inc., 1960), pp. 1–126.

4. A. A. Lumsdaine and Robert Glaser, *Teaching Machines and Pro-grammed Learning* (Washington: National Education Association, 1960), pp. 94–113.

FOR FURTHER READING

Denmark, Thomas, and Robert Kalin, "Suitability of Teaching Geo-metric Construction in Upper Elementary Grades—A Pilot Study," *The Arithmetic Teacher* 11 (February 1964) 73–80.

Gagne, Robert, and Otto Bassler, "Study of Retention of Some Topics of Elementary Non-metric Geometry," *Journal of Educational Re-search* 54 (June 1963) 123–131.

———, and staff, "Some Factors in Learning Non-Metric Geometry," *Monograph of the Society for Research in Child Development*, Vol. 30, No. 99 (1965), pp. 42–49.

Lerch, Harold H., "Fourth Grade Pupils Study a Number System With Base Five," *Journal of Educational Research* 57 (October 1963) 59–63.

Ojemann, Ralph H., James E. Maxey, and Bill C. Snider, "The Effect of a Program of Guided Learning Experiences in Developing Probability Concepts at the Third Grade Level," *Journal of Experimental Education* 33 (June 1965) 321–330.

Olander, Clarence E., "The Use of a Readiness Test in Teaching a Unit of Signed Numbers," *School Science and Mathematics* 57 (February 1957) 131–138.

Suppes, Patrick, and Blair A. McKnight, "Sets and Numbers in Grade One, 1959–60," *The Arithmetic Teacher* 8 (October 1961) 287–290.

———, and Frederick Binford, "Experimental Teaching of Mathematical Logic in the Elementary School," *The Arithmetic Teacher* 12 (March 1965) 187–195.

Arithmetic Achievement in Iowa and the Netherlands *

KLASS KRAMER

This study is significant since both educators and the general public are interested in how American school instruction compares with instruction in other countries. While it compares only students in Iowa and the Netherlands, a wider survey on arithmetic achievement has been conducted recently (see Husen, cited in "For Further Reading"). Studies somewhat similar to Kramer's have been made in other subject areas, like reading and spelling. (See Preston and Personke cited in "For Further Reading.")

The first part of this straightforward and understandable study deals with testing of pupils from the two cultures and the analysis of the data. The latter part deals with relevant data concerning American and Dutch educational procedures—student selection policy, time spent on arithmetic, and placement of topics.

The researcher, in speaking of the representativeness of his Dutch sample, said the schools were drawn from "upper social classes" and "lower social classes," but it is not clear whether these would be comparable for Iowa and the Netherlands. The measuring instrument used was the *Iowa Test of Basic Skills* for grades 6, 7, and 8. All items with a uniquely American background were eliminated as were items dealing with money and measurement. One might wonder if this would affect the validity of the resulting test. Though the arithmetic achievement of Netherland pupils exceeded that of Iowa pupils, the writer concluded "that a direct comparison is not very meaningful." Some interesting questions come to mind upon reading this study: Should American schools follow some European practices, considerably increasing arithmetic time, adding to the amount of retardation in our schools, and gearing instruction to passing examinations at end of grade 6? Or will later studies of American children now learning the "new mathematics" indicate less superiority for foreign pupils?

Critics of American schools sometimes make unsubstantiated comparisons of the achievement of pupils in the United States and in Europe.

* From *Elementary School Journal* 59 (February 1959) 258–263. Reprinted with the permission of the University of Chicago Press © 1959 and Klass Kramer, Professor of Education, State University of Brockport, New York.

This report is based on a study that compared achievement in arithmetic in the upper grades of schools in Iowa and in The Netherlands (1).

To make it possible to interpret properly the data on arithmetic achievement, other important data on the school systems involved in the study are reported. This information includes the amount of time devoted to the study of arithmetic, selective factors that are at work in one school system and absent in the other, and other major features of each school system.

To collect data for comparing achievement, two tests were constructed. The tests were prepared by selecting and modifying items from the arithmetic section of the Iowa Tests of Basic Skills for Grades 6, 7, and 8.

Test 1 was a test of the ability to solve problems. Thirty-five items were selected from the 57 in the original test (61 per cent). In the international test, competence was tested in a functional setting through problems chosen as challenging and practical.

Test 2 was designed to measure understanding of concepts and processes in arithmetic. For this test, a total of 59 of the 84 items (70 per cent) in the original test were approved. Skills involving children's understanding of the following were tested:

The number system	7 items
Whole numbers	5 items
Fractions	22 items
Decimals	5 items
Per cents	5 items
Standard measures	3 items
Geometric figures	9 items
Ratio and proportion	3 items

As nearly as could be ascertained, the tests were equally fair to pupils in both countries. Items of the original test that were eliminated from consideration for the international test included the following: items dealing with units of measure that differ in the two countries; items with a unique American background; items involving articles with prices that were not comparable in the two countries; and items involving abbreviations that are more common or easier to understand in one country than in the other. Professional teachers familiar with the languages of both countries checked the translation of the Dutch version for comparability with the American version. Reactions to the test from administrators in Dutch schools were all favorable.

To secure a representative sample of schools, thirteen district school superintendents in The Netherlands (at least one in each of the eleven provinces) were asked to enlist the cooperation of at least two school principals. One school in each district was to be drawn from an area serving the upper social classes and one from an area serving the lower social classes.

Ten superintendents from eight provinces co-operated. In all, twenty-one schools were enrolled, two of which administered the tests to their sixth grades only. The tests were given to forty fifth- and sixth-grade classes with a total of 1,511 pupils.

How representative the sample was of Dutch schools is not known. A request was sent to the superintendents to enrol schools whose pupils differed in socioeconomic status. Beyond that request, it was impossible to exercise control over the characteristics of the sample. For the Dutch schools, no information on relative achievement was available that could be used as a means for selection.

In Iowa, sixteen schools were selected for the study. A letter was sent to the superintendent of each of these schools explaining the purpose of the proposed study and requesting his co-operation. Fifteen schools with a total of 1,530 pupils in Grades 5, 6, 7, and 8 took part in the experiment.

The sixteen schools were originally invited to take part on the basis of two criteria: the schools had taken part in the Iowa Basic Skills Testing Program in January, 1956, but the schools had not taken part in the program in 1957. Thus, it was possible to select schools according to the percentile ranks of school averages on the arithmetic test in Grade 6 in the 1956 program and at the same time avoid practice effects. With respect to achievement in arithmetic, therefore, the schools were representative of those that regularly take part in the annual Basic Skills Testing Program in Iowa.

Tests were administered in both countries in February or March of 1957. A practice test was administered in Dutch schools to familiarize pupils with multiple-response items and methods of marking a separate answer sheet.

The principal results of the tests are summarized in Table 1. For purposes of analysis, the school was considered as the unit of sampling. The means shown are the unweighted averages of school means.

On both tests, pupils in Grades 5 and 6 in Dutch schools performed considerably better than their Iowa counterparts in corresponding grades. The differences are sizable and significant at better than the 1 per cent level. In fact, average performance for the sixth grade in The

TABLE 1

Mean Scores in Arithmetic Achievement of 1,511 Dutch Pupils and 1,530 American Pupils

Grade and Test	Mean Scores		Difference	Standard Error of Difference	t†
	Dutch Pupils*	American Pupils			
Test 1: Problem-solving (35 items):					
Grade 5	22.26	14.23	8.03	.93	8.63
Grade 6	27.25	19.19	8.06	.64	12.52
Grade 7		23.03			
Grade 8		25.02			
Test 2: Concepts and processes (59 items):					
Grade 5	27.88	17.64	10.24	1.55	6.33
Grade 6	38.69	26.41	12.28	1.53	8.00
Grade 7		33.18			
Grade 8		37.93			

* Mean scores for Dutch pupils in fifth and sixth grades only were used in the study.

† Significant at the 1 per cent level.

Netherlands is somewhat higher than the Iowa average for eighth grade.

To intrepret the data in Table 1, a knowledge of the major features of the program of instruction in the schools of The Netherlands and of Iowa is required. The Dutch elementary-school program consists of six grades (years) with a school year of forty to forty-two weeks and a school day of five hours. Children enter Grade 1 at age six, as in the United States. Dutch authorities recommend a weekly time allotment of 240 minutes in arithmetic (2). The average "preferred" time allotment for arithmetic in elementary schools in the state of Iowa is 154 minutes a week (3). In The Netherlands a greater share of time is devoted to reading, writing, and arithmetic at the expense of science, social studies, art, music, and health. Relatively little time is spent on the readiness program in arithmetic in the primary grades in The Netherlands. However, the Dutch schools are about a year ahead of the Iowa schools in the grade placement of concepts and processes in arithmetic.

In The Netherlands, the selection of pupils for higher levels of instruction takes place at the end of the sixth grade. In 1953, for example,

11 per cent of the children completing sixth grade went to a secondary school; 28 per cent went to a four-year school for more extensive elementary education; 34 per cent went to a vocational school; and 27 per cent went to a school with a two-year curriculum for continued elementary education.

In Iowa, there is no rigid or formal selection of elementary-school pupils for high-school entrance. Theoretically, all who finish the elementary-school program may enter high school. Actually, in 1957, over 90 per cent of those who finished eighth grade entered secondary schools.

In The Netherlands, the highly selective admission to secondary schools results in a differentiation in instruction at the fifth- and sixth-grade levels. This differentiation consists of extra instruction in arithmetic in the form of special exercises for those pupils who, in the opinion of the teacher, are likely candidates for the secondary school.

The incidence of failure in Dutch elementary schools is high. It is estimated that 40 per cent of the elementary-school pupils experience failure during the first six years (4). In Iowa, this figure is about 10 per cent (5). About 10 per cent of the Dutch elementary-school pupils fail to reach the end of the sixth-grade. It is estimated that the corresponding figure for Iowa is less than 5 per cent.

The Dutch pupil completes the study of arithmetic in elementary school at the end of Grade 6. During the previous two years he pursued a program designed to help him pass the entrance examinations to secondary school if he plans to attend such a school. The Iowa pupil does not complete his study of arithmetic until the end of Grade 8, and even then he does not have to prepare for a secondary-school entrance examination.

In addition, the average score of the Iowa schools is influenced more by the scores of the poorer pupils than scores in The Netherlands are. For in The Netherlands most of the poorer pupils either have been dropped from school or have been retained a year or more and are therefore not of normal age for Grade 6.

From these facts it can be seen that direct comparison of mean scores of sixth-graders in The Netherlands and in Iowa is not very meaningful. The differences in time allotments, the difference in grade placement of arithmetic topics, and the fact that the Dutch schools are more selective than the Iowa schools make direct comparisons difficult.

Percentile ranks were computed of raw scores on each test for each grade in both countries. Table 2 shows the scores corresponding to the selected percentiles.

TABLE 2

Mean Scores in Arithmetic Achievement at Selected Percentiles
of Dutch and of American Pupils

Percentile Rank and Test	Dutch Pupils*		American Pupils			
	Grade 5	Grade 6	Grade 5	Grade 6	Grade 7	Grade 8
Test 1: Problem-solving (35 items):						
99	34.5	34.5	27.5	31.5	35.0	35.0
90	28.3	31.7	21.7	26.3	30.1	31.8
75	25.9	30.1	18.1	23.5	27.2	29.7
50	22.6	27.9	14.2	19.5	23.8	26.7
25	19.3	25.5	10.6	14.9	19.5	21.7
10	15.5	22.3	7.4	11.7	15.2	16.6
Test 2: Concepts and processes (59 items):						
99	51.5	56.5	41.5	47.5	54.5	57.5
90	39.7	49.3	25.3	36.0	45.6	50.5
75	34.0	45.6	21.4	31.6	40.1	45.8
50	27.7	39.5	17.2	26.5	34.0	39.5
25	22.0	33.3	13.0	20.7	27.0	32.0
10	17.2	27.5	10.0	17.2	22.1	24.1

* Mean scores for Dutch pupils in fifth and sixth grades only were used in the study.

The evidence in Table 2 suggests that, at the top ability levels, the performance of sixth-graders in The Netherlands closely matches the performance of eighth-graders in Iowa. To permit a critical examination of the data in Table 2, the actual time allotments for arithmetic in Dutch and Iowa schools were compared. According to the data supplied by the Iowa superintendents, the average time given to arithmetic each week in the fifteen schools that took part in the study was 149 minutes for Grades 1 through 6 and 160 minutes for Grades 1 through 8. Data supplied by superintendents of Dutch schools reveal that the average time allotment for arithmetic in the participating Dutch schools was 266 minutes for Grades 1 through 6.

According to these figures, in six years of elementary school, the average Dutch pupil spends 1,064 hours of class time on arithmetic (figuring 40 weeks in the school year and disregarding non-promotion). During these six years, the average Iowa pupil spends 537 hours on arithmetic (figuring 36 weeks in the school year). Even at the end of the eighth grade, the average Iowa pupil has spent only 768 hours on arithmetic.

The educational program in the United States is designed to educate all children to the extent that their abilities allow. Content and teaching method are selected to accomplish the greatest good for the greatest number. All pupils are eligible to attend a common school for twelve years, and a majority do so. Selection and specialization occur relatively late. In the first eight grades, there is a considerable emphasis on social studies, health, music, and art.

On the other hand, the common school in The Netherlands is a six-year school. Selection and differentiation occur, for the most part, at the end of Grade 6. A relatively greater share of time and effort is devoted to reading, writing, and arithmetic. Relatively little time is devoted to science, social studies, art, music, and health. As a result, we would expect pupils to progress more rapidly in the basic subjects than pupils in America do. Selective examinations for the more able pupils at the end of Grade 6 have considerable influence on the elementary-school program and on pupil motivation.

Because of differences in philosophy, objectives, and methods, an objective comparison of achievement is valid only insofar as all these factors are taken into consideration.

The findings of this study show that, when pupils from the two countries are compared in achievement at corresponding grade levels, Dutch pupils outperform American pupils, at least pupils in Iowa. However, in interpreting this conclusion, it must be kept in mind that almost twice as much time is devoted to formal instruction in arithmetic in the first six grades in The Netherlands as in America.

There is nothing in the results of this study that could justify the conclusion that either country should adopt the program of the other. Each country has selected the content and the methods of teaching arithmetic consistent with its philosophy and with the aims this philosophy suggests. Levels of achievement reached by the two educational programs differ. This finding should result in a reconsideration of each program in terms of its own philosophy and aims. If the examination is carried out with thought and without prejudice, the result could be beneficial to the programs of both countries.

REFERENCES

1. This article is based on a Ph.D. thesis completed at the State University of Iowa in 1957.
2. Boswinkel, J. W., and Wedzinga, J. *Rekening en Verantwoording van de Rekenmethode voor de Lagere School,* p. 6. Groningen and Djakarta: J. B. Wolters, 1953.
3. *Resource Ideas for Planning Classroom Programs,* p. 27. Des Moines, Iowa: Department of Public Instruction, 1955.
4. "Kaleidoskopij," *Onze Vacatures* (November 23, 1955), 1.
5. Stroud, James B., *Psychology in Education,* p. 385. New York: Longmans, Green & Co., 1956.

FOR FURTHER READING

Bogut, T. L., "Comparison of Achievement in Arithmetic in England, California, and St. Paul," *The Arithmetic Teacher* 6 (March 1959) 87–94.

Brownell, William A., "Observations of Instruction in Lower-Grade Arithmetic in English and Scottish Schools," *The Arithmetic Teacher* 7 (April 1960) 165–177.

———, "The Evaluation of Learning Under Dissimilar Systems of Instruction," *The Arithmetic Teacher* 13 (April 1966) 267–274.

Buswell, Guy T., "A Comparison of Achievement in Arithmetic in England and Central California," *The Arithmetic Teacher* 5 (February 1958) 1–9.

Husen, Tortsen, *International Study of Achievement in Mathematics* (New York: John Wiley & Sons, Inc., 1967).

Personke, Carl, "Spelling Achievement of Scottish and American Children," *Elementary School Journal* 66 (March 1966) 337–343.

Preston, Ralph C., "A Comparative Study of the Reading Achievement of German and American Children," in J. Allen Figurel, editor, *Changing Concepts of Reading Instruction,* International Reading Association Conference Proceedings 6 (New York: Scholastic Magazines, 1961) 109–112.

Thomason, G. M., and A. F. Perrodin, "Comparison of Arithmetic Achievement in England, Central California, and Georgia," *The Arithmetic Teacher* (March 1964) 181–185.

A Description of Twenty Arithmetic Underachievers*

RAMON ROSS

Ross presents a case study report which involved much observation, of arithmetic underachievers. The problem is pertinent; the description of the 20 pupils is comprehensive; and it opens the way (or at least raises many questions) for future research.

A study of this nature attempts to identify the antecedents responsible for a phenomenon, in this case arithmetic disability. It represents one comprehensive means of studying the "whole child." It is recognized that bias may result since the researcher may be the only judge of some factors and only tentative generalizations can be applied. Yet this approach—being primarily clinical and only secondarily concerned with research techniques—can provide insight into the dynamics of human behavior and contribute a source of hypotheses to be verified by more rigorous investigation. If the experimental sample number is large enough, if the cases are typical, and if the hypotheses of probable antecedents of the difficulty can be identified—then one can safely move to the stage of suggested treatment and follow-up to check on response to treatment.

Some references in "For Further Reading" are included to draw attention to accelerated arithmetic programs for academically talented pupils. Also provided are references concerning diagnosis and treatment of arithmetic difficulties.

Researchers in the area of arithmetic have tended to investigate curricular sequence and scope, stressing particularly an analysis of the difficulty of the various arithmetical processes [1]. These studies have been of considerable value in the development of textbooks and programs of instruction enabling the majority of students to make satisfactory progress in arithmetic. But the findings have provided little direct information about children who experience unusual difficulty in mastering arithmetic in spite of adequate general learning aptitude.

* From *The Arithmetic Teacher* 11 (April 1964) 235–241. Reprinted with permission of The National Council of Teachers of Mathematics and Ramon Ross, Professor of Education, San Diego State College, California.

PURPOSE

In the present study, case studies were obtained of twenty sixth- and seventh-grade students of average or above-average intelligence who were two years or more below their mental grade level in arithmetic achievement as measured by standardized tests. Individual and group descriptions of the intellectual, social, emotional, familial, physical, educational, and specific arithmetical characteristics of these subjects were completed. Although the individual case report remains the primary outcome of such a study, attention will be focused in this article on group findings, due to the number of cases involved.

SUBJECTS

A total of 353 fifth, sixth, and seventh graders who were identified in the initial screening as possessing IQ's of 100 or more on the *California Test of Mental Maturity* and who were one year or more below grade level on the arithmetic section of the *Stanford Achievement Test* were the subjects of this study. The breakdown for grade and sex is shown in Table 1.

TABLE 1

Grade	Boys	Girls	Total
5	75	44	119
6	90	53	143
7	60	31	91
Total	225	128	353

The *Jastak Wide Range Achievement Test*, Arithmetic Subtest, was administered as the next step in screening. From this group of 353 students, twenty-six sixth-grade students and twenty seventh-grade students were indentified who had *CTMM* scores of 100 or over and *Jastak* arithmetic subtest scores two years below their mental age.† No fifth graders were identified who met these criteria.

Twenty students who were among those with the greatest disparity between obtained *Jastak* scores and expected *Jastak* scores were selec-

† Of the twenty-six sixth graders, sixteen were boys and ten were girls; of the twenty seventh graders, sixteen were boys and four were girls.

ted for case studies. Of these twenty, twelve were sixth graders and eight were seventh graders. Two of the sixth graders and three of the seventh graders were girls. The remainder of the report concerns itself with these twenty subjects.

CASE STUDY DESCRIPTIVE MEASURES

Various dimensions of human development were selected as particularly pertinent to the case study of these pupils. The dimensions and the instruments used to measure those variables were as follows:

1. Intelligence: *Wechsler Intelligence Scale for Children* (Full Scale).
2. General achievement: *Stanford Achievement Test,* Intermediate and Upper Level Batteries, Forms J and K.
3. Arithmetic performance: *Jastak Wide Range Achievement Test,* Arithmetic Subtest, and an "Informal Arithmetic Inventory" constructed by the author.
4. Reading performance: *Durrell Analysis of Reading Difficulty,* including the Spelling, Word Flash, Word Analysis, Oral Reading, Silent Reading, and Listening Comprehension subtests.
5. Personality: *California Test of Personality,* Elementary Battery, 1953 revision, and a modification of the *House-Tree-Person* Projective Technique.
6. Socioeconomic background: A parent interview was conducted for each case, obtaining information about the following ten factors: (1) the home, (2) the family constellation, (3) education of the parents, (4) opportunities for arithmetic in the home for the child, (5) school history of the child, (6) work experiences of the parents, (7) attitudes of the parents toward arithmetic, (8) attitudes of the parents toward the child, (9) educational and vocational goals of the parents for the child, and (10) family activities.
7. Physical characteristics: The *Keystone Telebinocular Visual Survey Test* provided a measure of binocular visual proficiency. The *Audivox Audiometer* was used to screen for hearing defects. Height, weight, and disease records were obtained from the cumulative folders. A statement of each child's physical development was obtained from the parents and present teacher.
8. Sociometric data: A sociometric test was conducted in the classroom of each of the students selected for the study. Subjects and peers selected one choice in each of three criteria: arithmetic helper, committee worker, and out-of-school companion.

9. Teacher assessment: Classroom teachers of sixth-grade subjects and mathematics teachers of seventh-grade subjects were asked to describe them in the following three areas: personal behavior characteristics, sources of major difficulty in arithmetic, and general academic aptitude.

10. Past school achievement and behavior: Cumulative records were examined to obtain information relating to past grades, sociometric data, illnesses and frequency of absence, past teachers' assessments, and anomalies that might affect school adjustment and achievement.

All of the assessment, with the exception of height and weight, teacher evaluation, general achievement testing, and sociometric measuring was completed by the writer during the spring of the 1960–1961 school year.

FINDINGS

The findings of this study are arranged by areas of investigation, and include information relating to arithmetic performance, general academic performance including reading, intellectual abilities, physical characteristics, personal-social behavior, and home and family background.

Arithmetical Performance

Table 2 shows *Jastak* grade equivalent scores earned by sixth- and seventh-grade subjects, together with the percentage worked correctly

TABLE 2
Median Grade Equivalent Scores and Mean Percentage Correct on Basic Processes on the Jastak *Arithmetic Subtest*

	Grade equivalent score	Addition of whole numbers	Subtraction of whole numbers	Multiplication of whole numbers	Division of whole numbers	Addition of fractions	Subtraction of fractions	Multiplication of fractions	Division of fractions
Sixth	4.67	83	76	61	33	12	3	8	4
Seventh	5.25	95	82	59	32	27	22	7	0
Mean		88	79	60	33	18	14	8	2

in each of the various processes. Although the grade equivalent score was computed from the entire test results, for the purpose of diagnosis only the four basic processes in whole numbers and fractions were reported.

Accuracy in computation generally decreased as subjects advanced from addition of whole numbers to the other processes. Both groups were very deficient in multiplication and division skills with fractions. Many of the subjects did not attempt these problems, so that the low scores reflected either incorrect computation or no attempt to solve the examples.

An "Informal Arithmetic Inventory" was administered individually to subjects in the study to provide insight into errors being made in reading and reasoning in verbal arithmetic problems. The most frequent oral reading error in these verbal problems was in the reading of large numbers and decimal fractions. Thirteen of the twenty subjects made one error or more in this category. The next most frequent error was in substitution of words, with nine subjects erring.

Four subjects manifested severe reading difficulties in verbal arithmetic problems. For the remainder of the subjects, poor reading skills did not appear to constitute a serious handicap in the story problems on the Informal Inventory. However, reading difficulties were minimized as much as possible in writing the verbal problems. Vocabulary and sentence structure tended to be simpler than that contained in sixth- and seventh-grade arithmetic texbooks.

After subjects had read the problems and described in their own words what the problem was about, they were asked to select the process by which the problem might be solved. Table 3 shows the

TABLE 3

Frequency of Errors in Selecting the Correct Process to Solve Verbal Problems

Process	Frequency of error
Addition of whole numbers	0
Subtraction of whole numbers	2
Multiplication of whole number	8
Division of whole numbers	14
Addition of fractions	4
Subtraction of fractions	7
Multiplication of fractions	15
Division of fractions	15

number of subjects making errors in this selection in one or more instances.

Not only were these subjects unwilling to attempt fraction problems when presented in computational form, as on the *Jastak;* they also tended to select the incorrect process to solve fractional problems when placed in a verbal setting.

Teachers of sixteen of the subjects indicated that "story problems" caused the most difficulty to subjects in their classes. This would tend to corroborate findings on the "Informal Arithmetic Inventory" in which subjects frequently chose incorrect processes to solve verbal problems.

Teachers were also asked to describe what they considered to be causes of arithmetic underachievement among subjects in their classes. Their responses were then categorized under four headings: educational factors, personality factors, physical factors, and home factors. A total of sixty-seven responses were recorded for these four factors. (See Table 4.)

TABLE 4

Factor	Frequency mentioned	Percentage mentioned
Personality	42	62.6
Educational	15	22.4
Physical	5	7.5
Home	5	7.5
Total	67	100.0

Nearly 63 per cent of the factors identified were related to personality characteristics, with fewer than 8 per cent of the causes named as originating from physical or home conditions. Relatively few of the teachers observed that poor work in arithmetic was caused by a lack of the fundamental skills, basic computational errors, poor reading comprehension, or similar educational factors. These subjects were apparently manifesting personality problems in their classrooms which were evident to the teachers. Educational deficiencies were seen by these teachers as originating mostly from personality factors.

Typical of the comments made by teachers were "tries to get by without exerting effort," "inattentiveness in class," "timidity," "immaturity of behavior," "needs confidence in himself."

General Academic Performance

The *Durrell Analysis of Reading Difficulty* was administered to provide information relating to the functional reading and language skills of the subjects. While all of the subjects were at or above middle-fifth-grade level in Listening Comprehension, seven of the twenty were below fifth-grade level in Oral Reading skills, and eight were below fifth-grade level in Silent Reading skills. Greatest deficiencies were observed in materials in which a selection of significant information was required. Students could read the words, as evidenced by success on the Word Flash and Word Analysis subtests, but were unable to answer questions about what they had read in the Oral and Silent Reading paragraphs.

Teachers' assessments indicated that the majority of the subjects were considered below or much below average in all academic areas, including reading, language, and spelling, as well as in arithmetic. Furthermore, the general scholastic aptitude of fourteen of the subjects was assessed as below or extremely below average, reflecting teachers' impressions that these subjects lacked functional capacity for school learning.

Intellectual Abilities

As measured by the *WISC*, little difference appeared in mean Total Verbal and Total Performance scale scores for the group. The mean Verbal IQ for the group was 108.05; the Performance IQ was 110.50. Mean Total IQ was 109.95.

Wider differences were found to exist among mean weighted subtest scores, as is shown by Table 5.

The precise intellectual and personality factors contained in these subtests has remained a source of debate among investigators. Previous researchers have suggested, for example, that low scores in Arithmetic and Digit Span subtests reflect a lack of concentration or attention to a school task [2]. Certainly these differences appear worthy of further investigation of a more definitive nature.

Physical Characteristics

Hearing of the subjects in the study was considered normal. Visual deficiencies appeared among eight of the subjects, with lack of fusion

TABLE 5

*Mean Weighted WISC Scores of Twenty Sixth- and
Seventh-Grade Arithmetic Underachievers*

Test	Score	Extremes
General information	10.55	7– 14
General comprehension	14.25	9– 19
Arithmetic	9.40	6– 13
Similarities	12.40	7– 20
Vocabulary	11.10	9– 13
Digit span	9.80	5– 13
VERBAL IQ	108.05	94–123
Picture completion	13.30	9– 18
Picture arrangement	11.40	7– 14
Block design	11.15	7– 15
Object assembly	11.15	5– 16
Coding	10.20	7– 14
Mazes	11.40	7– 15
PERFORMANCE IQ	110.50	90–131
TOTAL IQ	109.95	102–121

appearing as the most frequent visual anomaly observed. Teachers indicated that ten of the subjects possessed low vitality. Parents of thirteen subjects expressed in the family interview that they considered physical conditions as contributing to arithmetic disability, with the most frequent anomalies observed being a lack of vigor and "nervousness." These children, in general, gave the impression of lacking energy within the school environment, with more nervous tendencies and physical anomalies than would normally be expected among average children.

Personal and Social Adjustment Factors

The *California Test of Personality* was administered to provide an objective measure of personal and social adjustment. Table 6 provides median, Q1, Q3, and Q scores of the group for each of the subtests and composite scores. With the exception of Social Standards, medians for all the subtests were below the fiftieth percentile. The median for one score, Anti-Social Tendencies, was below the twentieth percentile.

Results of this test would suggest that these children were much below average in their social and personal adjustment.

To obtain a projective personality assessment, subjects were asked to draw a house, a person, and a tree, together with any other objects or

TABLE 6
Median, Q1, Q3, and Q on the California Test of Personality,
Form AA, Elementary Battery

Component	Median	Q1	Q3	Q
Self-reliance	35	23	57	17
Sense of personal worth	41	24	51	14
Sense of personal freedom	34	7	56	24
Feelings of belonging	31	13	39	14
Withdrawing tendencies	41	21	56	18
Nervous symptoms	31	14	48	17
PERSONAL ADJUSTMENT	27	17	41	12
Social standards	54	37	71	17
Social skills	49	27	69	21
Antisocial tendencies	18	7	36	15
Family relations	33	21	55	17
School relations	38	11	51	20
Community relations	39	21	55	17
SOCIAL ADJUSTMENT	35	27	40	7
TOTAL ADJUSTMENT	31	29	38	5

details they might wish to include in the picture. These drawings were then analyzed by a psychometrist** who had not been provided with information regarding the subjects. Three general conclusions regarding the group were posited by the psychometrist.

1. "Many of the homes appear empty. Most of the drawings of houses indicate the subjects' feelings of lack of security and structure within the home environment."
2. "There is a lack of integration among the subject, the home, and society."
3. "There is a low general intelligence and/or inadequate experiential background indicated in these drawings."

To summarize these three conclusions, it appeared to the psychometrist that these subjects were generally lacking in an experiential background, were withdrawn, immature, and limited in their family and peer relations.

Results of the sociometric assessment indicated that arithmetic underachievers were chosen infrequently in all categories. Only two of the twenty subjects received one or more choices as an arithmetic helper. Nine subjects each received one or more choices as a committee worker or an out-of-school companion. Nine subjects were unchosen in

** Mrs. Evelyn Watson, School Psychological Services, University of Oregon.

any of the categories. It would appear that the general deficiencies in relating to people as manifested by the sociometric technique are in accordance with the low scores in the Feelings of Belonging and Freedom from Anti-Social Tendencies subtests on the *California Test of Personality*.

Teachers were asked to complete a checklist of descriptive phrases for subjects in the study. Results of this check-list indicated that teachers considered these subjects as generally cheerful and manifesting a liking for school, but also as withdrawn and isolated from their classmates. Subjects were considered much below average in their work habits, their acceptance of responsibility, and their concern about their schoolwork.

Home and Family Background

The majority of these subjects were from lower socioeconomic class homes. One father was a successful merchant, two others owned small home businesses, two were salesmen in chain stores, and the remainder were skilled and unskilled workers. Seven mothers were employed at the time of the study, doing service work in restaurants and taverns, working in packing plants, and assisting the father in his business.

Families were larger than average, with none of them having fewer than three children, and two of them having six children. One home evidenced above-average prosperity, and eight others, while modest in construction, were neat and well-tended. The remaining eleven homes tended to be what Warner et al. would refer to as "fair" or "poor," located in generally "below-average" neighborhoods [3].

All but three of the parents had attended high school, although only ten fathers and eleven mothers had graduated. Four parents had some trade school, junior college, or college training, but none of them had completed more than two years of college work. Ten fathers and five mothers recalled personal difficulties in reading, spelling, or arithmetic when in school.

Job concerns, problems with finances, and a lack of outside interests appeared as common among these families. Poor communication seemed to exist between parents and children, particularly between male subjects and fathers, with both parents indicating that the majority of these boys appeared to get along better with the mothers.

Fifteen of the parents observed that their children had shown generally slow development or immaturity as infants and young children, and had been slow in school from the beginning. In twelve instances parents felt that arithmetic underachievement had been exacerbated by poor instruction at school, with teachers identified as "immature," "cranky," "too old," "picked on the kids," and other similar descriptions.

SUMMARY AND CONCLUSIONS

To measure various dimensions of human behavior among twenty sixth- and seventh-grade arithmetic underachievers of average or above-average intellectual ability, a battery of tests, interviews, checklists, and screening devices was utilized. The following results appeared during the course of the investigation and suggest need for further definitive study:

1. Mean per cents of accuracy in the basic computational processes were as follows: addition, 8 per cent; subtraction, 79 per cent; multiplication, 60 per cent; division, 33 per cent; addition of fractions, 18 per cent; subtraction of fractions, 14 per cent; multiplication of fractions, 8 per cent; division of fractions, 2 per cent.

2. Subjects evidenced satisfactory reasoning in word problems involving addition and subtraction of whole numbers, but made frequent reasoning errors in problems involving multiplication and division of whole numbers as well as in all the processes involving common fractions.

3. Sixteen of the subjects were one or more years below their mental grade level in functional reading ability as measured by the *Durrell Analysis*.

4. Teacher assessment and cumulative records indicated that subjects were underachieving generally in school subjects other than arithmetic.

5. Teacher assessment and personality tests indicated that subjects characteristically were withdrawn and defeated in their attitudes toward school and society.

6. Sixty-three per cent of the causes of underachievement identified by classroom teachers were of an emotional nature, involving lack of interest, home or school maladjustment, short attention span, or limited initiative.

7. Fifteen of the subjects had shown immaturity or slowness of general development, while thirteen of them manifested abnormal physical conditions, ranging from low vitality to rheumatic fever.

8. Parents tended to be from lower socioeconomic classes. Three parents owned small businesses, two were salesmen, twelve were skilled or unskilled laborers, and three were unemployed.

9. Parents of twelve of the subjects tended to hold one or more teachers responsible for their child's inadequacies.

In this study arithmetic underachievement appeared as a complex and multiple-factored disability. While broad patterns of behavior appeared among these subjects, further investigation is needed to determine the precise relationships extant between these factors and arithmetic underachievement.

REFERENCES

1. Hunnicutt, C. W., and Iverson, William J., *Research in the Three R's* (New York: Harper and Brothers, 1958), p. 348.
2. Richardson, Helen M., and Surko, Elise F., "WISC Scores and Status in Reading and Arithmetic of Delinquent Children," *Journal of Genetic Psychology,* LXXXIX (1956), 251–62.
3. Warner, W. Lloyd; Meeker, Marchia; and Eells, Kenneth, *Social Class in America* (Chicago: Science Research Associates, 1949), pp. 149–54.

FOR FURTHER READING

Aftreth, Orville B., "The Effect of the Systematic Analysis of Errors in the Study of Fractions at the Sixth Grade Level," *Journal of Educational Research* 52 (September 1958) 31–34.

———, and Donald MacEachern, "An Action Research Study in Arithmetic," *The Arithmetic Teacher* 11 (January 1964) 30–32.

Bernstein, Allen, "Library Research—A Study in Remedial Arithmetic," *School Science and Mathematics* 59 (March 1959) 185–195.

Blair, Glenn M., *Diagnostic and Remedial Teaching* (New York: The Macmillan Company, 1956).

Brueckner, Leo J., "Analysis of Difficulties in Decimals," *Elementary School Journal* 29 (September 1928) 32–41.

———, "Analysis of Errors in Fractions," *Elementary School Journal* 28 (June 1928) 760–770.

———, and Guy L. Bond, *Diagnosis and Treatment of Learning Difficulties* (New York: Appleton-Century-Crofts, 1955).

———, and Fred Kelly, "A Critical Evaluation of Methods of Analyzing Practice in Fractions," *Research in Arithmetic,* 29th Yearbook of

the National Society for the Study of Education, Part II (Bloomington; Public School Publishing Co., 1930), pp. 525–534.

Buswell, G. T., and Lenore John, *Diagnostic Studies in Arithmetic,*
Supplementary Educational Monograph No. 30 (Chicago: University of Chicago, 1926).

Haggard, Ernest A., "Socialization, Personality, and Academic Achievement in Gifted Children," *The School Review* 65 (Winter 1957)
388–414.

Harvey, Lois F., and George C. Kyte, "Zero Difficulties in Multiplication," *The Arithmetic Teacher* 12 (January 1965) 45–50.

Jacobs, James N., Althea Beery, and Judith Leiwohl, "Evaluation of an
Accelerated Arithmetic Program," *The Arithmetic Teacher* 12 (February 1965) 113–119.

Keough, John J., "The Relationship of Socio-Economic Factors and
Achievement in Arithmetic," *The Arithmetic Teacher* 7 (May 1960)
231–237.

Otto, Wayne, and Richard A. McNenemy, *Corrective and Remedial
Teaching* (Boston: Houghton Mifflin Company, 1966).

Suppes, Patrick, and D. N. Hansen, "Accelerated Program in Elementary School Mathematics—the First Year," *Psychology in the
Schools* 2 (July 1965) 195–203.

A Study of the Attitudes Toward Arithmetic
of Students and Teachers in the
Third, Fourth, and Sixth Grades*

VIRGINIA M. STRIGHT

This survey report was selected to represent attitude studies for all areas of the curriculum. It is thought in every subject area that the effectiveness of instruction will be heightened by the development of a program which recognizes the significance of each child's attitude— for his attitude affects what he learns, what he remembers, and what he does. Although little used, an arithmetic attitude test may provide valuable information for planning the instruction to try to build a positive attitude toward the subject. In Stright's study, the researcher adapted Dutton's *Arithmetic Attitude Scale* and provides the items of the scale for the reader. As the author notes, measurement in this area of attitude is not easy—current means for gathering data on pupil attitudes are not very refined. The organization and summary of data are clearly presented, though some readers may not agree that the researcher's third conclusion is supported by the data presented in the report.

The reader may find references in "For Further Reading" concerning pupil attitude toward other school subjects (for example, see Perrodin). Certainly, the limitations noted by Stright in her study suggest further topics for research.

In the last few years many changes have occurred in the teaching of arithmetic, with the result that today arithmetic has a place of much greater importance in the curriculum. However, even with these changes, much of the current literature about arithmetic in the elementary curriculum gives one the impression that arithmetic is still a much disliked subject. Statements such as these appear in periodicals:

* From *The Arithmetic Teacher* 7 (October 1960) 280–286. Reprinted with permission of The National Council of Teachers of Mathematics and Virginia M. Stright, Teacher, Horace Mann School, Indiana, Pennsylvania.

"It is only too certain that today's mathematically ill-prepared teachers, many of whom are ill-disposed toward the subject, are infecting too large a number of our boys and girls with an enduring fear and hatred of mathematics, which can rarely be overcome later on in high school" (1) and "Most students who have a fear and dislike of mathematics met with some frustration in the elementary grades." (2)

In the *New York Times* this statement has appeared:

Attitudes of frustration build up because of insufficient challenge or because of too difficult work in the elementary grades. The students of today's classroom represent widely different capacities and interests which cannot be satisfied through uniform content and method. . . . The future of many American scientists and mathematicians depends on how they feel about mathematics in the early grades. (3)

B. R. Buckingham says:

One of my colleagues at Ohio State University used to dismiss arithmetic with the remark—often repeated—that the subject had come to a standstill, that there was little more to be learned about it, and that those who concerned themselves with it were dealing with trivialities. We knew all we needed to know, said he, about arithmetic, and all of any consequence that we were ever likely to want to know. I fancy too that my colleague, if he had spoken his full mind, would have said that arithmetic is a hard subject, an unlovely subject, and a subject altogether ungrateful, demanding the strength of the young and repaying with disappointment. (4)

Just what is the attitude taken by children in the elementary school today? Are teachers really infecting fear and hatred into a large number of our boys and girls? Is arithmetic still a much disliked subject with little practical application in our everyday life?

It was with these questions and others in mind that the writer undertook a study to attempt to discover within a limited field the present-day attitudes of children and teachers toward arithmetic.

The writer will feel justified in having made the study if an elementary teacher who reads this report asks herself, "Is this the attitude of the children in my arithmetic class?" "Is arithmetic meaningful to my group?" "Do 17% of the children in my room find arithmetic boring?"

What can the teacher do for the child who wishes he didn't have to be submitted to arithmetic? Is it possible through carefully planned lessons to change or at least modify a child's negative attitude?

STATEMENT OF THE PROBLEM

Most educators agree that attitude plays an important part in the learning process. Attitudes formed early in life quite often persist throughout life. Elementary schools, therefore, seem to have a great responsibility in helping to create favorable attitudes toward school subjects.

How are attitudes formed? Do children as early as third grade have rather firm attitudes toward arithmetic? Do teachers work to establish a wholesome frame of mind in children concerning the need for and importance of arithmetic? Does the teacher use many devices and employ different methods with different children, or is arithmetic still merely the drill subject that it once was in the curriculum?

The purpose of this project is to study the attitudes of children and teachers today, to note changes, if any, from third grade to fourth grade to sixth grade, to note trends in attitudes of both children and teacher, and to compare the attitudes of boys and girls toward arithmetic.

NATURE OF THE STUDY

The study was begun by searching for an attitude scale for school subjects. There have been many scales devised and used successfully for elementary school subjects. Dutton's Attitude Scale appeared adequate, but careful study proved the need of revision for the purpose the writer had in mind.

Dr. H. E. Remmers of Purdue University's Division of Educational Reference has tried many types of attitude scales and graciously supplied samples for study. Dr. N. L. Gage of the University of Illinois also supplied information which was helpful.

After careful study of these samples and after several trials with small groups of children and a sample of teachers, the Dutton Attitude Scale was revised for purposes of this study.

LIMITATIONS OF THE STUDY

The writer realizes that this research study has definite limitations.

1. No attempt has been made to compare achievement with attitude.
2. There has been no provision made for individual differences in children's abilities to read and interpret the attitude scale.
3. No attempt has been made to discover why some children take unfavorable attitudes toward arithmetic.
4. There has been no follow-up to note change in attitude from month to month or year to year.
5. The area studies have been limited to selected school districts in Pennsylvania and one in Ohio.

PROCEDURE

The writer selected for this study children from grades three, four, and six. The study was pursued through the co-operation of the teachers and elementary supervisors from the following schools in Pennsylvania: Benjamin Franklin Joint School, Indiana County; the Penns Manor District, Indiana County; West Deer Fraser School in Allegheny County; Latrobe City Schools, Westmoreland County; West Chester School District, Chester County; and Franklin Street School, Elyria, Lorain County, Ohio.

In most of the schools the questionnaire was distributed by the elementary supervisor so that the children would perhaps feel freer to give a true answer and not merely the answer he thought would please his teacher. It was explained that the teacher would not see the answers, and because neither the child's nor the teacher's questionnaire asked for names, there was no pressure for approval or disapproval on certain questions. Grade placement and sex were indicated on the questionnaires. The elementary supervisor supplied such information as was necessary regarding the teacher's experience, training, and recent study in the field of arithmetic.

The composite results showed that 29 teachers and 1,023 students participated in the study. The graphs, charts, and summaries which follow describe the results of the study.

TABULATIONS OF QUESTIONNAIRE DATA

The number of students involved in this study included 335 third grade students, 327 fourth grade students, and 361 sixth grade students, or a total of 1,023 students.

Each school's questionnaires were tabulated according to grade, then according to sex within the grade. Since there were no significant differences in the responses from the separate school districts, the tabulations were then combined to include the totals from each grade for all the school districts surveyed.

The attitude scale included 25 items to be checked as to whether the child agreed or disagreed with the statement. In the third grade the supervisor was instructed to read the statements if she felt the reading might prove too difficult for the youngsters, but she was instructed to read without comment as to meaning. The writer realizes that attitudes are not easily measured but felt nevertheless that this type of scale, if properly used, would yield a satisfactory measure, since there was no immediate and personal issue at stake. It will be recognized in the interpretation of the data that some error of measurement exists. However, the tabulations are from a fairly wide sampling and should offer stable results. The child was under no pressure as he might be in taking a test, for the questionnaire had no means of identifying him except by age, grade and sex. This was an effort to get an unbiased response from the child.

Responses to the 25 questions on the attitude scale are tabulated according to both sex and grade. In order to make comparisions of the responses, the data was also converted into percentages and shown by both grade and sex. The original tabular and graphic information is available with the original manuscript, on file at the Library, State College, Indiana, Pennsylvania.

The first chart shows responses to the 25 items on the scale for all the students involved in the study. The second chart presents in graphic form the responses of the twenty-nine teachers to the thirty-five items on the teacher attitude scale.

Responses on Arithmetic Attitude Scale of
1023 Students in Grades Three, Four, and Six

1. If I had my way, everybody would study arithmetic.

2. Arithmetic is one of the most useful subjects I know.

3. All people should know arithmetic.

4. Arithmetic will help us in our daily lives.

0 10 20 30 40 50 60 70 80 90 100

5. Arithmetic has its faults, but I still like it.

0 10 20 30 40 50 60 70 80 90 100

6. Arithmetic is very uninteresting.

0 10 20 30 40 50 60 70 80 90 100

7. Nobody in our room likes arithmetic.

0 10 20 30 40 50 60 70 80 90 100

8. Arithmetic might be worth while if it were taught right.

0 10 20 30 40 50 60 70 80 90 100

9. Arithmetic is dull and boring.

0 10 20 30 40 50 60 70 80 90 100

10. I wouldn't take arithmetic if I didn't have to.

0 10 20 30 40 50 60 70 80 90 100

11. I don't even try to do my best in arithmetic.

0 10 20 30 40 50 60 70 80 90 100

12. I can't see how arithmetic will help me.

0 10 20 30 40 50 60 70 80 90 100

13. I really enjoy arithmetic.

0 10 20 30 40 50 60 70 80 90 100

14. I wish we'd miss arithmetic more often.

0 10 20 30 40 50 60 70 80 90 100

15. I like to figure and reason out problems in this class.

0 10 20 30 40 50 60 70 80 90 100

16. I've found arithmetic is useful at home.

0 10 20 30 40 50 60 70 80 90 100

17. I sometimes do extra work in arithmetic just for fun.

0 10 20 30 40 50 60 70 80 90 100

18. Arithmetic is just too hard for me to understand.

0 10 20 30 40 50 60 70 80 90 100

19. We get too much arithmetic.

0 10 20 30 40 50 60 70 80 90 100

20. I can't see how arithmetic will be very useful to me out of school.

0 10 20 30 40 50 60 70 80 90 100

21. Arithmetic teaches me to be accurate.

22. Arithmetic is a waste of time.

23. Arithmetic is the best subject in school.

24. Arithmetic is okay.

25. I wish we had arithmetic more often.

Responses of 29 Teachers on Arithmetic Attitude Scale

1. No matter what happens, arithmetic comes first.

2. Arithmetic is of great value.

3. Arithmetic develops good reasoning ability.

4. I can teach arithmetic well without reading arithmetic magazines and methods books.

5. Arithmetic is very practical.

6. If some class has to be skipped, arithmetic is usually it.

7. I really enjoy teaching arithmetic.

8. Arithmetic is profitable to everybody who takes it.

9. I like to have the pupils try several ways of solving problems rather than to follow a suggested pattern.

10. I look forward to teaching arithmetic.

11. Arithmetic will benefit only the brighter students.

0 10 20 30 40 50 60 70 80 90 100

12. Arithmetic is one of the most useful subjects I know.

0 10 20 30 40 50 60 70 80 90 100

13. Arithmetic serves the needs of a large number of boys and girls.

0 10 20 30 40 50 60 70 80 90 100

14. A good teacher needs to keep up with modern methods in teaching arithmetic.

0 10 20 30 40 50 60 70 80 90 100

15. I spend more time on arithmetic than my schedule calls for.

0 10 20 30 40 50 60 70 80 90 100

16. If the teacher is sure she can solve the problems and exercises in arithmetic, she does not need to plan the arithmetic lessons.

0 10 20 30 40 50 60 70 80 90 100

17. I skip over arithmetic whenever I can.

0 10 20 30 40 50 60 70 80 90 100

18. Arithmetic is just a skill with little practical application.

0 10 20 30 40 50 60 70 80 90 100

19. Sometimes I give extra assignments in arithmetic as punishment.

0 10 20 30 40 50 60 70 80 90 100

20. I didn't like arithmetic in school and I still don't.

0 10 20 30 40 50 60 70 80 90 100

21. I can't seem to get arithmetic across to my students.

0 10 20 30 40 50 60 70 80 90 100

22. A good teacher follows the textbook very closely.

0 10 20 30 40 50 60 70 80 90 100

23. I give homework as a way of getting it across.

0 10 20 30 40 50 60 70 80 90 100

24. I use many devices and ways to get my students interested in arithmetic.

0 10 20 30 40 50 60 70 80 90 100

25. Arithmetic is very hard for the slow student.

26. I thoroughly enjoy teaching arithmetic.

27. I see no practical purpose in emphasizing arithmetic.

28. I wish I did not have to teach arithmetic.

29. Methods of teaching arithmetic have changed very little since 1930.

30. I have the feeling that my students hate arithmetic.

31. I always schedule arithmetic at a time when there will be no interruptions.

32. Arithmetic is never slighted. One time or another I fit it into my schedule each day.

33. I feel that I make arithmetic interesting to most of the children.

34. Arithmetic is the subject I like least of all to teach.

35. Arithmetic is not receiving the attention it deserves in school.

SUMMARY OF DATA

Third Grade

Since several studies seem to support the hypothesis that attitudes are formed as early as third grade, the following conclusions seem significant. However, one must take into consideration the lack of complete accuracy in third grade children's responses, part of which may be due to reading difficulty and part to the immaturity of the eight-year-old.

1. 19% of third grade children said arithmetic was dull and boring.
2. 20% thought arithmetic an uninteresting subject.
3. 25% said they wouldn't take arithmetic if they didn't have to.
4. 63% felt it was the best subject in school.
5. 65% sometimes do arithmetic just for fun.
6. 71% wished they had arithmetic more often.
7. 84% really enjoyed arithmetic.
8. 85% liked to figure and reason out problems.

Fourth Grade

Study of the responses of fourth grade children to the attitude questionnaire seemed to justify the following statements. Again one must take into consideration inaccuracies due to lack of meaningful concepts.

1. 17% of fourth graders felt arithmetic was dull and boring.
2. 18% thought they got too much arithmetic.
3. 21% found arithmetic uninteresting.
4. 23% wouldn't study arithmetic if they didn't have to.
5. 63% wished they had arithmetic more often.
6. 79% really enjoyed arithmetic.
7. 86% liked to figure out problems.
8. 87% thought arithmetic one of the most useful subjects they knew.
9. 88% thought arithmetic helped them to be accurate.
10. 93% found arithmetic useful at home.

Sixth Grade

After a study of the results of sixth grade children's responses, the following conclusions seemed significant.

1. 14% thought arithmetic dull and boring.
2. 14% felt they got too much arithmetic.
3. 18% found arithmetic uninteresting.
4. 53% thought it was the best subject in school.

5. 63% wished they had arithmetic more often.
6. 66% liked to do arithmetic for fun.
7. 81% really enjoyed arithmetic.
8. 85% liked to figure out problems.
9. 87% felt it taught them to be accurate.
10. 91% thought arithmetic was one of the most useful subjects in school.
11. 93% had found it helpful at home.
12. 98% thought arithmetic would help in our daily lives.

SUMMARY STATEMENTS OF DIFFERENCES

From the tables and charts that have been tabulated from the data received, the following conclusions seem significant.

1. A small percentage in all three grades felt arithmetic was a waste of time.
     Third grade—13%
     Fourth grade—8%
     Sixth grade—6%
2. In third grade 23% couldn't see how arithmetic would be very helpful out of school, but in fourth grade this attitude was held by only 12% and in sixth grade 10%.
3. 25% of third graders and 23% of fourth graders said they wouldn't take arithmetic if they didn't have to, while only 13% of sixth graders gave this reply.
4. 61% of third graders felt that all people should know arithmetic, while by fourth grade this response had increased to 94% and by sixth grade to 98%.
5. In all three grades more than 80% of the children really enjoyed arithmetic.
6. In third grade 84% found arithmetic useful at home; in the fourth and sixth grades, 93% found it useful at home.
7. As for thinking arithmetic the best subject in school, 63% of the third graders agreed; 59% of fourth graders; and 53% of sixth graders.

SUMMARY OF ALL STUDENTS

When the attitudes of all the students were totaled from the data received from the attitude scale, the following conclusions seemed to be the most interesting and worthwhile:

1. Only 9% of the children checked felt that arithmetic was a waste of time.
2. 17% felt they got too much arithmetic.
3. 20% thought arithmetic uninteresting.
4. 58% said it was the best subject in school.
5. 66% wished they had more arithmetic.
6. 69% liked to do extra arithmetic just for fun.
7. 81% said they really enjoyed arithmetic.
8. 86% classified arithmetic as the most useful subject in school.
9. 87% felt that arithmetic taught them to be accurate.
10. 95% of all the children felt that arithmetic would help them in their daily lives.

COMPARISONS BETWEEN BOYS AND GIRLS

Since studies show that boys tend to achieve better scholastically in arithmetic, the results of the questionnaire made for an interesting comparison between the attitudes of boys and girls.

1. 20% of both boys and girls felt arithmetic was an uninteresting subject.
2. 54% of the boys and 63% of the girls thought arithmetic was the best subject in school.
3. 61% of the boys and 71% of the girls wished they had arithmetic more often.
4. 65% of the boys and 73% of the girls did extra arithmetic just for fun.
5. 76% of the boys and 84% of the girls stated that they really enjoyed arithmetic.
6. 76% of the boys and 94% of the girls felt everyone needed to know arithmetic.
7. More than 85% of both boys and girls agreed that arithmetic was one of the most useful subjects they knew.

SUMMARY AND CONCLUSIONS DRAWN FROM THE TEACHERS' DATA

It has already been stated elsewhere in this study that the teachers who completed the attitude scale were not identified by name. It was felt that perhaps this would tend to present a truer picture than if the teacher were under pressure to give the answer he felt was wanted or that he knew was acceptable in the light of present-day methods of teaching. The elementary supervisor did supply enough information so that the writer might ascertain whether or not the teachers' age, training, experience, and recent study made any significant difference in attitude. The years of experience ranged from thirty-two years to one. Several teachers were near retirement age while others were recent college graduates. Of the teachers surveyed fourteen held a Bachelor of Science degree, six had the Master of Education degree, and nine no degree and no recent college work. The writer realizes that true attitudes are very difficult to measure. However, from the data tabulated the following conclusions may be significant.

1. 90% of all teachers said that no matter what happens, they fit arithmetic into their schedule each day.
2. 93% stated that they really enjoyed teaching arithmetic, while 97% indicated that they thoroughly enjoy teaching arithmetic. Several questions were repeated in different form as a check. This was one which varied slightly.
3. 90% of teachers felt that a good teacher should keep up with modern methods, but 21% felt they could teach arithmetic well without reading periodicals and methods books.
4. 17% felt that methods of teaching arithmetic had not changed in the past thirty years.
5. All of the teachers agreed that arithmetic is of great value.

CONCLUSIONS AND IMPLICATIONS

After analyzing the results of the study of pupil attitudes by grade and by sex, as well as the teachers' responses, the writer draws the following conclusions and implications:

1. A large percentage of elementary teachers really enjoy teaching arithmetic and use many devices to make it interesting.
2. All teachers felt that lessons should be carefully planned. It was not felt sufficient that the teacher just know how to solve the problems and exercises. This does not imply that all of these teachers do plan each arithmetic lesson carefully, but that they know the value of careful planning.
3. The teacher's educational background, recent training, age, or years of experience seemed to make no significant difference in his attitude toward the teaching of arithmetic, nor of the attitude of the children in the group.

4. Contrary to popular opinion, a very large percentage of both boys and girls do like arithmetic and feel it is a very useful subject.

5. The majority of the teachers answering the questionnaire really enjoy teaching arithmetic. This does not imply that all of the teachers are good teachers of arithmetic.

6. Definite attitudes in students have developed by the third grade.

7. As children grow older they develop more meaningful concepts in arithmetic.

8. According to previous studies, girls tend to make consistently better scores than boys in general studies. Boys seem to have a slight edge in arithmetic, geography and science. However, in all three grades measured in this study, girls liked arithmetic better than boys, and 22% more of the girls thought everyone should know arithmetic. No attempt has been made to check the correlation between arithmetical achievement and attitude toward arithmetic.

REFERENCES

1. Marshall Stone, "Fundamental Issues in the Teaching of Elementary School Mathematics," *The Arithmetic Teacher*, VI (October, 1959) 177.

2. Leon McDermott, "A Study of Factors That Cause Fear and Dislike of Mathematics," Dissertation Abstract 19, July, 1958, M.Ed., Michigan State University, p. 71.

3. "Feel For Science Develops in Youth," *New York Times* (February 18, 1957).

4. B. R. Buckingham, "Perspective in the Field of Arithmetic," *The Arithmetic Teacher*, II (February, 1955) 1.

FOR FURTHER READING

Bassham, Harrell, *et al.*, "Attitude and Achievement in Arithmetic," *The Arithmetic Teacher* 11 (February 1964) 66–72.

Dutton, Wilbur H., "Attitudes of Prospective Teachers Toward Arithmetic," *Elementary School Journal* 52 (October 1951) 84–90.

———, "Attitudes of Junior High School Pupils Toward Arithmetic," *School Review* 64 (January 1956) 18–22.

Lowery, Lawrence F., "Developing an Attitude Measuring Instrument for Science Education," *School Science and Mathematics* 66 (May 1966) 494–502.

Lyda, Wesley J., and Evelyn C. Morse, "Attitudes, Teaching Methods, and Arithmetic Achievement," *The Arithmetic Teacher* 10 (March 1963) 136–138.

Perrodin, Alex F., "Children's Attitudes Toward Elementary School Science," *Science Education* 50 (November 1966) 314–318.

6

NATURAL SCIENCE

In the elementary school the content of botany, zoology, physics, chemistry, geology, and astronomy is unified into one subject called "science" (or "natural science" to distinguish it from social science). There appears to be a fair degree of agreement on this unification of science in the elementary school, in contrast to the language arts or social studies, in which the content is often segmented. As a school subject, science has not yet been accorded the importance it deserves as one of the two "idea" subjects. An "idea" subject is one that deals with content or ideas about the physical or social world, as opposed to "tool" subjects which deal with *how* to express these ideas. Science also deserves a more important role in the school because ours is a technical society requiring such knowledge.

The researches in this chapter have been selected to deal with the topics of: historical overview, children's readiness, children's interest, information sources, grade placement of content, methods, special science teachers, and evaluation. The types of research found in this chapter include four experimental studies, three surveys, and one historical study. Classified by grade level of coverage, these research studies include: one covering K–8; one 1–6; one 1–2; two 4–5–6; and one each for K, 4, and 6.

There appears to be not nearly as much research in science education as in other subject areas of the elementary school curriculum. Of the research available the intermediate grades (4–6) seem to be favored, while the lower grades are comparatively neglected. It is particularly difficult to find good reports of research on broad experimental projects. The elementary school science program appears not to be as greatly affected by the foundation and federally supported projects as the secondary school science program. Many researches reach the stage of a dissertation on microfilm, or a government report, but are not made more widely available through journals. The reader may be interested to know that the journals in which the writers found the most reports on research in elementary science education are *Science Education, School Science and Mathematics, The Journal of Research in Science Teaching, The Science Teacher,* and *Elementary School Journal.* Readers who are particularly interested in science might wish to consider the following sources (all of which cover grades 1–12):

Journal of Research in Science Teaching (John Wiley & Sons, Inc., 605 Third Avenue, New York, N.Y. 10016) published quarterly.

Mallinson, George G., editor, *School Science and Mathematics* (Western Michigan University, Kalamazoo, Michigan 49007) published nine times a year.

Pruitt, Clarence M., editor, *Science Education* (University of Tampa, Tampa, Florida 33606) published five times a year.

The Science Teacher, the official journal of the National Science Teachers Association (1201 Sixteenth St., N.W., Washington, D.C. 20036) published nine times a year.

A listing of sources follows for the benefit of those wishing to pursue some aspect of elementary school science research. Several recent comprehensive professional textbooks have also been included to give the reader guidance on topics on which there is little or no research.

American Educational Research Association, "Natural Sciences and Mathematics," *Review of Educational Research* 34 (June 1964), 31 (June 1961), 27 (October 1957), 21 (October 1951).

Blackwood, Paul E., *Science Teaching in The Elementary Schools* (Washington, D.C.: U.S. Office of Education, 1965).

Blough, Glenn O., and Julius Schwartz, *Elementary School Science and How to Teach It,* 3rd edition (New York: Holt, Rinehart & Winston, Inc., 1964).

Buck, Jacqueline, "Summary of Published Research 1929–52 in Teaching Elementary Science," *Science Education* 38 (February 1954) 81–101.

———, and George M. Mallinson, "Some Implications of Recent Research in the Teaching of Science at the Elementary School Level," *Science Education* 38 (February 1954) 81–101.

Carin, Arthur, and Robert B. Sund, *Science Teaching Through Discovery* (Columbus, Ohio: Charles E. Merrill Books, Inc., 1964).

Craig, Gerald S., "Science in the Elementary School," *What Research Says to the Teacher*, No. 12 (Washington, D.C.: National Education Association, 1957).

———, *Science for the Elementary School Teacher*, 5th edition (Waltham, Mass.: Blaisdell Publishing Co., 1966).

Cummings, Howard H., editor, *Science and the Social Studies*, 27th Yearbook (Washington, D.C: National Council for the Social Studies, 1957).

Department of Elementary School Principals, *Science for Today's Children*, 32nd Yearbook (Washington, D.C.: National Education Association, 1953).

Dunfee, Maxine, *Elementary School Science: A Guide to Current Research* (Washington, D.C.: Association for Supervision and Curriculum Development, 1968).

Gega, Peter C., *Science in Elementary Education* (New York: John Wiley & Sons, Inc., 1966).

Hone, Elizabeth B., Alexander Joseph, Edward Victor, and Paul F. Brandwein, *Teaching Elementary Science: A Sourcebook for Elementary Science* (New York: Harcourt, Brace & World, Inc., 1962).

Hurd, Paul D. and James J. Gallagher, *New Directions In Elementary Science Teaching* (Belmont, California: Wadsworth Publishing Co., 1968).

Keesler, Oreon, "A Survey of Research Studies Dealing with the Elements of Scientific Method as Objectives of Instruction in Science," *Science Education* 29 (October 1945) 212–216.

Kuslan, Louis I. and A. Harris Stone, *Teaching Children Science: An Inquiry Approach* (Belmont, California: Wadsworth Publishing Co., 1968).

National Society for the Study of Education, *Rethinking Science Education*, 59th Yearbook, Part I (Chicago: National Society for the Study of Education, 1960).

Navarra, J. Gabriel, and Joseph Zaffaroni, *Science Today for the Elementary-School Teacher* (New York: Harper & Row, Publishers, 1963).

Piltz, Albert, and Robert Sund, *Creative Teaching of Science in the Elementary School* (Boston: Allyn and Bacon, Inc., 1968).

Ramsey, Gregor A., and Robert W. Howe, "An Analysis of Research Related to Instructional Procedures in Elementary School Science" *Science and Children* 6 (April 1969) 25–36.

Renner, John W., and William B. Ragan, *Teaching Science in the Elementary School* (New York: Harper & Row, Publishers, 1968).

Smith, Herbert A., and Kenneth E. Anderson, "Science" in Chester W. Harris, editor, *Encyclopedia of Educational Research* (New York: The Macmillan Company, 1960), pp. 1216–1232.

Sullivan, John J., and Calvin W. Taylor, *Learning and Creativity, With Special Emphasis on Science* (Washington, D.C.: National Science Teachers Association, 1967).

Tannenbaum, Harold E., Nathan Stillman, and Albert Piltz, *Science Education for Elementary School Teachers*, 2nd edition (Boston: Allyn and Bacon, Inc., 1965).

Victor, Edward, *Science for the Elementary School* (New York: The Macmillan Company, 1965).

Watson, Fletcher G., "Research on Teaching Science," in N. L. Gage, editor, *Handbook of Research on Teaching* (Chicago: Rand NcNally & Co., 1963), Chap. 20, pp. 1031–1059.

Elementary School Science in the Past Century*

GERALD S. CRAIG

To enable the reader to place the elements of this chapter in perspective, an historical overview of elementary school science is presented. In our mad rush to go somewhere, it is often useful to take time out to look at where we have been, and to get some sense of where we seem to be headed. This article is a good illustration of historical research, relating important events, movements, and people in science with each other and with broader areas of education psychology, and the whole of society. More studies of this nature are needed in education.

The reader may wish to compare events as recorded in this article with those mentioned in Smith's review of the development of reading instruction (Chapter 2), Mackintosh's history of language arts instruction (Chapter 3), and Wade's perspective on social studies education (Chapter 4). In addition, the reader will find other excellent overviews in the field of science education in the list "For Further Reading." Of particular interest may be the broad surveys of elementary school science instruction in Illinois, Minnesota, Virginia, and Florida.

Although he could not gracefully speak of it himself, it should be mentioned that Craig, in his long and significant career, has made a most outstanding contribution to elementary science education through repeated editions of his professional textbook, his elementary school text series, his teaching at Teachers' College, Columbia University, and his study of children's science interests.

The National Education Association is observing its first 100 years of service to the nation and the world. It seems altogether fitting in this Centennial Year that persons interested in the improvement of science education give some attention to the history of American education. Through a knowledge of the origins and developments of science in education, we as teachers may be wiser in designing the science in future programs of education. It is the purpose of this rticle to discuss briefly

* From *Science Teacher* 24 (February 1957) 11–14. Reprinted with permission of the publisher and Gerald S. Craig, Professor Emeritus of Natural Sciences, Teachers' College, Columbia University, New York.

a few of the events of the past 100 years and relate these events to the present trends in the development of science in the elementary school.

The present elementary school science was initiated in the 1920's and 1930's by a number of public school systems and teacher educational institutions as it became evident that nature study was not well designed for the educational needs of children. This development is so recent that many, if not most, of the teacher educational institutions of the nation are still in the process of retooling; that is, reorganizing their staffs and curricula in order to meet the demands for science in the professional education of classroom teachers.

Science during the period of the late 18th and for a considerable portion of the 19th century was frequently labeled "natural history" or "natural philosophy." The natural history consisted of the study of plants, animals, minerals, and other natural objects. The natural philosophy was the study of nature in general. The natural history became the biology of today and the natural philosophy became the physics and chemistry.

The late Professor Orra E. Underhill, in a scholarly study published in 1941, revealed that the roots of our modern elementary school science are deep in the history of American education and American science. Instruction in science, according to Dr. Underhill, can be traced to the late 18th century when children's literature (known as the didactic literature) was designed for the purpose of instruction. Some of this literature directed children's observation and study of natural phenomena. Although these books were largely of British origin, many were brought to the United States and were adapted to the new world and reprinted by American publishers. Underhill has traced this literature to the influence of Francis Bacon, John Locke, and other writers who stimulated democratic thought on both sides of the Atlantic Ocean.

This instructional literature was designed for use with parents or tutors teaching the children at home. Only the upper class families could afford to give the children the advantages of such an education. At the time the NEA was being organized (1857), some of this literature was being adapted for use in schools.

PESTALOZZIAN TEACHING

At the same time (1857), "Pestalozzian object teaching" was attracting the attention of both European and American educators. The NEA was instrumental a few years later in securing the almost universal adoption of the "Oswego object teaching" which was an American version of the Pestalozzian methods. With the introduction of this new method, there was an upsurge of interest in the revision of content and method of the elementary school. This came at a time when there was increased growth in the elementary school enrollment and the newly-organized NEA was directing efforts toward the development of the elementary school as the great common school—common in that it was the institution intended for all the people regardless of social class, religion, nationality, or race.

As we look back on the period of object teaching, it is easy to emphasize its obvious weaknesses rather than its contributions. In any appraisal of this method, we should keep in mind that object teaching was an international educational development. In Germany, it evolved into Heimatkunde. In both England and the United States, object teaching was supplanted by nature study. The English and American versions of nature study differed greatly.

During the period of the development of object teaching (1860–1880), the emphasis on a highly formal methodology obscured the direction and the purpose of science. In many ways object teaching was an intrusion in the development of elementary school science. The continuity that had grown from the promotion of science by our forefathers who were interested in the development of science in elementary education, such as Franklin and Jefferson, was interrupted by the introduction of object teaching. It might be said, too, that as an importation from Europe it lacked the vigor and support of a movement which was associated with the American frontier. As far as instruction in science in the elementary school was concerned there was a mere emphasis on descriptions of animate and inanimate objects rather than on interpretations of phenomena or events. In most cases the organization of questions about the objects were dictated by the formal organization of the separate sciences and as a result represented an adult imposition of learning upon a child. Object teaching was designed to encourage a description of obvious and trivial matters to the neglect of the profound and challenging meanings.

Object teaching was based upon the principles of faculty psychology. Assumptions of a serial development of the faculties led to the emphasis on observations and memorizing in the primary years. It was assumed on the basis of faculty psychology, that young children were able to observe and identify objects but they lacked the ability to interpret phenomena. The specialized methodology of object teaching together with the exclusion of the use of books made heavy demands upon the ability and knowledge of the teacher. Object teaching was not well designed for either children or teachers. It was not realistic and lacked the challenging ideas and purposes needed for an education of children living in an industrial democracy.

However, from the point of view of the evaluation of the origins of elementary school science, object teaching made a significant contribution to the development of techniques which were utilized in a long list of research studies from 1920 to the present time. These studies were instrumental in the selection and evaluation of the purposes of elementary school science and in analyzing these purposes into component learning elements. Beginning in the 1930's, these techniques have been adapted more intensively to use in the study of behavior as related to learning in science and to experiential meanings.

OBJECT TEACHING WANES

As the interest in object teaching waned and emphasis again became more specifically directed to the nature of content, a strong demand for science in the elementary school program became evident. Following the depression of 1873, the schools were severely attacked as the pinch of taxes made the citizens ask what they were getting for their money. There was scarcely an educational journal of that day that did not carry at least one article pleading for more science in the school program. The chief emphasis during this period was in terms of giving a wider knowledge and understanding of the rapidly increasing science and technology.

The attempts to formulate an elementary school science curriculum met with a clash of points of view. Changes were occurring in the social and economic patterns which tended to influence the accepted purposes of an educational program. There were also changes in psychology which brought about changing conceptions as to the nature of the learning process.

Materials for pupil use and teacher planning were not common until nearly the end of the 19th century. Such leaders as G. Stanley Hall and Colonel Francis W. Parker furnished a general philosophy of education which strongly supported the study of nature and provided opportunity for others working under them to experiment and work out detailed programs, as did Wilbur S. Jackman and Henry H. Straight under Parker and Clifton F. Hodge under Hall. Others translated philosophy and educational theory into specific details of a program, as did William T. Harris and Charles, Frank, and Lida Brown Mc-Murray.

PARKER'S INFLUENCE

The great influence of Parker came from his desire to use science as a unifying principle for the elementary school curriculum and his support of the work of Jackman and Straight along this line at the practice school of the Cook County Normal School, later Chicago Institute, and finally the School of Education at the University of Chicago.

Harris prepared the first detailed and extensive elementary science curriculum which offered specific help to teachers. This curriculum represented an organization emphasizing the subject matter of the science as a guide to organization within a framework suggested by educational theory.

To Jackman belongs the distinction of being the father of modern elementary science. His point of view in regard to both children and science corresponds remarkably to our recent conceptions. Much of Jackman's writing indicates a positive and dynamic view of children rather than the negative ideas so prevalent in the latter part of the 19th century. He was the author of the third yearbook (1904) of the National Society for the Scientific Study of Education later known as the National Society for the Study of Education. This was the first yearbook of this society that was devoted to the problems of the teaching of science. Jackman represents the connecting link between the early writers of children's literature and the modern elementary science. He laid the basis for the developmental approach of elementary school science in the closing years of the 19th century and the first decade of the 20th century.

NATURE STUDY

About the same time, there came into the picture of science education a new phase known as the nature study movement. This movement obscured the contributions of Jackman for a time. Nature study, like object teaching, was an intrusion in the development of elementary science. However, in judging nature study, those interested in elementary school science should realize that there were many points of view of nature study and the leaders of nature study were in continuous debate. Nature study may be thought of as a movement in two senses. First, it may be considered part of a broad and general development resulting from the combined influences of Romanticism and the "new" education. Second, it may be thought of more specifically as a school program initiated and largely directed by Dr. Liberty Hyde Bailey and his associates at Cornell University. In either case one must think of nature study as a development of great vision. Bailey and many others involved in the nature study movement were men of high purpose. Furthermore, it must be said that the nature study movement was an American movement. It was homespun. It carried with it many of the ideals and thinking of the frontier. The main purpose of the nature study movement was a utilitarian one, namely, to improve agriculture and to overcome the desire of farmers' children to leave the farm for the city. Mrs. Anna Botsford Comstock, in the preface to one edition of her remarkable book, *Handbook of Nature Study,* which ran through edition after edition beginning in 1911, states that the nature study movement began during the depression of 1891–1893 in an attempt to prevent young people from migrating from the farms to New York City, thus adding to already crowded relief rolls.

From the beginning, the Cornell group recognized the importance of teacher education. The publications of Bailey, Mrs. Comstock, and others were among the most courageous and most comprehensive attempts at teacher education in the field of science education that have ever been undertaken.

Prior to 1870, elementary science was the commonly accepted term used to designate science work in the elementary school. By 1900, nature study had become the accepted term. During the ten-year period of transition the two terms were used more or less interchangeably and synonymously. Because of the extreme formalism to which science teaching had gone in the elementary school, leaders in the educational reform chose the term "nature study" as a means of setting up their program as different from, or opposed to, the formalism associated with the earlier elementary science. This division of opinion as symbolized by choice of terminology is seen to rest upon (1) differences in meaning carried by the term "science," and (2) a difference in underlying philosophy as to the nature of "truth" and how it is secured.

Nature study received much criticism almost from its inception. The most valid and significant of these criticisms were directed towards its emphasis upon incidental items, its lack of organization, its limitation of children's capacity to reason, and its extravagant claims for aesthetic and emotional values.

DIVERSITY AND EXTREMES

In the nature study movement, statements of purpose are characterized by wide diversity and extreme comprehensiveness. Such statements carry no suggestion of the content and method by means of which the purposes are to be achieved.

Assumptions as to the nature of children's interests and their part in motivating learning led to the assumption that the immediate and casual interests of children should be the guiding factor in the selection of what is to be studied. Nevertheless, the details of programs as given in nature study manuals reveal that the organization of the specialized sciences was an influential factor in the selection of materials and methods of presentation.

Continued emphasis on firsthand observation and "nature, not books" led in practice to seasonal organization of materials, theoretical emphasis on field trips and out-of-door nature experiences, and identification as an end in itself. In spite of this emphasis (in theory) on firsthand experience, much of the material classified as nature study was in the form of reading materials and stories about nature, and a great deal of this was fable, myth, and fairy tale.

Although theoretical discussion usually advocated a well-rounded program including the physical sciences, in practice nature study came to be considered as treating almost wholly with biological nature. This was probably owing to the greater ease with which such materials could be obtained and handled by teachers untrained in science, and to the fact that those most interested in introducing nature study into the schools were largely specialists in the biological sciences.

MORE NATURE STUDY

Nature study was largely the development of specialists in science and was not properly designed for the classroom. The earlier elementary school science movement was guided by men such as Jackman who not only were specialists in the field of science but were experienced teachers of children.

Nature study was also constructed on the basis of faculty psychology and serial development. The outlook on children was a negative outlook in that the leaders were prone to think of the child in terms of his limitations rather than his potentialities.

By the 1920's, it was quite evident that nature study was not succeeding in the elementary school. As we have said earlier, new attempts were made to design a curriculum in science. In the writings of Jackman, Dewey, and Kilpatrick were bases for a new outlook on science and children. The material in the present day elementary science curriculum is better designed for children and classroom teachers than was that constructed in Jackman's time. This, of course, would be expected because some 40 years have rolled around since the peak of Jackman's writings, and hence the human race has had more experience with science and the meanings of science.

CHAPTERS OF INTEREST

One of the chapters of interest in the development of elementary science relates to pressure groups. In the earlier periods there was pressure from various theologians to prescribe denominational science for children. There was also an urging for the development of a natural theology. There is much less of this kind of pressure in evidence today.

There have been other pressure groups such as humane societies, temperance societies, and more recently the aviation industries. These interests are not all to be condemned, except in so far as they seek to force the school to distort its purpose.

For almost two centuries it has been recognized that science is essential to the education of children in a democracy. Various informal experimentations have been conducted to establish a suitable basis for the development of science in the elementary school program. Few of these experimentations prior to 1920 were supported by adequate research.

Some of the problems encountered in developing elementary science in the past have arisen from the fact that science in its modern aspects has been both novel and profound for adult society. The problem of selecting purposes and procedures for teaching and learning experiences of children has been a perplexing one. However, as mankind has learned more about science, it has become more intelligent about the role of science in elementary education.

Other difficulties have arisen from inadequate views of the abilities of children to interpret the events of the universe. The psychological thinking of much of the 19th and early 20th centuries was negative about children and tended to place limitations upon their potentialities for growth and development in understanding natural phenomena.

Science was thought by many educators and scientists as beyond the comprehension of children in the elementary school. As a result, science in many elementary schools was relegated to a more casual or trivial place in the curriculum with an emphasis on its correlation with other elementary school subjects. Science became in many schools an incidental and accidental matter of little value to children or to society.

In recent years a more dynamic psychology of science education has been developed which recognizes the interpretation of the physical environment as a natural facet of child growth and development.

REFERENCES

A *Half Century of Science and Mathematics Teaching*. Central Association of Science and Mathematics Teachers, Inc., Oak Park, Ill., 1950.

Hindle, Brooke. *The Pursuit of Science in Revolutionary America, 1735–1789*. The University of North Carolina Press, Chapel Hill, 1956.

Robertson, M. L. "Emerging Curricula in Elementary Science." *Science Education*, XXVI (December 1942), pp. 178–186.

Underhill, Orra E. *The Origins and Development of Elementary-School Science*. Scott, Foresman and Co., Chicago, 1941.

FOR FURTHER READING

Challand, Helen J., "An Appraisal of Elementary School Science Instruction in the State of Illinois," *Science Education* 42 (October 1958) 363–365.

Dubins, M. Ira, "Curriculum Makers' Emphases in Elementary School Science 1940–1952," *Science Education* 43 (October 1959) 318–324.

Hedges, William D., and Mary Ann MacDougall, "An Investigation of the Status of Science Education in Selected Public Elementary Schools of Virginia," *Science Education* 48 (February 1968) 59–64.

Johnston, Jane, "Achievement in Elementary School Science in a Representative Sampling of Minnesota Schools," *Science Education* 45 (February 1961) 58–61.

Kuslan, Louis I., "Elementary Science in Connecticut, 1850–1900," *Science Education* 43 (October 1959) 286–289.

Mallinson, Jacqueline V., "The Current Status of Science Education in the Elementary School," *School Science and Mathematics* 61 (April 1961) 252–270.

McKibben, Margaret J., "Elementary School Science and Mathematics Education in Western Europe," *School Science and Mathematics* 61 (June 1961) 404–417.

Newport, John F., "Are Science Objectives Changing?" *School Science and Mathematics* 65 (April 1965) 359–362.

——, "The Distribution of Science Facts in Three Editions of an Elementary Science Series," *Science Education* 49 (December 1965) 485–487.

Piltz, Albert, "An Investigation of Teacher-Recognized Difficulties Encountered in the Teaching of Science in the Elementary Schools of Florida," *Science Education* 42 (December 1958) 440–443.

Rosen, Sidney, "A Bold Experiment in Elementary School Science: 1871," *Elementary School Journal* 62 (November 1967) 66–76.

Smith, Eugene H., "An Analysis of Some Prominent Viewpoints on Teaching Elementary School Science," *Science Education* 47 (March 1962) 188–193.

Children's Understanding of Natural Phenomena*

DONALD INBODY

Studies leading to decisions as to what to teach appear to be fewer in number than those concerned with how to teach, when it would seem that the reverse should be true. What to teach is both a prior and a very significant question. Curricula have many sources, including demands placed by: (1) A technological society; (2) the nature of knowledge in the disciplines; (3) children's interests, which are outgrowths of their environments; and (4) children's understandings, which are outgrowths of their maturation and experience. The following study, in the tradition of Piaget, examines the latter source and, from its results, draws curricular implications. It is a survey type research which uses very careful data-gathering procedures.

Examinations of curricular trends, or sources for curricular decisions, are also reflected in other studies in this volume, including Wade's analysis of trends in the social studies (Chapter 4), Joyce and Weinberg's consideration of the use of the strategies of sociology in social studies curriculum development (Chapter 4), Coxford's replication of Piaget's study (Chapter 5), Craig's history of the science curriculum (Chapter 6), Perrodin's study of children's science interests (Chapter 6), and Schenke's survey of the information sources children use (Chapter 6). "For Further Reading" points up other studies of children's understandings, particularly of young children's concepts and knowledge in science.

It is generally agreed that the school's curriculum should provide children with experiences which will utilize knowledge and understandings they possess and lead them on to new and more advanced understandings. The folly of attempting to teach children things for

---

*From *Science Education* 47 (April 1963) 270–278. Reprinted with permission of the publisher and Donald Inbody, Director of Instruction, Corinth District Schools, Prairie Village, Kansas. This paper is based on the author's doctoral dissertation "The Understanding of Selected Physical Phenomena Possessed by Suburban Kindergarten Children," submitted in partial fulfillment of the requirements for the Ed.D. degree at University of Kansas, Lawrence, Kansas, 1961.

which they have not obtained an experiential background is also commonly acknowledged. And, it is recognized that school experiences which merely duplicate the child's previous experiences and do not lead him to increased understanding are wasteful.

With these issues in mind, educators have for many years been concerned with the content and sequence of the elementary science program. Several approaches have been used in attempting to find the solution.

Studies as early as 1774 were concerned with concept development, "the contents of children's minds." Underlying that approach has been the premise that if we know enough about how children think and how their concepts develop, we can provide learning experiences at the optimum time. The approach has had varying amounts of popularity. G. Stanley Hall's work in the late nineteenth century stimulated many related studies then and in the early years of this century. Attention then apparently turned to other subjects until Piaget's books appeared in the late 1920's and early 1930's. His reports also stimulated many additional studies, the results of which seemed to contradict Hall. From about 1937 until just recently, one seldom finds Piaget or his work mentioned in the science education literature.

It appears that findings of investigations of children's concept development have had relatively little influence on the science curriculum. This may well be because of the lack of any agreement among the various investigators.

Beginning in the 1920's, other approaches to determination of the curriculum were tried. Children's interests were studied and science programs were designed which would utilize them. Most notable of these was Craig's investigation which probably has had more influence on elementary science than any other single piece of research. More recently, however, investigations of children's interests seem to have had less influence on the science program, perhaps because of conflicting evidence. There have been many investigations of children's interests, but it seems that the only outstanding implication is that environment is the principal factor influencing the acquisition of interests.

Children's environment has been the subject of another approach to the determination of the curriculum. Understandings possessed by children of different socio-economic backgrounds have been studied recently, although to a rather limited degree. Results of these studies seem to indicate significant differences among children from varying environments, but the extent and nature of these differences is not yet clear. There seems to be practically no evidence regarding the relationship between environment and children's understanding of natural phenomena.

From about 1940 until recently, the major research effort in determination of the nature of the elementary science program was through grade placement studies. These have been relatively fruitless, consistently producing the conclusion that there is little or no agreement about the grade placement of science topics.

Another recent approach to the problem has been through experimental placement of topics. In this method, a given topic is presented to children on two or more grade levels, and an attempt is made to learn which is the optimum level. This method, also, has had little influence on the curriculum, probably because there are too many variables which cannot be controlled, and the results of the experiments have only limited application.

In general, recent studies of science aims and objectives have indicated that the trend is away from subject matter objectives and toward the aim of developing suitable scientific aims and behavior, and on concept development as opposed to the learning of information. The present study was an attempt to learn something of the nature of children's understandings of natural phenomena before they entered the first grade, and sought to learn if current curriculum practices in elementary school science:

1. Provide opportunities for children to extend and enlarge their understandings.
2. Require children merely to repeat experiences they have had already, leading to little or no new understanding.
3. Provide experiences for which children have little or no background of experience.

PLAN AND PROCEDURE OF THE STUDY

To answer the questions posed above, 50 kindergarten children were examined regarding the extent of their understanding of selected physical phenomena. The children were questioned individually, using a demonstration-interview technique which has proven useful for many investigations.

Selection of Phenomena

Phenomena to be investigated were selected by an analysis of textbooks. The books were representative of widely used series published from 1955 through 1960. Books for grades one and two were included, as were the books for kindergarten and a "primer" provided with two of the series. All books were read and all physical phenomena presented were tabulated.

This analysis resulted in a list of 55 physical phenomena which were presented at least once in the collection of 18 books. As it seemed infeasible to investigate children's understandings of all 55 phenomena, it was decided to select only those presented one or more times by at least one-half of the textbook series. This selection produced the following list of 16 phenomena which formed the basic framework of the investigation.

1. Air is everywhere.
2. We cannot see, smell, or taste air.
3. Wind is moving air.
4. Wind can do work.
5. Air has weight.
6. Air occupies space.
7. Rain comes from clouds.
8. Rain is water.
9. Water may evaporate into the air.
10. Sun and wind speed evaporation.
11. Water which evaporates may form clouds and rain.
12. Water freezes into ice when it is cooled enough.
13. Ice melts and becomes water when it is warmed enough.
14. Electricity may produce light, heat, and do work.
15. Electricity may be carried by wires.
16. Some things float in water, others do not.

The Demonstration-Interview

Data concerning children's understandings of the above phenomena were collected by individual interviews with children. The interview technique was similar to that used by Piaget and others. Situations and questions were developed which would elicit children's explanations, and require a minimum of factual, one-word responses. Wherever possible, commonplace materials were used to demonstrate the phenomena. In a few cases pictures were used, and in two instances verbal questions with no accompanying materials were used.

Several guiding principles were formulated and followed throughout the interviews. These were based on a study of the professional literature and the investigator's own experience with young children.

1. To help reduce anxiety, each interview began with casual conversation about subjects of interest and concern to the child.
2. Questions were worded carefully to avoid influencing the child's response by giving him clues to the anticipated answers.
3. The interviewer attempted to be casually permissive and to avoid communicating any anxiety of his own about the child's responses, yet not appear disinterested.
4. The interviewer made every effort to convey to the child genuine liking and acceptance while maintaining a sense of neutrality and objectivity.
5. Interviews were conducted in a room which was quiet and free of distractions.
6. The interviewer attempted to adapt his behavior to the subject and the situation according to his evaluation of the motivations and defenses that might be influencing the child's responses.

With the above list of guiding principles, a tentative interview schedule was given an extensive try-out. Several procedures were tried and found to be of no value to the investigation, as were several of the proposed demonstration situations. After nearly 50 children were interviewed, and several modifications of procedure and technique had been made, it appeared that a workable instrument had been developed.

The final form of the schedule consisted of 12 topics or experiences. Eight involved demonstrations of natural phenomena with commonplace materials. Two used pictures and two were purely verbal. The time needed for each interview was 25 to 30 minutes, including general conversation with the child to put him at ease and to establish rapport. Each interview was tape recorded and a minimum of notes were made during the interview.

A brief description of each of the 12 experiences presented to children follows:

1. Each child was shown a toy sailboat and tank of water. They were asked to tell how to make the boat move without touching it or the

water. If the child did not suggest blowing, the investigator blew on the sail. This action was followed by several questions about the nature and sources of the air or wind that made the boat move.

2. The children were shown a balloon and asked to explain what made the balloon get big when it was inflated. The balloon was allowed to deflate and questions were asked about what happened to the contents of the balloon.

3. An inverted glass tumbler with a paper napkin inside it was shown to each child. He was asked to predict what would happen when the tumbler was forced into the water with the open end down, to observe what was happening while the tumbler was completely submerged, and to explain why the napkin did not get wet. The napkin was removed from the tumbler and the tumbler was again inverted and submerged. The children were asked to explain why water did not come into the tumbler, to predict what would happen when the tumbler was tipped, and to explain the nature and source of the bubbles which formed.

4. Each child was shown two identical sheets of paper. One of them was wadded into a ball. The child was then asked to predict what would happen if the two sheets were dropped at the same time, and then to explain why the sheets fell differently.

5. Air was forced onto each child's skin from a hollow rubber ball which had a small hole visible to the child. He was then asked about the source of the air and how it got there. The ball was deflated and the child was asked to place his finger over the hole and explain why it reinflated when he removed his finger. The last part of this experience consisted of having the child mash the ball by pushing with one finger on any place on the surface of it, then by placing his finger directly over the hole and pushing. He was asked to explain the different reactions.

6. The children were shown two pictures in which it was obvious that the wind was blowing. Questions were asked about the nature of wind and why certain objects in the pictures were moving.

7. Children were shown two pictures in which it was obviously raining, and they were asked what was happening in the pictures. After they had recognized that it was raining, they were asked the following typical questions: "What can you tell me about rain?" "What is rain?" "Where does rain come from?" "How did it get there?" "What makes it rain?"

8. Each child was shown a four-part picture in which the first scene showed rain falling on a sidewalk. In succeeding scenes, the rain was no longer falling, but water puddles remained. The puddles were shown successively smaller and in the last scene, no water was shown, and shadows indicated that the sun was shining. The children were questioned about

their ideas of what happened to the puddles, where the water could have gone, and why the water disappeared.

9. A picture of clothes hanging on a clothes line was shown. The children were asked to explain why the clothes were there, what made them get dry, where the water went, and the kind of day on which the clothes would dry the fastest.

10. Evidence of children's understandings of the freezing and thawing of water was obtained by direct questioning. The six basic, or control, questions were: (1) What will happen if we place a jar of water outdoors on a real cold night? (2) Will anything else happen? (3) What can you tell me about ice? (4) What would happen to a piece of ice if we placed it here on the table and left it alone? (5) What makes ice melt? (6) What makes water turn into ice?

11. Each child was shown six objects: a piece of wood about three-fourths inch square by about three inches long, a cork stopper, a rubber stopper the same size and shape as the cork, a small, oddly shaped piece of aluminum, a wooden spring clothes pin, and a penny. The children were asked to predict whether each object would float or sink. After the predictions were made for all six objects, the objects were placed in water, and the children were asked to explain why each object floated or sank.

12. The children were questioned directly concerning their understandings of electricity. The basic questions asked were: (1) What makes the lights in this room light? (2) What can you tell me about electricity? (3) What do you have in your home that uses electricity? (4) How does electricity get to the things that use it?

Each interview followed the prepared schedule in general, but not necessarily in detail. For each topic, the pattern was one of (a) showing the child certain materials and asking him to predict what would happen under given circumstances, (b) performing the demonstration and having the child state what happened, and (c) eliciting the subject's explanation of the phenomenon.

Most questions were worded in a manner which would require explanatory answers rather than brief one-word, factual responses. Every attempt was made to get the child to explain the reason or reasons for the event. The interview schedule was considered as suggestive, and if the subject's responses were such that it seemed profitable to do so, deviations were made. For example, one part of the schedule was intended to determine if the child knew that he could cause a toy sailboat to move by blowing on it, and that his breath was comparable to the wind. Often, in that part of the interview, the discussion became involved with wind, and the questions listed in another part were used. Certain questions, however, were considered control questions, and were asked during the interview, even though perhaps not in the order appearing on the schedule. At all times questions were worded in a manner that harmonized with the child's preceding response. Questions which suggested possible answers were avoided if at all possible.

Some conclusions seem justified regarding the interview process used, although it is difficult to produce empirical evidence to support them. These are based on study of the professional literature and the investigator's experience during the try-out and the investigation proper:

1. Children's responses were sincere. There was little or no indication of flippant or off-hand responses, nor of responses intended only to please the investigator.

2. The sample was adequate. By the end of the investigation, no new types of responses were being observed. Early in the investigation certain patterns seemed to emerge. During the process, however, a point was reached when no new patterns were discernable.

3. The demonstration-interview provided a realistic and reasonably accurate insight into children's understanding of most phenomena investigated.

Description of the Children Interviewed

Children selected for the study attended kindergarten classes in three school districts in a large residential suburb of Kansas City, Kansas and Kansas City, Missouri. There were very few families of upper or lower socio-economic classes in the area served by the three districts. Protestant, Roman Catholic, and Jewish faiths were represented. The population is almost entirely white, native American.

Interest and concern for schools and education is quite high. Evidence of this is the financial support for schools. In spite of a low tax base and high levies, all districts have more than adequate buildings, and the teachers' salaries are among the highest in the state. Other aspects of the educational programs are generally considered to be among the best in the state.

After the try-out procedure had been completed, a sample of 50 children, 21 boys and 29 girls, was randomly selected. Children interviewed during the try-out were not included. Chronological ages of the subjects ranged from 64 months to 80 months at the time of the interview.

FINDINGS

The 50 tape recorded interviews were played back and analyzed. Children's responses were analyzed in two ways. First, an attempt was made to learn how much the children understood about the various phenomena.

Then the responses were analyzed as to the nature or types of explanations presented. Summaries of these two analyses are presented here.

Children's Understandings of Natural Phenomena

AIR AND WIND

1. Twenty-six per cent of the children seemed to understand that air is everywhere. The rest apparently conceived of air as being outdoors, by or at windows or doors, or present only when there was evidence of motion.

2. Nearly two-thirds of the children seemed well aware that air is invisible. It is possible that some of the remaining 19 children may have been aware of this phenomenon, but had no opportunity to express themselves due to inadequate questioning procedure.

3. There was no indication that any of the children understood that air has weight.

4. Evidence regarding children's understanding that air is a substance occupying space appeared somewhat contradictory. When moving air was involved, such as inflating a balloon, over four-fifths apparently recognized that air was the causal factor. When no motion was evident, as with the inverted tumbler in water, the presence of air was recognized by ten per cent or less.

5. Approximately 90 per cent of the children indicated that they understood that wind involved motion. It was less clear whether they understood that it was air which was in motion. A factor which makes it difficult to reach any definite conclusion about the issue was the prevalence of the concept that air involved motion. It appeared that for about one-half of the children an acceptable definition of air would be "wind."

6. About 90 per cent of the children indicated an awareness that wind can move objects and that it does so by blowing against them.

EVAPORATION AND RAIN

7. All children were aware that rain is water.

8. Only 40 per cent of the children seemed to realize that rain falls from clouds. Over half characterized rain as falling from the sky, apparently without any awareness that clouds are the important factor. Two of the 50 children explained that rain comes from God or Jesus.

9. The children's understandings of evaporation are difficult to summarize. It appears that when the water being considered was in a visible, liquid form, such as in puddles, etc., about one-half realized that water could evaporate into air, although only a few used the term "evaporate." When water was in a less obvious situation, such as in wet clothing, explanations of drying implied considerably different understandings of evaporation. Nearly all children explained that clothes on a line dried because the water fell to the ground or that it "soaked in."

10. Twenty per cent of the children seemed to have some understanding of the water cycle as a factor in rainfall. Nearly two-thirds could give no explanation for the source of water in clouds. Of the 38 children who did give explanations, over one-half stated that God or Jesus was responsible.

FREEZING AND THAWING OF WATER

11. Nearly three-fifths of the children understood that water will freeze and become ice when it is cooled enough. The most commonly used descriptions of ice were "cold" and "water."

12. Most children, 92 per cent, explained that ice will melt at room temperature and become liquid water, but only 42 per cent appeared to understand that heat was necessary to cause melting.

13. Apparently none of the children were aware that freezing water will expand and possibly break its container.

BUOYANCY

14. The children predicted whether common objects would float or sink with only slightly greater accuracy than would have been expected from guessing.

15. About 60 per cent of the explanations for floating and sinking were in terms of the weight of the objects, and about 20 per cent were in terms of form or shape, size, or material composition of the objects. Only one child gave any indication that he was comparing the weight of the objects to the weight of the water. About 17 per cent of the children gave no plausible explanations.

16. There was considerable confusion about the meaning of "light" and

"heavy." Both terms were used as reasons for the actions of all objects. Thirteen children generalized that light objects floated and heavy objects sank, but nine stated that heavy objects floated and light objects sank. It appeared that children tended to consider "light" and "heavy" as absolutes.

ELECTRICITY

17. About 60 per cent of the children knew that electricity may produce light. Only 16 of the 50 children mentioned uses of electricity involving the production of heat and/or the operation of motors.

18. About 44 per cent of the children seemed to understand that wires may conduct electricity to things that use it. About 20 per cent of the children considered the wires as sources of electricity.

THE NATURE OF CHILDREN'S EXPLANATIONS

There seems to be little doubt that the nature of children's thinking changes with maturity and experience. It also seems that the kind of thinking a child can do at any given time places limitations on the type of instruction he can profitably utilize. With this hypothesis in mind, an attempt was made to analyze the quality or nature of the children's explanations.

It was found that the young children's explanations could be classified roughly into six general types:

1. Explanations which were fairly complete, generally correct, causal in nature, and with a minimum of verbalization.
2. Explanations which were plausible, causal in nature, but with incorrect causative factors given.
3. Explanations which were generally correct, but appeared to be largely verbalistic because of the lack of additional explanation or justification.
4. Explanations which were generally incorrect, involving no causation, animistic, or referring to God or Jesus.
5. Explanations which were merely descriptions or restatements of observations.
6. Responses which provided no explanation.

Because of the nature of the questioning procedure, it is difficult to make definite statements about the quantity or quality of children's explanations as such. Any tabulation by categories must of necessity be very subjective. Because of the flexible questioning procedure, responses had to be considered within the context of the entire interview or at least an entire questioning sequence. Due to those factors, the following statements about the types of children's responses must be considered as tentative, although they are based on careful study of the data.

To rank the types of explanations in order according to the number of times used is difficult, but it appears that the order from most-used to least-used was: 2, 4, 1, 5, 3, 6.

Although no child gave explanations of all types, all children used several types. There was a marked tendency for each child to use more of one or two types than any others. This became apparent during the interviews. After interviewing about half of the sample, the investigator was able to predict with fair accuracy the general nature of each child's explanations after two or three experiences had been presented. No serious attempt was made to do this, however, and no record was kept of such predictions in order to avoid the possibility of influencing the children's responses.

All but two children offered explanations involving causality, although about one-half did so in a very limited way. About one-fourth of the children gave explanations which were predominately causal in nature. Although their explanations of the causes were often erroneous, those children did show an awareness of cause and effect.

Phenomena with which children had had direct, physical, contact were most often explained correctly and with an awareness of causality. Freezing and thawing were explained correctly by most children, as was blowing up a balloon and objects blown by wind.

With less familiar phenomena, causality apparently was not an issue with most children. An example of this was the experience with the inverted tumbler in water. Most children had not seen that demonstration or any related to it. To nearly all children, nothing *kept* the water from entering the tumbler. When pressed for explanations, they made incorrect ones. When shown that their explanations could not be correct, they had no answers. Causation apparently was not part of their thinking in this type of situation.

Another instance of the same type of thinking was that related to rain. All children were aware that rain came "down," and several knew it came from clouds. Many, however, had no notion of causality. That water had to get into a cloud had not occurred to them. It was just there. For many children, evaporation presented a similar situation. They were aware that the water disappeared, but not that it went someplace. It just disappeared.

CURRICULAR AND INSTRUCTIONAL
IMPLICATIONS

This investigation revealed that some instructional experiences typically provided for young children are quite appropriate, but others are either too simple or too difficult to be of value. It is realized that there are variations of understanding from child to child, and that understandings possessed by individual children vary from phenomenon to phenomenon. However, it is the writer's contention that the following implications should receive serious consideration when planning instruction for young children. Perhaps they could be considered as working hypotheses.

1. It appears that science instruction for young children is most profitable when concerned with observable phenomena. Children can understand cause and effect in events with which they have direct contact. With less observable events, children are likely to do any or all of the following:

   a. Confuse cause with effect.

   b. Attribute causation to animistic or metaphysical factors.

   c. Consider the event as unique and without causation.

2. Instruction based on deduction which seems logical to the adult may be pointless to the child. What appears to be an obvious contradiction to the adult may be only another unique event to the child because of the child's limited experience.

3. A child's understanding of a phenomenon cannot be assumed even if he uses correct terms and gives correct explanations. A child's explanation may be a repetition of adult language and quite inconsistent with his understanding of the underlying principles. He may not be aware of the relationship which exists between his explanation and the underlying principles.

4. Children need many experiences involving different manifestations of the same phenomenon. Because of their limited experience and imperfect notions of causality, it is easy for them either to overgeneralize or fail to apply a known principle to similar events.

5. Children should be taught to observe physical phenomena carefully, and they should be helped to interpret their observations correctly, looking for correct causative factors.

6. Some phenomena are difficult for young children to interpret because they do not understand the underlying related phenomena. For example, many phenomena concerning air cannot be explained without understanding the nature and location of air. Instruction about the more com-

plex phenomena often leads to overgeneralized or even erroneous concepts.

CONCLUSION

As was mentioned above, the matter of determining the proper scope and sequence of the elementary school science program has received much attention. Most efforts have produced relatively little or no lasting effect on the curriculum. It is this writer's contention that the matter must be based upon children's understandings. Perhaps as we learn more of what children are capable of understanding, and how their concepts develop, we will be able to provide better instruction.

Evidence produced in the present study has shown that young children are capable of understanding cause and effect relationships. It has also shown that adult logic is often meaningless to children, and may well lead to overgeneralization and verbalization.

There seemed to be little doubt that when planning science instruction for young children, every effort should be made to take into consideration the real, not voiced, understandings of the children, and the way children think and reason.

SUGGESTIONS FOR FURTHER STUDY

Throughout the investigation, several unresolved issues arose. These lead the writer to suggest several areas needing further study.

1. It is pointed out that this investigation dealt only with children from a single socio-economic background. This is also true of previous studies. There appears to be little or no knowledge of the relationship between socio-economic background and understanding of natural phenomena. Rural and urban children should also be compared to determine if their environments have any effect on their understandings of natural phenomena.

2. A study similar to the present one conducted either before children enter kindergarten or in the early weeks of the kindergarten year should prove helpful in planning instruction. Perhaps if more were known about what young children understand and how they think, instruction could be presented in a manner which would help avoid verbalisms and misconceptions.

3. Little is known about the breadth of young children's understandings of natural phenomena. Most investigations have dealt with a limited number of phenomena in depth, as the present study attempted to do. Perhaps better instruction would result if more were known about the extent and scope of children's experiences.

4. Informal conversations with the teachers of the children used as subjects in this investigation indicated to the investigator that there may be a rather low correlation between what teachers intend to teach and the understandings gained by the children. The procedure used in this investigation but based on teacher's objectives instead of textbook material, could be useful in determining the actual outcomes of instruction.

5. The present study dealt with children of a limited age range. There is need for more knowledge about how children's understandings and thinking change with increasing age and with instruction. The technique employed by this investigation could be used in a longitudinal study extending over several years with the same children.

6. This investigation has dealt primarily with what children understand and secondarily with how they think. It may be that how children think is the more pertinent issue in planning instruction. The procedure used in this study, along with some scheme of classification and interpretation, could be useful in investigating children's thinking in greater depth.

FOR FURTHER READING

Butts, David P., "The Degree to which Children Conceptualize from Science Experience," *Journal of Research in Science Teaching* 1 (June 1963) 135–143.

Charles, C. M., "Bicultural Children in Science Achievement," *Science Education* 48 (February 1964) 93–96.

Cox, Louis T., Jr., "Working With Science in the Kindergarten," *Science Education* 47 (March 1963) 137–144.

Garone, John Edward, "Acquiring Knowledge and Attaining Understanding of Children's Scientific Concept Development," *Science Education* 44 (March 1960) 104–107.

Harlan, W., "The Development of Scientific Concepts In Young Children," *Educational Research* 11 (November 1968) 4–13.

Haupt, George W., "Concepts of Magnetism Held by Elementary School Children," *Science Education* 36 (April 1952) 162–168.

King, W. H., "The Development of Scientific Concepts in Children," *British Journal of Educational Psychology* 31 (February 1961) 1–20.

Lovell, Kenneth, *The Growth of Basic Mathematical and Scientific Concepts in Children,* 2nd edition (London: University of London Press, Ltd., 1962).

————, and E. Ogilvie, "A Study of the Conservation of Substance in the Junior School Child," *British Journal of Educational Psychology* 30 (June 1960) 109–118.

Scott, Norval C., Jr., "Science Concept Achievement and Cognitive Functions," *Journal of Research in Science Teaching* 2 (March 1964) 7–16.

Smith, Frank, and James H. Dougherty, "Natural Phenomena as Explained by Children," *Journal of Educational Research* 59 (November 1965) 137–140.

Young, Doris, "Atomic Energy Concepts of Children in Third and Sixth Grade," *School Science and Mathematics* 58 (June 1958) 535–539.

Yuckenburg, Laura M., "Children's Understandings of Certain Concepts of Astronomy in the First Grade," *Science Education* 46 (March 1962) 148–150.

Children's Interests in Elementary School Science*

ALEX F. PERRODIN

As the list "For Further Reading" suggests, interest studies abound in many subject areas, science being only one. Since interests are partly a function of children's experiences, they may not reflect what the child has not experienced, or may negatively reflect unsatisfactory experiences. If a child has not done any work with principles of sound, he will probably not know whether he is interested or not. As the sole basis for curriculum selection, therefore, interests are rather shaky, but along with other criteria they may be quite useful.

This is a survey type research. It is particularly noteworthy for its projective instrument, in which the respondent completes a sentence fragment to reveal his interests. The device is also useful in measuring attitudes or values as well as knowledge of subject matter. Since it is relatively easy to develop and administer, teachers can use it readily.

Studies of children's understandings provide another basis for curriculum selection (see Inbody's study preceding this one), and studies of grade placement of content (see Smith's study following this one) suggest still another basis for curriculum building. Joyce and Weinberg's study (Chapter 4) suggests analysis of the content as a basis. Wade (Chapter 4) and Craig (Chapter 6) in their historical studies provide a broader perspective on the task of curriculum building.

What do fourth, sixth, and eighth grade pupils indicate as their interests in science? Do these interests correspond to the course of study in science? Do their science interests change as they move through the elementary school years?

Five hundred fifty-four children in fourth, sixth, and eighth grades were studied in an effort to gain some answers to questions such as the above. The children were enrolled in three different Georgia school systems—one a large metropolitan area school system, one a school system for a city of 50,000 population, and one in a rural area which

* From *School Science and Mathematics* 65 (March 1965) 259–264. Reprinted with permission of the publisher and Alex F. Perrodin, Associate Dean of Instruction, College of Education, University of Georgia, Athens.

had one consolidated elementary school for an entire county. The children studied were completing either the fourth, sixth, or eighth grades. All systems operate within the framework of a state science guide (1) which recommends a spirally-organized curriculum based upon selected concepts in eleven science areas.

In the large school system science is taught primarily by television in grades one through six. Classroom teachers are provided guides in preparing pupils for the lesson with suggested follow-up activities. In the other two school systems science instruction is provided by professionally certified teachers in self-contained classrooms through the first four or five grades, and by a special teacher in a departmental organization in sixth through eighth grades.

PROCEDURE

A projective-type instrument consisting of twenty sentence fragments was devised and tested with pilot groups. The investigator then administered the revised instrument personally in each classroom instructing pupils to complete each sentence with their first thought. If the fragment did not immediately suggest a sentence ending, students were told to leave the item and go on to the next. Although the test was untimed most students responded as directed and completed the instrument in twenty to thirty minutes. The pupils' names were not included in the instrument, and in all classrooms pupils gave evidence of serious cooperation with the investigator.

The projective type instrument was used in order to encourage complete freedom of responses. Multiple choice items were considered by the investigator as possibly limiting the responses or suggesting responses to the pupil. Thus, another purpose of this study was to determine the usefulness of the sentence fragment technique in determining pupils's science interests.

Responses were tabulated and then categorized with the assistance of a doctoral student in science education.

FINDINGS

Favorite Unit

One item on the instrument was, "My favorite unit in Science is . . . ." Responses to this item were categorized according to the divisions of concepts listed in the state science guide. Table 1 summarizes the findings. It is interesting to note that the area "Health, Safety, Human Body" is extremely popular with boys and girls at both fourth and sixth grades, and although this item declines somewhat as a preference by the eighth grade, it is still suggested as a favorite unit.

Unit topics dealing with "Living Things" were mentioned by 25.8% of the boys and by 31% of the girls at the fourth grade level. These percentages dropped to a low level at the sixth grade and then increased greatly again at the eighth grade level.

Girls at both fourth and eighth grade levels indicated preference for units in the area of "Rocks, Soils, and Minerals" to a greater degree than did boys. Boys at the eighth grade level showed a decided preference for units on "Electricity and Magnetism" in comparison with boys and girls at fourth and sixth grade and with girls at the eighth grade level. Interest in units on "Heat, Light, or Sound" showed a great increase at the sixth grade for both boys and girls. Boys at fourth, sixth, and eighth grade levels indicated greater interest than did girls in units dealing with the area of "Transportation, Communication, or Machines."

TABLE 1

Responses to Item "My Favorite Unit in Science is . . ."
of Fourth, Sixth, and Eighth Grade Pupils

	Fourth Grade		Sixth Grade		Eighth Grade	
Category	Boys %	Girls %	Boys %	Girls %	Boys %	Girls %
Living Things	25.8	31.0	3.2	5.1	16.7	25.0
Rocks, Soils, Minerals	2.2	13.8	4.3	2.0	6.6	8.4
Air, Water, Weather	5.6	2.3	3.2	3.0	2.2	10.4
Universe, Solar System, Space	7.9	12.6	14.0	11.1	7.8	12.5
Electricity and Magnetism	4.5	1.1	5.4	0.0	17.8	4.2
Heat, Light, and Sound	1.1	0.0	11.8	12.1	2.2	1.0
Matter, Energy	5.6	1.1	9.7	5.1	4.4	3.1
Health, Safety, Human Body	28.1	27.6	39.8	59.5	16.7	21.9
Transportation, Communication, Machines	9.0	5.7	6.5	0.0	17.8	5.3
No Preference	10.1	4.6	2.2	2.0	7.8	8.4
No. of students responding	89	87	93	99	90	96

In summary, this item reflects only the favorite unit choice of fourth, sixth, and eighth graders. These choices appear to indicate that these elementary school children have preferences for the biological rather than the physical sciences. The study of the topic "Human body" which is most closely related to their own person and the changes taking place during preadolescence received mention most frequently. The data should be interpreted as an indication of the first reactions of the pupils, and do not imply that areas of low frequency of mention are necessarily unpopular.

Part of Science Liked Best

In completing the sentence fragment "The part I like best about Science is . . ." a majority of pupils at each grade level with the exception of the fourth grade boys named an activity as indicated in Table 2. The most frequently named activity is "experiments" and again with the exception of fourth grade boys these appeared to be equally favorite activities of both boys and girls. Other science activities frequently listed included discussing, reading, field trips, making booklets, drawing, films, TV, reports, making things, projects, studying, working, and preparing for a science fair.

Quoting from the pupils' responses to this item, this is what some of the pupils said: "When we discover things," "that you learn about amazing things," "finding out about things and what causes it to hap-

TABLE 2

Responses to Item "The Part I Like Best About Science is . . ." of Fourth, Sixth, and Eighth Grade Pupils

	Fourth Grade		Sixth Grade		Eighth Grade	
	Boys %	Girls %	Boys %	Girls %	Boys %	Girls %
Category						
Named a unit or area	47.2	25.1	30.2	24.1	18.7	11.4
Named an activity	29.2	54.0	58.1	68.7	55.6	58.3
Indicated desire to learn, pursue curiosities, etc.	16.9	18.4	8.6	7.1	8.9	21.9
No preference	6.7	2.3	3.2	0.0	17.8	7.3
No. of students responding	89	87	93	99	90	96

pen," "there is always a reason for everything you do," "that there are still things we do not know," "you can study things that have always puzzled you," and "you get to discover something new each day." Responses such as these were categorized as "learning or curiosity." 16.9% of fourth grade boys, 18.4% of fourth grade girls, and 21.9% of the eighth grade girls completed this item with statements such as the above. It is gratifying to note how closely these responses relate to one of the major goals of elementary school science education.

There were some negative responses to this item and most of these, 17.3%, appeared among the eighth grade boys.

Of those who responded with a name of a unit or science area, the category of "Health, Safety, and Human Body" was indicated again as the favorite of fourth and sixth grades, both boys and girls.

Part Liked Least About Science

In completing the sentence fragment, "The Part I like least about Science is . . ." a majority of the pupils at all grade levels listed a specific type of activity as shown in Table 3. Tests were disliked more by the girls than the boys, while other written work was disliked in general more by boys than by girls. Boys in the schools where science was taught by television objected to the taking of notes or copying

TABLE 3
Responses to Item "The Part I Like Least About Science is . . ." of Fourth, Sixth, and Eighth Grade Pupils

	Fourth Grade		Sixth Grade		Eighth Grade	
Category	Boys %	Girls %	Boys %	Girls %	Boys %	Girls %
Named a unit or area	37.1	31.0	35.5	24.2	25.6	27.1
Named an activity	50.6	57.5	57.0	66.7	66.7	62.5
e.g. tests	(6.7)	(17.2)	(15.1)	(27.3)	(11.1)	(28.1)
Written work	(12.3)	(14.5)	(18.3)	(13.1)	(14.4)	(9.4)
Named an undesirable teacher trait	1.1	3.4	4.3	4.0	3.3	2.1
Liked everything about Science	11.2	8.0	3.2	5.1	4.4	8.4
No. of students responding	89	87	93	99	90	96

the notes about the TV lesson. Some of the respondents made statements such as these: "copying off the board," "when you have to answer questions," "writing down everything," "when the TV teacher talks too fast to take notes," "when the TV teacher sometimes doesn't make sense and won't explain," "just listening to something in class not doing anything myself," "listening to the teacher read something," "having to read something I don't understand," "the long, boring lectures," "just studying and not working together," "writing down study questions at end of chapters," and "the worksheets we have to do."

Of the units or topics which students listed as being the part liked least about science, fourth grade boys and girls, and the sixth and eighth grade boys most frequently listed topics in the area of "Living Things." Sixth grade boys more than any other group indicated a dislike of topics in the area of "Health, Safety, and the Human Body." By contrast, sixth grade boys more than any other group indicated this area as their favorite in responses to the previously discussed item. Possibly this reflects the great differences in physical development appearing among sixth grade boys.

SUMMARY

By means of certain items included in a projective type instrument 554 fourth, sixth, and eighth grade pupils in three school systems gave an indication of their science interests. The area of study which appears to be the favorite is that of "Health, Safety, and the Human Body" with interest in this area, especially a study of the body, reaching a peak at the sixth grade level. The study of "Living Things" is popular, but the girls' interests exceed that of the boys in this area.

Fewer pupils listed a favorite unit in the areas dealing with physical science and in general more boys were interested in these than were the girls.

Pupils in general indicated that the part liked best as well as the part liked least in science are the activities. They indicated that they liked to do "experiments," but they disliked tests and written work. A study of the responses seems to indicate that both boys and girls want an opportunity to do things in science, to discuss what they are learning, to explore their curiosities, and to be able to ask questions. Lecturing, listening, copying notes, writing answers to the teacher's questions are not popular learning activities.

CONCLUSIONS

The instrument used in this study could be helpful if used early in the school year as an aid to the teacher in determining pupils' science interests. It could also serve the purpose of an aid in evaluating factors other than achievement as schools examine the effectiveness of their science instructional programs.

For the schools involved in this particular study it would appear that teachers need to plan better motivational procedures if elementary school science is to encourage the development of a broad background of science knowledge and contribute to expanded science interests.

The responses to this instrument reveal that children express a liking for what is generally considered to be a major goal of science instruction. The children indicate they are curious, they want to question, to discuss, and to experiment. They appear to be saying that they prefer experiences in which they can take an active part to those experiences which are largely teacher directed as copying notes and listening to lectures. This study has implications not only for the content of the elementary school science program but also for the methods of teaching most related to the goals of elementary science education.

FOR FURTHER READING

Blanc, Sam S., "Critical Review of Science Interest Studies," *Science Education* 42 (March 1958) 162–168.

Fitzpatrick, F. L., "Pupil Testimony Concerning Their Science Interests," *Teachers College Record* 38 (February 1937) 381–388.

Jungeblut, Ann and John H. Colemen, "Reading Content that Interests Seventh, Eighth, and Ninth Grade Students," *Journal of Educational Research* 58 (May–June 1965) 393–401.

LaDue, Donald C., "Social Studies Interests of Children," *Peabody Journal of Education* 40 (May 1963) 345–347.

McAulay, J. D., "Social Studies Interests of the Primary Grade Child," *Social Education* 26 (April 1962) 199–201.

MacCurdy, Robert D., "Science Interest Grows," *Science Education* 44 (December 1960) 401–407.

Norvell, George W., "The Reading Interests of Children" in *Reading in the Content Areas*, A Report of the 15th Annual Conference and Course on Reading (Pittsburgh: University of Pittsburgh, 1959), pp. 125–135.

Peterson, Rita W. and Lawrence F. Lowery, "A Study of Curiosity Factors in First Grade Children" *Science Education* 52 (October 1968) 347–352.

Stanchfield, Jo M., "Reading Interests of Eighth Grade Boys," *Journal of Developmental Reading* 5 (Summer 1962) 256–265.

———, "Boys' Reading Interests as Revealed Through Personal Conference," *The Reading Teacher* 16 (September 1962) 41–44.

Young, Doris A., "Some Techniques for Identifying Children's Science Interests," *School Science and Mathematics* 57 (June 1957) 462–464.

Information Sources Children Use*

LAHRON H. SCHENKE

This study was included because of the insight it gives into where and how children learn science information and the implications for methods of teaching science. It seems important that educators keep in mind that children derive their knowledge from many sources, that the major part may not be from school and reading, and that they may, if allowed, be an important learning resource to each other. This suggests a methodology in which teachers may do less talking and children more. If direct experience is the major source for children's knowledge, then perhaps the role of textbooks needs to be reevaluated in comparison with laboratories, projects, units, field experiences, and other activities.

This study is a survey type research, of particular interest because of the depth with which the researcher has explored each child's information sources, interviewing each first grader five times and each second grader nine times.

Several other studies in this volume have relevance to the questions raised here; for example, Inbody's survey of children's understandings, Perrodin's survey of children's interests and Carpenter's comparison of reading and activity methods (all in Chapter 6), and Adams' evaluation of multi-age grouping (Chapter 7).

This is a summary of a project which was an investigation of the sources of information children use for answering their questions and supporting their beliefs in science. Certain science areas were selected for discussion by children, the selection based on those areas in science which were believed to be familiar to first and second grade children. The selection of items to be included in the discussion was based, for the most part, on a list of science areas for the primary level by Craig.

* From *Science Education* 40 (April 1956) 232–237. Reprinted with permission of the publisher, and Lahron H. Schenke, Associate Professor of Education, Eastern Illinois University, Charleston. Based on doctoral study "Information Sources Children Use" for Ed.D. degree at Teachers College, Columbia University, 1954.

(1) As the children talked about these topics they were interrupted and asked where or how they learned what they just said.

The most significant work in relation to this project is the one by Bergen (2) who used two techniques in securing information concerning the sources of information children choose in relation to various types of problems. They were running records of regular classroom sessions, and individual interviews in which children were asked a set of previously selected questions.

In the present study it was decided that a tape recorder would be used in gathering the data. A semi-nondirective interview was used in an attempt to avoid the containment feeling of a set of questions. It was thought that such a technique might prove more efficient as to indications of sources of information than classroom observation. (It was later found by trial classroom observation that children seldom indicate the source of their belief or information unless specifically asked for it. To ask for it in class then, would have been more upsetting than to ask for it during an interview.) To help develop a semi-nondirective interview technique the writings of Erickson (3) and Axline (4) were consulted. Both authors describe interviews of a non-directive nature, but in both instances for a different purpose than to determine sources of information children use. Their guidance was useful however. For example, Erickson warns of the danger of jumping to early conclusions, of the restriction imposed when one asks questions with a yes or no answer, of the guiding effect of agreement or disagreement either by words or some other sign. (5) Axline stresses the importance of the attitude of the interviewer, with kindliness, patience, understanding, steadiness, and placing confidence in the pupil as the keys to a fruitful interview. (6)

The data for this study were gathered in an elementary school in Wisconsin, in a city of about 40,000 people. After permission for the study was granted by the school authorities, the first and second grade teachers were consulted and they selected children for the study. These teachers were urged to try to select as representative and typical group of children as possible. Following the selection the parents were asked for permission for their children to be interviewed.

Twenty two children were interviewed, nine in first grade, thirteen in second. Of the 9 from the first grade, four were boys and five were girls. Of the 13 from the second grade, four were boys and nine were girls. The average age of the first graders at the time of the interview was 7–2 (seven years, two months) and the average age of the second graders was 8–1. The average I.Q. of the children was 108.9 as determined by the California Mental Maturity Test. Seventeen of the children had a television set in their homes, four others were able to view television often enough so that it was a factor to be considered in their sources of information. The other child did not indicate television as a source of information during the interviews although she did say she sometimes saw television.

From a socio-economic standpoint, the children were quite similar, typical occupations of their fathers being factory workers, truck drivers, salesmen, sales clerks, tavern keepers, etc. The group included two whose parents held professional positions.

A schedule of interviews was set up so that each first grader was interviewed once a week and each second grader once or twice each week. The interviews were scheduled before school in the morning or after school in the afternoon for those who lived in the city. During the noon lunch period, nearly two hours long, those who came on buses and brought their lunches were interviewed. Before the interviews began all the children came in together for an explanation of the interviews to follow. Briefly, during this explanation the children were told that they would be given a chance to talk about various things related to science. They would be interrupted at times to find out if they remembered where they learned a particular fact or belief. If they remembered, they were to tell where they learned it; otherwise they were to feel free to say they didn't remember and it would be all right. (7) They were also told that it was preferred that they not tell other children about the things talked about in the interviews, and that their talks would not affect their grades. Their teacher would not be informed as to how well they were doing or how well they behaved, and they were free to discontinue the interviews at any time they wished, without penalty. There were to be no rewards or punishment connected with the interviews.

The interviews took place in a vacant room with a tape recorder set up within easy reach of the interviewer and the microphone placed on the table between the interviewer and the child. It was originally thought that the tape recorder and microphone should be concealed, but since all the children were familiar with a tape recorder and its use from previous experience, concealment was deemed unnecessary.

All of the first grade children were interviewed at least five times and the second grade children nine times. The interviews were directed or channeled as little as possible except to indicate the areas for discussion for each interview. These areas were quite broad or quite limited, depending on the particular areas of discussion and the child's knowledge of that area.

The main topics finally used for each interview are indicated below. The complete list differed for first and second grade, although the first grade list contained only items that were also found on the second grade list. In one interview the term "mammals" was not used because none of the children understood the word. They interpreted the word "animal" to mean mammal. It was not the purpose of these interviews to change or increase the knowledge of the children interviewed. It should also be explained that the children did not regard insects as being animals.

Topics for Interviews

1. Trees   Birds
2. Animals (mammals)   Insects
3. Electricity   Weather
4. Plants   Fish
5. Heat   Fire   Water   Superstitions
6. Cars   Trains   Airplanes
7. Astronomy   Optical instruments
8. Day and night   Health
9. Protective coloration of living things
10. Optional—children's choice of topics (limited to science)

During the time when the children were in class or between interviews the tape recordings were played back and the pertinent parts of the interviews transcribed. It was a simple matter, once the interviews were typed, to read through the interviews and indicate the sources in the outer margin for ease in later tabulation.

The excerpt which follows, the beginning of the third interview with a second grade child, gives some idea how the interviews evolved.

I: Today I would like for you to begin by telling me what you know about electricity.

C: If a plug goes out sometimes the lights go off.

I: How do you know about that?

C: Cause our light went off and daddy had to go down and fuss around and we had to see by candlelight. And once on our birthday a telephone pole came down and we had to have candlelight because the lights went out. The boys used flashlights and boy, we had fun.

I: Do you know where electricity comes from?

C: It comes along wires.

I: How do you know that?

C: Cause there's wires strung up, and I heard it on TV. They are strung up on poles and the steps are high up so you can't climb up there and get electrocuted.

It was necessary, especially during the early interviews, to ask probing questions concerning the sources. For example, when a child said he saw it in a book, he was questioned as to whether the book was a school book, his own book, or a library book. This meant that the source would be specific rather than general. The children soon became accustomed to indicate the specific source, and as the interviews went on they would usually say "a library book" or "a book at home" so that it became unnecessary to ask for further delineation of the source.

When the interviews were completed, a tabulation sheet was designed so that comparison and summary of results could be accomplished. One copy was used for each child. Later a number of these tabulation sheets, slightly modified, were used to get various summaries of the total results of the interviews. The tables which follow show some of the results.

In the analysis of the data it was found that nearly half, or 46 per cent of the science knowledge of the children in this study was learned from direct sources; that is, by personal observation or individual ex-

TABLE 1
Per Cent of Indications for Each Source,
Grouped into Major Areas

Major Areas	Per Cent
Direct Sources	46.0
School	8.8
People	22.8
Television	7.8
Radio	0.3
Commercial movies	1.9
Books	8.7
Comic Books	1.0
Others	3.0

TABLE 2

Total Indications for Each Source Expressed in Per Cent

Source	Per Cent		
	First Grade	*Second Grade*	*Both Grades*
Direct:			
Personal observation	35.6	31.4	32.8
Individual experience	11.9	13.9	13.2
Secondary:			
School:			
Teacher	6.8	2.9	4.2
Class discussion	0.3	1.5	1.1
Classmates	0.7	0.6	0.6
Weekly Reader	1.9	0.6	1.0
Movies (at school)	3.3	1.1	1.9
Television	9.2	6.9	7.8
Radio	0.1	0.3	0.3
Church	0.3	0.2	0.2
Adult magazines	0.1	0.3	0.3
Newspapers	0.4	0.7	0.6
People:			
Father	4.7	7.9	6.8
Mother	7.9	7.7	7.8
Brother	1.1	3.7	3.1
Sister	1.1	1.9	1.6
Grandparents	1.1	0.9	0.9
Other relatives	0.4	0.4	0.4
Neighbors	2.2	2.3	2.2
Movies, commercial	2.5	1.5	1.9
Books			
School	1.3	2.9	2.4
Library	0.9	4.6	3.4
Own, or in home	2.3	3.2	2.9
Comic books	0.5	1.3	1.0
Miscellaneous	2.8	1.3	1.6
Totals	99.4	99.8	100.0

periences. In almost half the instances, then, these children learned their science knowledge and beliefs with no assistance other than incidental help from other people. This confirms the Bergen study which indicated that neither empirical nor authoritative sources were predominant, based on records of classroom sessions. (8)

The term direct sources as applied in this study refers to instances where a child: (1) sees something happen; (2) is involved in a thing happening; (3) has something happen to himself; (4) causes something to happen such as a test, trial, experiment, or experience.

Secondary sources as applied in this study refer to all sources not classified as direct. Secondary sources are all those in which someone else has had the use of direct or other sources, and by some means of communication has passed on the information. People can be a direct source if they are watched by a child, but people are a secondary source if they tell about what they are doing or have done.

A summary of findings based on this study is as follows:

1. The first and second grade children in this study had a wide knowledge of their physical environment.

2. There was a great variation among the children in this study in regard to their knowledge of science.

3. In this study there was no marked sex difference in the reference to sources of information.

4. The children in this study obtained their science information from a wide variety of sources.

5. In this study, nearly half the science information that had been learned by the children had been derived from direct sources; that is, by personal observation and individual experience of each child, and without the help of anyone else.

6. Based on percentages, the second most significant source of science knowledge and beliefs was other people. Of these, two-thirds of the responses referred to mother or father.

7. Nearly one out of ten responses indicated the school as the source of science information. Since children study science about one hour per week, but are viewing television, playing, etc. many more hours per week, this would seem to indicate that the school was a highly efficient source.

8. Books were indicated as a source by these children in 8.7 per cent of the responses. The responses of the first grade children for books was 4.5 per cent. Of the second grade children's responses, 10.7 per cent had been derived from books.

9. These children had gained an appreciable amount of science information from viewing television. Some of this information could not have been readily obtained in other ways.

10. Radio was very rarely mentioned as an information source in this study.

11. The children in this study did not, for the most part, seem to realize that, if the immediately available source did not furnish the wanted information, there might be other sources available. The source had to be near at hand, or it was not used.

12. The encouragement and example of an interest in science by parents and older siblings seemed to help to develop an early habit of using books as a source of science information.

13. Many of the children in this study had a critical attitude toward superstitions and fairy tale characters.

14. Comic books were an inefficient source of science information since most of the children in this study read several comic books each week but rarely mentioned comic books as a source.

15. The simple question, "How did you learn that?," when asked in an atmosphere of acceptance by the interviewer, elicited answers which revealed considerable depth of thinking and reasoning on the part of these children.

16. The tape recorder was very useful in getting the words of children exactly as expressed.

If most children are similar to the children in this study, then the following are the more significant things for the elementary teacher. To begin with, children have a wide knowledge of their surroundings, and the sources used to learn any specific bit of information may vary from child to child. So the knowledge of the class as a whole will be wide; so wide that one of the best resources for teaching science in the elementary school will be the children themselves. They will, under proper guidance, also be able to evaluate the sources.

For the children in this study, the source used was usually the nearby source, the one most readily and easily available. It would seem highly desirable then to have resources and reference materials in the classroom and readily available for use by the children.

Older siblings, by example, are able to show younger children the usefulness of books as references and sources of information. Elementary teachers, knowing this, and having such younger children in their classrooms, can by like example have them show the way for the rest of the class.

There is some indication in this study that challenging questions may tend to lead children to turn to reference materials. If these reference materials are in the classroom the children could more readily learn to use such materials and rely on them.

Another point of significance for the elementary teacher is the technique of letting children talk in an atmosphere of acceptance by the teacher. Verbalization by the children may bring out science information and may also reveal how children think. These would help the teacher in teaching science more effectively.

Television is a source to be considered by the elementary teacher. The children in this study referred to it often as a source. It is possible that certain television programs can be used to bring out interests of children as a motivation for several days' study in science. It would probably be wise for the teacher to watch television herself to be acquainted with the next day's science interest! There will come a time too, when some child will indicate a dislike for a particular television program. With careful direction such a statement can be the basis for developing an evaluation of television programs by children.

SUGGESTIONS FOR FURTHER RESEARCH

1. A study parallel to this one with older children should be of value to get the picture of how the emphasis on the sources of information changes.
2. Would the percentages for each source change if some other field of knowledge such as social science, geography, or arithmetic were investigated in a similar manner?
3. How well do adults remember where they learned their knowledge of science?
4. Would the sources change if the children of different socio-economic levels were interviewed?
5. If the children in this study learned as much as they did from commercial television programs how much more could they learn from educational television? This question needs investigation. Is there a possibility that the children would learn very little more from educational television—that they are already getting nearly all they can and should from one educational medium?

REFERENCES

1. Gerald S. Craig. *Science for the Elementary-School Teacher*. Boston: Ginn and Company, 1947. pp. 527–530.

2. Catherine M. Bergen. *Some Sources of Children's Science Information,* Contributions to Education No. 881. New York: Bureau of Publications, Teachers College, Columbia University, 1943.

3. C. E. Erickson. *The Counseling Interview.* New York: Prentice-Hall, Inc., 1950.

4. Virginia M. Axline. *Play Therapy.* Boston: Houghton Mifflin Company, 1947.

5. Erickson, p. 69.

6. Axline, p. 65.

7. It is estimated that the instances when the children did not remember the source varied between 10 and 40 per cent.

8. Bergen, p. 63.

GRADE PLACEMENT

Replication of Study
*of Normative Grade Placement of Light Concepts**

GARY R. SMITH

One of the major efforts in curriculum development in the elementary school in recent years has been the attempt to introduce traditional topics earlier in the school program—though not everyone agrees that this should be done. Another effort has been to develop new elements of content for the elementary school curriculum, and with this effort comes the question as to what age or grade to assign the new content. In either case, placement of content becomes a critical issue. This study was selected as illustrative of some of the attempts to deal with the problem.

Smith's research is of an experimental type in which a pretest is followed by experimental teaching of a unit to three different grade levels, then posttesting, and finally an analysis of the data from each grade level for placement decisions. The researcher is to be commended for the replication of a study to further verify and refine his findings—a fairly unusual practice. It is significant that the procedure developed in this study dealing with science content is applicable to other subjects as well. Other efforts to deal with the problem of content placement may be found in the list "For Further Reading."

In a previous article it was suggested that the normative grade categories of a standardized science achievement test might be used to classify the difficulty of science concepts for elementary school pupils. (1) Perhaps a suitable analogy would be to compare such a normative grade scale to the Mohs hardness scale for minerals. Knowing that a mineral is hardness five or hardness seven doesn't tell the geologist anything about the chemical composition of the unknown specimen. It doesn't identify the mineral. All that the hardness rating can do for the geologist is to place the unknown mineral in a rank order relative

* From *Science Education* 47 (March 1963) 183–187. Reprinted with permission of the publisher and Gary R. Smith, Associate Professor of Education, Wayne State University, Detroit.

to the hardness of all of the other minerals. A difficulty scale for science concepts could be expected to provide a similar kind of ranking of all science concepts which might be considered for the elementary school science program.

The writer's original research on this problem seemed to indicate that such a rank order scale was feasible. (2) This paper is a report of an additional study to determine if similar results would be obtained when the normative grade placement approach was applied in a new situation and with a different sample of intermediate grade pupils. If comparable results were obtained with a new sample, then an increased confidence in the reliability and stability of this approach would appear to be justified.

INSTRUCTIONAL PROCEDURE

Wherever it was possible, the same conditions which had been present in the original study were established in the replication. The pupils in both samples were fourth, fifth, and sixth grade children. The same unit of instruction on reflection of light, refraction of light, and color was used. Table 1 indicates the sub-topics which were included

TABLE 1

Topics Included in Unit of Instruction on Light and the Number of Test Questions Used to Check Comprehension of Those Topics

Major Topic	*Sub-topic*	No. Questions on Light Test
A. Reflection and Transmission of Light	1. Transmission of light	4
	2. Reflection of light from smooth and rough surfaces	4
	3. Reflection of light from plane mirrors	5
	4. Reflection of light from concave mirrors	5
	5. Reflection of light from convex mirrors	3
B. Refraction of Light	1. Passage of light through different media	4
	2. Refraction of light by convex lenses	12
	3. Refraction of light by concave lenses	3
C. Color	1. Spectrum	6
	2. Primary colors of light	7
	3. Primary pigment colors	7

in the unit of study as well as the number of questions on the light test which checked pupil understanding of those sub-topics. The plan of instruction required approximately 15 school days of 30 to 45 minute periods. All classes had similar text material, film strip and apparatus to conduct experiments.

There were some conditions which were changed. In the original sample, the 12 cooperating teachers had the responsibility for teaching all subjects in the usual self-contained classrooms of elementary schools. In the new sample, the two cooperating teachers were only responsible for teaching science in their respective schools.

TESTING PROCEDURE

All tests were conducted by the researcher and his assistant, who is regularly employed as a test administrator by Wayne State University. In the original study, fourteen separate tests were administered to all pupils. In the present study, only seven tests were used. These are identified in Table 2.

A Pre-unit Test on Light was administered to pupils before they received instruction. The Post-unit Test on Light was given to the pupils after instruction had been completed. The same 60-item test on light was used for the pre-test and the post-test. When the pupils took the examination on light, they had copies of the test and separate an-

TABLE 2
Tests Used in Study

Test	Variable Measured
Stanford Achievement, Intermediate Battery, Form JM	Paragraph Meaning
Stanford Achievement, Intermediate and Advanced Science Test, Form JM	Science Achievement
Lorge-Thorndike Intelligence Test, Level 3, Verbal and Non-verbal	Intelligence Quotient
Pre-unit Test on Light	Information about light prior to instruction
Post-unit Test on Light	Information about light after instruction
General Science Test	Science Achievement

swer sheets. Each question was read aloud by the examiner along with the possible answers to the question. This was done to avoid handicapping poor readers. Pupils recorded their preferred answers on separate answer sheets.

ANALYSIS OF DATA

Test results for the two samples were examined to identify significant differences at each grade level for each of the following variables: (1) Pre-unit Test on Light, (2) Post-unit Test on Light, (3) Standardized Science Achievement Test, (4) Reading Comprehension, (5) Intelligence Quotients. Heeding the counsel of Siegel (3) the researcher elected to use non-parametric statistics, i.e. Chi-square, Spearman rank correlation, rather than use an analysis of variance, Pearson correlation analysis, and other parametric statistics.

All pupils in the new sample were classified according to their normative grade scores on the Standardized Science Achievement Test. The number of pupils in each normative grade category is shown in Table 3. An item analysis of the Post-unit Test on Light was conducted for each normative grade group.

TABLE 3
*Classification of Pupils into Normative
Grade Groups*

Grade Norm	Number of Pupils
Fourth grade or lower	39
Fifth grade	33
Sixth grade	36
Seventh grade	50
Eighth grade	33
Ninth grade or higher	50
Total	241

The item analysis identified the percentage of pupils in each normative grade group who responded correctly to each question on the Post-unit Test on Light. Because each question was associated with a specific concept or sub-topic in the unit of instruction, these percentages of correct responses provided estimates of the difficulty of the concepts and topics.

Graphs were plotted to show the relationship between percentages of pupils answering a test item correctly and the normative grade group of those pupils. Because similar graphs had been plotted for the original sample, it was possible to compare the graphs of the two samples for each item.

As shown in Table 1 the unit of instruction contained eleven sub-topics. For each of these sub-topics there was a percentage rating which reflected the difficulty of the sub-topic in terms of the pupils' correct responses to questions about the sub-topics. The difficulty of the sub-topics for one sample was correlated with the difficulty of the same concepts for pupils in the second sample.

The complete report of the original study (4) included tentative recommendations for grade placement of the concepts included in the study. Following the suggestion of Starrett, (5) it was decided that an arbitrary cut-off point of 60 per cent would be used. If more than 60 per cent of the pupils in a normative grade group appeared to understand a particular sub-topic, then it was accepted for consideration for the elementary school science program. If 60 per cent or fewer pupils understood the sub-topic, then it was not recommended for the elementary school science program. Using this arbitrary cut-off point, a sub-topic was either accepted or rejected for each normative grade.

The number of sub-topics which were recommended to be included in the program at each normative grade level were counted. A rank was assigned to each normative grade level according to the number of sub-topics recommended for it. A Spearman rank correlation coefficient was computed to compare the number of favorable recommendations made at each grade level for the original sample and the number of favorable recommendations made at each normative grade level for the new sample. The number of sub-topics rejected for each normative grade group in the original study was correlated with the number of sub-topics rejected for each normative grade group in the replicated study.

RESULTS

Table 4 indicates that there were significant differences in the scores made on the Post-unit Test on Light and the Reading Comprehension Test. Sixth grade pupils in Sample #1 scored significantly higher on the Post-test than did sixth grade pupils in Sample #2. However, the sixth grade pupils in Sample #2 scored significantly higher on

TABLE 4
Results of Chi-square Tests for Significant Differences between Two Samples

| | Grades | | |
Variable	4	5	6
Pre-unit Test on Light	NS	NS	NS
Post-unit Test on Light	NS	NS	S
Standardized Science Achievement Test	NS	NS	NS
Reading Comprehension	NS	NS	S
Intelligence Quotients	NS	NS	NS

(S)—Significant difference in scores made by pupils in the two samples.
(NS)—No significant difference in scores made by pupils in the two samples.

the Reading Comprehension Test than did the sixth grade pupils in Sample #1. There were no significant differences between the two samples for any of the other variables included in this study.

When the item graphs for the two samples were compared they were found to be very similar. In order to provide a statistical estimate of the relationship, the rank order difficulty of the sub-topics for Sample #1 was correlated with the rank order difficulty of the sub-topics for Sample #2. Table 5 shows the correlation coefficients for each normative grade group. Obviously, there is substantial relationship between the difficulty of the various sub-topics for pupils in Sample #1 and the difficulty of the same sub-topics for pupils in Sample #2.

Although the difficulty of the concepts might even be identical for pupils in the two school systems, this still does not mean that the recommendation for the grade placement of those concepts would be the same in both school systems. Therefore, the recommendations for

TABLE 5
Spearman Rank Correlation of Difficulty of Sub-topics for Pupils in the Two Samples

Normative Grade Group	Correlation Coefficient
Fourth	.92
Fifth	.87
Sixth	.94
Seventh	.88
Eighth	.91
Ninth	.81

grade placement using the arbitrary 60 per cent cut-off point were compared for the two samples. When favorable recommendations made at each normative grade level for one sample were correlated with favorable recommendations made for the second sample, the correlation coefficient was r = + .94. A similar correlation coefficient was computed to determine the relationship between sub-topics which were rejected at each normative grade level because of data collected in the two samples. This correlation coefficient was also r = + .94.

CONCLUSIONS AND IMPLICATIONS

This study provides support for the use of a normative grade placement approach to estimate the difficulty of science concepts. The relative stability of these estimates of difficulty when the procedure has been applied to a new sample is encouraging. This infers that a rank order "hardness" scale for science concepts may be derived empirically. Such a scale would have at least two definite advantages.

First, it would be based upon evidence as to those concepts which elementary school children could understand, when given competent and efficient instruction for a reasonable period of time. Leonelli, (6) Dubins (7) and others have documented the lack of agreement among authorities and curriculum groups on the difficulty of science concepts for elementary school pupils. The present study seems to suggest that the pupils' capacities to understand selected science concepts is more uniform and reliable than is the considered opinion of authorities regarding those capacities.

Secondly, the value of a rank order scale may be more significant in resolving our grade placement dilemma than is generally recognized. Non-parametric statistics is playing an increasingly important role in research in the social sciences. It may be expected to be more influential in future curriculum decisions. Moreover, the rapid development of Decision Theory (8) and Game Theory (9) may be a formative influence upon the entire curriculum of the elementary school. In both of these areas, rank order measurement is adequate to make valid probability statements and decisions.

It is the obligation of any researcher to point to fundamental limitations and deficiencies in his research. It should be noted that these conclusions and implications are based upon only two samples of approximately 500 pupils. In both instances the pupils were above average in native ability and academic achievement. It *has not* been demonstrated that this approach is serviceable with pupils with "average" or "below average" native ability and scholastic achievement. The writer is preparing to extend his research into these areas.

Normative grade categories have all of the limitations implied in the words "average" or "norm." At best, the normative grade approach has the properties of a rank order scale, and is serviceable only with specific statistical methods.

Finally, there are several facets of an excellent elementary school science program which are omitted in a classification system such as this. The normative grade placement approach makes no provision for problem solving skills, critical thinking, or the matrix of competencies which are loosely referred to as the "scientific method."

In conclusion, this study seems to indicate that a reliable scale of difficulty can be developed for these selected concepts of light. If this proves to be correct, then it may be possible to empirically derive estimates of the difficulty of other science concepts and topics which have been suggested for the elementary school science program. Such an accomplishment would merely be a preliminary stage in the meticulously careful organization of the elementary school science curriculum.

REFERENCES

1. Gary R. Smith and Edward Victor, "Science Concepts of Light," *The Science Teacher*, 28:11–14, February, 1961.

2. Gary R. Smith, "An Examination of Selected Measures of Achievement and Aptitude for use in Normative Grade Placement of Science Concepts on Light," unpublished doctoral dissertation, Northwestern University, Evanston, Illinois, 1960.

3. Sidney Siegel, *Non-Parametric Statistics*. McGraw-Hill Book Co., Inc., pp. 1–34, 1956.

4. Gary R. Smith, *ibid.*, pp. 114–172.

5. George Starrett, "Determination of Grade Placement of Heat Principles in Junior High School," unpublished doctoral dissertation, University of California, Los Angeles, California, 1957.

6. Renato Leonelli, "The Selection and Grade Placement of Physical Science Principles in the Elementary School Curriculum," unpublished doctoral dissertation, Boston University, 1952.

7. M. I. Dubins, "Current Practices in Elementary School Science, with Reference to Courses of Study, Published from 1940 to 1952, and the

Extent of Activities Undertaken for the Improvement of Instruction," unpublished doctoral dissertation, Boston University, 1953.

8. David W. Miller and Martin K. Starr, *Executive Decisions and Operations Research*, Prentice-Hall, Inc., 1960.

9. J. D. Williams, *The Compleat Strategyst*, McGraw-Hill Book Co., 1954.

FOR FURTHER READING

Atkin, J. Myron, "Teaching Concepts of Modern Astronomy to Elementary School Children," *Science Education* 45 (February 1961) 54–58.

Bruns, Richard F., and Alexander Frazier, "Scope and Sequence of Elementary School Science," *School Science and Mathematics* 57 (October 1957) 560–568.

Burger, Joanna, "An Experiment with Aquatic Animals in an Elementary School," *Science Education* 50 (March 1966) 175–183.

Cantrell, Sue Rowe, and Loren T. Caldwell, "A Selection and Evaluation of Physics and Chemistry Concepts to Be Used in the Seventh and Eighth Grade Science Program," *Science Education* 47 (April 1963) 264–270.

Cressman, Harry E., "Results of a Study on Teaching General Science to Pupils in the Intermediate Grades," *Science Education* 47 (April 1963) 304–308.

Harris, William., "A Technique for Grade Placement in Elementary Science," *Journal of Research in Science Teaching* 2 (March 1964) 43–50.

McNeil, John D., and Evan R. Keislar, "An Experiment in Validating Objectives for the Curriculum in Elementary School Science," *Science Education* 46 (March 1962) 152–156.

Nelson, Pearl A., "Concepts of Light and Sound in the Intermediate Grades," *Science Education* 44 (March 1960) 142–145.

Pella, Milton, "Development of Concepts in Elementary Science," *Science Education* 33 (October 1949) 269–272.

Smith, Gary R., "Use of Probability Statements," *Science Teacher* 29 (March 1962) 33–37.

Ulrich, Arthur H., "A Comprehension Level Determination of a Basic Science Concept," *Science and Children* 1 (April 1964) 12–13.

Weaver, Edward K., and Sara Gannoway Coleman, "The Relationship of Certain Science Concepts to Mental Ability and Learning of First Grade Children," *Science Education* 47 (December 1963) 490–494.

A Reading and an Activity Method in Elementary Science Instruction*

REGAN CARPENTER

The question of the textbook-recitation method versus the problem or activity method is important not only in science teaching but in other subjects as well. The textbook-recitation method persists, although it is a long time since most teacher education institutions have advocated it. Perhaps it survives because it requires the teacher to do less study and lesson preparation; because the teacher lacks confidence in his mastery of the subject matter; because there are too few materials available to carry on an activity method; because the teacher does not have the time to do the extra preparation the activity method requires; or because he feels too much pressure to "cover the book." The results of the Carpenter study and others suggest that teachers, administrators, and supervisors should give further thought to helping teachers reevaluate their methodology. This research is focused on only one aspect of methodology in teaching science; for other dimensions see "For Further Reading."

The following is an experimental research, noteworthy because the experimental factor is switched from one group of teachers to the other so as to cancel out teacher differences as a variable. The "Hawthorne effect" might still persist, however. A related study in this volume is Schiller's on study skills (Chapter 4).

The problem in this investigation was simply to compare (experimentally) two methods of teaching science to elementary pupils. The pupils who participated in this investigation were all of the fourth grade pupils in four Honolulu (Hawaii) elementary schools. There were two fourth grade classrooms in each school, with a total of 321 pupils. All of these children retained their regular classroom teachers;

* From *Science Education* 47 (April 1963) 256–258. Reprinted with permission of the publisher and Regan Carpenter, Associate Professor of Education, Southern Illinois University, Edwardsville. Based upon doctoral dissertation "A Study of the Effectiveness of the Problem-Solving Method and the Textbook-Discussion Method in Elementary Science Instruction," submitted in partial fulfillment for the Ed.D. degree, University of Colorado, Boulder, Colorado, 1958.

they maintained their scheduled academic programs except for this experiment in science instruction.

These eight classes of fourth grade pupils were arranged into two groups of approximately equal size (easy to manage, since all of the classes contained roughly the same number of children). An overall equation between the two groups of pupils was effected on these bases:

Intelligence (as measured by the Kuhlman-Anderson group intelligence test)
Age
Sex

The teachers who were involved in the experimentation were also matched on a group basis, with regard to amount of college education, years of teaching experience, and ratings of their administrators. All of the teachers maintained their regular classroom programs, except for their science classes.

The teaching methods which were compared are referred to in this paper as the "Textbook-Recitation Method" and the "Problem Method." The "Textbook-Recitation Method" simply means treating science more or less as an extension of the reading program; teaching the material by reading and discussing a basic textbook, and requiring the pupils to answer the questions found in the textbook. A great many elementary teachers teach science in this manner. The term "Problem Method" is used in this paper to describe a teaching method based upon classroom experimentation and demonstration. In this method, questions or problems expressed by the pupils, with teacher guidance, form important study guidelines. Reading, of course, remains important but is not the chief means of obtaining information. Choice of both terms was arbitrary, and perhaps neither is appropriately descriptive. But the two methods involved, term them whatever you will, are clear-cut bodies of instructional procedure, at opposite poles of pedagogical philosophy.

The science content which was covered in this investigation represents a balance between physical science content and biological science content, in harmony with the current thinking concerning science content. "Magnetism" was the first topic studied, and "The Adaptations of Animals" was the second. Both of these are common elementary school science topics. The experimenter prepared a resource unit upon each of these topics, copies of which were available to all teachers using the Problem Method. Also, the experimenter discussed this method with the teachers before they utilized it, and demonstrated some of its techniques and procedures. Nothing of this nature was attempted with regard to the Textbook-Recitation Method, since the teachers were accustomed to using this method.

The pupils in one of these matched groups (Group A) studied the topic "Magnetism" for three weeks in their science classes by the "Textbook-Recitation Method." The pupils in the other group (Group B) studied the same topic the same length of time by the "Problem Method." Then the same test, an objective test of factual material upon "Magnetism," was administered to both groups. The average scores compiled by the groups were compared by means of the "t technique." The mean score of the group which had been taught by the Problem Method was higher than that achieved by the group taught by the Textbook-Recitation Method. The t test revealed that the higher mean score achieved by the Activity Method Group was statistically significant. More will be stated later about the results of the statistical treatment.

Next the roles of the two matched groups were reversed. Group B, which had been taught about magnetism by the Problem Method, was taught "Adaptations of Animals" for three weeks by the Textbook-Recitation Method. The pupils of Group A, who had studied about magnetism through the Textbook-Recitation Method, now studied "The Adaptations of Animals" for three weeks along the lines of the Problem Method. Again, a test of factual information was administered to both groups after the topic had been studied. The pupils of Group A, who were taught by the Problem Method, achieved a higher mean score than did the pupils who were taught by the Textbook-Recitation Method. (Remember that Group A had scored lower than Group B in the study of Magnetism.)

GROUP A	GROUP B
161 pupils	160 pupils
I.Q. average 103.3	I.Q. average 102.7
Studied "Magnetism" by Textbook-Recitation Method	Studied "Magnetism" by Problem Method
Achieved a lower mean score on objective test taken by both groups	Achieved a higher mean score, significant at the .05 level
Studied "Adaptations of Animals" by the Problem Method	Studied "Adaptations of Animals" by the Textbook-Recitation Method
Achieved higher mean score on this test, significant at the .02 level	Achieved a lower mean score on same objective test taken by both groups

SUB-GROUP ANALYSES

The main stream of this experiment was, as described, the comparison of two contrasting methods of teaching science. However, having assembled the data, the investigator was intrigued to analyze them still further. Specifically, he obtained from each teacher involved in the experiment the names of the 25 per cent of her pupils who ranked highest in general academic achievement, and the 25 per cent who ranked lowest.

Then the investigator conducted the following analyses of the test scores recorded by the pupils in their study of magnetism:

(a) He compared the mean score achieved by the top 25 per cent of the Problem Method Group with that of the top 25 per cent of the Text-book-Recitation Group, again using the t test. The mean score of the Problem Method sub-group was higher than that of the Textbook-Recitation sub-group, but the difference was not statistically significant.

(b) He compared the mean score achieved by the lowest 25 per cent of the Problem Method Group with that of the lowest 25 per cent of the Textbook-Recitation Group, using the t test. The mean score of the Problem Method sub-group was higher, and the difference was statistically extremely significant.

After the study methods of the two groups had been reversed, the investigator conducted the following analyses of the test scores recorded by the children in their study of the Adaptations of Animals:

(a) He compared the mean score achieved by the top 25 per cent of the Problem Method Group with that of the top 25 per cent of the Text-book-Recitation Group. The mean score of the Problem Method sub-group was higher than that of the Textbook-Recitation sub-group, but the difference was not statistically significant.

(b) He compared the mean score achieved by the lowest 25 per cent of the Problem Method Group with that of the lowest 25 per cent of the Textbook-Recitation Group, using the t test. The mean score of the Problem Method sub-group was higher, and the difference was statistically extremely significant.

CONCLUSIONS

1. This study indicates that elementary pupils learn science factual matter more readily when taught by a method based upon classroom demonstra-

tions and experimentation than when taught by a method based upon reading and discussing a basic science textbook. Admittedly, this study covers only one experimental situation; however, the reversal of the group of children in the methodological roles, and the subsequent test results, definitely strengthens the study. One is willing to generalize more widely from the results than one otherwise would.

2. This activity-type teaching method offers real and unquestionable promise for teaching slower learning children. (At the elementary level, slow learners are primarily poor readers. The Sub-group Analyses in this investigation point out that good academic achievers—capable readers—learn almost as well by a reading-type method as by an activity-type method.)

3. Further experimentation of this same type is needed, since this investigation involved only one particular sample of the population. Would the same results obtain in *your* grade level? In *your* geographic area? With several such studies recorded, perhaps we could cease saying, "I *think* that my method of teaching science is best." We could make some definite statements based upon research findings.

4. Further research in experimentally comparing teaching methods is needed along these lines:

   (a) The retention of learned material, and

   (b) The development of desirable science attitudes.

5. The writer strongly recommends the technique of reversing the control and experimental roles of matched groups, whenever this is at all feasible. Of course, there are many experiments comparing two groups which (because of conditioning or other factors) do not lend themselves to this procedure.

FOR FURTHER READING

Atkin, J. Myron, and Robert Karplus, "Discovery or Invention," *Science Teacher* 29 (September 1962) 45–51.

Bennet, Lloyd, and Cherie Clodfelter, "A Study of the Integration of an Earth Science Unit Within the Reading Program of a Second Grade by Utilizing the Word Analysis Approach," *School Science and Mathematics* 66 (March 1966) 729–736.

Bohnhorst, Ben A., and Prentiss M. Hosford, "Basing Instruction in Science on Children's Questions: Using a Wonderbox in the Third Grade," *Science Education* 44 (March 1960) 146–149.

Boyer, Donald Allen, "A Comparative Study of the Science Achievement of Pupils in Elementary Schools," *Science Education* 39 (February 1955) 3–12.

Butts, David P., *An Inventory of Science Methods* (Austin: University of Texas, Science Education Center, 1966).

Heathers, Glenn, "A Process-Centered Elementary Science Sequence," *Science Education* 45 (April 1961) 201–206.

Herbert, Clarke L., "Outdoors With Title III," *National Elementary Principal* 46 (November 1966) 71–75.

Hollenbeck, Irene, "Outdoor Education in Oregon," *Science Education* 47 (March 1963) 113–121.

Jackson, Joseph and George R. Stuteville, "A Survey of Time Allotment and of Services For Science in the Elementary Schools" *Science Education* 52 (October 1968) 389–399.

Munch, Theodore W., *How To Individualize Science Instruction in the Elementary School* (Washington, D.C.; National Science Teachers Association, 1965).

O'Toole, Raymond J., "The Effectiveness of Individualized Elementary School Science" *Science Education* 52 (October 1968) 381–384.

Pella, Milton O., and Jack Sherman, "A Comparison of Two Methods of Utilizing Laboratory Activities In Teaching The Course I P S" (Introductory Physical Science) *School Science and Mathematics* 69 (April 1969) 303–314.

Robertson, Martin L., "An Investigation to Determine the Relative Effectiveness of Two Methods of Teaching Elementary Science in 5th Grade," *Science Education* 16 (February 1932) 182–187.

Schramm, Wilbur, "Classroom Out-of-Doors" *The National Elementary School Principal* 48 (April 1969) 70–81.

A Comparison of the Science Achievement of Sixth Grade Pupils Instructed by Regular Classroom and Special Science Teachers*

LOUIS T. DiLORENZO and JOSEPH W. HALLIWELL

This study was selected to raise one of the controversial issues facing not only science teaching but mathematics, reading, and other subjects in the elementary school curriculum—the issue of whether to use special subject teachers in the elementary school. There are several dimensions to the problem, including the questions of separate subjects versus a unified curriculum, the self-contained classroom versus a modified or departmentalized organization, the middle school versus a 1–6 or 1–8 self-contained school, and emphasis on subject matter versus emphasis on meeting the needs of the whole child. Illustrating some of these areas in this volume are the studies of Powell on the Joplin plan (Chapter 2), Schwartz on the core program (Chapter 7), and Cuff on middle schools (Chapter 7).

This is an experimental type research in which the experimental factor operated for a seven-month period. It would have been helpful if some sort of pretest had been given to add confidence that the differences were due to the experimental factor. One would know more about the applicability of the results if one knew a little more about the sample; i.e., was it limited to a white, middle-class group in addition to being bright and suburban? It is hoped that more research will be done on this very important and controversial issue.

The purpose of this study was to compare the science achievement of sixth grade pupils who were instructed in science by the regular classroom teacher with the science achievement of sixth grade pupils who were instructed in science by a special science teacher.

In all probability there has never been any era in the history of American education characterized by such ferment in science education as is the current post-Sputnik period. Intensive study and extensive

* From *Science Education* 47 (March 1963) 202–205. Reprinted with permission of the publisher and Louis T. DiLorenzo, Director, New York State Education Department and Joseph W. Halliwell, Professor of Educational Administration, St. John's University, New York City.

revision of science curricula at all levels of education are commonplace. The preponderant majority of the recent articles and studies concerned with science education stress the need for adequately trained teachers of science. While the need for thoroughly trained teachers in the science areas is not solely indigenous to the elementary school it is most acute at this level of education. There is ample evidence attesting to the inadequate preparation of elementary school teachers for the teaching of science [3, 4, 7, 11].

There is also serious doubt that the teaching of science in the elementary schools of tomorrow will not be seriously handicapped by teachers who are lacking an adequate science background. Very few teacher training institutions devoted to the training of elementary school teachers require the twenty semester hours in science recommended by the National Society for the Study of Education [10]. In fact, Chamberlain [3] found that only 442 of the 765 colleges training elementary teachers listed courses in elementary science, and that the mean number of semester hours required in all of the science areas was 9.21, hardly sufficient in view of the greater demands of the newer elementary school science curriculums.

In the light of the increased emphasis on science in the schools and the inadequacy of the science training of elementary school teachers more and more school systems are relying upon special science teachers to provide science instruction [8]. Certain authorities have maintained that a science specialist is essential to an effective science program in the elementary school [4]. Other authorities while acknowledging the weak science background of most elementary school teachers, advocate better science training in the general education of all teachers as the best approach to the improvement of elementary school science programs [11].

Although the problem of utilizing either classroom teachers or science specialists in elementary school science program is receiving a great deal of attention today, it is actually a problem that has confronted educators for a number of years. Several facets of this problem have been investigated by researchers for over a quarter of a century. Studies such as that reported in 1938 by Russell [12] indicated that while more educators favored special science teachers rather than classroom teachers instructing in science, the differences were not statistically significant. A survey of a similar nature today might or might not yield a significant difference in the attitudes of educators. It is of paramount importance, however, to note that the ultimate decision on which of these approaches is the more desirable should be based upon the objective findings of carefully controlled experimental research. Unfortunately, this, the most important aspect of the problem, has been neglected. It is certainly ironic that the approaches to the teaching of science, the scientific method, and the scientific spirit of inquiry have been selected without the benefit of scientific inquiry into the efficacy of the approaches [8]. The need and significance of such research has been underlined by the study, currently in progress, being conducted by the Science Teaching Improvement Program of the American Association for the Advancement of Science [13].

PROCEDURE

This investigation was conducted in four elementary schools in a public school system in suburban Long Island. The subjects of the study were 258 pupils distributed among ten sixth grade classes. In three of the schools comprising 188 of the sixth grade pupils seven classes were instructed in science by the regular classroom teachers. In the fourth, or experimental school, seventy pupils distributed in three classes were taught by the same special science teacher from September to April. A basic text, *Science for Today and Tomorrow*, was assigned to all of the classes in both the experimental and control groups. During the course of the investigation, the following six units of instruction were covered: the senses, communication and inventions that have facilitated communication, the functioning of various systems of the body and their relation to health and hygiene, food plants and the way in which they grow, and the history of the changing earth.

The special science teacher in this study had been observed by a school survey team of specialists in elementary education and elementary science, and had been rated as outstanding. The teachers in the control group had slightly more teaching experience than the special science teacher. There were no data available concerning the science backgrounds of the teachers involved in the study.

The Otis Quick Scoring Mental Ability Test was administered to all of the pupils and an I.Q. was calculated for each pupil. In April, the Metropolitan Achievement Tests: Intermediate Science Test was administered to all of the subjects, and standard scores and grade equivalents were calculated for each pupil. In view of the fact that boys tend to be more science-minded than girls, all of the data were tabulated and analyzed separately according to sex. Before testing for the significance of the differences between the mean science scores of the experimental and control groups, allowance was to be made, if necessary, for the differences in intelligence test scores between the groups by employing analysis of covariance.

THE FINDINGS

The data concerning the distribution of science achievement scores classified according to sex are presented in Table 1.

TABLE 1
*A Grouped Frequency Distribution of Sixth Grade Science
Achievement Scores Classified According to Sex*

Standard Scores	Boys	Girls	Totals
75–79	2	1	3
70–74	12	15	27
65–69	28	20	48
60–64	26	25	51
55–59	28	27	55
50–54	21	24	45
45–49	6	12	18
40–44	1	3	4
35–39	3	4	7
Totals	127	131	258

It is fairly obvious from the data in Table 1 that the distributions of science scores for both boys and girls are quite bell-shaped, that the boys' scores exceed the girls' scores, and that the students in this investigation are markedly superior to the norm group.

The data concerning the mean I.Q. and science achievement scores are classified according to sex and instructional group in Table 2.

It is readily apparent from the data presented in the last two rows in Table 2 that the decision to treat the findings for boys and girls separately in this study was justified. The mean I.Q. of the girls was 3.55 points higher than that of the boys, a difference resulting in a critical ratio of 2.53 which is significant at the .05 level of confidence. The mean standard score in science of the boys was 1.83 points higher than that of the girls despite the significantly higher I.Q. of the girls.

TABLE 2

The Means and Standard Deviations of the Experimental and Control Groups on
the Intelligence and Science Achievement Tests Classified According to Sex

Groups	N	Mean I.Q.	Standard Deviation	Mean Standard Score in Science	Standard Deviation
Experimental-Boys	29	108.53	11.41	61.41	7.60
Control-Boys	98	109.31	11.81	59.71	7.83
Experimental-Girls	41	112.04	10.64	58.42	6.82
Control-Girls	90	113.00	12.03	58.23	8.42
Total-Boys	127	109.14	11.41	60.09	7.80
Total-Girls	131	112.69	11.10	58.26	7.83

The difference in achievement yielded a critical ratio of 1.83 which is not significant. However, when allowance was made for the higher I.Q. of the girls through analysis of covariance, the adjusted mean of the boys' scores in science were significantly higher, at the .05 level of confidence, than the girls' scores.

Further analysis of Table 1 indicates that the boys in the experimental group obtained a mean standard science score of 61.41 while the boys in the control group obtained a mean standard science score of 59.71. The mean difference between these scores resulted in a non-significant critical ratio of 1.05. The data in rows 1 and 2, however, indicate a difference in mean I.Q. of .78 in favor of the control boys. Although this difference was not significant, allowance for the difference was made through analysis of covariance to determine whether the adjusted means in science achievement might approach significance. The resultant adjusted mean scores in science yielded a non-significant critical ratio of 1.33. Therefore it was concluded that there was no true difference in the achievement of these two groups.

The data in Table 1 also indicate that the girls in the experimental group obtained a higher mean standard science score than the girls in the control group. The difference in mean scores was .19, a difference resulting in a non-significant critical ratio of .14. Although there was a non-significant difference of .96 in mean I.Q. between the groups, analysis of covariance was not employed since it was obvious that significant differences between the adjusted science means could not possibly be found in the light of the small critical ratio, the small difference between the mean I.Q.'s and the limited sample. Therefore, it was concluded that there was no true difference in the achievement of these two groups.

SUMMARY AND RECOMMENDATIONS

When this study was initiated, the hypothesis of the investigators was that the students who were instructed by the special science teacher would manifest significant superiority in science achievement over the pupils who were instructed in science by the regular classroom teachers. While on the basis of the evidence obtained in this study such a hypothesis must be rejected, it is extremely important not to minimize the effects of two aspects of this study. The first aspect to be considered is the limited duration (seven months) of the study. The second aspect to be considered is the test which was employed to measure science achievement. It is of paramount importance for educators and scientists to analyze standardized achievement tests in science in order to ascertain whether they are providing valid appraisals of the desired objectives of the newer programs in science.

REFERENCES

1. Boyer, Donald. "Comparative Study of the Science Achievement of Pupils in Elementary Schools," *Science Education,* 39 (February 1955), 3–12.

2. Buck, Jacqueline. "Summary of Published Research 1929–52 in Teaching Elementary Science," *Science Education,* 38 (February 1954), 81–101.

3. Chamberlain, W. D. "The Development and Status of Teacher Education in the Field of Science for the Elementary School," unpublished doctoral dissertation, Wayne University, 1954.

4. Fitzpatrick, Frederick L. (Ed.). *Policies for Science Education.* Bureau of Publications, Teachers College, Columbia University, 1960.

5. Harris, C. W. *Encyclopedia of Educational Research.* Third Edition. New York: Macmillan, 1960.

6. Mallinson, George Griesen. "The Relationship between the Work of Elementary Science and Geography Teachers," *Journal of Geography,* 49 (May 1950), 206–10.

7. Mallinson, George Griesen and Sturm, H. E. "The Science Backgrounds and Competencies of Students Preparing to Teach in the Elementary Schools," *Science Education,* 39 (December 1955), 398–405.

8. Mallinson, Jacqueline. "The Current Status of Science Education in the Elementary Schools," *School Science and Mathematics,* 61 (April 1961), 252–70.

9. N.S.S.E. "A Program for Teaching Science," *Thirty-First Yearbook,* Part 1, 1932.

10. N.S.S.E. "Science Education in American Schools," *Forty-Sixth Yearbook,* Part 1, 1947.

11. N.S.S.E. "Rethinking Science Education," *Fifth-Ninth Yearbook,* Part 1, 1960.

12. Russell, D. W. "How 51 Well Known Educators Answered a Questionnaire Concerning the Teaching of Science in the Elementary Grades," *School Science and Mathematics,* 38 (November 1938), 907–21.

13. Science Teaching Improvement Program. *Study on the Use of Special Teachers of Science and Mathematics in Grades 5 and 6.* Washington: American Association for the Advancement of Science, 1960.

FOR FURTHER READING

Broadhead, Fred C., "Pupil Adjustment in the Semi-departmental Elementary School," *Elementary School Journal* 60 (April 1960) 385–390.

Gibb, E. Glenadine, and Dorothy C. Matala, "Study on the Use of Special Teachers of Science and Mathematics in Grades 5 and 6," *School Science and Mathematics* 61 (November 1961) 569–572; "Final Report," *School Science and Mathematics* 62 (November 1962) 565–585.

Morrison, R. Ruel, Jr., "Is Specialization the Answer? The Departmental Classroom Revisited," *Elementary School Journal* 68 (January 1968) 206–212.

A Test of Science Comprehension
for Upper Elementary Grades*

CLARENCE H. NELSON and JOHN MASON

This study is representative of the many concerned with evaluation in general, evaluation of science in particular, and the measurement of critical thinking more specifically. It is generally accepted that we should teach critical thinking and that we should do it in science classes, but it is not often that definite instruments are used to measure the results of such teaching. The reproduction of the complete test in this article should give ideas to many teachers as to how to construct tests of comprehension to go with their subject matter units. It is profitable to carefully examine the specific items for techniques of item construction. The reader will find references in "For Further Reading" on inquiry training as well as testing of critical thinking.

The first part of this article is a brief report of an experiment, although little is told about the experimental units. The second and major part is a description of a test used to evaluate the experiment, including information as to its reliability, ability to discriminate, and estimated difficulty. The evidence of validity is the face validity which can be obtained from a study of the actual test. It would be interesting to know how this test correlates with other tests of critical thinking.

Other studies in this volume which are related include McCracken's study of reading tests (Chapter 2), Lundsteen's study of critical listening (Chapter 3), and Schiller's study of study skills (Chapter 4).

Recent space exploration successes combined with many other significant breakthroughs, particularly in the field of medical science, have given new impetus to the study of science in the schools. This impetus has manifested itself in more ambitious curricular offerings in science, in more concern on the part of some parents that their

* From *Science Education* 47 (October 1963) 319–327. Reprinted with permission of the publisher; Clarence H. Nelson, Professor, Office of Evaluation Services, Michigan State University, East Lansing; and John M. Mason, Professor of Education, Michigan State University.

children's education—including training in science—be characterized by excellence and rigor, in increased motivation on the part of some children and youths to become involved in science in greater depth and with more thoroughness, and finally in a greater availability of facilities for the study of science now being provided by local school systems, the federal government, and private foundations.

Apropos of this surge in interest in science there would seem to be justification for the development of somewhat more sophisticated teaching units and for the creation of a measuring instrument capable of yielding data which would reveal whether or not pupils have indeed attained a more thoroughgoing comprehension of science and whether or not they have gained greater facility in the scientific skills of critical thinking.

In a report to be published subsequently the development and try-out of a series of such teaching units for grades 4–6 in the five Michigan school systems of Dearborn, East Lansing, Grosse Pointe, Lansing and Pontiac will be presented. The experimental design of that study was such as to include three groups of children at each grade level. These groups were designated (1) research, (2) experimental, and (3) control. Instruction for the research and experimental pupils was designed to set learning situations for the direct teaching of the skills and attitudes inherent in problem solving. The teachers instructing the classes comprising the research group had had some instruction in the direct teaching of critical thinking skills while the teachers of classes making up the experimental group were assumed to have had no previous experience with this method of presentation. The teachers of classes which constituted the control group taught without emphasizing the deliberate and constant involvement of pupils in critical thinking situations, though on occasion class discussion may have taken such a direction incidentally in connection with something brought up by the pupils.

The number of teachers and pupils in each group at each grade level is shown in Table 1.

A summary of the critical thinking pre-test and post-test variances, means, differences in means (which are interpreted as gains), and the critical ratios of these differences is presented in Table 2. Inspection of Table 2 shows that the pre-test means for each group (research, experimental, and control) were higher for each ascending grade. The post-test means for each group were also progressively greater for the pupils in grades four through six with the exception of the fifth grade

TABLE 1
Teachers and Pupils by Grades and Groups

Grade	Research Teachers	Pupils	Experimental Teachers	Pupils	Control Teachers	Pupils
4	4	105	8	182	6	139
5	7	177	11	256	5	130
6	8	190	9	213	7	165
	19	472	28	651	18	434

control group. When the scores of all the pupils at a given grade were treated as a whole, the pre- and post-test means were greater for each succeeding grade.

The pupils in the research and experimental groups at each grade level made significant gains between pre- and post-test scores as indicated by the critical ratios cited in Table 2. The only group that did not show a significant gain was the fifth grade control group, and being a control group it would not necessarily be expected to show a significant gain.

The estimated reliability coefficients of the tests were calculated from the test scores of the students for both pre- and post-test administrations in each group at each grade level. The formula used for estimating the reliability coefficient of each test at each administration was that developed by G. J. Froelich and cited by Garrett. Garrett says that the "Formula always underestimates to a slight degree the reliability of a test as found by the split-half technique and the Spearman-Brown formula, and the more widely items vary in difficulty the greater the underestimation." The reliability data are shown in Table 3.

A questionnaire, used to obtain teachers' reaction to the materials employed in the study, was sent to all the teachers who had participated in the experiment. The number of teachers to whom the questionnaire was sent and the number of returns by grades were as follows: fourth grade, 33–25; fifth grade 38–33; and sixth grade, 42–28. An analysis of the items designed to elicit teacher reaction to the critical thinking test indicated that at the fourth grade level three research, one experimental, and two control group teachers considered the critical thinking instrument to be too difficult for everyone. Seventeen teachers at this grade level thought the test to be difficult for most pupils. At the fifth grade level five research teachers and one experimental teacher con-

TABLE 2

Variances, Means, Differences in Means, and Critical Ratios

Grade	Group	N	Variance on Pre-test	Variance on Post-test	Mean Post-test	Mean Pre-test	Difference between means	Critical Ratio = Difference ÷ σD
4	Research	105	35	63	26.89	20.42	6.47	6.69*
	Experimental	182	40	47	21.68	17.47	4.21	6.09*
	Control	139	41	61	25.97	22.44	3.53	4.12*
	Total—Grade 4				24.36	19.82		
5	Research	177	57	77	28.15	26.06	2.09	2.40**
	Experimental	256	49	64	31.05	26.86	4.19	6.31*
	Control	130	49	72	25.13	25.55	-0.42	-0.44
	Total—Grade 5				28.77	26.31		
6	Research	190	59	73	33.61	29.89	3.72	4.46*
	Experimental	213	61	58	33.55	30.43	3.12	4.18*
	Control	165	57	62	33.64	30.98	2.66	3.13*
	Total—Grade 6				33.60	30.41		

* Significant at 1% level of confidence.
** Significant at 5% level of confidence.

TABLE 3
Reliability Coefficients—Critical Thinking Instrument

	Pre-test	*Post-test*
Grade 4	.70	.77
Research	.63	.77
Experimental	.70	.72
Control	.67	.77
Grade 5	.73	.82
Research	.75	.82
Experimental	.71	.79
Control	.71	.81
Grade 6	.76	.78
Research	.76	.81
Experimental	.76	.76
Control	.75	.77

sidered the test to be too difficult for everyone. Eighteen said it was difficult for most pupils. Three teachers in the research and three in the experimental groups felt that the test was about right in reading difficulty. At the sixth grade level one research and two experimental teachers said the reading difficulty was too high for everyone. Sixteen indicated that it was difficult for most pupils and two research and two experimental teachers felt that it was about the correct difficulty. One may infer, from teacher reaction, that the test was challenging and not beyond the reading capabilities of most pupils.

As a matter of general interest, comparisons were made between the scores of the pupils in the research and experimental, research and control, and experimental and control groups at the fourth, fifth and sixth grade levels. The scores were treated by analysis of variance and covariance with one independent variable (the pre-test score). The results of these analyses showed that the pupils in the research group in the fourth grade made significant gains in critical thinking skills over the pupils in both the experimental and control groups. At the fifth grade level the pupils in the experimental group showed significant gains over the pupils in the research and control groups. The research pupils also showed significant gains over the control pupils. There were no significant differences in means between any of the groups at the sixth grade level.

The remainder of this paper will concern itself with the development of the critical thinking test entitled A TEST OF SCIENCE COMPRE-

HENSION for Grades 4–6. In the development of this test cognizance was taken of a number of criticisms of objective testing for such a purpose as this and a deliberate attempt was made to avoid some of the more common faults of objective tests. Three of these criticisms and/ or alleged shortcomings of objective tests will be dealt with briefly before the rationale and actual construction details of the critical thinking test are discussed.

A rather frequently recurring criticism of objective testing centers around the belief that this form of test exercise can be devised only to measure the attainment of factual knowledge. There is no denying that mastery of factual knowledge is important and that the measurement of its attainment has a rightful place. However, surveys of measuring instruments devised by teachers tend to reflect an overemphasis on factual knowledge *per se* and a paucity of exercises that involve the student in critical thinking and the *application* of knowledge in problem solving situations. This imbalance of emphasis exists not because objective tests cannot be constructed to measure anything else, but largely because factual items can be written with the expenditure of less time and effort. Even though in actual practice the preponderance of testing is done at the factual level, it does not necessarily follow that this is desirable or that objective testing must be confined to the measurement of factual recall.

A second prevailing misconception, expressed repeatedly in some quarters, maintains that test exercises involving critical thinking and problem solving cannot be constructed to yield as sharp discrimination indices as those obtainable with exercises designed to measure attainment of factual knowledge. That many poorly constructed critical thinking items of the objective type do in fact yield results which lack incisive discrimination is all too evident. This does not imply, however, that it is impossible to construct highly discriminating items in the critical thinking category. Construction of high quality critical thinking items requires time, patience and a willingness to revise, re-think and refine the products of one's labors until a reasonably satisfactory standard is attained.

A third mistaken notion expressed by many critics of objective measuring instruments contends that objective test items are necessarily limited to the measurement of isolated, discrete, disjointed bits of information that bear little or no relationship to a central idea and little or no interrelationship among themselves. While this criticism is actually valid for many tests that are being used, it is nevertheless possible to create instruments that avoid these faults. With deliberate planning and by using a degree of imagination, it is possible to develop a sequential series of testing exercises which measure in stepwise fashion the systematic unfolding and progression of thinking required in the solution of a problem situation. Such a sequence of test items can touch upon many relevant facets and check upon the thorough understanding of each step along the way by delineating the same tasks for all the pupils. In the open-ended, free response testing exercise many of the significant and relevant details are often omitted by a large number of the respondees, leaving the teacher to wonder whether these individuals did not know or merely forgot to include these pertinent steps in their free response answers. In a series of sequential items of the objective type, on the other hand, all the pupils are confronted with the *same* series of pertinent steps. Each individual pupil must react to the significant facet incorporated in *each* item and thus all have the opportunity to demonstrate whether they do or do not understand each step in the sequence. The teacher then has a complete record to use as a basis for judging each individual pupil's performance and there is a comparability of standard from pupil to pupil.

To facilitate giving it, A TEST OF SCIENCE COMPREHENSION was set up in two parts, each part consisting of thirty items. Part I would be of appropriate length to occupy a class period one day and Part II could be given during a class period one or several days later. Each part consists of four situations arranged approximately in ascending order of difficulty. The items are so designed as to lead the pupils systematically through the situation. In some cases a problem is definitely stated, in others it is implicit in the situation. In each case the pupil must analyze the situation to arrive at answers to the questions about the situation.

To obtain the most meaningful results arrangements should be made to give the test as a pre-test early in the school year and again as a post-test near the end of the academic year. While some of the more perceptive pupils will be able to make moderately good scores on the pre-test, it is likely that the scores of the majority will be quite low. Nevertheless, establishing an initial reference point for each pupil gives more meaning to his end-of-year score. After a year's study of science which should include some opportunities for the pupils to think about, discuss and analyze situations of the kind included in the test, the year-end re-testing should be undertaken to ascertain what gain each pupil has made. This is determined by subtracting the initital pre-test score from the final post-test score. In rare instances a pupil may show retrogression instead of gain. But in most cases moderate to substantial gains will be in evidence. These gains can be partially attributed to the study of science during the year, but also in part to increased facility in reading attained during the year and to some extent to seven or eight months growth and maturity that each pupil has experienced in the interim between pre-testing and post-testing.

The test was deliberately designed to have a high ceiling, that is, it is difficult enough to yield a wide range of scores without a large clustering at or near the highest possible score level either during the pre-test or post-test administrations. While this tends to make the test seem quite difficult, nevertheless in order to obtain meaningful gains data for all the pupils, such a level of difficulty is necessary. If the test is too easy there will be a large clustering at the upper end of the range even on the pre-test. Those who earned high scores initially would not be adequately measured during the post-test administration for they could undoubtedly have earned higher scores than the test enabled them to do. For them the test would have been far too easy.

Each of the eight blocks of items centers around the interpretation of a situation, the application of scientific principles or theory in accounting for what has happened, and analysis of the situation as a basis for arriving at a solution to the problem inherent in the situation presented. In working through the test items relating to the situations the pupils become involved in making distinctions between what is given and what must yet be learned by making further observations, between facts and assumptions, between problems and hypotheses, and between inductive generalizations (a kind of theoretical assumption) and deductions from such assumptions or generalizations. A deliberate attempt has been made to use descriptive phraseology for the above-enumerated terms and to couch this phraseology in language that is meaningful to children of the upper elementary school age level. The chief concern throughout has been to measure the degree of understanding of an idea rather than the memorized meaning of a term. Whether or not the pupil understands the idea becomes evident in how he answers the questions involving the idea. As its name implies, therefore, this instrument was designed to be a test of science *comprehension* rather than a test of science information. The requisite background information would have been dealt with in the study of the units and tested for in the unit tests. Mastery of such information is essential. This should not, however, become the end goal in itself. It should be *contributory* to the ultimate goal of understanding or comprehension. Such comprehension manifests itself in demonstrating ability to apply what has been learned in the interpretation and analysis of new but related problem situations and in the ability to discern which of several alternatives constitutes the most appropriate conclusion to be drawn from the findings or the most appropriate solution to the problem inherent in the situation under consideration.

In the printed version of A TEST OF SCIENCE COMPREHENSION, which follows, the keyed answer for each item is indicated in parentheses following the item. In reproducing the test for classroom use, these would of course be omitted.

A Test of Science Comprehension

Grades 4–6

Part I

Directions: The purpose of this test is to find out how well you understand science. You will be asked to read a story situation. Then you will be asked to answer some questions about it. Your answers should be marked on the answer sheet. Use a soft lead pencil that makes a very black mark. Your teacher will show you how to make the marks on the answer sheet.

Numbers 1 through 6 refer to the following sketch which represents a city:

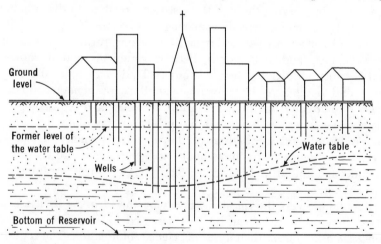

1. What is the total number of dry wells shown in the picture?
   1. Four
   2. Six
   3. Eleven   (2)

2. How many wells shown in the picture are still supplying water?

   1. One
   2. Two
   3. Five   (3)

3. How many wells shown in the picture have never supplied any water?

   1. One
   2. Two
   3. Four   (1)

4. The houses and other buildings stand on firm ground, but far down in the ground there is also water. We can, therefore, best describe the water table as

   1. a freely flowing underground lake of water with nothing else in it.
   2. a mixture of water and soil in the ground far down underneath the buildings.
   3. a ledge of rock far down underneath the ground.   (2)

5. Why has the level of the water gone down?

   1. This would happen only if the city is located in a desert.
   2. The city must be located on a hill causing the water to go down to lower ground.
   3. More water is used up in this city than is replaced by rainfall.   (3)

6. What helps to prevent the water in the water table from leaking away?

   1. The underground water table reaches down to the center of the earth.
   2. Constant pumping keeps the water near the top of the reservoir all of the time.
   3. The bottom of the reservoir

is made up of materials that water cannot pass through.

(3)

Numbers 7 through 11 refer to the following situation:

From 1944 to 1951 City A and City B both got their drinking water from Lake Michigan. In 1945 City A began to add a small amount of sodium fluoride to the water before the water was pumped through the water mains to the homes. In City B *no* sodium fluoride was added to the water.

Each year the school children's teeth were checked by dental officers in both cities. The average number of cavities (holes in their teeth) for each age of child is given below for the year 1944 and for the year 1951.

Average number of cavities each age of child	1944		1951	
	City A	City B	City A	City B
5 year olds	¼	¼	¼	¼
6 year olds	1	1	½	1
7 year olds	2	2	1	2
8 year olds	3	3	1½	3
9 year olds	4	4	2	3½
10 year olds	5	5	3	4¼
11 year olds	6	6	3½	5½
12 year olds	8	8¼	6	8
13 year olds	10	10	6½	9½
14 year olds	11½	12	8¼	11½
15 year olds	12½	13	9	13
16 year olds	13	14	11	13½

7. In 1944, how did the drinking water used in City A differ from the drinking water used in City B?

   1. It came from Lake Michigan.

   2. It had sodium fluoride added
      to it.

   3. There was no difference.

              (3)

8. During the years 1945 through
   1951 how did the drinking water
   used in City A differ from the
   drinking water used in City B?

   1. It was pumped through water
      mains.

   2. It had sodium fluoride added
      to it.

   3. There was no difference.

              (2)

9. Compare the number of cavities
   in 1944 in the children of City
   A with the number of cavities in
   the children of City B. How do
   they compare?

   1. There were very nearly the
      same for most ages of chil-
      dren.

   2. City A children had many
      more cavities than City B
      children.

   3. City B children had many
      more cavities than City A
      children.   (1)

10. Compare the number of cavities
   in 1951 in the children of City A
   with the number of cavities in
   the children of City B. How do
   they compare?

   1. They were very nearly the
      same for most ages of chil-
      dren.

   2. City A children had fewer
      cavities than City B children.

   3. City B children had fewer
      cavities than City A children.

              (2)

11. Which of the following is a conclusion that we might draw from
   the information given in the
   passage?

1. City B children must brush
   their teeth more often and
   more thoroughly than City A
   children do.
2. City A children probably eat
   more candy and drink more
   cokes than City B children
   do.
3. Adding sodium fluoride to
   drinking water may reduce
   the number of cavities in
   children's teeth.   (3)

For Number 12 through 16 decide
   which one of the following
   best applies to each statement:

1. Something that Dr. Fleming
   already knew (fact)

2. Something that Dr. Fleming
   saw (observation)

3. Something that puzzled Dr.
   Fleming (problem)

4. Something that Dr. Fleming
   predicted (hypothesis)

12. Bacteria S will grow on agar.
                               (1)

13. One day Dr. Fleming noticed a
    mold colony growing right in
    the center of one of his dishes
    of bacteria.   (2)

Numbers 12 through 16 pertain to
   the following situation:

   Dr. Fleming raised a certain kind
   of bacteria, which we shall call
   S. These bacteria grew on a
   jello-like substance known as
   agar. The agar is poured hot
   into round glass dishes. When it
   cools it sets up firm like jello,
   then bacteria are planted on the
   agar. When the bacteria grow
   normally the colonies or clusters
   are scattered in the dish of agar
   as shown at the right.

   One day, however, some mold
   had found its way into one dish

of bacteria. By the time Dr. Fleming discovered it, the mold had grown into a large colony in the middle of the dish. When he looked more closely, Dr. Fleming noticed that immediately surrounding the mold colony there was a clear zone in which the bacteria seemed to have been killed, as shown at the right.

"How did this happen?" he wondered. "Could the mold have given off some kind of substance that digests bacteria?"

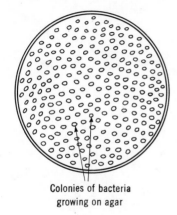

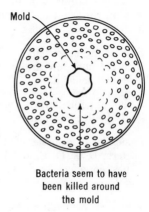

Colonies of bacteria
growing on agar

Bacteria seem to have
been killed around
the mold

14. Upon looking more closely, Dr. Fleming discovered that immediately surrounding this mold colony there were no living bacteria—only skeletons or shells of dead bacterial colonies. (2)

15. "Strange," he thought, "Now what could have caused these bacteria near the mold to die?" (3)

16. "Perhaps the mold is giving off some substance that eats up bacteria," he reasoned. (4)

Dr. Fleming began performing an experiment to find out why the bacteria near the mold had died. He wondered if the mold was giving off a substance that caused bacteria S to die. He managed to obtain from the mold a fluid which he called penicillin. This fluid did indeed kill bacteria S. But would it also kill other kinds of bacteria? *All* other kinds of bacteria? Or only *some* kinds? He would find out.

17. Penicillin kills all known kinds of bacteria. (4)

18. Two of the seven kinds of bacteria grew normally on the agar, even in the presence of penicillin. (1)

19. Five of the seven kinds of bacteria did not grow in the region near the penicillin. (1)

20. A shot of penicillin will cure any kind of infection in man. (4)

21. Penicillin is capable of killing bacteria B, C, D, E, and F, but it has no effect on bacteria A and G. (3)

22. Why does penicillin prevent certain kinds of bacteria from growing while it has no effect on other kinds? (2)

23. What does penicillin do to certain kinds of bacteria that makes them die? (2)

Dr. Fleming prepared a dish of agar and allowed it to cool. Along one side of the dish he cut out a strip of agar—a piece about the size of a strip of French fried potato. Into the furrow left when the strip of agar had been taken out he laid another strip of agar that contained some pencillin, as shown at the right.

Next he used a special needle with a handle on it, like this:

to make streaks on the surface of the agar in the dish. Before he drew the first streak he dipped the needle into a colony of bacteria A. For the second streak he dipped the needle into a colony of bacteria B, and so on for seven different kinds of bacteria. The agar dish with the streaks on the agar is shown at the right.

He put the dish in a warm place. Two days later when he took the dish out to look at it, this is how the seven different kinds of bacteria had grown. (See dish to the right.)

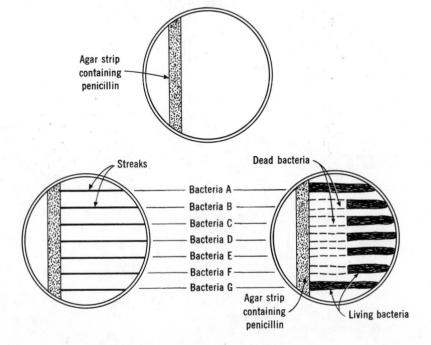

Agar strip containing penicillin

Streaks

Dead bacteria

Bacteria A
Bacteria B
Bacteria C
Bacteria D
Bacteria E
Bacteria F
Bacteria G

Agar strip containing penicillin

Living bacteria

For Number 17 through 23 decide which one of the following best applies to each statement.

1. Something that Dr. Fleming saw (observation)
2. Something that puzzled Dr. Fleming (problem)
3. Something that Dr. Fleming decided on the basis of what happened (conclusion)
4. Something that does not agree with the results of this experiment (false statement or false conclusion)

Numbers 24 through 30 are concerned with a comparison of two kinds of thermometers. One of these, known as Centigrade, is shown at the left. The other, known as Fahrenheit, is shown at the right.

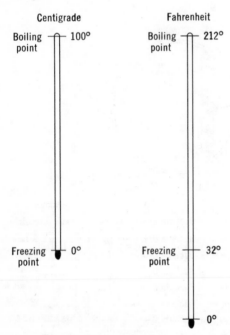

24. There are how many degrees between the freezing point and

the boiling point on the Centigrade thermometer?

1. 32
2. 100
3. 180   (2)

25. There are how many degrees between the freezing point and the boiling point on the Fahrenheit thermometers?

    1. 32
    2. 180
    3. 212   (2)

26. How does the number of degrees between the freezing point and the boiling point on the Centigrade and Fahrenheit thermometers compare?

    1. They are both the same.
    2. There are more Centigrade degrees.
    3. There are more Fahrenheit degrees.   (3)

27. There are 20 nickels or 100 pennies in a dollar. Since a dollar consists of fewer nickels than pennies, a nickel is larger than a penny. Now compare the number of Centigrade degrees to the number of Fahrenheit degrees between the freezing point and the boiling point. How does a Centigrade degree compare in size with a Fahrenheit degree?

    1. They are the same size.
    2. The Centigrade degree is smaller.
    3. The Centigrade degree is larger.   (3)

28. If a Centigrade thermometer reads 10 degrees above the freezing point, how many degrees above the freezing point would the Fahrenheit thermometer read?

1. 10 degrees
2. 18 degrees
3. 50 degrees   (2)

29. If the freezing point on a Fahrenheit thermometer is 32 degrees above zero, then how many degrees Fahrenheit above zero would a temperature of 10 degrees on the Centigrade thermometer be equal to? (Put marks on the pictures of the two thermometers to show these temperatures.)

     1. 50 degrees
     2. 18 degrees
     3. 10 degrees   (1)

30. How do you work out the answer to the previous question?

     1. $10 \times 9/5 + 32 =$ Number of degrees Fahrenheit.
     2. $10 \times 9/5 =$ Number of degrees Fahrenheit.
     3. 10 degrees Centigrade $= 10$ degrees Fahrenheit.   (1)

FOR FURTHER READING

Atkin, J. Myron, "A Study of Formulating and Suggesting Tests for Hypotheses in Elementary School Science Learning Experiences," *Science Education* 42 (December 1958) 414–422.

Boener, Charlotte N., "Picture Test for Comprehension of Science Concepts," *School Science and Mathematics* 66 (May 1966) 409–414.

Burmester, Mary Alice, "The Construction and Validation of a Test to Measure Some of the Inductive Aspects of Scientific Thinking," *Science Education* 37 (March 1953) 131–140.

Elkind, David, "Children's Discovery of the Conservation of Mass, Weight, and Volume: Piaget Replication Study II," *Journal of Genetic Psychology* 98 (June 1961) 219–227.

Hill, Katherine E., *Children's Contributions in Science Discussions* (New York: Teachers' College, Columbia University, 1947).

Mason, John M., "The Direct Teaching of Critical Thinking in Grades Four Through Six," *Journal of Research in Science Teaching*, Vol. 1, Issue 4 (December 1963), pp. 319–328.

Nelson, Clarence H. *Improving Objective Tests in Science* (Washington, D.C.; National Science Teachers Association, 1969).

Richardson, Evan C., "The Development of an Instrument for Evaluation of Elementary-School Science," *Science Education* 44 (March 1960) 112–118.

Suchman, J. Richard, "Inquiry Training: Building Skills for Autonomous Discovery," *Merrill-Palmer Quarterly of Behaviour and Development* 7 (July 1961) 147–169.

West, Joe Young, *A Technique for Appraising Certain Observable Behaviors of Children in Science in Elementary Schools* (New York: Bureau of Publications, Teachers' College, Columbia University, 1937).

Zapf, Rosalind M., "Superstitions of Junior High School Pupils, Part II: Effect of Instruction on Superstitious Belief," *Journal of Educational Research* 31 (March 1938) 481–496.

7

ADMINISTRATION OF
THE CURRICULUM

Administrative grouping is defined as the variety of efforts to assemble children into instructional groups for assignment to classroom teachers. Such grouping usually involves the principal and several teachers, if not the entire staff of the school, and calls for cooperative planning and group understanding. It is contrasted with instructional grouping, which is carried out by an individual teacher within one classroom and requires no particular coordination with other teachers.

As the reader studies the research in this chapter and possibly attempts, himself, to manipulate groupings, he may wish to consider the hypothesis that form itself (including the various forms of administrative grouping) may have little or no effect on children's learning. Perhaps only if the change in form brings about a significant change in instructional practice does learning improve.

Included in this chapter are the topics of entrance age, promotion and retention, ability grouping, nongraded, multi-age grouping, team teaching; the middle school, and core programs. Other closely related studies in this volume include Powell's study of the Joplin plan (Chapter 2), and DiLorenzo and Halliwell's study of the use of special teachers in science (Chapter 6).

It may be of interest to speculate as to why five out of the eight researches in this chapter are of the ex post facto type (of the other three, two are experimental, and one is a survey). Is it because public school officials are mainly interested in research "after the fact"? Is it because researchers in universities do not have the money or the control over school policies to set up larger experiments involving whole schools or several schools? Or is it that ex post facto research lends itself to the study of school-wide instructional organization? In terms of grade, the studies in this chapter distribute themselves as follows: two studies cover grades 1–6; one 1–2; one 1–2–3; one 4–8; one 7–8; one grade 5; and one grade 3.

Two journals account for almost half of the recently published researches on the topic of administrative grouping: *The Elementary School Journal* and *The Journal of Educational Research*. No other single journal yielded nearly as much research on this particular topic. Other useful sources in studying in this area are:

Association of Childhood Education International, *Toward Effective Grouping* (Washington, D.C.: The Association, 1962).

Dean, Stuart E., "School Organization in Historic Perspective," *Elementary School Organization 1961–1962*, National Education Association of Elementary School Principals Yearbook, pp. 49–59.

Franklin, Marion Pope, *School Organization: Theory and Practice* (Chicago: Rand McNally & Co., 1967).

Henry, Nelson B., editor, *Individualizing Instruction*, 61st Yearbook, Part I, National Society for the Study of Education (Chicago: University of Chicago Press, 1962).

Hillson, Maurie, editor, *Change and Innovation in Elementary School Organization* (New York: Holt, Rinehart & Winston, Inc., 1965).

———, editor, *Current Issues and Research in Education: Elementary Education* (New York: The Free Press, 1967).

Morgenstern, Anne, editor, *Grouping in the Elementary School* (New York: Pitman Publishing Corp., 1966).

Otto, Henry J., and David C. Sanders, *Elementary School Organization and Administration*, 4th edition (New York: Appleton-Century-Crofts, 1964).

Plowden, Lady Bridget, *Children and Their Primary Schools*, Report of Central Advisory Council for Education (England). (London: Her Majesty's Stationary Office, 1967).

Shane, Harold G., "Grouping in the Elementary School," *Phi Delta Kappan* 41 (April 1960) 313–319.

Thelen, Herbert A., "Classroom Grouping," in Alfred Yates, editor, *Grouping in Education* (New York: John Wiley & Sons, Inc., 1966), 143–150.

Wrightstone, J. Wayne, "Class Organization for Instruction," *What Research Says to the Teacher* (Washington, D.C.: National Education Association, 1957).

Yates, Alfred, editor, *Grouping in Education* (New York: John Wiley & Sons, Inc., 1966).

A Study of the Comparative Reading Achievements of Early and Late School Starters*

RICHARD S. HAMPLEMAN

There are many ways to improve reading and other school growths. Parent education, kindergartens, better teachers and methods, and improved materials are some of them—and changing the age of entrance is yet another. In spite of the fact that we have been struggling with the problem of admission for many years, and despite the unanimity of findings about the age of entrance, a major problem remains. Perhaps we are unwilling to institute a more flexible primary program which adapts to the individual differences of children.

Hampleman's study is an ex post facto type of research. It is noteworthy as an illustration of what can be done with relatively unsophisticated statistics. The follow-up study reported in the final footnote deserves mention. It is good to see a researcher attempt to pin down loose ends.

Related studies in this volume include those by Smith, Hillerich, and Hahn, in Chapter 2; and by Dobbs and Neville in Chapter 7. Of particular note in the list "For Further Reading" is the Halliwell review of reviews on entrance age.

INTRODUCTION

For approximately thirty years school people have been speculating about the problem of the best age at which to start teaching children to read. As a result of some early study of the problem, it was concluded that children were having difficulty with reading because they were being started too young. Some schools moved back the dates by which pupils had to be six years of age before they could start school in Sep-

* From *Elementary English* 36 (May 1959) 331–334. Reprinted with permission of The National Council of Teachers of English and Richard S. Hampleman, Professor of Education, North Texas State University, Denton. Footnote at end of the article is from *Readings on Reading Instruction*, p. 65, and is reprinted with permission of its publisher, David McKay Co., Inc., and the author.

tember, from February 15 or January 15 to January 1 or December 15, or even earlier. Other schools approached the problem from another angle—kept the same rule for entrance age, but saw to it that no pupils were put in beginning reading groups until they were six years of age or over.

Later studies began to indicate that perhaps other factors, more important than chronological age, also operate to affect the problem of the proper time to begin reading instruction. Mental age, teaching techniques, and certain reading readiness factors which might be strengthened by kindergarten and first grade pre-reading experiences, were now considered to be of more value in predicting readiness for reading than was chronological age.

It is the opinion of the author, however, that school people can get changes made in the chronological age requirement far more easily than they can get the public to accept school entrance on the basis of mental age or reading readiness test scores. Therefore, to be practical, more study should be concentrated on that chronological age at which beginning reading can be taught most successfully.

The question this study will attempt to answer is, "Are pupils who start school at the age of six years four months or over better readers in the sixth grade than those who start school below the age of six years four months?"

It is the opinion of the author that there should be some important difference between the two groups. Those who are approximately one-half year older should be more successful in reading than the younger ones for three main reasons. Since they are older chronologically they will (1) be somewhat more advanced in mental age, (2) have more experiences to assist with readiness, and (3) have better eye coordination. Thus, even though chronological age by itself may not be an excellent prognosis for reading success, other factors which may be more important are advanced, to some extent, as chronological age advances.

RELATED RESEARCH

A review of related studies shows that the bulk of them were done in the 1920's and 1930's. All but one of them has studied the relationship of various factors to reading achievement in grades one or two. One study uses fourth grade subjects.

One group of studies indicates that chronological age should be six years to give a child a satisfactory start in reading. Most of them say that age seven may be better if the child is immature physically, mentally, or emotionally. Correlations found between chronological age and reading achievement are .09 and .12.

Studies of the relationship between mental age and reading achievement show that a mental age of six to seven years is necessary for beginning reading. Correlations between these two factors range from .50 to .69.

The best predictors of reading success discovered in the literature were mental age, teacher rating in November, and various combinations of such factors as mental age, reading readiness tests, and teacher rating plans.

A number of studies point to other factors more important to success in beginning reading than any fixed chronological or mental age. These factors are individual attention to the needs of slow learners, rich experience background, reading programs centered around experiences, and quality of techniques and materials used. A conclusion running through these studies is that mere postponement in the time of beginning to teach reading will not in itself insure that all children will learn to read.

The present study is different in that it is the first to compare the relationship between school entrance age and eventual reading success as far along as the sixth grade.

METHODS OF RESEARCH

Data used in the study were obtained from the school office of the Bloomington, Indiana, Metropolitan School District. These facts were collected: date of birth, reading achievement score (age-equivalent) on the *Stanford Achievement Test, Intermediate Complete, Forms F and J*, date this test was administered, and all available intelligence quotient scores.

Data were collected only for those children who entered the first grade in September, 1947, finished the sixth grade in June, 1953, and had all of their schooling in the Bloomington schools. Working with these criteria, 58 pupils out of 181 in the class were selected for study.

All of those who were six years, three months of age or younger at entrance were put in Group 1, and those who were six years, four months of age or over were placed in Group 2. Mean and median reading achievement scores were then figured for each group.

In order to be able to compare the mean and median achievement of the first and fourth quarters of the whole group of subjects, Group 1 was divided into two equal parts, Group 1A and Group 1B. Group 2 was divided into two nearly equal parts, Group 2A and 2B.

Intelligence test scores were not used in this study to equate the two groups. They were used only to assist in the analysis and interpretation of results. In that connection, the score used was the median I.Q. score of the three to six scores found for each child.

ANALYSIS AND RESULTS

Table 1 will help clarify relationships in the analysis of the data which answer the main question of this study, "Are late school starters more successful in reading by the time they finish the sixth-grade than are early starters?" Group 2, the older children, have a mean reading

TABLE 1

Mean and Median Chronological Age, Intelligence Quotient, and Reading Achievement Score of Two Groups

Group number	Mean chron. age*	Median chron. age*	Mean I. Q. score	Median I. Q. score	Mean read. ach. score*	Median read. ach. score*
2	146.51	146.00	106.25	103.00	148.86	146.00
1	141.53	141.50	106.13	108.00	144.70	139.00
Difference	4.98	4.50	0.12	−5.00**	4.16	7.00

* Expressed in months
** This difference is marked minus (−) to indicate that it is the reverse of all the other differences shown.

achievement score slightly more than four months higher than Group 1. The median score for Group 2 shows them to be seven months superior. Intelligence quotients for the two groups are essentially the same, means both being 106, and medians being 108 for Group 1 and 103 for Group 2. In mean chronological age, Group 2 is five months older. As a result of this data it is clear that those children who started to school at age six years, four months or more, as a group are superior in reading achievement at the sixth-grade level to their younger class-mates.

The results shown by a comparison of data for Groups 1A and 2B (youngest and oldest quarters) are even more impressive. Table 2 shows the means and medians of these two groups along with the corresponding chronological ages. The mean of the oldest quarter, Group 2B, shows a superiority of almost seven months over the youngest quarter, Group 1A. Comparing these groups by medians shows an even greater superiority—eleven months. Intelligence quotients for the two groups are essentially the same in both mean and median scores. The older group has a mean difference in age from the younger group of almost eight months and a median difference of seven months.

TABLE 2

*Mean and Median Chronological Age, Intelligence Quotient, and
Reading Score for Upper and Lower Quartiles*

Group number	Mean age*	Median age*	Mean I. Q.	Median I. Q.	Mean reading score*	Median reading score*
2B	152.19	151.00	103.63	100.50	146.56	146.00
1A	144.27	144.00	103.27	100.00	139.73	135.00
Difference	7.92	7.00	0.36	0.50	6.83	11.00

* Expressed in months

Since the older group in this study, Group 2B, showed more superiority to Group 1A in reading achievement than might have been expected, the data was analyzed in one other way in an attempt to shed further light on the matter. Of the fifteen in Group 1A, there were only five up to grade level (143 months) in reading. Four of these five had an intelligence quotient of 110 or better. The fifth one had an I.Q. of 99, yet was up to grade level. One who was not up to grade level (eight months below) had an intelligence quotient of 115.

Of the sixteen in Group 2B, there were nine up to grade level and five of that nine achieved this with intelligence quotients below 110. One of these five had an intelligence quotient of 87. Six of the seven in Group 2B who did not achieve grade level had intelligence quotients below 100. The seventh one had a score of 102.

CONCLUSIONS

A comparison of the two groups, Group 1 and Group 2, indicates that there is an interesting difference between them in reading achievement. Although it has been well established by earlier research that many factors may influence reading readiness, it seems fairly certain, as a result of this study, that school administrators can advise parents that their children have a considerably better chance for success in reading by starting to school a few months later, rather than a few months earlier. This would be especially important in those cases where birthdate causes doubt as to the best time to send a child to school. The administrator can be more confident of a good prognosis if an intelligence test is given. Those children who have a considerably higher intelligence quotient than 100 would have an excellent chance for success in reading even if they were only six years, three months of age or below. Those children with intelligence quotients below 100 would have very little chance for success in reading if they were this young.

The differences in reading achievement between the older and younger groups observed in this study, although not statistically significant, are nevertheless interesting enough to merit further attention. It is possible that such differences would be significant if the number of cases studied were larger. Such a study is now in progress.*

NOTE

* The author reports that a replica of the above study was made with 323 sixth-grade pupils in Macomb, Illinois. A difference of 6.3 months was observed between the mean reading achievement scores of the older pupils (group 2) and the younger pupils (group 1). The difference favored the older pupils and was significant at better than the one per cent level. A difference of 7.7 months was observed between the mean reading achievement scores of the oldest one-fourth (group 2b) and the youngest one-fourth (group 1a). The difference favored the older one-fourth of the pupils and was statistically significant at better than the 1 per cent level. The mean I.Q. scores for these groups slightly favored the younger pupils (groups 1 and 1a).

    The correlation between intelligence and reading achievement in this study was .71. Among the older pupils (group 2), 30 per cent of those who had I.Q.'s below 100 were up to grade level, and 98 per cent of those who had I.Q.'s of 110 or better were up to grade level. Among the younger pupils (group 1), 10 per cent of those who had I.Q.'s below 100 were up to grade level, and 84 per cent of those who had I.Q.'s of 110 or better were up to grade level.

REFERENCES

1. Arthur, Grace, "A Quantitative Study of the Results of Grouping First-Grade Classes According to Mental Age," *Journal of Educational Research* 12:173–185, October, 1925.

2. Bigelow, Elizabeth B., "School Progress of Under-Age Children," *Elementary School Journal* 35:186–192, November, 1934.

3. Boney, C. DeWitt, and Agnew, Kate, "Periods of Awakening or Reading Readiness," *Elementary English Review* 14:183–187, May, 1937.

4. Davidson, Helen P., *An Experimental Study of Bright, Average, and Dull Children at the Four-Year Mental Level*, Genetic Psychology Monographs, Vol. 9, Nos. 3–4, Clark University, Worcester, Massachusetts, 1931, pp. 119–289.

5. Dean, Charles D., "Predicting First-Grade Reading Achievement," *Elementary School Journal* 39:609–616, April, 1939.

6. Deputy, E. B., *Predicting First-Grade Reading Achievement, A Study in Reading Readiness*, Teachers College, Columbia University, Contributions to Education, No. 426, New York, 1930, 61 pp.

7. Eames, Thomas, "Comparison of Children of Premature and Full Term Birth Who Fail in Reading," *Journal of Educational Research* 38:506–508, March, 1945.

8. Gates, Arthur I., "The Necessary Mental Age for Beginning Reading," *Elementary School Journal* 37:497–508, March, 1937.

9. Gates, Arthur, and Bond, Guy L., "Reading Readiness: A Study of Factors Determining Success and Failure in Beginning Reading," *Teachers College Record* 37:679–685, May, 1936.

10. Hilliard, George H., and Troxell, Eleanore, "Informational Background as a Factor in Reading Readiness and Reading Progress," *Elementary School Journal* 38:255–263, December, 1937.

11. Monroe, Marion, *Children Who Cannot Read, The Analysis of Reading Disabilities and the Use of Diagnostic Tests in the Instruction of Retarded Readers*, The University of Chicago Press, Chicago, 1932, 205 pp.

12. Morphett, Mabel V., and Washburne, Carleton, "When Should Children Begin to Read?" *Elementary School Journal* 31:496–503, March, 1931.

13. Peterson, Inez B., "The Reading-Readiness Program of the Ironwood Public Schools," *Elementary School Journal* 37:438–446, February, 1937.

14. Reed, Mary M., *An Investigation of Practices in First Grade Admission and Promotion,* Teachers College, Columbia University, Contributions to Education, No. 290, New York, 1927, 136 pp.

15. Samuels, Fra, "Sex Differences in Reading Achievement," *Journal of Educational Research* 36:594–603, April, 1943.

16. Thompson, J. L., "Big Gains from Postponed Reading," *Journal of Education* 117:445–446, October 15, 1934.

17. Wilson, Frank T., and Burke, Agnes, "Reading Readiness in a Progressive School," *Teachers College Record,* 38:565–580, April, 1937.

18. Wilson, Frank T., and Flemming, Cecile W., "Correlations of Reading Progress with Other Abilities and Traits in Grade I," *Journal of Genetic Psychology* 53:33–52, 1938.

19. Wright, Wendell W., *Reading Readiness—A Prognostic Study,* Bulletin of the School of Education, Indiana University, Vol. 12, No. 3, Bureau of Cooperative Research, Indiana University, June, 1936, 46 pp.

FOR FURTHER READING

Ahr, Edward, "Early School Admission: Our District's Experience," *Elementary School Journal* 67 (February 1967) 231–236.

Anderson, Irving H., *et al.,* "Age of Learning to Read and Its Relation to Sex, Intelligence and Reading Achievement in the Sixth Grade," *Journal of Educational Research* 49 (February 1956) 447–453.

Birch, J. W., "Early School Admission for Mentally Advanced Children," *Exceptional Children* 21 (December 1954) 84–87.

Halliwell, Joseph W., "Reviewing the Reviews on Entrance Age and School Success," *Journal of Educational Research* 59 (May–June 1966) 395–401.

——, and B. W. Stein, "A Comparison of the Achievement of Early and Late School Starters in Reading, Related and Non-Reading Areas in Fourth and Fifth Grades," *Education Digest,* 30–31 (September 1964), 31–37; in *Elementary English* 41 (October 1964) 631–639.

Hamalainen, Arthur E., "Kindergarten—Primary Entrance Age in Relation to Later School Adjustment," *Elementary School Journal* 52 (March 1952) 406–411.

Ilg, Frances, and Louis B. Ames, *School Readiness: Tests in Use in the Gesell Institute* (New York: Harper & Row, 1965).

King, Inez B., "Effect of Age of Entrance into Grade I Upon Achievement in Elementary School," *Elementary School Journal* 55 (February 1955) 331–336.

Larson, A., "The Early Admission Experiment of the Fund for the Advancement of Education," *Education Forum* 23 (November 1958) 101–108.

Pauley, Frank R., "Sex Differences and Legal School Entrance Age," *Journal of Educational Research* 45 (September 1951) 1–9.

"School Admission and Promotion," *National Education Association Research Bulletin* 37 (February 1959) 13–15.

Washburne, C. W., "When Should We Teach Arithmetic?: A Committee of Seven Investigation," *Elementary School Journal* 28 (May 1928) 659–665.

————, "Mental Age and the Arithmetic Curriculum—Summary of the Committee of Seven Grade Placement Investigations to Date," *Journal of Educational Research* 23 (1931) 210–231.

Weiss, Rosalee G., "The Validity of Early Entrance Into Kindergarten," *Journal of Educational Research* 56 (September 1962) 53–54.

PROMOTION AND RETENTION

The Effect of Nonpromotion on the Achievement of Groups Matched from Retained First Graders and Promoted Second Graders*

VIRGINIA DOBBS and DONALD NEVILLE

Either the system is rigid and the child adapts to it (or suffers the consequences) or differences in children are respected and the system is adapted to them. Promotion and retention are parts of a rigid system. Nongrading, multi-age grouping, and other provisions for individual differences are current attempts to modify that system to respect children's differences. There is much research on this topic and (unlike some other areas) there is consensus that retention seldom improves achievement. Yet the practice still continues in many elementary schools today. This study was included to point up the problem and to relate it to some of the proposed solutions.

In addition to providing a good bibliography, the following study is noteworthy as an illustration of the ex post facto type research. The researchers worked diligently to identify a group containing two subgroups that were comparable except for the one factor of retention. Valid and reliable instruments and sophisticated statistics were used to establish comparability and to examine differences.

Related studies which consider alternative solutions are Hampleman's study of admission; Jones, Moore, and Van Devender's study of nongraded programs; Adams' study of multi-age grouping; and Balow and Curtin's study of ability grouping (all in the present chapter). Also related are the studies of double promotion, enrichment, and acceleration cited in "For Further Reading" (Cook and Clymer, Criscuolo, Engle, and Ivey).

The nonpromotion of children in school is based on the assumption that it is of educational value. Yet research, since the early part of this century, has failed to substantiate such an assumption.

* From *The Journal of Educational Research*, 60 (February 1967) 472–475. Reprinted with permission of *The Journal of Educational Research;* Virginia Dobbs, Director of Pupil Personnel Services, Metropolitan Nashville Public Schools; and Donald Neville, Associate Professor of Education and Psychology, George Peabody College for Teachers, Nashville, Tennessee.

The educational advantages claimed for retention include that of aiding the academic achievement of the child, maintaining high achievement standards for each grade, and decreasing the variability of achievement within a classroom. In 1936 Arthur (1) found that the average repeater in Grade 1 learned no more in two years than the average nonrepeater of the same mental age learned in one year. For other grade levels, Saunders (14) concluded that nonpromotion for inadequate achievement was not justifiable, and research since that time has supported such a view (12, 5, 10). Research has also shown that retention did not raise grade level standards (6, 12, 5). As early as 1933, Caswell (3) concluded that nonpromotion did not decrease the variability of achievement levels in the classroom. This finding has been supported by later research (6, 14). Thus it appears that retention has not been effective as a means of achieving the major educational objectives for which it is allegedly used.

The conclusion that nonpromotion has no educational value is only one of the important considerations in deciding whether to retain a child. Several authors have pointed out the potential danger of failure on personal and social adjustment. According to research, some detrimental effects of failure experiences are: emotional instability (14), social rejection (7), delinquency (15), and school dropouts (2). School dissatisfaction, which has adverse effects on life adjustment, could be greatly reduced if school programs provided success experiences for all children.

Otto and Estes (13: 8), in their review of literature on nonpromotion in the *Encyclopedia of Educational Research*, concluded that nonpromotion had no significant educational value for pupils, and in 1962 Sister Josephine (8), in a comprehensive review of existing research, found a plethora of research results which indicated that the ultimate returns did not justify failing a pupil. Yet large numbers of children continue to be retained at the close of each school year. Apparently there has not been enough conclusive research to demonstrate that retention is not an aid to achievement, or the results of existing research have not been clearly communicated to educators. This indicates a need for further well-designed research which can clearly communicate the effects of nonpromotion to school personnel.

Since low achievement is a major cause of retention, the present study was designed to ascertain the effects of nonpromotion on the achievement of once-retained first graders as compared with never-retained second graders. From these two groups, pairs were matched on seven variables. This imposed a high degree of control on the major variables relevant to achievement. The study was done in eight elementary schools with an overall high first-grade retention rate; however, the rate of retention varied greatly from school to school, ranging from 2 per cent to 36 per cent.

PROCEDURE

Thirty pairs of children, each pair consisting of a once-retained first grader and a never-retained second grader, were matched on: (a) race, (b) sex, (c) socio-economic level, (d) type of classroom assignment, (e) age, (f) mental ability, and (g) reading achievement. Matching was done from an original pool of 74 once-retained first-grade children and 170 never-retained second-grade children enrolled in eight low socio-economic urban schools. Throughout the remainder of this report the once-retained first graders are referred to as the non-promoted group, and the never-retained second graders as the promoted group.

All children were Caucasian, and the original matched groups consisted of ten pairs of girls and 20 pairs of boys. The socio-economic variable of the school areas was controlled by equating the mean income level within $1,000 of districts in which the eight schools were located. The 1960 Bureau of the Census Report (4) provided the information relative to mean income levels. Classroom assignment of the children used in the study was made on the basis of homogeneous or nonhomogeneous grouping, and pairs were matched on the same basis. As can be seen in Table 1, there were no significant differences between the two groups on the variables of age, derived IQ, or reading achievement level. The latter two variables were measured by the

TABLE 1

Age, Mental Ability, and Achievement of the Non-Promoted Group as Compared with the Promoted Group for Matched Pairs

	Non-Promoted Mean	Promoted Mean	Mean Difference	Standard Error Mean Difference	t
Age in Months	88.13	88.43	.30	.49	.61
Derived IQ	84.16	85.80	1.63	1.09	1.50
Reading Gr. Level	1.42	1.43	.013	.018	.72
Arithmetic Gr. Level	1.36	1.57	.203	.076	2.67*

* Significant, df = 29, p < .02.

Lorge-Thorndike Group Intelligence Test and the Metropolitan Achievement Test.

The entire subject pool from which the pairs were matched was given the Lorge-Thorndike Group Intelligence Test in groups of not less than ten or more than 15 children. The mean IQ levels of both groups, it can be noted in Table 1, are within the slow learner category; however, the range in IQ was such that some of the matched pairs fell within the average and borderline classifications.

Pairs were not matched on arithmetic achievement. Table 1 shows that the promoted group was .2 of a school year higher than the non-promoted group in arithmetic achievement, as measured by the Metropolitan Achievement Test. This difference was significant (t = 2.67, df = 29, p. < .02). It was decided, however, that it would be useful to compare the arithmetic and reading achievement gains of the two groups, and the arithmetic achievement scores of the matched pairs were handled in the same way as the reading achievement scores throughout the study.

About six weeks before the close of each school year the Metropolitan Achievement Test was administered simultaneously by grade level in the classrooms of the schools used in the study. These tests provided the achievement data used throughout the study. The difference between the 1962 and 1963 achievement test scores was used as a measure of both the reading and arithmetic gain of the 30 matched pairs. One year later, in a follow-up of the reading and arithmetic achievement of the matched pairs, scores were available on 24 of the original 30. The grade level scores of these 24 matched pairs for the years 1962, 1963, and 1964 were used for a comparison of the reading and arithmetic achievement of the two groups over the two-year period of the study.

RESULTS

A t test for matched pairs (16: 151) was used to test the significance of the mean difference between the 1962 and the 1963 reading and arithmetic achievement test scores of the nonpromoted and promoted groups. This test showed both the reading achievement gain and the arithmetic achievement gain of the promoted group to be significantly greater than the corresponding gains of the nonpromoted group. It can be seen from Table 2 that a comparison of the reading achievement gain of the two groups yielded a t value of 6.01 (df = 29, p < .01), and a

TABLE 2

*Achievement Gains of the Non-Promoted Group as Compared
with the Promoted Group*

	Non-Promoted Mean Gain	Promoted Mean Gain	Mean Difference	Standard Error Mean Difference	t
Reading 1962–63	.32	.62	.297	.049	6.06*
Arithmetic 1962–63	.69	1.14	.447	.116	3.85*

* Significant, df = 29, p < .01.

comparison of the arithmetic achievement gain yielded a *t* value of
3.85 (df = 29, p < .01).

An analysis of the achievement data on the 24 matched pairs, whose
achievement test scores were available the second year of the study,
provided a comparison of the reading and arithmetic achievement
gains of the two groups over the two-year period. Figure 1 gives a
graphic representation of the 1962, 1963, and 1964 mean grade level
achievement of the nonpromoted and promoted groups in both reading
and arithmetic. Table 3 gives the means and standard deviations of the
grade level scores represented on the graph.

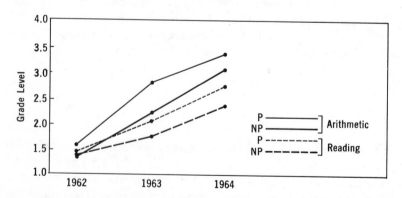

Two analyses of variance, using repeated measures on the same
subjects under two experimental conditions (11: 237), were employed
to test for the interaction of the nonpromoted and promoted conditions
with the 1962, 1963, and 1964 achievement test measures.

TABLE 3
*Grade Level Means and Standard Deviations of the
Reading and Arithmetic Scores*

| | Non-Promoted | | | | | |
| | 1962 | | 1963 | | 1964 | |
	M	SD	M	SD	M	SD
Arithmetic	1.43	0.11	1.78	0.25	2.44	0.87
Reading	1.42	0.34	2.15	0.39	3.09	0.39
	Promoted					
	1962		1963		1964	
	M	SD	M	SD	M	SD
Arithmetic	1.46	0.12	2.08	0.36	2.80	0.58
Reading	1.65	0.42	2.76	0.57	3.37	0.84

The analysis of variance using the three reading achievement grade level scores of the 24 matched pairs over the two-year period showed that the reading achievement of the promoted group was significantly greater than that of the nonpromoted group both from 1962 to 1963 ($F = 4.00$, df = 2/46, $p < .025$) and from 1963 to 1964 ($F = 5.28$, df = 2/46, p = .01). There was a significant interaction between groups and the three reading achievement test measures ($F = 5.28$, df = 2/46, p < .01).

The analysis of variance using the three arithmetic achievement grade level scores over the two-year period showed a significant difference in the overall arithmetic achievement of the nonpromoted and the promoted groups ($F = 15.56$, df = 1/23, p < .001). The arithmetic achievement of the promoted group was significantly greater than that of the nonpromoted group ($t = 3.85$, df = 71, p < .01). There was no significant interaction between groups and the three arithmetic test measures.

The t tests used to determine the significance of the mean difference in the reading achievement of each group from year to year showed the reading achievement gain of both the nonpromoted group and the promoted group to be significant from 1962 to 1963 and from 1963 to 1964. The t values ranged from 3.68 to 14.11 (df = 23, p < .01). The t tests used to determine the significance of the mean difference in the arithmetic achievement of the combined groups from year to year showed a significant difference in the arithmetic achievement gain from 1962 to 1963 and from 1963 to 1964. The t values ranged from

8.11 to 17.89 (df = 47, p < .001). Since there was no interaction between groups and the three arithmetic achievement test measures, it was not appropriate to examine the significance of the difference in the arithmetic achievement gain of the two groups separately.

DISCUSSION

During the first year of the present study, using the achievement data on the original 30 matched pairs, both the reading achievement gain and the arithmetic achievement gain of the promoted group were found to be significantly greater than that of the nonpromoted group.

An analysis of the achievement data, over a two-year period, on the 24 matched pairs whose achievement test scores were available the second year of the study showed: (a) a significant difference in the reading achievement level of the nonpromoted and promoted groups in both 1963 and 1964, with the reading achievement level of the promoted group being higher, (b) a significant difference in the overall arithmetic achievement gain of the nonpromoted and promoted groups over the two-year period, with the arithmetic gain of the promoted group being greater, (c) the reading achievement gain of both the nonpromoted and promoted groups was significant from year to year, and (d) the arithmetic achievement gain of the two groups combined was significant from 1962 to 1964.

Since an attempt was made to control variables other than promotion which could have influenced achievement gain, strong support is provided for concluding that promotion led to the increased achievement gain of the promoted group. The present study provides no information concerning the factors associated with promotion which could have influenced achievement gain. The findings of previous research suggest that the feeling of success associated with promotion may have provided the added incentive for greater achievement (11).

Previous research cited indicated that nonpromotion is not advantageous to achievement. In the present study, results indicated that nonpromotion was actually a disadvantage to achievement. Conclusions based on the findings of the present study, however, must be considered in relation to the limits set by the research. Only white, low socio-economic children were used, and a majority of the matched pairs were slow learners. Research on such children concerning the effects of nonpromotion should, however, be most pertinent, since retention is commonly used by schools as a means of curriculum adjustment for low achievers.

Personal and social adjustment factors are also to be considered in relation to the present research. These adjustment factors were not among the variables on which pairs were matched. Personal and social adjustment factors as a consistent influence in the original decision to promote or retain these children is questionable, however, because of the high variability in the retention rate (2% to 36%) of the eight schools used in the study. There were undoubtedly many children promoted in schools with low retention rates who would have been retained in schools with high retention rates. This suggests that the difference in promotional practices from school to school was a more important influence on the decision to promote or retain than was the personal and social adjustment of the individual child.

It is of interest to consider the pattern of the arithmetic achievement gain of the promoted group over the two-year period. The promoted group was .2 of a school year higher in arithmetic achievement than the nonpromoted group when the pairs were matched. At the end of the first year of the study the promoted group was .7 of a school year higher in arithmetic achievement than the nonpromoted group. At the end of the second year of the study, however, the promoted group was only .3 of a school year higher than the nonpromoted group. Apparently the initial superiority in arithmetic achievement of the promoted group did not indicate a lasting difference in the arithmetic ability of the two groups.

Previous research and the present study could suggest that continued promotion is best for all children. This, however, may be an erroneous conclusion. The continued promotion of a child who is unable to gain about one grade level in achievement each school year eventually places him at a grade level where he has difficulty functioning. Neither group of children used in the present study was academically ready for their present grade placement. Although the promoted group gained significantly more each year in both reading and arithmetic achievement than did the nonpromoted group, it is to be remembered that the grade placement of the promoted group was one level higher than the non-promoted group. Low achievers, therefore, experience failure through retention or through continued promotion unless classroom activities are adjusted to the ability level of the individual child.

Although attempts have been made to provide maximum educational opportunity for low achievers, the problem of low achievers in the classrooms remains unsolved. There have been some efforts to abolish grade levels and institute systems of continuous progress (8). Pilot studies using this approach in the primary grades are now being conducted. (2) Other fruitful approaches might be ungraded classes, team teaching or track systems, achievement or ability grouping, remedial reading provisions, or smaller class enrollment with teachers who have attitudes and skills which permit them to vary instruction according to individual progress. The needs of low achievers will not be met until they have an educational setting which provides for maximum academic growth and fosters a more positive life adjustment through satisfying success experiences.

NOTES

1. Grateful acknowledgement is due the Nashville Public Schools, in which this study was conducted. Special thanks are due the teachers and other school personnel who so willingly and competently assisted in the research.

2. Personal communication from Dr. Rupert Klaus cited one such program being carried on in the Murfreesboro Public Schools in Murfreesboro, Tennessee.

REFERENCES

1. Arthur, Grace. "A Study of the Achievement of Sixty Grade 1 Repeaters as Compared with that of Non-repeaters of the Same Mental Age," *Journal of Experimental Education*, V (1936), pp. 203–205.

2. Berlman, Mildred. "Why Boys and Girls Leave School," *American Teacher*, XXXIII (1949), p. 20.

3. Caswell, H. L. *Nonpromotion in Elementary Schools*. Division of Surveys and Field Studies (Nashville: George Peabody College, 1933).

4. "Census Track Committee of the Nashville Standard Metropolitan Statistical Area," in *1960 Census Population Handbook* (Nashville: Bureau of the Census, 1960).

5. Coffield, W. H., and Blommer, P. "Effects of Nonpromotion on Educational Achievement in the Elementary School," *Journal of Educational Psychology*, XLVII (1956), pp. 235–250.

6. Cook, W. W. "Some Effects of the Maintenance of High Standards of Promotion," *Elementary School Journal*, XLI (1941), pp. 430–437.

7. Goodlad, J. I. "Some Effects of Promotion and Nonpromotion Upon the Social and Personal Adjustment of Children," *Journal of Experimental Education*, XXII (1954), pp. 301–328.

8. Josephine, Sister. "Promotion, a Perennial Problem," *Education,* LXXXII (1962), pp. 373–376.

9. Klene, Vivian and Branson, E. P. "An Experiment in Long Beach, California, Schools," Editorial comment in *Elementary School Journal,* XXIX (1929), pp. 564–566.

10. Kowitz, G. T. and Armstrong, C. M. "Effect of Promotion Policy on Academic Achievement," *Elementary School Journal,* LXI (1961), pp. 435–443.

11. Lindquist, E. F. *Design and Analysis of Experiments in Psychology and Education* (Boston: Houghton Mifflin, 1956).

12. Otto, H. J. "Grading and Promotion Policies," *National Educational Journal,* XL (1951), pp. 128–129.

13. Otto, H. J., and Estes, D. M. "Accelerated and Retarded Progress," in Harris, A. J. (Ed.), *Encyclopaedia of Educational Research,* 3rd Edition (New York: Macmillan Co., 1960).

14. Saunders, C. M. *Promotion or Failure* (New York: Teacher's College, Columbia University, 1941).

15. Stryker, Sue B. "Undergrading as a Cause of Delinquency," *School and Society,* XXVI (1927), pp. 821–822.

16. Walker, Helen M., and Lev, J. *Statistical Inference* (Chicago: Holt, Rinehart & Winston, 1953).

FOR FURTHER READING

Chase, John A., "A Study of the Impact of Grade Retention on Primary School Children," *Journal of Psychology* 70 (November 1968) 169–177.

Cook, Walter W., and Theodore Clymer, "Acceleration and Retention," in Nelson Henry, editor, *Individualizing Instruction,* National Society for the Study of Education Yearbook, Part I (Chicago: University of Chicago Press, 1962), pp. 179–208.

Criscuolo, Nicholas P., "Enrichment and Acceleration in Reading," *Elementary School Journal* 68 (December 1967) 142–146.

Engle, Thelburn L., "A Study of the Scholastic Achievement in High School of Pupils Who Have Had Double Promotions in Elementary School," *Elementary School Journal* 31 (October 1930) 132–135.

———, "Achievement of Pupils Who Have Had Double Promotions in Elementary School," *Elementary School Journal* 36 (November 1935) 185–189.

Goodlad, John I., "Research and Theory Regarding Promotion and Nonpromotion," *Elementary School Journal* 53 (November 1952) 150–155.

Ivey, John O., "Computation Skills: Results of Acceleration," *Arithmetic Teacher* 12 (January 1965) 39–42.

Lobdell, Lawrence O., "Results of a Non-Promotion Policy in One School District," *Elementary School Journal* 54 (February 1954) 333–337.

Scott, Betty A., and Louis Bates Ames, "Improved Academic, Personal, and Social Adjustment in Selected Primary School Repeaters," *The Elementary School Journal* 69 (May 1969) 431–439.

Snipes, Walter T., "Promotion and Moving," *Elementary School Journal* 65 (May 1965) 429–433.

Steadman, E. R., "Fifteeen Who Were Not Promoted," *The Elementary School Journal* 59 (February 1959) 271–276.

Worth, Walter H., "Promotion vs. NonPromotion: I. The Earlier Research Evidence," *Alberta Journal of Educational Research* 5 (June 1959) 77–86.

———, "Promotion or NonPromotion," *Educational Administration and Supervision* 46 (January 1960) 16–26.

———, "Promotion vs. NonPromotion: II. The Edmonton Study," *Alberta Journal of Educational Research* 5 (September 1959) 191–203.

———, and J. Harlan Shores, "Does NonPromotion Improve Achievement in the Language Arts?" *Elementary English* 37 (January 1960) 49–52.

Ability Grouping of Bright Pupils*

BRUCE BALOW and JAMES CURTIN

Perhaps the most controversial aspects of administrative grouping are the questions of ability grouping and how to provide for the gifted child. The length of the list "For Further Reading" and the diversity of titles attests to the interest in the topic. Many elements make the issue complex, such as: Whether it is possible to create homogeneous groups, the effects on the bright or disadvantaged child who is isolated from his peers, the impact on the egos of the teachers who are assigned to the slow and fast groups and those of the parents of the bright and less bright children, and the "reputation" of the school to "uphold standards." There is an abundance of research, but some of the most vital questions can only be answered by serious thought concerning the hierarchy of the values sought through school programs.

Balow and Curtin report a well-executed ex post facto type of research employing a large quantity of data, sophisticated statistics, good instruments, and a large sample.

The Joplin plan, discussed in Chapter 2 by Powell, is one form of ability grouping. The Clarks' study of Negro children (Chapter 4) shows how one segregated group, which may be similar to an intellectually segregated group, looks at itself. Within this chapter, Dobbs' and Neville's study of retention is another look at ability grouping and Adams researches its opposite—multi-age grouping. While ability grouping is listed as an administrative grouping problem, it is also an instructional problem. (See Wallen in "For Further Reading.")

The research literature on ability grouping is almost as old as the procedure itself. Rarely has the research offered any support for this method. Negative results were reported at least as early as 1927 (1). Yet ability grouping persists to this day with undiminished strength. Indeed, with the vast increase in special classes for mentally retarded

* From *Elementary School Journal* 66 (March 1966) 321–327. Reprinted with permission of The University of Chicago Press, © 1966; Bruce Balow, Professor of Educational Psychology and Special Education, University of Minnesota, Minneapolis; and James Curtin, Professor of Elementary Education, University of Minnesota.

pupils and for gifted pupils, ability grouping has come into a rena-
scence of sorts. The upper-middle-class suburban school district appears particularly susceptible to the notion of segregation of pupils of
high ability, while urban districts have been in the forefront in establishing classes for pupils of very low ability. Such special classes,
created in response to practical problems that face school districts,
have always been appealing because of the apparent ease and simplicity with which they "solve" curriculum problems.

In theory, ability grouping reduces the range of achievement for
which a given teacher must prepare lessons, allowing him to more
readily teach the entire class. When lessons are at one level of difficulty,
the belief is that the class move ahead rapidly with no waiting for
laggards. Improved achievement is thought to be a natural outcome
of such grouping.

The research literature is relatively clear regarding mentally retarded pupils. Special classes for retarded pupils have much to recommend them, but increased achievement is not one of the demonstrated
outcomes of these classes (2, 3). The same may be said for ability
grouping of pupils whose intelligence quotient is between 70 and 130.
Many studies have compared the three ability groups—below average,
average, and bright—and found so much overlap in achievement as to
make the groupings meaningless. Variability is reduced slightly or not
at all, and the gain in achievement is not significantly different from
that in heterogeneous control groups (4–7). However, it is difficult to
find evidence on the very bright pupils who are represented in large
numbers in the upper-middle-class suburban districts now in the forefront of grouping by intelligence quotient.

The study by Goldberg and Passow investigated the effect of various
grouping patterns on pupils at all levels of ability but gave particular
attention to the very bright pupils (6). Goldberg and Passow found the
teacher more important than the grouping arrangement and concluded
that simply narrowing the range of intelligence quotient in a class does
not result in greater achievement.

The present study was designed to investigate the effect of grouping
by intelligence quotient on the distribution of basic school skills among
bright third-grade pupils. The principal question to be answered was
whether grouping bright pupils by narrow intelligence quotient bands
would significantly reduce the range of achievement over that represented by a heterogeneous group. The hypothesis to be tested was that
there would be no significant differences in achievement means or in
achievement variances between groups classified according to intelligence quotient.

The records of pupils who had attended third grade in the University of Minnesota Elementary School were sampled until 150 complete sets were obtained. Results from the Stanford-Binet Scale (in a very few instances the Wechsler Intelligence Scale for Children) were available for the measure of intelligence, while achievement scores were obtained from the Iowa Every-Pupil Tests of Basic Skills.

The families represented in this school are similar in many respects to suburban families. The parents are bright, verbal people who are interested in schools and anxious that their children obtain a high quality education. Many appear to reflect a value system of high striving for attainment and position and see education as one important avenue of upward mobility.

The pupils attending this school had been taught in classes of 25, with no special ability grouping. However, as Tables 1 and 2 show, nearly all the pupils are quite bright. Although they are not representative of the usual school population, they are representative of many suburban districts.

The 150 sets of records were randomly separated into two equal groups, Group A and Group B. The seventy-five pupils in Group A represented a heterogeneous group of bright pupils who ranged in intelligence quotient from 98 to 163, while the 75 pupils in Group B were separated by intelligence quotient into three groups of 25 each; B1 included pupils whose intelligence quotients ranged from 100 to 122; B2, from 123 to 141; and B3, from 142 to 181.

The statistical analysis was then carried out on these four groups. The means were tested with an analysis-of-variance procedure for subgroups of unequal size (8: formulas 9.13, 9.14, and 9.15). Variances were compared using Hartley's method (9). In this method the largest variance is contrasted with the smallest, and a special F max table is entered with the columnar value equal to the number of groups and the row value equal to the degrees of freedom for the largest group.

The question of concern in this investigation was the degree to which ability grouping would reduce variation within groups. Thus, the test of differences in variances was more important than the test of mean differences. When variances were found to be significantly different on Hartley's test, the analysis of variance was carried out, nonetheless, as an approximate test of means. The bias resulting from the significant variance ratios obtained in these data increases only very slightly the probability of incorrectly obtaining a statistically significant result on the test of differences between means (10, 11).

The data for each ability group on all the variables tested are summarized in Tables 1 and 2.

TABLE 1

Means of Raw Scores and Results of the Analysis of Variance for Differences between Means of Ability (Intelligence Quotient) Groups in Age, Intelligence Quotient, and Skill Areas

VARIABLE	HETEROGENEOUS GROUP Group A	HOMOGENEOUS GROUPS			F	P*
		High Intelligence Quotient 100–122 Group B1	Superior Intelligence Quotient 123–141 Group B2	Very Superior Intelligence Quotient 142–181 Group B3		
Number of Pupils	75	25	25	25		
Chronological Age (months)	106.40	106.44	106.32	106.24		NS
Intelligence Quotient	128.71	115.36	129.88	157.20	61.6070	<.01
Reading Comprehension	38.20	31.68	38.96	45.04	7.5116	<.01
Reading Vocabulary	23.95	17.88	26.12	31.84	8.6191	<.01
Map Reading	8.56	6.04	8.68	9.68	5.9572	<.01
Use of References	11.39	8.36	11.48	13.32	6.4233	<.01
Use of Dictionary	9.28	7.04	9.04	10.72	3.7848	<.05
English Usage	39.31	37.28	40.24	43.52	6.0459	<.01
Spelling	24.83	20.36	24.48	29.68	3.3837	<.05
Arithmetic Computation	14.63	11.84	14.08	14.80	1.8284	NS
Arithmetic Knowledge	17.44	13.32	17.60	21.64	10.2873	<.01
Arithmetic Problem Solving	15.09	11.76	15.52	16.28	3.5296	<.05

* With 3 and 146 degrees of freedom. $F.99 = 3.91$, $F.95 = 2.67$.

TABLE 2

Raw Score Variance and Results of Hartley's Test for Equality of Variance among Ability Groups in Age, Intelligence Quotient, and Skill Areas

| Variable | Heterogeneous Group Group A | Homogeneous Groups | | | F max | P* |
		High Intelligence Quotient 100–122 Group B1	Superior Intelligence Quotient 123–141 Group B2	Very Superior Intelligence Quotient 142–181 Group B3		
Number of Pupils	75	25	25	25		
Chronological Age (months)	14.1891	17.0900	14.3933	9.9400	1.7193	NS
Intelligence Quotient	201.7506	33.4900	28.3600	95.3333	7.1139	<.01
Reading Comprehension	96.4594	108.9766	138.7900	60.0400	2.3116	<.01
Reading Vocabulary	100.7268	85.6933	133.5266	65.2233	2.0472	<.05
Map Reading	10.8983	10.6233	11.3100	6.9766	1.6211	NS
Use of References	16.9160	14.9900	22.7600	10.6433	2.1384	<.05
Use of Dictionary	13.8800	9.5400	18.7900	22.2100	2.3280	<.01
English Usage	31.3506	27.2100	34.9400	18.1766	1.9222	NS
Spelling	102.8209	105.1566	128.5100	102.8933	1.2498	NS
Arithmetic Computation	28.6965	24.3900	28.9100	36.5000	1.4965	NS
Arithmetic Knowledge	29.3848	33.0600	17.5000	29.4900	1.8891	NS
Arithmetic Problem Solving	28.5181	23.9400	27.7600	35.7100	1.4916	NS

* With $k = 4$ and degrees of freedom $= 60$, F max $.99 = 2.3$; F max $.95 = 1.96$.

With the exception of Arithmetic Computation, all the achievement means are significantly different at the .05 level or less. As Table 1 shows, the achievement level increases as intelligence quotient increases, although in many instances the increase is only two or three raw score points. Several raw score points are sufficient to provide statistical significance but do not argue a practical difference that would be particularly noticeable if these pupils were to be taught in their separate ability groups. The differences in mean reading scores, however, are particularly wide, reflecting a practical difference in this very important skill. The only other skill area to show a difference between groups clearly large enough to be of value in the classroom is Arithmetic Knowledge.

Neither of the findings offers any support for ability grouping (12). However, the fundamental argument for such grouping rests on the belief that it drastically reduces the wide variation in achievement found in a heterogeneous group. The data of the present study do not support such an argument for these bright pupils. Four of the ten comparisons of variances were significant at the .05 level or less, but six were not significant. As Table 2 shows, even when the variances were unequal, the variance in the heterogeneous group was by no means the largest. Generally, the largest variance was found in the group of superior ability. Rarely did one of the pupils score at the bottom or at the ceiling of any of the tests. Thus, the variance was not artificially truncated in any of the groups.

A more practical way to consider the question of reduction in range of achievement is to compare the four ability groups across all ten achievement areas rather than one skill at a time, since ability grouping is meant to provide homogeneity in all areas of the curriculum. This comparison can be made by examining Table 3. The smallest total variability in any one ability group, from the highest grade

TABLE 3
Total Range in Grade Equivalents over Ten Skill Areas by Intelligence-Quotient Groups

| | HETEROGENEOUS GROUP | HOMOGENEOUS GROUPS | | |
VARIABLE	Group A	Group B1	Group B2	Group B3
Number of Pupils	75	25	25	25
Extreme Scores	1.0–10.7	1.0–8.0	1.0–11.6	1.6–11.6
Range	9.7	7.0	10.6	10.0

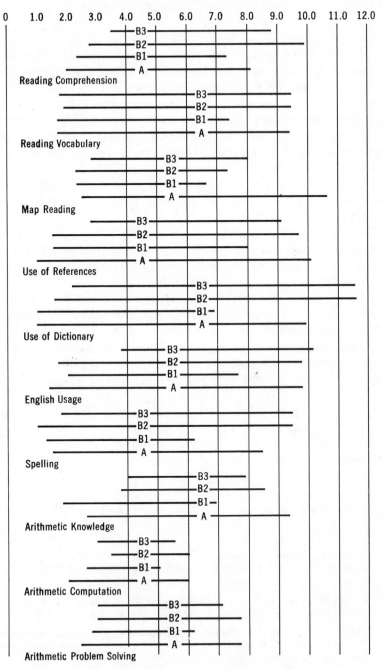

FIG. 1.   Range of grade equivalents in ten skill areas
          by intelligence-quotient group.

equivalent on any achievement test to the lowest on any achievement test, is found in Group B1 (intelligence quotient 100 to 122). The range in that group is 7.0 grades. The largest total variability—10.6 grades—is found in Group B2. For the three ability groups, the average reduction in range, by comparison with the heterogeneous group, is 5 per cent. The relative uniformity of total spread demonstrated in Figure 1 and Table 3 again emphasizes the fact that grouping by intelligence quotient among these relatively bright pupils did not produce any practical homogeneity in achievement.

This study does not support the practice of sectioning bright pupils into classrooms by relatively narrow ability bands in hope of attaining homogeneous achievement groups.

While achievement means are statistically significantly different (except for Arithmetic Computation), the differences between these groups are generally not of a magnitude to have a practical influence in the classroom.

Within any one skill area, the spread in achievement for which the teacher must teach is not significantly reduced by grouping based on intelligence quotient.

When a large number of achievement areas are inspected simultaneously, the total variation within ability groups is not greatly different among the groups. Every group has high, average, and low achievers in a number of skill areas.

If ability grouping based on intelligence quotient is to be used with pupils of average to very superior ability, the justification for such grouping will have to depend on reasons other than homogeneity of achievement.

REFERENCES

1. Helen Ruhlen. "The English Curriculum," *English Journal*, XVI (1927), 440–45.

2. G. Orville Johnson. "Special Education for the Mentally Handicapped," *Exceptional Children*, XXIX (October, 1962), 62–69.

3. Thelma Thurstone. *An Evaluation of Educating Mentally Handicapped Children in Special Classes and in Regular Grades*. Chapel Hill, North Carolina: University of North Carolina, 1959.

4. Irving H. Balow. "Does Homogeneous Grouping Give Homogeneous Groups?" *Elementary School Journal*, LXIII (October, 1962), 28–32.

5. Irving H. Balow. "The Effects of Homogeneous Grouping in Seventh Grade Arithmetic," *Arithmetic Teacher,* XI (March, 1964), 186–91.

6. Miriam Goldberg and A. H. Passow. "The Effects of Ability Grouping," *Education,* LXXXII (April, 1962), 482–87.

7. W. G. A. Rudd. "The Psychological Effects of Streaming by Attainment," *British Journal of Educational Psychology,* XXVIII (February, 1958), 47–60.

8. Helen M. Walker and Joseph Lev. *Statistical Inference.* New York: Henry Holt and Company, 1953.

9. H. O. Hartley. "The Maximum F Ratio as a Short Cut Test for Heterogeneity of Variance," *Biometrika,* XXXVII (1950), 308–12.

10. S. N. David and N. L. Johnson. "The Effect of Nonnormality on the Power Function of the F Test in the Analysis of Variance," *Biometrika,* XXXVIII (June, 1951), 43–57.

11. B. L. Welch. "The Significance of the Difference between Two Means When the Population Variances Are Unequal," *Biometrika,* XXIX (June, 1937), 350–62.

12. The study reported in this article was supported by a research grant from the Graduate School of the University of Minnesota.

FOR FURTHER READING

Amaria, Roda P., L. A. Biran, and G. O. M. Leith, "Individual versus Cooperative Learning," *Educational Research* 11 (February 1969) 95–103.

Balow, Irving H., and Arden K. Ruddell, "The Effects of Three Types of Grouping on Achievement," *California Journal of Educational Research* 14 (May 1963) 108–117.

Barbe, Walter B., "Evaluation of Special Classes for Gifted Children," *Exceptional Children* 22 (November 1955) 60–62.

———, "Homogeneous Grouping for Gifted Children," *Educational Leadership* 13 (January 1956) 225–229.

Barthelmess, Harriet M., and Philip A. Boyer, "An Evaluation of Ability Grouping," *Journal of Educational Research* 26 (December 1932) 284–294.

Bettelheim, Bruno, and Kenneth Mott, "Grouping the Gifted," *Education Digest* 30 (May 1965) 4.

Bicak, Laddie J., "Achievement in Eighth Grade Science by Heterogeneous and Homogeneous Class," *Science Education* 48 (February 1964) 13–22.

Bonar, Hugh S., "Ability Grouping in the First Grade," *Elementary School Journal* 29 (May 1929) 703–706.

Borg, Walker R., "Ability Grouping in the Public Schools," *Journal of Experimental Education* 32 (Winter 1965) 1–97.

———, "An Evaluation of Ability Grouping," abstracted by Loretta D. Foxman and A. H. Passow in Alfred Yates, editor, *Grouping in Education* (New York: John Wiley & Sons, Inc., 1966), pp. 181–187.

Bremer, Neville, "First-Grade Achievement Under Different Plans of Grouping," *Elementary English* 35 (May 1958) 324–326.

Burt, Cyril, "The Differentiation of Intellectual Ability," *British Journal of Educational Psychology* 24 (February 1954) 76–90.

Clarke, S. C. T., "The Effect of Grouping on Variability in Achievement at the Grade III Level," *The Alberta Journal of Educational Research* 4 (September 1958) 162–171.

Deitrich, Francis R., "Comparison of Sociometric Patterns of Sixth-Grade Pupils in Two School Systems: Ability Grouping Compared with Heterogeneous Grouping," *Journal of Educational Research* 57 (July–August 1964) 507–512.

Dvorak, August, and J. J. Rae, "A Comparison of the Achievement of Superior Children in Segregated and Unsegregated First-Grade Classes," *Elementary School Journal* 29 (January 1929) 380–389.

Dyson, Ernest, "A Study of Ability Grouping and the Self-Concept," *Journal of Educational Research* 60 (May–June 1967) 403–405.

Eash, Maurice, "Grouping: What Have We Learned?," *Educational Leadership* 18 (April 1961) 429–434.

Gallagher, J. J., and Thora Crowder, "The Adjustment of Gifted Children in the Regular Classroom," *Exceptional Children* 23 (April 1957) 306–312, 317–319.

Goldberg, Miriam L., A. Harry Passow, and Joseph Justman, *The Effects of Ability Grouping* (New York: Teachers College Press, 1966).

Goldworth, M., "The Effects of an Elementary School Fast-Learner Program on Children's Social Relationships," *Exceptional Children* 26 (October 1959) 59–63.

Holmes, D., and Harvey L., "An Evaluation of Two Methods of Grouping," *Educational Research Bulletin* 35 (November 14, 1956) 213–222.

Husen, Torsten, "Loss of Talent in Selective School Systems: The Case of Sweden," *Comparative Education Review* 4 (October 1960) 70–74.

Johnston, A. Montgomery, "Intellectual Segregation," *Elementary School Journal* 67 (January 1967) 207–212.

Karnes, M. B., George McCoy, R. R. Zehrboch, J. P. Wollersheim, and H. F. Clarizio, "The Efficacy of Two Organizational Plans for Underachieving Intellectually Gifted Children," *Exceptional Children* 29 (May 1963) 438–446.

Koontz, William F., "A Study of Achievement as a Function of Homogeneous Grouping," *Journal of Experimental Education* 30 (December 1961) 249–253.

Luchins, Abraham, and Edith Luchins, "Children's Attitude Toward Homogeneous Grouping," *Journal of Genetic Psychology* 72 (March 1948) 3–9.

Mann, Maxine, "What Does Ability Grouping Do to the Self-Concept?" *Childhood Education* 36 (April 1960) 357–359.

Martinson, Ruth A., "The California Study of Programs for Gifted Pupils," *Exceptional Children* 26 (March 1960) 339–343.

Miller, W. S., and Henry J. Otto, "Analysis of Exceptional Studies in Homogeneous Grouping," *Journal of Educational Research* 21 (February 1930) 95–102.

Millman, Jason, and Mauritz Johnson, Jr., "Relation of Section Variance to Achievement Gains in English and Mathematics in Grades Seven and Eight," *American Education Research Journal* 1 (January 1964) 47–51.

Passow, A. Harry, "The Maze of the Research on Ability Grouping," *The Education Forum* 26 (March 1962) 281–288.

Pinney, Grant C., "Grouping by Arithmetic Ability—An Experiment in the Teaching of Arithmetic," *The Arithmetic Teacher* 8 (March 1961) 120–123.

Roberts, J. L., "Homogeneous Grouping: An Exception," *Chicago School Journal* 29 (September 1947) 30–32.

Tilman, Rodney, and J. H. Hull, "Is Ability Grouping Taking Schools in the Wrong Direction?" *Nation's Schools* 73 (April 1964) 70–71, 128–129.

Wallen, Norman E., and Robert O. Vowles, "The Effect of Intraclass Ability Grouping on Arithmetic Achievement in the Sixth Grade," *Journal of Educational Psychology* 51 (June 1960) 159–163.

Willig, C. J. "Social Implications of Streaming in the Junior High School," *Educational Research* 5 (1963) 151–154.

A Comparison of Pupil Achievement After One and One-Half and Three Years in a Nongraded Program*

J. CHARLES JONES, J. WILLIAM MOORE, and FRANK VAN DEVENDER

Nongrading is an administrative grouping practice that appears to be gaining in popularity, although there are wide variations in its definition. The movement constitutes a protest against many of the deficiencies of the graded structure, making provisions for individual differences. Some feel that it is a bandwagon movement without valid justification. (See Lewin, listed in "For Further Reading.") Others feel that there are good and bad nongraded programs—the creation of many specific levels within a group being cited by some as one element of poorer design.

The following experimental study is noteworthy for the length of time it treats (three years) and also for its list of references. It has the shortcoming of using only one experimental group (26 pupils). The results might therefore be attributable to chance or to other factors such as the teacher or the community. It would be useful to know something of the differences in classroom practices between the two groups, particularly since there is no agreement as to just what constitutes nongraded instruction.

Related studies in this chapter include Adams' of multi-age grouping, Balow and Curtin's of ability grouping, Dobbs and Neville's of promotion and retention.

Two general criticisms have been directed at educational innovations. It has been contended that many of them have been instituted on the basis of the subjective estimates or favor of their advocates rather than because of sound evidence of their effectiveness. Other critics have maintained that even where prior experimentation has appeared

* From *The Journal of Educational Research* 61 (October 1967) 75–77. Reprinted with permission of *The Journal of Educational Research;* J. Charles Jones, Professor of Education, Bucknell University, Lewisburg, Pa.; J. William Moore, Chairman, Department of Education, Bucknell University, Lewisburg, Pa.; and Frank Van Devender, Assistant to the Superintendent, Shamokin Public Schools, Shamokin, Pa.

to demonstrate the superiority of some innovation, this advantage is not maintained after the procedure has become an established part of the educational program.

One educational innovation in which many public elementary schools have shown an increasing interest is the nongraded plan of organization for the primary grades. (2) The proponents of nongrading have stressed the fact that pupil achievement is increased at *all* levels of pupil ability and that nongrading reduces tensions and anxieties for both pupils and teachers because children are allowed to progress at a rate appropriate to their own abilities and without the disorganizing effects of the threat of failure. Other specific advantages have also been claimed for the nongraded system: instruction can be easily adjusted to individual spurts and lags in development; pupils can compete with their own records rather than with each other; teachers need not fear encroaching on materials for the next grade or being required to raise all pupils, regardless of their ability, to the same level of achievement. It has also been contended that pupils, after an absence from school, may easily resume their studies at the point where they had left off.

In a previous article (5), the authors raised the possibility that some of these claimed advantages might be attributable to the fact that more able teachers have been selected for these programs, and that they have been given additional preparation and special instructional materials. Goodlad (4) had previously stated that "nongrading is supported by some plausible sounding claims and theories rather than by research."

Although several studies (8, 7) had reported superior pupil achievement under a nongraded organization, others (2, 6) had found either no differences or an advantage for the graded plan. In the study reported by Hopkins *et al.* (6) the nongraded organization was abandoned after four years because the results were not significantly better and there were more administrative problems.

The purpose of this investigation was to assess in a controlled experimental situation, the effects of a nongraded program on the reading achievement of a group of elementary school pupils and to determine if these effects remained stable after the nongraded organization had become an established part of a school's program.

METHOD

Subjects

All first-grade students entering the Washington Elementary School (Shamokin, Pennsylvania, Public Schools) for the academic year 1960–61 were assigned randomly to either experimental (N = 26) or control groups (N = 26). These subjects remained in their respective groups for the academic years 1960–61, 1961–62, and 1962–63. All transfers or new entries were assigned randomly to experimental or control groups. Reading readiness levels for all children in both experimental and control groups were determined during the first two weeks of the school year. Nine reading levels were established for the experimental group.

Teachers

All teachers, whether assigned to experimental or control groups, were selected by the administration of their school on the basis of their excellence in teaching, and were assigned randomly to experimental or control groups. All teachers, whether experimental or control, participated in workshops in preparation for the nongraded program and received the assistance of a reading consultant from Bucknell University in selecting materials, carrying on their programs, and observing and assessing the pupils for placement in reading groups.

Procedure

Pupils in both experimental and control groups were initially assigned to one of three reading levels upon their entrance into first grade. However, for the experimental group the distinction between first and second grade was eliminated at the end of the first year. Three additional reading levels were created and a pupil in his second year of school could be in any one of the six existing reading levels, depending upon his progress. At the end of the second year the designation of third grade was abandoned and another three reading levels created. Pupils in the experimental group, regardless of their rate of progress, began reading instruction each fall at the point where they had finished the previous year.

Grade designations were retained for the control group and pupils could move only within the three reading levels for their grade. Except for those classified as failures, all pupils in the control group moved on to the next grade at the end of each school year and were again assigned to one of three reading groups.

Results

The effects of the nongraded organization on pupil achievement were evaluated at the end of one and one-half school years, and again at the end of the third year by means of reading achievement tests. The achievement tests used for the first evaluation were the Lee Clark Reading Test and the Paragraph Meaning and Word Meaning Tests of the Primary Battery of the Stanford Achievement Tests. The second evaluation at the end of the third year employed the Reading and Language Tests of the California Achievement Test. In addition, questionnaires were given to the teachers, the pupils who participated in this experiment, and to their parents.

The results of the comparisons of the mean grade placement using the t-test analysis (two-tailed test), for the experimental and control groups at the end of one and one-half and three academic years are presented in Table 1.

TABLE 1
A Comparison of Mean Grade Placement in Reading Achievement at the End of One and One-Half Years

Test	Experimental Group N = 26	Control Group N = 26	t	p
Paragraph Meaning	3.27	2.90	1.95	.06
Word Meaning	3.33	2.86	3.13	.01
Reading	3.19	2.81	2.71	.01

A Comparison of Mean Grade Placement in Reading Achievement at the End of Three Years

Test	Experimental Group N = 27	Control Group N = 22	t	p
Paragraph Meaning	4.46	4.22	1.06	.20
Word Meaning	4.60	4.27	1.35	.10
Reading	3.93	3.76	1.07	.20

Table 1 indicates that the scores of the E group were higher than those of the control group on all measures of achievement at both evaluation points. However, the differences between the two groups were statistically significant at the end of one and one-half years but not at the end of the third year.

Since the Language test of the Stanford Achievement Tests was not administered at the one and one-half year point, this comparison could not be made. The mean grade placement score on this test at the end of the third year for the experimental group was 4.25 and for the control group, 3.98. This difference was not statistically significant at the .10 level.

A composite reading score at the end of three years for each pupil was obtained by combining his four scores from the Stanford and California Achievement Tests. The results of the comparison of the mean composite scores using the t-test (two-tailed test) and a median test on the composite scores are shown in Table 2 for the experimental and control groups. The results of both of these tests were significant at the .10 level, although there was a greater number of pupils with scores above the median in the experimental group than in the control group.

TABLE 2

A Comparison of Mean Composite Scores of the Four Scores
from the Stanford and California Achievement Tests

	Experimental Group N = 27	Control Group N = 22
Composite score	17.23	16.23
	t = 1.139; df = 47; p > .10	

Median Test on Composite Scores

Combined median for experimental and control groups = 17.2

	Experimental Group N = 27	Control Group N = 22	Total N = 49
Above median	16	8	24
Below median	11	14	25
Totals	27	22	49
	$x^2 = 1.709$; df = 1; p > .10		

In addition to reading achievement tests, questionnaires were administered to the participating teachers, to pupils in both experimental groups, and to their parents. The results of this subjective evaluation are contained in Table 3.

In general, teachers, whether in the experimental or control groups, favored the nongraded pattern. Pupils in the nongraded group had slightly more favorable attitudes toward their reading classes than did those in the control group. Parents, however, deviated from this pattern: The majority preferred whichever program their child was in.

DISCUSSION

This present study had a double purpose: to obtain reliable data on the effects of nongrading on reading achievement and to determine if these effects are stable over an extended period of time. Whether this first objective was achieved is dependent upon the soundness of the experimental design as well as the statistical analysis of the data. In general, variables were adequately controlled. Although Hopkins and others (6) judged this the best experimental design to date, greater control over teacher variability would have been desirable. Even though care was exercised in the matching and random assignment of teachers, the small number of teachers (N = 6) involved raises the possibility of the existence of some systematic differences.

The grade placement scores of the nongraded group were higher than those of the control group on all of the reading achievement tests, yet the results were much less favorable to the nongraded group at the end of the third year than at the end of one and one-half school years. A number of possible explanations can be advanced to account for this apparent decline in the effectiveness of the nongraded pattern of organization. Since different tests were used at each evaluation point, it is possible that part of the change may be attributed to this factor. However, both tests measure essentially the same behaviors, the Stanford and California tests provide sufficient ceiling at this level so that statistically significant differences are possible, and the direction of the differences were the same at both testing periods.

A possibly more plausible explanation is that part of the difference in reading achievement between the nongraded and the control groups is due to the interaction between experimental conditions and the independent variable. Both pupils and teachers were aware that they were participating in an experiment. Moreover, for both pupils, teach-

TABLE 3
Summary of Evaluations by Pupils, Teachers, and Parents

PUPIL EVALUATION

1. Responses to the question "do you enjoy reading?"
   100% of the E pupils responded "yes"
   96.4% of the control pupils responded "yes"

2. Responses to the question "do you think you read about as well as others in your class?"
   82.1% of E pupils answered "yes"
   75.0% of control pupils answered "yes"

3. Responses to the question "do you enjoy reading class?"
   100% of both groups responded "yes"

4. Responses to the question "do you think others in your class like reading class?"
   82.1% of E pupils answered "yes"
   85.7% of control pupils answered "yes"

5. Responses to the question "do you think you should be in a higher reading group than the one in which you are now reading?"
   39.3% of E pupils responded "yes"
   42.9% of control pupils responded "yes"

TEACHER EVALUATION

1. The three E teachers and the three control teachers agree that most of the students were working to capacity in reading class.

2. Two E teachers and two control teachers felt that students in non-graded classes learn to read better (two were undecided).

3. All three of the E teachers and two of the control teachers felt that the students were emotionally more secure in the non-graded classes (one was undecided).

4. All six teachers favored the non-graded program.

PARENTAL EVALUATION

In response to the question "If I had my choice, I would favor having my child go to school in a non-graded primary organization," the following was determined:

	Agree	Disagree
E parents	16	3
Control parents	3	15

A chi square analysis yielded $x^2 = 16.88$; $p < .01$.

ers, and, to some extent, parents, the non-graded organization presented a novel situation which may have stimulated greater interest and effort. This would tend to account for the greater differences between the E and C groups on the dependent variable at the end of one and one-half years than at the end of three years.

A third possibility is that the nongraded organization with its minimal threat of failure is more effective with younger children and pupils in the first year or two of school than it is with children in their third year of school. Five of the six teachers, it will be noted, felt that pupils were emotionally more secure in the nongraded classes. Such emotional security (if the teachers' judgments are accurate) may have a greater effect upon the achievement of younger children. It is conceivable that simply removing the threat of failure without any change in grade organization, might have similar effects upon reading achievement. And last, it may be that the effects of graded organization may be limited to an interaction effect. For example, it could be hypothesized that grade organization (nongrading) has a positive effect only on low ability pupils. Since the N of the E and C groups was so small in the present experiment it was not possible to stratify on variables of ability and/or sex to determine the possibility of interaction effects. Thus the small differences obtained in the present study should not be considered conclusive when considering the possible effects of grade organization.

More positively, it could be stated that perhaps the real advantage of the nongraded organization lies in the fact that teachers and pupils are better satisfied even though achievement may not be significantly higher. An interesting aspect of this study was the acceptance of experimentation by the teachers, parents, and participating pupils.

CONCLUSIONS

Pupils participating in a nongraded primary organization achieved at a significantly higher level on measures of reading ability at the end of one and one-half academic years than did pupils enrolled in a conventional graded program. However, these results were not stable; at the end of the third academic year while differences which favored the nongraded group still existed, none of the differences were statistically significant. It was concluded that the initial superiority of the nongraded organization could have been due to transient novelty effects, to its greater suitability for very young and beginning students, to variables not uniquely associated with nongrading, or to some combination of these factors.

These results raise a question not only about the intrinsic advantages of nongrading but about the advisability of generalizing from data obtained under conditions where the participants are aware that they are involved in an experiment. It is suggested that further research of a controlled experimental variety is needed, directed at determining the effects of grade organization on a variety of pupil behaviors with special emphasis on interaction variables.

NOTES

1. This work was supported in part by the Upper Susquehanna Valley Program, Bucknell University, through a grant from the Ford Foundation.
2. For a comprehensive discussion of nongraded programs see John I. Goodlad and Robert H. Anderson, *The Nongraded Elementary School* (New York: Harcourt, Brace & World, 1959).

REFERENCES

1. Anderson, R. H., and Goodlad, J. I., "Self-Appraisal in Nongraded Schools: A Survey of Findings and Perceptions," *Elementary School Journal*, LXII (1962), pp. 261–69.
2. Carbone, Robert F., "A Comparison of Graded and Non-Graded Elementary Schools," *Elementary School Journal*, LXII (1962), pp. 82–88.
3. Eldred, D. M., and Hillson, M., "The Nongraded School and Mental Health," *Elementary School Journal*, LXIII (1963), pp. 218–222.
4. Goodlad, John I., "Classroom Organization," *Encyclopedia of Educational Research, 3rd Edition*, The American Educational Research Association (New York: The Macmillan Co., 1960), p. 22.
5. Hillson, M., Jones, J. C., Moore, J. W., and Van Devender, F., "A Controlled Experiment Evaluating the Effects of a Non-Graded Organization on Pupil Achievement," *The Journal of Educational Research*, LVII (1964), pp. 548–550.
6. Hopkins, K. D., Oldridge, O. A., and Williamson, M. L., "An Empirical Comparison of Pupil Achievement and Other Variables in Graded and Ungraded Classes," *American Educational Research Journal*, II (1965), pp. 207–216.

7. Ingram, Vivien, "Flint Evaluates Its Primary Cycle," *Elementary School Journal,* (1960), pp. 76–80.

8. Shapski, Mary K., "Ungraded Primary Reading Programs: An Objective Evaluation," *Elementary School Journal,* LXI (1960), pp. 41–45.

FOR FURTHER READING

Anderson, Richard C., "The Case for Non-Graded Homogeneous Grouping," *Elementary School Journal* 62 (January 1962) 193–197.

Anderson, Robert H., "The Non-Graded School: An Overview," *National Elementary Principal* 47 (November 1967) 4–10.

Barnickle, Donald W., and Ruth T. Lindberg, "The Unwilling Accelerate—A Problem of the Non-Graded School," *Elementary School Journal* 67 (November 1966) 84–87.

DiLorenzo, Louis T., and Ruth Salter, "Cooperative Research on the Non-Graded Primary," *Elementary School Journal* 65 (February 1965) 269–277.

Dipasquale, Vincent C., "The Relation Between Dropouts and the Graded School," *Phi Delta Kappan* 46 (November 1964) 129–133.

Glogau, Lillian, and Murray Fessel, *The Non-Graded Primary School: A Case Study* (West Nyack, N.Y: Parker Publishing Co., 1967).

Goodlad, John I., "Individual Differences and Vertical Organization of the School," in Nelson Henry, editor, *Individualizing Instruction,* National Society for the Study of Education Yearbook, Part I (Chicago: University of Chicago Press, 1962), pp. 209–238.

———, and Robert H. Anderson, *The Non-Graded Elementary School,* revised edition (New York: Harcourt, Brace & World, 1963).

Halliwell, John W., "A Comparison of Pupil Achievement in Graded and Non-Graded Primary Classrooms," *Journal of Experimental Education* 32 (Fall 1963) 59–64.

Hart, Richard H., "The Non-Graded Primary School and Arithmetic," *The Arithmetic Teacher* 9 (March 1962) 130–133.

Kelly, Frances C., "Ungraded Primary School," *Educational Leadership* 18 (November 1960) 79–81.

Lewin, David, "Go Slow on Non-Grading," *Elementary School Journal* 67 (December 1966) 131–134.

Miller, Richard I., *et al., The Non-Graded School: Analysis and Study* (New York: Harper & Row, Publishers, 1967).

"Non-Graded School Organization," *National Education Research Bulletin* 43 (October 1965) 93–95.

Shearron, Gilbert F., and Hazel Wait, "Non-Graded Elementary Schools: A Survey of Practices K–6," *National Elementary Principal* 47 (November 1967) 39–42.

Smith, Lee L., *A Practical Approach to the Nongraded Elementary School* (West Nyack, N.Y.: Parker Publishing Co., 1968).

Tewksbury, John L., *Non-Grading in the Elementary School* (Columbus, Ohio: Charles E. Merrill Books, Inc., 1967).

Williams, Wilmajean, "Academic Achievement in a Graded School and in a Non-Graded School," *Elementary School Journal* 67 (December 1966) 135–139.

Zerby, John R., "Comparison of Academic Achievement and Social Adjustment of Primary School Children in the Graded and Non-Graded School Program," *Pennsylvania State Review of Educational Research* 13 (May 1961) 33.

Achievement and Social Adjustment of Pupils in Combination Classes Enrolling Pupils of More Than One Grade Level*

JOSEPH J. ADAMS

Multi-age grouping may come about as a result of an imbalance in enrollments at two or more grade levels, resulting in a "split fourth and fifth" for example. Or it may result from a deliberate choice to provide greater heterogeneity as an added resource for learning. The assumption in this latter case is that children do and should learn from each other, and that it is the educators' duty to provide as rich and varied a learning environment as possible. Another related assumption is that individuality can best be fostered by providing as diversified a social environment as possible—one in which provisions for individual differences are inescapable.

Research in general indicates that there are no disadvantages to the learner in being in multi-age groups, and some of the researches indicate there are slight to significant advantages, depending on the factors being examined. Adams' research, of the ex post facto type, is noteworthy because it studies not only academic achievement but social structure and adjustment, and because it uses a large number of cases (150 pairs from 19 class groups).

Related studies in this volume include an evaluation of the Joplin plan by Powell (Chapter 2); promotion and retention by Dobbs and Neville; the nongraded school by Jones, *et al.;* team teaching by Lambert, *et al.*, and ability grouping by Balow and Curtin—all in this chapter.

Elementary school principals are frequently faced with the decision as to whether to set up a combination class (including children from more than one grade level) or to permit wide variation in class size, with some classes being undesirably large. When a principal decides

* From *The Journal of Educational Research*, 47 (October 1953) 151–155. Reprinted with permission of *The Journal of Educational Research* and Joseph J. Adams, Deputy Public Guardian, Los Angeles County, California. Article based on Master's project, University of Southern California.

in favor of setting up a combination class, he faces the additional problem of counseling with parents who protest the assignment of their children to the new class situation.

Teachers of combination classes are frequently faced with public relations problems of the same type. A parent expresses undue concern about the achievement of his child, or, in some instances, asks for a transfer to a regular class. Parents pose such questions as:

1. In a combination class, can sufficient instructional time be given to developing the skills with both grade level groups?
2. Will instruction be geared to the level of the lower grade level group to the disadvantage of pupils in the higher grade level?
3. Why does my child have to be separated from his friends?

PROBLEM AND PROCEDURES

This study was essentially composed of two different research projects—one on achievement in the skills, and the other on class social structure and the social adjustment of pupils. For this reason, the groups studied and techniques used in the two sub-projects are described separately.

Study of Growth in Achievement in the Skills

For the purposes of comparing achievement in the skills in combination and regular classes, use was made of the test data from class record sheets on file in the Research Office of the Pasadena City Schools for the school years, 1946–47 through 1951–52.

In an attempt to eliminate the effects of other factors on achievement, the following precautions were observed in selecting cases for study:

1. All pupils studied were fifth-grade pupils.
2. The pupils from combination classes were all from classes of grades 4–5 so that in each case they represented the older or more advanced group. This procedure was followed since parent concern about achievement is greatest when their children are placed in classes with a lower-grade-level group.
3. Only native-born white children were included from schools serving middle-class neighborhoods.

TABLE 1

Comparison of Gains in Achievement Made by Fifth-Grade Pupils in Combination Classes and their Pairs in Regular Classes

| Sub-test | Mean gain during fifth grade by: | | Difference |
	Combination classes	Regular classes	
Reading Vocabulary	1.20 ± .18	1.12 ± .18	+.08 ± .25
Reading Comprehension	.67 ± .14	.71 ± .14	−.04 ± .20
Reading Total	.91 ± .14	.83 ± .14	+.08 ± .20
Arithmetic Reasoning	.52 ± .09	.49 ± .09	+.03 ± .13
Arithmetic Fundamentals	.90 ± .07	.87 ± .06	+.03 ± .09
Arithmetic Total	.74 ± .07	.72 ± .06	+.02 ± .09
Language	.86 ± .11	.69 ± .11	+.17 ± .16
Total	.75 ± .08	.68 ± .08	+.07 ± .11

4. No child was included who had not attended the same school the preceding year.

5. In order to minimize the effects of differences in teaching ability, the pupils were selected from nineteen different combination classes and the same number of regular classes.

6. Pupils in combination classes were paired with pupils of the same sex in regular fifth-grade classes who had approximately the same Expected Grade Placement. (1) Usually, it was possible to pair pupils within one month. The mean Expected Grade Placements for pupils in combination and regular classes were 4.94 and 4.97 respectively.

When the 150 pupils and their pairs in combination classes had been selected, their achievement test results for the first months of the fifth grade and the first month of the sixth grade were recorded. Forms A and B of the *Progressive Achievement Test*, Elementary Battery, had been given in grades 5 and 6 respectively. Results were then tallied for each group for each sub-test, and mean gains were computed.

Study of Social Structure of Classes

For the study of social structure, it was necessary to study pupils who were in combination and regular classes at the present time. Nine classes were selected, all in schools which enrolled only white children from middle-class neighborhoods. Three classes were regular fifth-grade classes; three included pupils of grades four and five; and three included pupils of grades five and six.

In each class, a sociometric test was administered which included the three following questions:

1. Write the name of the boy or girl whom you wish to sit nearest you in the classroom. If you have a second or third choice, you may write their names.

2. If you were choosing the president or chairman of this class, who would be your

> First choice
> Second choice
> Third choice

3. Write down the names of your very best friends in this school. You may write down one or two or three names. You may choose children in this class or in other classes.

The first question was included as a basis for judging the social structure within the class, while the third provided an opportunity for pupils to choose outside the class. The percentage of choices outside the class is frequently used as negative evidence concerning the degree of group integration. The second question was included as a basis for judging the extent to which pupils of different sub-groups were chosen for leadership roles by their classmates. Since the questionnaires were administered in the seventh month of the school year, pupils were well acquainted, and the social structure of each class was well established.

Comparative Achievement in Reading

Gains in Reading Comprehension were almost identical for combination and regular classes, while gain in Reading Vocabulary and Reading Total was negligibly higher for combination than for regular classes. In no case did the differences found approach statistical significance.

Comparative Achievement in Arithmetic

When gains were compared for Arithmetic Reasoning, Arithmetic Fundamentals, and Arithmetic Total, they differed by only .02 or .03 month. In other words, it can be said that with respect to both fundamentals and reasoning, the average gains of fifth-grade pupils in regular and combination classes were identical.

Comparative Achievement in Language

The combination class and regular groups were almost identical with respect to initial achievement. When their gains during the fifth grade were compared, however, there was a difference of .17 month in favor of the pupils in combination classes. Although the largest difference was found between combination and regular classes, it lacked statistical significance.

Social Structure of Combination and Regular Classes

Comparison of different measures of integration or cohesiveness of combination and regular classes indicated that:

1. The percentages of choices outside the class were almost identical for combination and regular classes.
2. There were no consistent differences between combination and regular classes with respect to percentages of mutual choices.
3. Percentages of pupil choices not utilized were approximately the same for combination and regular classes.
4. In combination classes, approximately three-fourths of best friend and seatmate choices were within grade level. The tendency for four distinct groups to form (as a result of sex and grade level cleavages) is sufficiently evident that a teacher of a combination class should strive to provide a maximum number of activities in which pupils of both grade levels work and play together.
5. In combination classes, there was a trend for upper-grade pupils to receive more leadership choices than did lower-grade pupils, and for girls to receive more leadership choices than did boys. The trend for leadership choices to pyramid toward the girls, however, was even more marked in regular fifth-grade classes.
6. Combination and regular classes had approximately the same percentages of boy isolates, while a lower percentage of girls were isolated in combination, as compared to regular classes.

CONCLUSIONS

The fifth-grade children enrolled in the nineteen combination 4th–5th grade classes tended to achieve as well in the skills as did the fifth-grade pupils in regular classes. In other words, the data gave no support to the hypothesis that children are "held back" in their achievement in the skills by being grouped with children of a lower grade level.

Although combination classes showed no inferiority to regular classes with respect to number of choices outside the class, number of mutual choices and other indices of group integration, there did appear a tendency for pupils in combination classes to separate into four groups on the basis of sex and grade level cleavages.

REFERENCE

1. Alice McAnulty Horn, *Uneven Distribution of the Effects of Specific Factors* (Southern California Education Monographs, No. 12. Los Angeles, California: The University of Southern California Press, 1941), p. 68.

FOR FURTHER READING

Dreier, William H., "Differential Achievement of Rural Graded and Ungraded School Pupils," *Journal of Educational Research* 43 (November 1949) 175–186.

Finley, Carmen J., and Jack Thompson, "A Comparison of the Achievement of Multi-Graded and Single-Graded Rural Elementary School Children," *The Journal of Educational Research* 56 (May–June 1963) 171–175.

Franklin, M. P., "Multigrading in Elementary Education," *Childhood Education* 43 (May 1967) 513–515.

Gilbert, Jerome H., "Multigraded Developmental Plan Focuses on Pupil Achievement, Tesla School Breaks Through Traditional Graded Structure," *Chicago Schools Journal* 43 (February 1962) 209–214.

Hamilton, Warren W., "Multigrade Grouping With Emphasis on Differences," *Toward Effective Grouping* (Washington, D.C.: Association for Childhood Education International, 1962), pp. 54–56.

———, and Walker Rehwoldt, "By Their Differences They Learn," *National Elementary Principal* 37 (December 1957) 27–29.

Hull, J. H., "Multigrade Teaching," *The Nation's Schools* 62 (July 1958) 33–36.

Metfessel, Newton S., "The Saugus Experiment in Multi-Grade Grouping," *California Journal of Educational Research* 11 (September 1960) 155–158.

White, W. D., "Pupil Progress and Grade Combinations," *National Association of Secondary School Principals Bulletin* 51 (February 1967) 87–90.

A Comparison of Pupil Achievement in Team and Self-Contained Organizations*

PHILIP LAMBERT, WILLIAM L. GOODWIN,
RICHARD F. ROBERTS, WILLIAM WIERSMA

Team teaching is a popular, although highly controversial, topic (see particularly Fraenkel and Olson in "For Further Reading"). This controversy may be due to the lack of agreement as to just what constitutes team teaching. It may also be attributed to team teaching's association with other controversial issues such as ability grouping, undue subject matter emphasis, large group instruction, and hierarchical arrangements of teachers. Certainly a great deal more clarification and research is needed before team teaching can be conclusively defined as a desirable elementary school practice.

This study describes an experimental type research which is commendable for its sophisticated statistics, the length of the experimental period, and the good bibliography in its report. The reader should be cautioned from over-generalizing from the results, since it involves only two teams. As the researchers suggest, the findings could be a function of the nature of the personnel on the teams or many other factors.

Related researches in this volume include Powell's study of the Joplin plan (Chapter 2), DiLorenzo and Halliwell's study of the effectiveness of special teachers (Chapter 6), Schwartz' study of the core program, Adams' study of multi-age grouping, and Balow and Curtin's study of ability grouping, all in this chapter.

Early work by Pistor (21) and Wrightstone (25) suggests that any thoughtful attempt to improve elementary education will show gains in pupil attitude, adjustment, and, most probably, achievement. Pitruzzello (22) lamented that achievement was often the only depen-

* From *Journal of Experimental Education*, 33 (Spring 1965) 217–224. Reprinted with permission of *The Journal of Experimental Education*; Philip Lambert, Professor of Education, University of Wisconsin, Madison; William L. Goodwin, Assistant Professor, Bucknell University, Lewisburg, Pa.; Richard F. Roberts; and William Wiersma, Director, Center for Educational Research, University of Toledo.

dent variable investigated when comparing teaching methods. However, the general public would probably look askance at any new teaching method that improved pupils' personality, social adjustment, and interacting capabilities, yet lowered their academic achievement. Holmes and Harvey (8) felt that an effective teacher, sensitive to children's individuality, influenced achievement more than any type of grouping arrangement.

There has been a serious lack of carefully controlled studies in this area. Most sources have reported no marked difference in achievement between team and self-contained organizations (1, 2, 3, 4, 5, 6, 10, 12, 15, 16, 19, 20). A few authors (17, 18) reported significantly better achievement on the part of the team organization.

Only five of the sources listed above have direct reference to elementary school teams. Adams (1) reported especially favorable achievement for a fourth grade team, but Crandell and Piel (5) believed that fourth graders in their project would benefit more from a self-contained organization. The three other sources (3, 12, 16) found no significant differences between elementary team and self-contained organizations. At this time the literature does not provide evidence that achievement is superior under either organizational approach, team or self-contained, on the elementary level.

Although these writers considered achievement, personality adjustment, and classroom interaction in the main Office of Education, U.S. Department of Health, Education and Welfare report (14), only achievement is discussed here due to lack of space.

METHOD

Subjects

The experimental population for this study consisted of 299 elementary school students the first year and 381 students the second. Since the study was conducted over a two-year period, the number of pupils in particular classes changed slightly from month to month and year to year. Washington School, Madison, Wisconsin, housed 60 per cent of these pupils while Longfellow School, also in Madison, enrolled the remaining 40 per cent. Both schools are located in an economically depressed area of the city; 25 per cent of the families receive aid under the Public Assistance Program, 60–70 per cent of the fathers work in unskilled or semi-skilled occupations, etc.

Design

Pupils from Washington School were randomly assigned to either a team or a self-contained organization. Within the team organization, two multi-grade teams were formed. These teams corresponded to grades 1–3 and 4–6, and were referred to as the Primary and Intermediate Teams, respectively. Each team had five members: a team leader, a regular teacher, two graduate teacher-interns, and a half-time instructional secretary. Each team's cost was approximately equal to that of three regular teachers.

Longfellow School, the second control organization, continued a self-contained approach. Longfellow was included in the project to detect possible contamination of variables at Washington School and to lend greater power to the statistical analyses.

PROCEDURE

In the first year of the experiment, different forms of the *California Achievement Test* (24) were given as pretests to grades two through six in October, 1961, and then as post-tests to the same grades in May, 1962. Post-test scores were available in reading, arithmetic, language, and total achievement and were subjected to an analysis of co-variance using pretest and IQ scores on the *California Short Form Test of Mental Maturity* (23) as covariates.

Several changes were made for the second year's achievement study. The achievement test was changed to the *Iowa Test of Basic Skills* (9) for grades three through six. This test measures five major areas which, along with an average or composite score, were reported and analyzed. In addition, the covariates were eliminated; a comparison of the mean IQ's for the three organizations showed only small between-organization differences (107.8, 105.4, and 107.5), although noticeable between-cell differences were evident. With IQ no longer a covariate, the first grade was also used in the statistical analysis; both first and second grades took the *California Achievement Test*. The data were subjected to analyses of variance, run separately for first grade, second grade, and grades three through six. (Although first and second grades both took different levels of the same basic test, these writers developed several misgivings about the articulation between levels of the test; hence separate analyses were conducted for first and second grades.)

In both years' analyses, sex and organization served as independent variables; grade was also treated as an independent variable except when a single grade was analyzed separately (e. g., first and second grades the second year). When a significant organizational effect was found, a Duncan Multiple Range Test was used to locate the precise comparison(s) which provided the significant difference (see Edwards, 7). However, since the cell frequencies were unequal, a modification of the Duncan procedure outlined by Kramer (11) was used.

RESULTS

Academic Year 1961–62; Second through Sixth Grades

The Bi-Md 14 computer program, which handles cells with unequal n's, was used to run analyses of covariance for the four subject areas on the 299 subjects.

The sources of organizational significance included overall organizational pre- and post-test means as well as total gains for each score. The Duncan Range was actually computed on the gain scores using the results of the analysis. This is an approximation procedure, yet reasonable since IQ turned out to be a randomly distributed covariate. The Duncan Range has been computed in each case to determine which differences are significant.

In all scores, Washington Self-Contained gained significantly more than Washington Team; and in language and total scores, Washington Self-Contained gained significantly more than Longfellow Self-Contained. In arithmetic and total score, Longfellow Self-Contained gained significantly more than the Team.

The cause of grade level significance was simply the fact that each grade's achievement was correspondingly higher than the previous grade's. (For a full discussion of the significant interactions, see the Office of Education, U.S. Department of Health, Education, and Welfare Report, 14).

Academic Year 1962–63: First Grade

Separate analyses of variance were computed for each of the four subject areas. The division of the first grade analysis was 3×2 for three organizations and two sexes (total $N = 72$), and the resultant F-ratios were determined.

The sources of organizational significance were analyzed by organization, the average placements in reading, language, and total.

Both Washington Team and Longfellow Self-Contained were significantly higher than Washington Self-Contained in all three scores. Interestingly, the boys did significantly better than the girls in language and total achievement; this is a reversal of the usual findings at this level.

Academic Year 1962–63: Second Grade

As in the first grade analysis, a 3×2 factorial ANOVA was computed for each of the four subject areas (total $N = 63$). F-ratios were determined.

The sources of organizational significance in reading, language, and total achievement scores were examined. In these scores, as in the first grade scores, Longfellow Self-Contained was always significantly higher than Washington Self-Contained and never significantly different from Washington Team. However, Washington Team was significantly higher than Washington Self-Contained in only one score for the second grade, language.

There were no significant main effects for sex.

Academic Year 1962–63: Third Through Sixth Grades

The analysis of variance division was $3 \times 4 \times 2$ for three organizations, four grades, and two sexes (total $N = 246$). Separate analyses were computed for each of the six scores. F-ratios were computed.

Organization was significant in all subjects. In the scores of the average grade placements by organization there is a marked shift from the first and second grade scores: Longfellow Self-Contained is always significantly higher than *both* other organizations, while there are no significant differences in scores between Washington Team, and Washington Self-Contained.

Grade, of course, showed significance due to the successively larger grade placement scores from grade three through grade six.

Girls were significantly higher than boys in over-all composite ($p < .05$) and in total language ($p < .001$).

DISCUSSION

When comparing the results of the first and second years, it should be remembered that an analysis of covariance was used to analyze the first year's data, while analyses of variance were used with the second year's. Therefore, the main effects and interactions of the first year analysis were based on adjusted means, and primarily reflected the gain between pre- and post-test scores, while those of the second study were based entirely on post-test scores.

There were significant differences in achievement between organizations in all scores except first and second grade arithmetic the second year. In both years the first grade of the Team was higher than the first grades of the Self-Contained organizations (although the first grade was not included in the statistical analysis as explained above, it was given achievement tests); in the second year the second grade of the Team was higher than its self-contained counterparts, although in both cases the Team was only significantly higher than Washington Self-Contained. Grades three through five in the Team moved slightly ahead of Washington Self-Contained in the second year. In all grades, except the first two, the class achievement of Longfellow Self-Contained was higher than the other two organizations in both years. The only exception was Washington Self-Contained's fifth grade, which was higher the first year.

Achievement scores for team students in the third and sixth grades leveled off in comparison to other grades in the Team and the control groups. The achievement at the upper levels of the Primary and Intermediate Teams seemed to be checked relative to other grades in the same teams as if an artificial ceiling had served as a barrier to their achievement. It is not unreasonable to assume that these differences would disappear by extending the team concept to additional grades— even to an entire ungraded 1–8 elementary school.

Achievement results as well as results of a concurrent classroom interaction study suggested the possibility of important effects due to an uncontrolled teacher variable. Particularly noticeable were the differences between the organizations' third grades in both years of the study. However, in addition to the teacher variable, other unidentified factors may have contributed to these differences.

The gains that the Team made the second year suggested that further improvement might follow. Possibly the appearance of strong gains for the Team would require a longer period of time than the two years allotted to this investigation. Certainly the team organizational concept should not be evaluated until it has time to reach operational stability and is strong and effective. The team and its new teaching framework must compete with teachers having two to thirty years' experience under a self-contained organizational framework. Differences between the inexperienced interns and experienced certified teachers, cited in the main report (14) would imply that a team made up entirely of experienced teachers might be more desirable, although cost would increase.

There were definite indications that student achievement did improve under a team organization that had been functioning longer than a year. For example, it is noteworthy that both interaction and achievement results pointed to instability within the Intermediate Team (13). The Primary Team kept its experienced teachers, but both the team leader and regular teacher of the Intermediate Team were replaced during the two-year study. This lack of continuing personnel on the Intermediate Team may have been reflected in its poor achievement gains which were far less substantial than those of the Primary Team.

It is felt that the team organization concept warrants further development and research. This study does not demonstrate that the team structure leads to significantly better achievement, but it does suggest that such improvement might come by continuing development of the team concept, especially if the development is supported by teachers who accept the task of molding a team that is characterized by polished desk-side manners and professional interrelationships among its members.

REFERENCES

1. Adams, A. S. "Operation Co-teaching, Dateline: Oceano, California." *Elementary School Journal*, LXII (January, 1962), pp. 203–212

2. Anderson, H. H., and Brewer, J. E. "Studies of Teachers' Classroom Personalities, II: Effects of Teachers' Dominative and Integrative Contacts on Children's Behavior." *Applied Psychology Monographs*, No. 8, 1946.

3. Anderson, R. H. "Team Teaching." *Education Digest*, XXVI (May, 1961), pp. 5–7.

4. Bloomenshine, L. L. "Team Teaching in San Diego—The First Year." *National Association of Secondary School Principals Bulletin*, XLIV (January, 1960), pp. 181–196.

5. Crandell, E., and Piel, W. "Birmingham Tries Team Teaching Experiment." *Michigan Education Journal*, XXXVIII (January, 1961), pp. 344–345.

6. Dillion, C. L. "Taylorville, Illinois, Senior High School Uses Tape Recorders, Team Teaching, and Large Group Instruction to Improve Staff Utilization." *National Association of Secondary School Principals Bulletin*, XLV (January, 1961), pp. 178–188.

7. Edwards, A. L. *Experimental Design in Psychological Research* (New York: Holt, Rinehart, and Winston, 1960).

8. Holmes, D., and Harvey, L. F. "An Evaluation of Two Methods of Grouping." *Educational Research Bulletin*, XXXV (November, 1956), pp. 213–222.

9. *Iowa Test of Basic Skills*. (Boston, Mass.: Houghton Mifflin Company, 1956).

10. Johnson, R. H., Lobb, M. D. and Swenson, L. G. "An Extensive Study of Team Teaching and Schedule Modification in Jefferson County, Colorado, School District R-1." *National Association of Secondary School Principals Bulletin*, XLIV (January, 1960), pp. 79–93.

11. Kramer, C. Y. "Extension of Multiple Range Tests to Group Means with Unequal Numbers of Replications." *Biometrica*, XII (September, 1956), pp. 307–310.

12. Lambert, P. "Team Teaching for the Elementary School." *Educational Leadership*, XVIII (November, 1960), pp. 85–88.

13. Lambert, P., and Goodwin, W. L. "Interaction Variations in an Unstable Team Organization." Paper read at AERA Convention, Chicago, February, 1964.

14. Lambert, P., Wiersma, W., Goodwin, W. L., and Roberts, R. F. *Classroom Interaction, Pupil Achievement and Adjustment in Team Teaching as Compared with the Self-Contained Classroom*. CRP No. 1391 (Madison, Wis.: University of Wisconsin, 1964).

15. Loretan, J. O. "Team Teaching: Plus and Minus in New York City's Junior High Schools." *National Association of Secondary School Principals Bulletin*, XLVI (January, 1962), pp. 135–140.

16. Mahoney, W. M. "Try Co-ordinate Teaching." *American School Board Journal*, CXXXIX (November, 1959), pp. 13–14.

17. Noall, M. F., Riggle, W., and Jensen, L. "Teacher-team Project, Roosevelt Junior High School, Duchesne County School District, Utah." *National Association of Secondary School Principals Bulletin*, XLV (January, 1961), pp. 234–238.

18. Noall, M. F., and Rose, G. "Team Teaching at Wahlquist Junior High School, Weber County, Utah." *National Association of Secondary School Principals Bulletin*, XLIV (January, 1960), pp. 164–171.

19. *Norwalk Plan of Team Teaching, Third Report*. (Norwalk, Conn.: Norwalk Board of Education, 1961).

20. Partridge, A. R. "Staff Utilization in Senior High School." *Educational Leadership*, XVIII (January, 1961), pp. 217–221.

21. Pistor, F. A. "Evaluating Newer School Practices by the Observational

Method." *Appraising the Elementary-School Program,* 16th Year book, Department of Elementary Principals, NEA (1937), pp. 377–389.

22. Pitruzzello, P. R. "A Report on Team Teaching." *Clearing House,* XXXVI (February, 1962), pp. 333–336.

23. Sullivan, E. P., Clark, W. W., and Tiegs, E. W. *California Short Form Test of Mental Maturity.* (Monterey, Cal.: California Test Bureau, 1957).

24. Tiegs, E. W., and Clark, W. W. *California Achievement Test.* (Los Angeles, Cal.: California Test Bureau, 1957).

25. Wrightstone, J. W. *Appraisal of Newer Elementary School Practices.* (New York: Teachers College, 1938).

FOR FURTHER READING

Beggs, David W., editor, *Team Teaching: Bold New Adventure* (Indianapolis, Indiana: Indianapolis Unified College Press, 1964).

Borg, Walker R., "Teaching Effectiveness in Team Teaching," *The Journal of Experimental Education* 35 (Spring 1967) 65–70.

Carlin, P. M., "A Current Appraisal of Team Teaching," *Education* 85 (February 1965) 348–353.

Drummond, Harold D., "Team Teaching: An Assessment," *Educational Leadership* 19 (December 1961) 160–165.

Fraenkel, Jack R., "Opinions Differ: Team Teaching: A Note of Caution Is in Order," *National Education Association Journal* 56 (April 1967) 16–17.

Georgiades, William, "Opinions Differ: Team Teaching: A New Star, Not a Meteor," *National Education Journal* 56 (April 1967) 14–15.

Heathers, Glen, "Research on Implementing and Evaluating Cooperative Teaching," *National Elementary Principal* 44 (January 1965) 27–33.

Hillson, Maurie, *Change and Innovation in Elementary School Organization* (New York: Holt, Rinehart & Winston, Inc., 1965).

Jackson, J., "Analysis of a Team Teaching and of a Self-Contained Homeroom Experiment in Grades 5 and 6," *Journal of Experimental Education* 32 (Summer 1964) 317–331.

Jarvis, Galen M., and Roy C. Fleming, "Team Teaching as Sixth-Graders See It," *Elementary School Journal* 66 (October 1965) 35–39.

Klausmeier, Herbert J. and William Wiersma, "Team Teaching and Achievement," *Education* 86 (December 1965) 238–242.

————, "A Study of the Elementary School Teaching Team," *Elementary School Journal* 66 (October 1965) 28–34.

Olson, C. O., Jr., "Why Teaching Teams Fail," *Peabody Journal of Education* 45 (July 1967) 15–20.

Paige, D. D., "A Comparison of Team Versus Traditional Teaching of Junior High School Mathematics," *School Science and Mathematics* 67 (April 1967) 365–367.

Palos, Nicholas C., *The Dynamics of Team Teaching* (Dubuque, Iowa: William C. Brown Company, Publishers, 1965).

Shaplin, Judson T., and Henry F. Olds, Jr., editors, *Team Teaching* (New York: Harper & Row, Publishers, 1964).

Sweet, R., and P. Dunn-Rankin, "An Experiment in Team Teaching Seventh Grade Arithmetic," *School Science and Mathematics* 62 (May 1962) 341–344.

Zweibelson, I., M. Bahnmuller, and L. Lyman, "Team Teaching and Flexible Grouping in the Junior High School Social Studies," *Journal of Experimental Education* 34 (Fall 1965) 20–32.

MIDDLE SCHOOLS

*Middle Schools on the March**

WILLIAM A. CUFF

The topic of middle schools was included in this volume because the movement toward such a school organization is growing rapidly. It is a controversial movement, and the editors feel it is important for elementary school personnel to think the issues through and to be prepared to guide the movement in the best directions. Middle schools may be desirable, depending largely upon the curriculum and methods which are carried on in them. Will the program be designed to better serve the unique needs of the children involved, or will it be a downward extension of the high school program? Will it be a meaningless token of some administrators' ability to "keep abreast of the times," or a device for solving building, integration, or athletic needs? The reader will note the differences of opinion from some of the titles listed in "For Further Reading."

Cuff's survey does an excellent job of identifying a movement and some of the problems related to it. It might have helped the reader if the researcher had told a little about his data-gathering instrument. There are other studies in this volume which bear on aspects of the same problem, including DiLorenzo and Halliwell's evaluation of use of special teachers (Chapter 6), and Schwartz' presentation of the effects of the seventh and eighth grade core program (Chapter 7).

The thirty-eighth annual Junior High School Conference at New York University was opened last spring by Chairman Myron Jacobson with this prediction: "We may be attending not one, but two meetings today—the last Junior High School Conference, and the first Middle School Conference."

Dr. Jacobson was alluding, without bitterness, to the subject of that 1966 conference, "The Middle School." In the sessions which followed,

* From *National Association of Secondary School Principals Bulletin* 51 (February 1967) 82–86. Reprinted by permission of the National Association of Secondary School Principals (Copyright: 1967 by the National Association of Secondary School Principals) and William A. Cuff, Associate Professsor of Education, Montclair State College, Upper Montclair, New Jersey.

leading educators from Maine to Florida explored the purposes, problems, and potential of our new intermediate institution.

To clarify the status and trend of the middle school movement, a nationwide survey was undertaken by this writer. Since the U.S. Office of Education did not have the information, each state department of education was asked to report on the middle schools in its state during the 1965–66 school year. Replies from 36 states and reports in various publications produced data about middle schools in 44 states. Incomplete information from these and missing data from six states should not, in the opinion of the writer, invalidate the findings seriously.

For the purpose of this survey, a middle school had grades 6 and 7 and did not extend below grade 4 or above grade 8. In this way it was expected to obtain a picture of an institution not dominated by the problems and goals of either the primary or the high school grades. A small number of private middle schools came to light; these, however, have been eliminated from the data.

MIDDLE SCHOOLS IN 1965–66

Last school year 446 public school districts in 29 states were reported to be operating 499 middle schools. Ninety-seven per cent of them were located in 16 states of the Maine-Maryland strip, the Great Lakes border, the Pacific Northwest, and the western Gulf coast. Ohio, Maine, New Jersey, and Illinois, with just over 50 middle schools apiece, and Texas, with over 100, comprise about two-thirds of the total.

Most middle schools were in small school districts. Ninety-four per cent of the communities cited had but one, usually the sole building in the system housing the stipulated grades. Only eight large cities were reported, and they accounted for 27 middle schools.

The number of middle schools is presently increasing, accompanied by a decrease in the number of junior high schools. Several state education officials reported middle schools in the process of planning or construction. Boston, New Haven, Pittsburgh, and Newark (N.J.) have publicized their intentions of incorporating middle schools throughout their school systems. The New York City Board of Education will exchange all of its 138 junior high schools for a middle school network by 1972. A survey showing that 24 out of 227 junior high schools sampled in 1954 were no longer junior high schools in 1964 is evidence of the trend.

Middle Schools in the United States by States, 1965–66

State	No. of Middle Schools	No. of School Districts	State	No. of Middle Schools	No. of School Districts
Alabama	4*	1*	Montana	1	1
Alaska	0	0	Nebraska	1	1
Arizona	0*	0*	Nevada	0	0
Arkansas	0*	0*	New Hampshire	0	0
California	3**	1**	New Jersey	54	52
Colorado	0	0	New Mexico	0	0
Connecticut	15	15	New York	20**	18**
Delaware	2*	2*	North Carolina	6	5
Florida	1	1	North Dakota	0*	0*
Georgia	1*	1*	Ohio (1964–65)	58	52
Hawaii	1	1	Oklahoma	0	0
Idaho	0	0	Oregon	32	28
Illinois	51	51	Pennsylvania	4	4
Indiana	7	7	Rhode Island	0	0
Iowa	0	0	South Carolina	1*	1*
Kansas	0	0	South Dakota	0	0
Kentucky	0	0	Tennessee	0*	0*
Louisiana	15(*)**	15(*)**	Texas	112(*)**	92(*)**
Maine	58	55	Utah	0*	0*
Maryland	(6)	(6)	Vermont	0*	0*
Massachusetts	5	5	Virginia	1*	1*
Michigan	15*	5*	Washington	19	19
Minnesota	1	1	West Virginia	0	0
Mississippi	1	1	Wisconsin	1	1
Missouri	2	2	Wyoming	1	1
			Totals	499	446

* Unofficial   ** Probably incomplete   ( ) Indefinite.

MIDDLE SCHOOL CURRICULUM

Examination of the literature and a sample of middle schools revealed a diversity of daily programs. Eighth graders usually follow the departmental plan commonly associated with secondary schools. For seventh graders, departmentalization is sometimes modified by blocking one or two pairs of subjects. Sixth graders most often operate in the one-room, one-teacher comprehensive plan common in elementary schools, but varying degrees of departmentalization were encountered. Fifth and fourth graders generally have comprehensive instruction except for nonacademic subjects which are departmental at all levels. It should be noted, however, that purposeful deviations were found at the upper and lower extremes.

Middle school course offerings show a general uniformity and conformity. English, social studies, mathematics, science, physical education, art, and music are standard in all grades. Conversational foreign language, mostly French and Spanish, industrial arts, and home economics start by the eighth grade in all the schools studied, as early as the fourth grade in some. Some middle schools have all, and all have some of the following subjects: health, reading, typing, arts and crafts, homemaking for boys, library, and homeroom guidance. Extra-class activities are usually limited to band, orchestra, chorus, student council, and intramural sports. Instances of interscholastic athletics were not found. Activities are scheduled at lunchtime, after school, during a special period, or in competition with regular classes.

A NUMBERS GAME

This century has witnessed a continuous reorganization of public education which has revolved around the junction of elementary and secondary education. Sixty years ago, four-year high schools and eight-year elementary schools were standard in the United States. Since then, the junior high school movement has presented several alternatives for housing the seventh, eighth, and ninth grades, but no consensus has been reached as to the best way to do it. Now, just under half of these students are in 6-6 or 6-3-3 school systems, and about one-third remain in the traditional 8-4 set-up. The rest attend two-year junior high schools (6-2-4) or middle schools.

The most common form of organization where middle schools were located was the 5-3-4, which occurred in 55 per cent of the districts. Thirty per cent used the 4-4-4 plan, and nine per cent had 3-5-4. In isolated cases, 5-2-5, 4-3-5, and 3-4-5 were found.

Removal of the ninth grade from junior high schools focuses attention on the classification of the middle school. In New Jersey, for example, this converts the school from a secondary to an elementary school, and has created certification problems for the building principal. In a sample of 17 state departments of education, the middle school is on the secondary level in 10 of them. Moreover, the National Association of Secondary School Principals apparently considers middle schools its domain, judging from the program of the 1966 NASSP convention, research criteria in a study of junior high school principals, and a recent NASSP publication entitled "Guidelines for Junior High and Middle School Education." The position of the National Elementary School Principals is not clear.

WHY THE MIDDLE SCHOOL?

In seeking a rationale for the rise of middle schools, the writer studied developments in cities and fast-growing suburbs of the northeastern states. Simple arithmetic created a middle school in some districts when enrollments increased, suggesting that these middle schools may be only temporary arrangements. Few middle schools in the survey were the result of specific middle school planning, but a trend towards this was observed.

In some cities integration was clearly a factor, as new attendance districts were made to cross old neighborhood boundaries and bring a diverse population into the intermediate grades. Part of the controversy surrounding New York City's Intermediate School 201 stems from the refusal of the Board of Education to locate this new structure strategically for integration. The retirement of ancient school buildings and population shifts within cities have played a part in the establishment of middle schools.

Pressure from organizations of high school teachers and administrators for the restoration of the four-year high school has been strong, especially in New York City. The dominant patterns of school systems with middle schools indicate a return to the traditional high school as the middle school movement progresses. Some critics of the junior high school have discovered in the middle school better solutions to the problems of early secondary education.

PROBLEMS AND ISSUES

State departments of education and schools of education have not yet come to grips with the middle school. In two cases, departmental spokesmen were unaware of middle schools operating within the borders of their states. Teacher-preparation courses are either elementary or secondary, with emphasis polarized in generalism or specialization. Certification and in-service training do not seem to reflect the unique characteristics of middle school students or programs, for either teachers or administrators. The beginnings of activity at the state level were observed in the states of New York, Connecticut, and Washington, with publications, conferences, and experimental certification in the past year.

To the teacher and administrator in a school district which faces a move towards establishment of a middle school, some questions need to be answered:

1. Should the middle school curriculum be a simple combination of lower secondary and upper elementary school programs, or should a unique curriculum be developed?
2. How should the middle school utilize such concepts as departments, grades, grouping, marks, and schedules?
3. How should musical and other voluntary activities be scheduled?
4. Should the middle school become the stage for a host of innovations and experiments in curriculum and facilities?
5. Is the middle school elementary, secondary, both, or neither?
6. What about training and certification of teachers and principals?
7. What shall we call it—middle, intermediate, junior high, junior?
8. Do the characteristics and problems warrant the establishment of a separate professional group and periodical literature for the middle school?

FOR FURTHER READING

Alexander, William M., and Emmett L. Williams, "Schools for the Middle School Years," *Educational Leadership* 23 (December 1965) 217–223.

Alexander, William M., Emmett L. Williams, Mary Compton, Vynce A. Hines, and Dan Prescott, *The Emergent Middle School* (New York: Holt, Rinehart & Winston, Inc., 1968).

Brod, Pearl, "The Middle School: Trends Toward Adoption," *Clearing House* 40 (February 1966) 331–333.

Douglas, H. R., "What Type of Organization of Schools?," *Journal of Secondary Education* 41 (December 1966) 358–364.

Educational Research Service, *Middle Schools in Action* (Washington, D.C.: National Education Association, 1969).

Eichorn, Donald H., *The Middle School* (New York: The Center for Applied Research in Education, 1966).

Grooms, M. Ann, *Perspectives on the Middle School* (Columbus, Ohio: Charles E. Merrill Books, Inc., 1967).

Howard, Alvin W., "Which Years in Junior High?," *Clearing House* 33 (March 1959) 227–230.

Jennings, W., "Middle School? No!," *Minnesota Journal of Education* 47 (January 1967) 73–74.

Kindred, Leslie W., editor, *The Intermediate Schools* (Englewood Cliffs, N.J.: Prentice-Hall, Inc., 1968).

Mehit, George, "The Middle School," *Ohio Schools* (October 1966) 23–24, 39.

Mills, George E., "The How and the Why of the Middle Schools," *The Nation's Schools* 68 (December 1961) 43–49.

Moss, Theodore C., *Middle School* (Boston: Houghton Mifflin, 1969).

National Education Association, *Middle Schools,* Educational Research Service Center Bulletin No. 3 (Washington, D.C.: National Education Association, 1965), 15 pp.

"Planning and Operating the Middle School," *Education Executive Overview* 4 (March 1963) 52–55.

Popper, Samuel H., *The American Middle School: An Organizational Analysis* (Waltham, Massachusetts: Blaisdell Publishing Co., 1967).

Vars, Gordon F., "Junior High School or Middle School? Which Is Best for the Education of Young Adolescents?," *High School Journal* 50 (December 1966) 109–113.

White, William D., "Pupil Progress and Grade Combinations," *National Association of Secondary School Principals Bulletin* 51 (February 1967) 87–90.

An Investigation of the Effects
of a Seventh and Eighth Grade Core Program*

BERNARD SCHWARTZ

Core is a form of administrative grouping used with departmentalization in the junior high or middle school, as well as in high schools. Good elementary schools (K–6) have for many years organized their instructional programs using core ideas, including major emphasis on process goals (such as problem solving, self-understanding, attitudes), units of work, integration of learning, functional learning, and activity. The core is still considered an important and viable alterrative for the upper grades.

The ex post facto type of research, of which this is one example, has the advantage of being realistic because it is extracted from current practice, of being applicable to field conditions (because it is drawn from real situations), and of having no Hawthorne or halo effects because the data are gathered after the conditions were implemented. As a research report, one might wish that this article had included a description of the core program being evaluated; however, some of the references in "For Further Reading" (as Aiken, Alberty, Faunce and Bossing, and Giles *et al.*) include excellent descriptions.

Related studies in this volume include Hahn's study of the language experience approach (Chapter 2), Schiller's study of study skills (Chapter 4), DiLorenzo and Halliwell's study of the use of special teachers (Chapter 6), and Cuff's study of the middle school (Chapter 7).

Within the past two dacades, many new instructional ideas have appeared upon the educational scene and, though these ideas have differed in their approach to curriculum and method, they have all revolved around one aim, that of fulfilling more effectively the educa-

* From *The Journal of Educational Research* 53 (December 1959) 149–152. Reprinted with permission of *The Journal of Educational Research* and Bernard Schwartz, Professor of Education, Trenton State College, Trenton, New Jersey. The material presented in this paper is based on the author's doctoral dissertation accepted in August, 1958 by Temple University. A more complete analysis of the data may be found upon examination of the dissertation.

tional needs of children. One of the most promising of the newer approaches to curriculum has been labeled the "core program" approach.

Recognizing the crucial need for obtaining factual evidence about the effects of the core program in the educational field, an attempt was made in this study to shed some light on the relationship between participation in a core program and success as a high school student. The initiation and operation of a core program thrusts heavy burdens upon the shoulders of school administrators and teachers. The transformation from the traditional teaching system to the core system greatly affects all who are either directly or indirectly involved in the field of education. Therefore it is cogent to evaluate the effects that the core program produces upon its students, as compared with those elicited by the conventional method.

THE PROBLEM

The major purpose of this study was to evaluate the effectiveness of the core program at Pennsbury High School, Yardley, Pennsylvania. Specifically, it was hypothesized that the following characteristics would be noted when children who have learned through a core program in junior high school were compared in senior high school with an equated group of students who did not learn through the core program:

1. High school students who have learned through a core program will achieve significantly higher scores in various selected subject matter and skill areas as measured by standardized achievement tests.

2. High school students who have learned through a core program will achieve higher final marks in grades ten, eleven and twelve.

3. High school students who have learned through a core program will exhibit more favorable personality and behavior traits when rated by their teachers.

4. High school students who have learned through a core program will participate in a greater number of extra-curricular activities, a greater variety of extra-curricular activity, and will devote more time to these activities.

5. High school students who have learned through a core program will maintain or increase their advantage over non-core experienced students in all of the above factors, as they progress from grade ten to grade eleven, and then to grade twelve.

6. High school students who have learned through a core program will exhibit more favorable social attitudes and more favorable attitudes toward various aspects of school life as measured by a standardized student attitude scale.

THE POPULATION

The population for this study consisted of the 236 seniors in the Pennsbury High School graduating class of 1957. Of this number, 168 met the requirements established for inclusion in the study. These requirements were: 1) availability of either sixth grade class marks, or of some acceptable standard indication of intelligence level in the sixth grade; 2) attendance at Pennsbury High School for grades ten to twelve inclusive; and 3) availability of data on the various factors investigated. Of the 68 students excluded from the study, 45 were eliminated because it was not possible to secure either their sixth grade school marks or an intelligence quotient obtained in the sixth grade. Also excluded were 19 students who entered Pennsbury High School after the beginning of grade ten. Four students were eliminated after being selected for the study because their test results on important factors, selected for comparison of the two groups, were missing.

The 168 students ultimately used in the study were then divided into two groups. The first group had all participated in the core program in grades seven and eight at Pennsbury. This experimental group consisted of 80 students, 38 males and 42 females. The students of the second group, which shall be referred to as the control group, did not have core program experience. This control group totaled 88 students, 42 males and 46 females. For the purpose of this study it was assumed that they received instruction of equal quality in grades seven and eight although they came from different school systems in Pennsylvania and other states.

EQUATING THE CONTROL AND
EXPERIMENTAL GROUPS

The entire core group had been in the Pennsbury Schools from grades seven to twelve. Most of the control, or non-core group entered Pennsbury in grade nine. A small number of non-core students entered

Pennsbury at the beginning of the tenth grade. It was deemed advisable to eliminate ninth grade data in making comparisons between the control and experimental groups. It was assumed that the results of such comparisons would be spurious because the core group was better acquainted with the high school, since it is actually an extension of the junior high school, in school climate, tone, philosophy, and even in physical plant. To minimize the core group's advantage in school orientation, group comparisons were not made for the ninth grade. This gave the non-core students a year to become adjusted to the school and its manner of operating.

It is important to note that although the experimental group had participated in the core program in grades seven and eight, they were intermingled with non-core students in the high school classes. Thus the homeroom and instructional classes of the tenth, eleventh, and twelfth grades consisted of both experimental and control group students. In this manner those designated as non-core students had the same teachers and received the same instruction and attention as did the core students in the same class. This eliminated the possibility of attributing differences found between the two groups in high school to special instruction or attention on the part of the teachers.

Briefly, the two groups were equated on the following factors:

1. Number within the group.
2. Sex.
3. Chronological age.
4. High school instruction.
5. High school areas of concentration.
6. Intelligence (measured in grade eleven.)
7. Sixth grade evaluations.
    a. School marks.
    b. Standardized achievement test results.
    c. Intelligence quotients.
8. Socio-economic status.
    a. Educational level of parents.
    b. Occupation of chief wage earner.

No statistically significant differences were found between the control groups on any of the above factors. Substantial similarity between the core and non-core groups was established for each of these factors.

FACTORS INVESTIGATED

It was the aim of the investigator to make statistical comparisons between the control and experimental groups on as many relevant factors as possible. The factors selected for investigation and their sources of data were as follows:

1. *Subject matter and skill areas achievement in high school as measured by standardized tests.* The core and non-core groups were compared on each of the nine sub-tests comprising the Iowa Tests of Educational Development. This battery was administered twice to all the participating students in the tenth grade and again in grade twelve. Results of the California Reading Test, administered in grade eleven, were also analyzed. Comparisons between the two groups were made for scores obtained in the reading vocabulary section, the reading comprehension section and the total reading score.

2. *High school report card marks.* Final report card marks, listed numerically, for grades ten, eleven and twelve were obtained from the school files. The control and experimental groups were then compared for each year by averaging the marks achieved in the five major subjects carried by each student. In addition, separate comparisons were made of the two groups on marks achieved each year on the two subjects which all students were required to take—English and social studies.

3. *Personality and behavior traits.* In grade ten and again in grade twelve all participating students were rated on a variety of personality and behavior traits. The ratings were performed for each student by the five teachers he had in his five major subjects. By assigning numerical weights to each step within each attribute scale, it was possible to adapt these evaluations for statistical analysis. Comparisons were then made between the control and experimental groups for each of the six personality and behavior characteristics rated in the tenth grade and for each of the seven attributes rated in the twelfth grade.

4. *Amount and extent of extra-curricular participation in high school.* Three approaches were employed in determining differences between the core and non-core groups on the topic of extra-curricular participation. The first approach involved noting the number of activities in which each student participated each year. The second appraisal involved examination of the types of extra-curricular activities in which the students were participants. The final approach entailed determining the amount of time (hours per week) the students devoted toward extra-curricular participation. Employing the last approach it was possible to compare the control and experimental groups in grade twelve only. However, group com-

parisons in grades ten, eleven and twelve were made for the first two types of extra-curricular activity appraisals.

5. *Determination of the degree to which the investigated factors are maintained through each high school grade.* It was deemed important to ascertain whether results and significant differences noted in the tenth grade comparisons of core and non-core groups also persisted through grades eleven and twelve. Included in this phase of the investigation were: results of standardized achievement tests in subject matter and skill areas; high school marks; four of the rated personality and behavior traits, and number and types of extracurricular activities participated in by the students.

6. *Social and school attitudes.* The investigator adopted and revised a questionnaire for the purpose of obtaining indications of the social adjustment and school attitudes of the participating pupils. The following four areas were derived by further adaptation of the attitude scale: 1) personal-social adjustment, 2) attitude toward classmates, 3) attitude toward teachers, and 4) attitude toward school administrators and school operation. An appropriate scoring system was devised by the investigator. Comparisons between the control and experimental groups were made on the total scale scores and on the scores for each of the four established areas.

FINDINGS

In the attempt to obtain valid information about the established hypotheses, appropriate statistical procedures were applied to the data. The results are presented in the light of statistically significant differences obtained by comparing the experimental and control groups on the various factors investigated.

1. *Subject matter and skill areas.* The results of the standardized achievement tests used in the study revealed that:
   a. The results of the Iowa Tests of Educational Development, administered in grade ten, revealed that the core group achieved significantly higher scores in Reading—Natural Science and General Background—Natural Sciences.
   b. The results of the same battery of tests, administered again in grade twelve, showed that the experimental group's scores were significantly higher in Quantitative Thinking, as well as Reading—Natural Science and General Background—Natural Sciences.
   c. Statistically significant differences in favor of the experimental group were also found for the Total Vocabulary and Total Reading scores of the California Reading Test administered in grade eleven.

2. *High School Report Card Marks.* An examination of report card marks revealed:
   a. The core group received significantly higher final averages in grades ten, eleven and twelve.
   b. The core group received significantly higher final marks in the required social studies courses in grades ten, eleven and twelve.
   c. The core group obtained significantly higher final marks in the required English courses in grades ten and twelve. No statistically significant difference was found in grade eleven in this area.

3. *Personality and Behavior Traits.* Personality and behavior trait findings revealed that:
   a. The core group, both in grades ten and twelve, received significantly higher ratings in Responsibility, Influence, and Seriousness of Purpose.
   b. The experimental group members rated significantly higher in grade ten in Creativeness and Adjustability.
   c. Statistically significant differences in favor of the core group were found in grade twelve in Industry and Initiative.
   d. The two groups received similar ratings in both grades in the attributes Concern for Others and Emotional Stability.

4. *Extra-Curricular Participation.* The topic of extra-curricular participation was analyzed by employing three distinct approaches in making experimental and control group comparisons. The following results were obtained by these approaches:
   a. Number of activities participated in—The core group engaged in a significantly greater number of extra-curricular activities in grades ten and eleven. No statistically significant difference was found in grade twelve.
   b. The two groups did not differ in the types of extra-curricular participation (e.g. athletic, honorary, social, etc.) in any of the three investigated grade levels.
   c. The twelfth grade investigation of the number of hours per week devoted to extra-curricular activities by experimental and control students revealed no statistically significant differences.

5. *Degree of Maintenance of Factors Through High School Grades.* Results of this phase of the study indicated that:
   a. Statistically significant superiority exhibited by the core group in Natural Science in grade ten was maintained in grade twelve.
   b. The significantly higher total final averages achieved by the core group in grade ten persisted through grades eleven and twelve.
   c. The core group's statistical superiority in social studies final marks in grade ten was maintained through grades eleven and twelve.
   d. The core group's superiority in English marks in grade ten, though not maintained through grade eleven, did reappear in grade twelve.

e. Of the four personality and behavior traits which were measured, the core group achieved significant superiority in both the tenth and twelfth grade ratings of Seriousness of Purpose, Influence, and Responsibility. The other attribute, Concern for Others, was not found to be significantly different between the two groups in either the tenth or twelfth grade ratings.

6. *Social and School Attitudes.* No statistically significant differences appeared between the experimental and control groups when total scores of the social and school attitude scale were examined. This was also the case when the two groups were compared on scores of each of the four-sections of the scale.

CONCLUSIONS

Within the limitations of this study, the following conclusions, based upon statistical findings, can be drawn regarding the specific hypotheses established:

1. The hypothesis that high school students who have learned through a core program in junior high school achieve significantly higher scores in various subject matter and skill areas as measured by standardized tests can be accepted in part.

2. The hypothesis that high school students who have learned through a core program in junior high school achieve higher final marks in grades ten, eleven and twelve can be accepted.

3. The hypothesis that high school students who have learned through a core program in junior high school exhibit more favorable personality and behavior traits when rated by their teachers can be accepted in part.

4. The hypothesis that high school students who have learned through a core program in junior high school participate in a greater number of extra-curricular activities can be accepted. However, the hypotheses that they participated in a greater variety of extra-curricular activity and that they devote more time to these activities must be rejected.

5. The hypothesis that high school students who have learned through a core program in junior high school maintain or increase their advantage over non-core experienced students in the above factors as they progress from grade ten, to grade eleven, and then to grade twelve can be accepted in part.

6. The hypothesis that high school students who have learned through a core program in junior high school exhibit more favorable social attitudes and more favorable attitudes toward various aspects of school life as measured by a standardized student attitude scale must be rejected.

FOR FURTHER READING

Aikin, Wilford M., *The Story of the Eight Year Study* (New York: Harper and Bros., 1942).

Alberty, Harold, "A Sound Core Program," *National Education Association Journal* 45 (January 1956) 20–22.

Cramer, Roscoe V., "How Effective Is the Core Curriculum in the Junior High School?", *National Association of Secondary School Principals Bulletin* 38 (April 1954) 172–179.

Fair, Jean, "The Comparative Effectiveness of a Core and a Conventional Curriculum in Developing Social Concern," *The School Review* 62 (May 1954) 274–282.

Faunce, Roland C., and Nelson L. Bossing, *Developing the Core Curriculum*, 2nd edition (Englewood Cliffs, N.J.: Prentice-Hall, Inc., 1958).

Flanders, Ned A., "English and Social Studies—or Core? Which for Better Basic Skills?," *School Review* 66 (September 1958) 351–360.

Giles, H. H., S. P. McCutchen, and A. N. Zechiel, *Exploring the Curriculum*, (New York: Harper and Bros., 1942).

Hopkins, L. Thomas, *Interaction: The Democratic Process* (Boston: D. C. Heath & Company, 1941).

Stratemeyer, Florence B., Hernden L. Forkner, Margaret G. McKim, A. Harry Passow, *Developing a Curriculum for Modern Living*, 2nd edition (New York: Bureau of Publications, Teachers' College, Columbia University, 1957).

Wright, Grace S., *Core Curriculum Development Problems and Practices* (Washington, D.C.: United States Office of Education, 1952).

———, *The Core Program Abstracts of Unpublished Research: 1946–1955* (Washington, D.C.: United States Office of Education, 1956).

INDEX OF NAMES

INDEX OF TOPICS